McGRAW-HILL SERIES IN PSYCHOLOGY
CLIFFORD T. MORGAN, *Consulting Editor*

CLINICAL PSYCHOLOGY

The Study of Persons

McGRAW-HILL SERIES IN PSYCHOLOGY

CLIFFORD T. MORGAN, *Consulting Editor*

BARKER, KOUNIN, AND WRIGHT · Child Behavior and Development
BARTLEY · Beginning Experimental Psychology
BLUM · Psychoanalytic Theories of Personality
BROWN · The Psychodynamics of Abnormal Behavior
BROWN AND GHISELLI · Scientific Method in Psychology
CATTELL · Personality
CRAFTS, SCHNEIRLA, ROBINSON, AND GILBERT · Recent Experiments in Psychology
DEESE · The Psychology of Learning
DOLLARD AND MILLER · Personality and Psychotherapy
DORCUS AND JONES · Handbook of Employee Selection
FERGUSON · Personality Measurement
GHISELLI AND BROWN · Personnel and Industrial Psychology
GRAY · Psychology Applied to Human Affairs
GRAY · Psychology in Industry
GUILFORD · Fundamental Statistics in Psychology and Education
GUILFORD · Psychometric Methods
HAIRE · Psychology in Management
HIRSH · The Measurement of Hearing
HURLOCK · Adolescent Development
HURLOCK · Child Development
HURLOCK · Developmental Psychology
JOHNSON · Essentials of Psychology
KARN AND GILMER · Readings in Industrial and Business Psychology
KRECH AND CRUTCHFIELD · Theory and Problems of Social Psychology
LEWIN · A Dynamic Theory of Personality
LEWIN · Principles of Topological Psychology
MAIER AND SCHNEIRLA · Principles of Animal Psychology
MILLER · Experiments in Social Process
MILLER · Language and Communication
MISIAK AND STAUDT · Catholics in Psychology: A Historical Survey
MOORE · Psychology for Business and Industry
MORGAN AND STELLAR · Physiological Psychology
PAGE · Abnormal Psychology
REYMERT · Feelings and Emotions
RICHARDS · Modern Clinical Psychology
SEASHORE · Psychology of Music
SEWARD · Sex and the Social Order
SHAFFER AND LAZARUS · Fundamental Concepts in Clinical Psychology
SIEGEL · Nonparametric Statistics: For the Behavioral Sciences
STAGNER · Psychology of Personality
TOWNSEND · Introduction to Experimental Method
VINACKE · The Psychology of Thinking
WALLEN · Clinical Psychology: The Study of Persons
ZUBEK AND SOLBERG · Human Development

John F. Dashiell was Consulting Editor of this series from its inception in 1931 until January 1, 1950.

CLINICAL PSYCHOLOGY

The Study of Persons

Richard W. Wallen, Ph.D.

ASSOCIATE PROFESSOR OF PSYCHOLOGY
WESTERN RESERVE UNIVERSITY

McGRAW-HILL BOOK COMPANY, INC.

New York   Toronto   London

1956

CLINICAL PSYCHOLOGY: THE STUDY OF PERSONS

Library of Congress Catalog Card Number 55-11937

Preface

A first course in clinical psychology can hardly lay claim to any distinctive content. Although the clinical trainee needs many kinds of information, most of them are supplied by courses with other titles. Thus, abnormal psychology, personality theory, testing, and research methodology may all be considered clinical courses. Clearly, however, a clinician is something more than a specialist in these areas of study; he is a practitioner, one who applies his information.

Courses in clinical psychology, then, should help students put their knowledge to work. Since this can be done in many ways, first courses in clinical psychology vary greatly in their informational content. Some are essentially courses in differential diagnosis, others stress intelligence testing, and still others deal mainly with behavior problems in children. Perhaps the most useful kind of course, however, is one which attempts to develop skill in eliciting and integrating many kinds of data about a single person.

I have tried to write this book around the idea that the first clinical course should aid students to think creatively about the many kinds of data obtained in studying persons. I have pointed out some of the practical problems faced by clinicians and have suggested ways of thinking about dress, gesture, case histories, and psychological tests. I have also tried to give the student a foundation for further and more specialized courses in clinical methods. Seriously disturbed cases are not emphasized because it seems to me that the clinical method should be taught as a way of understanding all kinds of people. It is not just the practical side of abnormal psychology.

While writing, I have kept the professionally oriented student of psychology foremost in my thoughts; but there is much that will interest students of educational administration, of personnel work, or of social work. Many of them will work with clinicians someday, and they may be conducting interviews and interpreting background data themselves. They should find profit in a course using this text.

As teachers we are not entirely sure when students should be introduced to clinical psychology. Appropriate placement depends on both the formal education and the life experiences of the students. In some schools, the course is given to advanced undergraduates; in others, it is offered only in graduate school. Consequently I have tried to write in a way that would be roughly suitable for either advanced undergraduates or first-year graduate students. My assumption is that students using this text will have some background in abnormal psychology, psychological testing, and the psychology of personality. Obviously, however, some parts of the book will be too easy for some classes and too hard for others. Some teachers will want to spend more time on the problem of prediction, and others will want to supplement the treatment of projective methods.

At his best, a clinician seeks to understand people rather than to classify cases. To do this he must be a sensitive observer of clients and of himself. He must be skillful in eliciting useful information. These sensitivities and skills are not conferred by the study of books on psychology. Given intelligent students, such achievements depend largely upon guided experience and upon overcoming repressions that have desensitized them or hampered their creativity. A textbook cannot do these two jobs. Dealing with words and ideas cannot substitute for dealing with people. But I hope this book will draw the student's attention to himself and to the people he studies in a way that will make his experiences clearer and more meaningful.

I think that students can be helped somewhat to gain sensitivity and the ability to think creatively by trying to solve the problems met in interviewing and in interpreting projective test data. Therefore, I have interspersed problems throughout the text. They are meant to initiate clinical thinking, speculation, and interpretation, rather than to recall the points that have been made. Some are too difficult for students in the first clinical course, and some have no single correct answers. I do not believe that they are thereby less valuable, for in these respects they resemble problems actually met in clinical work. Perhaps the problems can serve to stimulate teachers to create additional ones of their own; for I have only hinted at what can be done to provide experiences in interviewing, observing, and in interpreting drawings, written material, and tests.

Although I have not attempted extensive documentation of the text, I have referred to a sufficient number of primary and secondary sources to orient students who want more information. For the most part the end-of-chapter references, cited by number throughout, will be available in the average college library and can serve as reading lists or as starting points for the detailed study of special topics.

A clinical psychologist must depend upon some theory of personality for his final, explicit formulations. Currently, no single theory seems acceptable to most clinicians. Freudian principles are popular, but the ideas of Karen Horney and H. S. Sullivan are also influential. Many clinicians are trying to adapt psychological learning theory to clinical work, especially in the field of psychotherapy. I suppose this book leans toward neo-behaviorism. Even in the chapters on psychotherapy where subjective experience is stressed, there are traces of it. But the book is not so clearly oriented toward one viewpoint that it cannot be used by teachers who are persuaded differently.

I have introduced a number of ideas from social psychology. We know now, I think, that the study of persons cannot be carried out without taking culture and community into account. The structure and aim of the public school is just as much a fact in the lives of most people in the United States as is the law of gravity. And the small, crowded urban family leaves its special mark on the individual. The clinician needs to be aware of these cultural givens in order to understand his client.

I should like to have written more explicitly on the way that clinicians integrate their various data. I do not think I am equipped to write it. The way that facts and fantasies finally fit together is too subtle and, so far as I know, too unexplored to describe in a manner helpful to students. Perhaps it resembles a multiple regression equation; but I don't really believe that, because the presence of one variable transforms a clinician's perception and use of others. In several places I have tried to show how clinical inferences can be made. The trouble is that clinicians rarely seem to draw deliberate formal inferences. Rather, their understanding emerges without forcing; then the data are checked more analytically to decide whether the understanding is correct.

My thanks are due to many people who have contributed to this text directly or indirectly. Continuously, I have interviewed my inner consultants, those images and memories of teachers, friends, and colleagues who help me speculate about people. There are all the students who keep asking questions that make me reexamine my assumptions. There are the therapists who helped me recover some sensitivity. And there are the clients who involved me in their living, let me feed upon data they provided, and made me realize that clinicians study persons rather than behavior.

I also want to acknowledge my debt to Western Reserve University for granting me a leave of absence to make the completion of this book possible. My colleagues in the Department of Psychology have unwittingly contributed much to my thinking by their willingness to discuss psychological issues with me even when I had not clearly formulated them.

Miss Marjorie Taylor devoted great care and skill to preparing the final copy of the manuscript, and I appreciate her effort.

My special gratitude goes to several people: to Dr. Henry Haines for teaching me that the uniqueness of people defies our neat schemes of classification; and to Dr. Marjorie Creelman for spending many patient hours helping me to trust my own perceptions, feelings, and wants. Special gratitude is far from enough, however, to express to my wife for teaching me that there is more to people than science describes, for her encouragement, and for her help in reaching some directness and clarity in the writing.

RICHARD WALLEN

Acknowledgments

Thanks are due to the following publishers and journals for permission to quote from the copyrighted sources indicated.

American Psychological Association, Inc.: *Journal of Abnormal and Social Psychology,* S. Rosenzweig, A transvaluation of psychotherapy—a reply to Hans Eysenck, Vol. 49, 1954; A. Roe, Two Rorschach scoring techniques: the inspection technique and the basic Rorschach, Vol. 47, 1952; A. Korner, Theoretical considerations concerning the scope and limitations of projective techniques, Vol. 45, 1950. Also *Journal of Consulting Psychology,* J. H. Sacks and H. S. Lewin, Limitations of the Rorschach as sole diagnostic instrument, Vol. 14, 1950. Also *Psychological Bulletin,* R. B. Cattell, The measurement of adult intelligence, Vol. 40, 1943.

Case Reports in Clinical Psychology: L. Chalfen, Organic factors in a maladjusted young male, Vol. 1, 1950; M. A. Wexler, A diagnostic and therapeutic study of a schizophrenic woman, Vol. 2, 1951; A. M. Zeichner, Alcoholism as a defense against social isolation, Vol. 2, 1951.

Educational and Psychological Measurement: A. Anastasi, The concept of validity in the interpretation of test scores, Vol. 10, 1950.

Farrar, Straus and Cudahay, Inc.: Theodor Reik, *Listening with the third ear,* 1948.

Harper and Brothers: F. E. Howard and F. L. Patry, *Mental health,* 1935.

Harvard University Press: H. A. Murray, *Thematic Apperception Test manual,* 1943.

Paul B. Hoeber, Inc.: Flanders Dunbar, *Psychosomatic diagnosis,* 1943.

Henry Holt and Company: J. Dewey, *Human nature and conduct,* 1922; G. W. Allport, *Personality,* 1937.

Houghton Mifflin Company: C. R. Rogers, *Counseling and psychotherapy,* 1942; C. R. Rogers, *Client-centered therapy,* 1951; W. U. Snyder, *Casebook of non-directive counseling,* 1947.

International Universities Press: L. S. Kubie, *Practical and theoretical aspects of psychoanalysis,* 1950.

Journal of Projective Techniques: M. R. Hertz, Current problems in Rorschach theory and research, Vol. 15, 1951.

Journal of the American Medical Association: Resolution on relations of medicine and psychology, Vol. 156, 1954.

The Journal Press: *Journal of Social Psychology,* M. L. Farber, Prison research: techniques and methods, Vol. 14, 1941.

McGraw-Hill Book Company, Inc.: L. E. Cole, *General Psychology*, 1939; J. Dollard and N. E. Miller, *Personality and psychotherapy*, 1950; A. Lief (Ed.), *The commonsense psychiatry of Dr. Adolph Meyer*, 1948.

The New Yorker: Stanley Hyman (in The Talk of the Town, June 30, 1945).

W. W. Norton and Company: D. M. Levy, *New fields of psychiatry*, 1947.

Oxford University Press: H. A. Murray, *Explorations in personality*, 1938.

Rinehart and Company, Inc.: C. Brown, *Brainstorm*, 1944; OSS Assessment Staff, *Assessment of men*, 1948.

Ronald Press Company: Kenneth Mark Colby, *A primer for psychotherapists*, 1951; J. McV. Hunt (Ed.), *Personality and the behavior disorders*, Vol. I, 1944.

Contents

Contents

CHAPTER 1

The Study of Persons

For centuries the study of persons has interested thoughtful people; only recently has it come to be a practical and primary occupation. In the last century great energy has been invested in the study of man, but relatively little has been expended on ways to study *a man*—concrete, particular, and unique. Scientists have mainly concerned themselves with variables, with diseases, with social structures, with general principles and laws. Even that part of psychology that came closest to the individual, the psychology of individual differences, found out more about the differences than about the individual. We do not intend to disparage the real advances that have resulted from the creation of abstractions and generalities; that is the proper task of scientists. We are emphasizing the point that the study of persons is not the same as the study of organs, conditioned responses, problem solving, or social structures. Knowledge about these areas of investigation is indispensable for the expert study of persons; but the study of the individual requires that this knowledge be applied to the doings, sayings, and surroundings of a particular person with a history of his own.

Perhaps writers, particularly novelists, have devoted themselves more completely to the observation of individuals than has any other group. With innocent disregard for academic distinctions, they follow their heroes through sickness and health, conflict and certainty, war and peace, and show them as unique centers of social events. Since novelists and dramatists have no direct responsibility for their subjects, they have a freedom to err, to omit, and to invent which is not permitted the expert who must deal with the distress of real people. For writers want to create interesting and moving stories and to meet artistic requirements that do not concern practical specialists. Nevertheless, you can learn from writers the largeness of view and the concreteness of detail needed to understand one human being.

Four qualities of great novels stand out as guideposts for the study of individual persons. In the first place, the great novelist shows his central character as part of a social network. The person is revealed, in part, by his relationships with people and by his use of these relationships to

1

get what he wants. In the second place, the person in literature is viewed over a period of time. Hardly ever does a novelist content himself with describing a central person in cross section at one moment of his life. Writers find, or else create, a sense of continuity between one week and the next, between one year and the next. Thirdly, writers are concerned with the coherence and the unity of the person as he participates in the varied activities of living. And fourthly, the novelist strives for concreteness of detail. He may be selective and inventive, but he sees to it that individuality is finally expressed in the specific acts and words of his character.

The free-ranging and detailed studies of persons by literary writers often yield penetrating insights that make the reading of literature rewarding to anyone who wants to understand people. Reik reminds us of these insights by discussing a case of a woman with insomnia, obsessional ideas, and a hand-washing compulsion. He says:

Hers was a simple and rather common case, very well understood today—thanks to Freud—but misunderstood or not understood by the psychiatrists of his time. Who understood it? A poet by the name of William Shakespeare, who presented the identical case on the stage four hundred years ago. At least the Doctor of Physic who observes Lady Macbeth confessed: "This disease is beyond my practice," whereas the psychiatrists of 1907 would have treated it. . . . What the physicians until Freud did not understand, a playwright who had not studied medicine did understand. He recognized the hidden motives and mechanisms of obsession neurosis more clearly and deeply than did the psychiatrists four hundred years later (9, p. 103).

Insights from literature are hardly enough, however, to serve as a basis for studying and helping people. We need, at least, a body of empirical generalizations derived from actual work with persons; and, ideally, we need systematic generalizations based on scientific investigations. Fortunately, some of both are now available. We also have a few methods of study that yield data beyond the reach of casual observation.

The Rise of Concern with Persons. The professional study of persons is a relatively new occupation, dating no earlier than the latter part of the nineteenth century. It does not seem correct to say that it began with the birth of scientific psychology in the 1870s, since that science purported to study consciousness, not people. Nor can the study of persons be appropriately dated from the beginning of psychiatry, since prior to the end of the nineteenth century, psychiatric interest centered around diagnosis and disease, not persons. Yet both psychology and psychiatry were intimately involved in the rise of concern with persons. Without trying to give the history of what happened around the turn of the century, we shall suggest some influences and trends of thought that contributed most to the study of persons.

One of the important influences in the development of the professional study of persons was the work of Sigmund Freud. As physician, he was concerned with relieving the distress of patients, particularly those whose complaints had no obvious organic basis. As he worked with unhappy, neurotic people he began to inquire more and more into their thoughts and feelings, their early life, and their relationships with others. It is true that, as the first psychoanalyst, Freud could be thought of as interested mainly in "the unconscious" and in the irrational basis of symptoms. But his method of inquiry and his insight into causal relationships led him inevitably, as it seems now, into the study of his patients' lives. In the famous case of Dora, reported in 1905, Freud remarks: "It follows from the nature of the facts which form the materials of psycho-analysis that we are obliged to pay as much attention in our case histories to the purely human and social circumstances of our patients as to the somatic data and the symptoms of the disorder" (8, pp. 39 f). This statement appears tame enough now, half a century later, but it was far from conventional when it was made. And it was this willingness to follow where the paths of free association led that resulted in the intensive studies of individuals, perhaps more intensive than any made before that time.

Around the turn of the century, another neurologist who had turned to psychiatry began to emphasize the study of persons. Adolph Meyer urged that American psychiatrists give up a preoccupation with supposed organic disturbances and heredity in behavior disorders; he encouraged them to study in detail the facts of the patient's life and his development instead. He refused to study "mind" in the limited way it was defined by most academic psychologists. In 1908 he argued against the artificial division of activity into mental or physical.

Mind [he said] . . . is a *sufficiently organized living being in action;* and not a peculiar form of mind stuff. A sufficiently organized brain is the main central link, but mental activity is really best understood in its full meaning as the adaptation and adjustment of the individual as a whole, in contrast to the simple activity of single organs such as those of circulation, respiration, digestion, elimination, or simple reflex activity (6, p. 172). [By 1917 he had come to define the sphere of psychiatry as the study of the patient as a person]: . . . that whole which we know as the personality of the patient, the subject of the life history, the entity to which we as physicians appeal when we give advice and map out a routine behavior and adjustment; that entity which we try to bring into health- and success-bringing relations with ourselves, the environment, and personal life problems (6, p. 406).

Here we can see, even more clearly than in Freud's work, a broadened perspective as to the kinds of facts to be sought by professional helpers and a deliberate centering on the person as the point of concern.

Another one of the roots of the study of persons is the beginning of clinical psychology in 1896. Lightner Witmer, at the University of Pennsylvania, was asked in that year to study a poor speller (4). In the same year, he made a formal announcement of his conception of the clinical method in psychology, and in 1908 he founded a journal called *The Psychological Clinic*. Other psychologists became interested in the study of the individual and established clinics (7). This phase of the development of clinical psychology was marked by concern with educational problems and so, quite naturally, with children as patients. The emphasis on personal difficulties connected with schooling was strengthened by the appearance of the intelligence test in 1905 in France. A translation of the 1908 revision of the Binet-Simon scale was made by Goddard in the United States, and by 1916 Terman had worked out a thoroughgoing revision of the test which was suitable for the examination of school children in this country.

The introduction of quantitative methods for the study of the individual certainly ranks as one of the chief contributions of psychology to clinical work. In fact, the clinical psychologist was actually regarded as a "mental tester"; in the two decades following Terman's revision, the study of persons by psychologists too often degenerated into the study of test scores. Occasionally, it still happens that a clinician loses his perspective, but most professional workers use tests as aids, not ends, in the study of individuals.

Another influence leading to the study of persons has been the development of social work as a vocation. Prior to the early years of the twentieth century, social workers were concerned almost entirely with giving assistance to needy and distressed persons. This assistance was usually money, food, or clothing, and the early social workers wanted to be sure that these "gifts" were delivered to people who were truly deserving of them. As experience in relief agencies accumulated, social workers came to see that helping others was not just a matter of deciding who was worthy of help. They found that some people resented the welfare agency and its workers, and they discovered that others became increasingly unable to help themselves as outside assistance continued. Furthermore, when social workers turned their attention to the reasons for the unfortunate state of their clients, they soon learned that they needed to understand them as persons trying to cope with a complex social structure. Gradually social work lost its moralistic tone, and the individual caseworker began to study the lives of his clients. The modern social caseworker knows that financial assistance is only one kind of help; and he knows, too, that the way in which help should be given, its kind and amount, can be determined only by studying the individual client.

The Study of Persons as an Occupation. The three streams of influence we have briefly mentioned have finally resulted in occupations having common concerns and common methods. If you were to observe psychiatrists, clinical psychologists, and social caseworkers as they deal with their clients, you would find that it is often hard to distinguish among them. Of course, you would soon discover that the special training given to each professional group had left its mark. Each kind of specialist would have proficiencies and information not found in the others. But there would also be a clearly discernible common orientation among them that marks them as professionals in the study of persons. Let us note some of the features of this common approach.

1. Their work is directed toward an immediate and practical end. They are concerned with producing some change in the person and his human relationships. They are not primarily concerned with the development of general principles of human conduct and personality, although they may formulate such principles as a secondary function. In this respect, their occupation differs from the work of scientific investigators who are concerned with long-range problems, theory building, and the establishment of general principles.

2. Their work is guided by ethical considerations as to the kinds of human changes that are desirable. The ethical values may not have been clearly formulated by the specialist, but they are implicit in both the ends he seeks and the methods he uses. Even though he may deny that his aim is to do more than help people become happy and effective, the specialist is thus expressing his conception of certain desirable values. When a consultant agrees to study and assist a person who is depressed and suicidal, he is subscribing to an ethical conception that regards suicide as undesirable. If he believes that certain information given by his client should not be disclosed to others, his belief expresses an ethical code. In this respect, the study of persons is similar to other professional occupations, although it has special ethical problems of its own.

3. The center of attention in the study of persons is the individual, not a subject-matter area. The whole range of his functioning is the source of potential data for understanding him. Consequently you will find the professional consultant investigating such diverse things as nutritional intake and literary preferences. He feels justified in considering physiological, intellectual, cultural, emotional, and sociological facts about the lives of his clients. These facts do not all have equal significance in every case. In some instances physical disease or defects will be more important than any other consideration, but in others the sociological facts will have the greatest relevance for the practical goal. The point is that the student of persons holds himself ready to incorporate many kinds of information into his final conception of the person he studies.

4. The professional consultant considers the social realities of the human environment. Whether he is psychiatrist, psychologist, or social

worker, he is interested in the persons with whom his client interacts, in the opportunities afforded him by the community, and in the demands imposed by the social group and its customs. No study of a person can afford to investigate only the inner biological and psychological workings of the individual without regard for their relationship to the social environment; for it is in this setting that the difficulties of living are noticed. The problems of persons are distinguishable from other kinds of problems because they have social outcomes.

Some Consequences of This View. We gain some advantages by adopting the person as the focus of attention. In the first place we can adopt a view toward the mind-body problem which Stern (11) calls "psychophysically neutral." Instead of parceling out observations under the dubious headings of "mental" or "physical," you can devote yourself to the understanding of the doings of a person. You attempt to perceive his total behavior in the light of his history. When you study some emotion, say hatred, the changes in blood pressure, the restless activity, and the plans for revenge are all part of the pattern. You need not assume that you are observing surface evidence of a mental state.

Cancer is clearly a "physiological" disorder, but if the victim knows he is doomed by it we shall observe emotional changes and perhaps even changes in religious beliefs. Religious belief is clearly "psychological," but did it not play an important role in the "physiological" death of martyrs? The student of persons, faced with such interrelationships, cán hardly assume that he is studying "mind" or "body." In psychiatric and psychological literature, you will meet with expressions such as "disorders of the psyche." Such phrases are awkward and inaccurate. They actually refer to disorders of the person. A psychophysically neutral view aids in discovering a variety of causes and effects in any human problem. Some are cultural, some are intellectual, some physiological, some emotional.

A second advantage of placing the person at the center of interest is that it provides a way of integrating the contributions of specialists with different backgrounds. No one field of knowledge has sole ownership of the study of persons; different human problems require the services of differently trained consultants. Since it is hard for one person to master the intricacies of a number of different fields of knowledge, the obvious way to proceed is to use a team of specialists. This practice has been followed in mental hygiene and child-study clinics for many years. In the usual team of psychologist, psychiatrist, and social worker each person contributes what he can according to his training, experience, and special inclinations. Sometimes administrators assign tasks to team members on the basis of incorrect and stereotyped conceptions of their skills. It may be assumed, for example, that psychologists should do testing and psychiatrists should carry on psychotherapy. Such a view overlooks individual proficiencies and special abilities in favor of traditional distinctions. A more defensible position is that the responsibility for various cases should be assigned on the basis of the characteristics of the client and the special talents of individual clinicians. Some experts in each of the three fields will have particular skill in diagnosis, others in research, others in treatment, and so on. Each clinic or agency must decide how its manpower resources can be most effectively deployed.

Often the team will need the services of other specialists such as speech therapists, teachers, lawyers, or dentists. It is not feasible to keep all these specialists on the staff of a single agency, but clients can be referred to them for special study or treatment. In such cases, effort should be made to integrate the outside consultant into the team. Case conferences can help each team member to see his own findings in the light of the total information about the client.

THE AIMS OF THIS BOOK

In the chapters that follow we shall try to present the study of persons from the viewpoint of clinical psychology. The book tells how clinicians trained in psychology can contribute to the understanding of people. Other kinds of clinicians would be able to supply useful methods of a different sort, but there is undoubtedly some overlapping in both method and knowledge.

The procedures discussed in the book are not intended to be used solely with abnormal persons, although clinical psychologists are usually more concerned with such people. Increasingly, clinical methods are regarded as methods for the intensive study of individuals, whether or not they show behavior disorders. Vocational counselors are not satisfied to measure and interpret abilities and interests without trying to understand the persons they counsel. Industrial psychologists use clinical methods in selecting executives and managers. Even consumer-preference studies sometimes use modified clinical methods to find the key factors in product acceptance. There are good reasons for thinking that clinically trained psychologists can make valuable contributions in many places besides clinics and mental hospitals.

The chief aim of this book is to help you develop your ability to think critically and creatively about persons. We hope you will be able to ask more significant questions about people when you have finished it. You should also be able to see possible meanings in apparently insignificant facts. You may find that you can write a better sketch of the personality of an individual you have studied. To help you acquire these proficiencies, we have interspersed problems among the chapters. These problems are part of the task of reading the book. They are not meant to test whether you have learned the specific material in the text; they are designed to give you exercise in thinking like a clinician. Occasionally a problem makes a point that has not been treated in the text, but most of the problems give you a chance to start thinking about applications of the ideas you have read. In other words, we have tried to construct this book so that your participation is required if you are to learn the beginning steps in clinical psychology. If your goal is limited to learning *about* clinical work, simply reading over the problems will do. But if you want to begin to *do* clinical work, you should write out your answers.

Another purpose of this book is to acquaint you with some of the tools used in the study of persons. You will be asked to think about test results of various kinds and speculate about their meaning. But you should not imagine that you will be sufficiently skilled in interpreting these tests to use them after reading this book. What you learn from this text should provide a background to help you in more advanced work with tests.

This book will not help you learn the skills required in actually dealing with people in a clinical setting. To meet clients in a friendly way, to be able to conduct an interview gracefully, or to administer a test without fumbling requires practice. Reading will not make you skillful. Real practice, critically evaluated, is an essential part of your training. You can make a beginning in acquiring these skills by getting nonclinical experience in dealing with people. For example, camp counselors and playground supervisors have many opportunities to learn how their behavior affects children and how to acquire poise in dealing with them. Other opportunities can be found in social-welfare agencies, industrial-employment offices, individual tutoring, and interviewing for public-opinion polls. Even assisting in the collection of data for psychological experiments can help you discover your strengths and weaknesses in face-to-face relationships.

PEOPLE WHO STUDY PEOPLE

A great many of us like to think of ourselves as "students of human nature." Often we think of choosing clinical psychology as a vocation because we are interested in people. The professional clinician, however, is not alone in having this interest. Many other professionals and nonprofessionals also claim it. The clinician is distinctive because of the special circumstances under which he studies people, the particular kinds of relationships he establishes with them, and the goals he is trying to reach. Perhaps we can see this better if we compare the ways different people study individuals.

Studying a Friend. Fred Norton [1] is thinking about asking Dottie to marry him. Fred is twenty years old, a high-school graduate, and is working as a clerk in a men's clothing store. He has dated Dottie a good deal in the last year and has spent a half-dozen evenings with her family. Since his own family frowns on divorce, he wants to be sure that his marriage will last and that Dottie is "the right girl." He feels that he knows her pretty well. She was in the high-school class following his own, and he knew her in school even before he began dating her.

Fred knows her tastes in clothes, foods, and movies. He knows what things upset her and what things please her. He knows a little about her attitude toward sex and having a family. He calls Dottie "good company" and "a lot of fun." He is sure that she loves children and will be a good mother. On the surface, Fred seems to know her pretty well, and you may think that there is little he couldn't discover about her.

How did Fred get his information? He has talked with her, kissed her, talked with her parents, and discussed her with friends. He has observed her in different situations. Actually, however, there are a good many things he doesn't know about her. Some things Fred will not learn, because he cannot ask certain questions. Discretion prevents some questions, such as those about her menstrual history or about mental disorder in her family. Other questions will never be asked, because Fred doesn't know enough about people to ask them.

Many facts that Fred does know are without significance for him. He knows that Dottie's grades in high school were consistently below average, although she studied about as much as average students. This fact raises no questions about Dottie's intelligence, because Fred simply assumes that she wasn't interested in school. Then, too, Fred has been told that she was pretty ill several years ago. She was out of school nearly a month suffering from "exhaustion due to overwork." It has not occurred to Fred to question this rather vague explanation.

Because Fred's own feelings are deeply involved, he cannot interpret relationships that he might have understood under other conditions. Dottie and her mother have quarreled frequently, and, naturally enough, Fred's sympathies are with his girl. Privately he thinks marriage may be good for Dottie, since it will take her away from her mother's nagging. He does not see that she is emotionally dependent upon her mother to a degree that could seriously affect her married life.

Our example is intended to show that intimate acquaintance with another person does not necessarily lead to a rich understanding of that

---

[1] People in many of our examples will be given names. These names are not intended to refer to actual persons. Possibly some examples will seem to refer to people you know, but that will be due to coincidence.

person. Indeed, a very close relationship may make it harder to understand him. Whether Fred is right or wrong in his judgment of Dottie, he must eventually make a decision about marriage. The decision which he makes will implicitly contain a prediction, perhaps a vague one, about Dottie and her future.

Psychological Research. John Marden is in his last year of graduate work in psychology and is collecting data for his doctoral dissertation. He wants to find the reasons why students fail in college and hopes that his findings may help failing students. He is twenty-six, unmarried, interested in chess and photography. He prides himself on his objective, scientific approach to this research.

He has constructed an autobiographical questionnaire to furnish the main information about his subjects. He also plans to use the interest-test scores, the intelligence-test scores, and the grade records of his subjects. After he has made a detailed analysis of the data from his passing and failing groups, he will be able to draw some conclusions about the reasons for failure.

Marden's data sheets cannot include certain kinds of information that Fred Norton could easily get. Fred has actually met the family of his "subject," and he has spent long hours talking with Dottie. If Marden meets his subjects individually, he will spend only an hour or so with them, and the relationship will be formal and academic. Nevertheless, Marden will probably be able to reach some conclusions about the reasons for failure, and to make predictions about new groups of students.

Professional Consultation. Dr. Harold Green is a consulting psychologist. One morning he is visited by Ted, a married man of twenty-three. Ted says that he is having a hard time with his college work because he can't concentrate. Dr. Green listens to Ted's story and then asks a few questions about the young man's health and vocational plans. During their talk, Ted says that he worries a bit about money, although he admits that his wife's earnings are adequate at present. She had finished college while Ted was in the Army and she has continued in the job she had when they were married a year ago.

At the end of the interview, Dr. Green asked Ted to return in a few days so they could talk further. In the next interview Ted showed that he resented his wife's working. He felt too obligated to her for supporting him. He also feared he could not match the grades she had earned in college. Dr. Green had no advice to offer, but he made it easy for Ted to talk about his feelings.

The next interview turned out to be the last one. Ted reported that he had finally brought himself to discuss the whole matter with his wife and that he felt better about things. He felt that he was studying better and that he could work out any remaining problems with his wife.

During these three interviews Dr. Green obtained a good deal of information about Ted. Probably the actual facts he possessed about his client were fewer than Fred Norton possessed about Dottie. On the other hand, he drew conclusions that Norton could not have reached.

When Green's information is compared with the information Marden collected about one of his subjects, it is clear that in many ways Marden's information was more precise. Green did not have Ted's actual test scores to assist him. But Green could see interrelationships among the facts in a way that Marden could not. Furthermore, he obtained information about Ted's feelings and desires which could not usually be obtained on tests and questionnaires.

Dr. Green had a number of decisions and predictions to make during these three contacts. He had to come to some conclusion about the seriousness of Ted's difficulty, about Ted's ability to do college work, and about the probable stability of the marriage. He also had to decide whether or not he was capable of helping Ted, whether any tests were needed, and whether Ted's wife should be interviewed. These decisions could be made without the intense emotional involvement of Norton, but they had to be made with reference to the welfare of his client.

Comparison of the Three Orientations. These three people—the nonspecialist, the scientist, and the consultant—are all dealing with people. Each collects data, draws conclusions, and comes to decisions. But there are differences in:

1. The kind of data available to each observer
2. The relationship between the observer and his subject
3. The degree to which each observer is personally involved in the outcome of the study
4. The immediate goals of the study

We should add one other difference that arises at the level of the verbal formulations made by each kind of observer. The nonspecialist is primarily interested in limited generalizations applying to one person at a time. His statements are like this: "John does not like parties but he wants to learn to dance." The consultant seeks wider generalizations but limits them to one person at a time: "John is fearful of social situations but desires social approval." The scientist reaches his goal when he can make even more general statements: "Simultaneous approach and avoidance tendencies lead to vacillating behavior." In this kind of statement, all reference to particular individuals has disappeared; it is a statement about the relationship among variables.

Our illustrations have been overdrawn to emphasize the distinctive qualities of the three kinds of study. Actually consultants often do research work, and investigators may use clinical methods in gathering data. You should keep the two functions separated in your thinking, however. In actual practice, the clinician must often sacrifice necessary research controls to insure the welfare of his client. Then his observations cannot serve to prove an hypothesis; they serve only as suggestive evidence in favor of it.

VARIETIES OF CLINICAL WORK

Clinical psychologists are engaged in many types of work. The specific details and immediate aims of their work differ from job to job, but they also have a good many tasks in common. The most adequate account of the kinds of clinical work available has been presented by Shartle (10). His analysis covers twenty-eight kinds of psychological positions, and lists the duties, qualifications, advancement possibilities, and range of income for each one. In order to show you what various clinicians are called on to do, we shall draw upon Shartle's descriptions of five different positions.

College Counselor. These specialists help students to select courses in accord with their plans and abilities. Also, they often deal with students who are on probation. Sometimes they are concerned with vocational guidance in a college setting. They depend heavily upon interviews, grades, reports from instructors, and test results in assisting their clients. Often they must confer with parents and instructors who feel that a particular student is having trouble. While they rarely have the time to do psychotherapeutic work, they may have a number of counseling interviews with a single student. Usually they have additional duties such as taking charge of an employment agency for student part-time work, administering entrance examinations, or teaching a few courses in psychology or guidance.

Employment Counselor. These positions may be found in connection with universities, governmental agencies, or private firms. The counselors advise clients about job opportunities, training opportunities, and the duties in various kinds of work. Interviews are used to evaluate the client's experience, education, and interests, although tests are often used in addition. The counselor surveys published occupational information and occupational statistics, and visits business firms and industrial plants to obtain knowledge of various jobs. Marked personality deviations in a client would influence the counselor's advice and could result in referring the client for treatment.

Psychologist in Penal Institutions. This specialist is usually in charge of test administration to groups of prisoners. He writes interpretations of the test results for the prisoners' records. This information, along with data from individual interviews, is used to plan educational and placement programs within the prison, and may influence decisions about parole. The psychologist attends staff meetings and supplies information about the prisoners that is helpful or required. He also works with other specialists in planning for cases of physical handicap or psychiatric disturbance. Research on psychological problems peculiar to prisons often occupies some of his time.

General Clinical Psychologist. The general clinical psychologist often works in a "mental-hygiene clinic," in an institution for the feeble-minded, or in court. Sometimes institutions for special purposes, such as drug-addiction hospitals, orphans' homes, or schools for the blind or deaf, employ a clinical psychologist. Although there is wide variation in the amount of time devoted to various duties in these different settings, a primary task is usually the preparation of case studies. The psychologist conducts interviews, gives and scores tests, and integrates his findings. At times he gives vocational guidance; at other times he conducts psychotherapy for individual clients. Many times he is asked to advise administrators and teachers about educational and training programs for individuals he has studied. In a good many clinics, the psychologist must supervise the training of student clinicians, evaluate their progress, and hold conferences with them about their work.

Psychologist in Mental Hospitals. This kind of position also requires case reports as an important duty. The psychologist may not take a complete case history but usually has it available from hospital files. He has a good deal of testing to do, and he presents the data he gathers to case conferences, to aid in diagnosis and treatment planning. He has the responsibility for keeping records and filing test and interview data. Occasionally he may make surveys of accumulated information in the files for some special purpose. He may collaborate in carrying out vocational therapy, speech therapy, and reeducation. Sometimes the hospital psychologist engages in individual or group psychotherapy. Planning and carrying out research investigations is often part of the job, particularly where there is a large staff. If student psychologists are being trained, the clinical psychologist may supervise their work or assist them in planning research.

Other Kinds of Positions. Of course, there are a good many other positions requiring training in clinical psychology. Child psychologists or school psychologists obviously have a good many responsibilities of a clinical nature. Even in industrial psychology, a clinical psychologist can make contributions to the intensive study of executive personnel. Clinical psychologists may have positions with agencies that are primarily concerned with parent education or the education of the general public in understanding emotional problems.

In contrast to these jobs, many positions do not require a fully trained clinician but do need people with a substantial knowledge of the psychological clinician's approach. Among the educational occupations, such positions include: dean of men, dean of women, high-school principals, and counselors. In the industrial field, personnel workers, counselors, and some industrial physicians are concerned with individual psychological problems. Indeed, people in any position that requires understanding the individual as a whole can profit from knowing how clinicians do their work.

Activities Common to Clinicians. As you read the descriptions of clinical work, you probably saw some duties that were common to nearly all the jobs. We can summarize them this way:

1. Administering and interpreting tests
2. Interviewing to find data for describing personality
3. Interviewing for counseling, guidance, or therapy
4. Writing and presenting case reports
5. Conferring with other specialists
6. Interviewing relatives and other persons especially interested in the client's welfare
7. Preparing reports of work completed or of original research

Taken together, these activities constitute a kind of definition of a clinical psychologist. The amount of time devoted to each one, however, will differ widely in different jobs.

PREPARATION FOR CLINICAL PSYCHOLOGY

By now you can see that the expert in the study of persons cannot do a good job without broad preparation. He must be able to talk to people from many different backgrounds and to understand how physicians, educators, and social workers think about human problems. On one day, he may have to decide whether his test results show that a patient has a damaged brain; on the next, he may be asked to work out a way of selecting the best hospital attendants from those who apply. Not only must the clinician be skillful in cooperating with others and be familiar with psychology, he must be able to put down his observations and conclusions in writing. Most clinicians spend much time writing or dictating reports for other people to read. Students who think they may want to do clinical work had better decide early to develop a clear expository style.

College Preparation.[2] Most students who plan to become professional psychologists choose psychology as their major field in college. Some students major in sociology or biology but take sufficient psychology courses to enter graduate school. It is important, however, to realize

[2] The remarks about preparation are based upon the 1947 report of the Committee on Training in Clinical Psychology of the American Psychological Association (1).

the value of broad undergraduate education. The specialized work in graduate school rarely affords time to learn much about subjects that were missed in college. Useful background courses for the future clinician include: genetics, physiology, statistics, sociology, philosophy, English composition, literature, and drawing or painting. If the graduate school to be attended requires a reading knowledge of foreign languages for the doctor's degree, the student should at least begin language study in college. Taking courses is not the only way to get the general background you need, however. You can plan your own reading to help overcome excessively narrow training.

Graduate Work. Increasingly, the Ph.D. in psychology is regarded as necessary for the practice of clinical psychology. The professional student must therefore expect to spend three to five years following his college work in a graduate school. Here he will aim at becoming a psychologist before he becomes a clinical psychologist. The history, methods, and general propositions common to all psychology are part of the equipment needed by those who specialize later in a particular kind of psychological work. This general background of information enables the clinician to meet the diverse requirements made of him. But perhaps more important is the fact that this background develops attitudes and habits of critical thought that enable him to make a distinctive contribution to a team of specialists.

For the clinician, graduate courses will include: personality theory, motivation, testing, interviewing, psychopathology, psychotherapy, and related courses in medical, educational, or sociological studies. Practical work in agencies as a psychological intern will be required to develop skill in dealing with clients. Learning research methods will require familiarity with statistics, laboratory methods, and with planning and carrying out investigations of psychological problems.

Informal Preparation. We have already suggested that future clinicians need work experience that exposes them to a variety of people. Most of us are in close contact solely with people much like ourselves. This narrow contact produces a narrow set of standards for judging normality and deviations. Moreover, many of us are uncomfortable when we interact with uneducated people or individuals from regional cultures unlike our own. We do not know the "social rules" in these groups. Whatever you can do informally to get a feel for the range of human differences can be turned to good account in clinical work. Even industrial jobs can serve as preclinical training if they enlarge your perspective on the human scene.

Another kind of preparation is getting to know the community in which you live or work. Local customs, forms of speech, recreation habits, and fads are part of the intimate culture that influences people.

Lacking this kind of information, you may be puzzled by behavior that should be easily understood. In military service, for example, psychologists found that they had to be familiar with service slang, drill commands, and daily routines in order to understand the men they studied.

One day a recruit was brought to a military psychiatric unit with the report that he had had a convulsion during rifle practice. The description of the seizure suggested that it was hysterical rather than epileptic. To aid in making the diagnosis, the recruit was hypnotized and asked to recall his thoughts just before the convulsion began. He started to mumble, "Maggie's drawers, Maggie's drawers, Maggie's drawers to him who missed the target." This bizarre remark puzzled the clinicians. It was not until later that they learned that "Maggie's drawers" was a slang term on the rifle range. It referred to a red flag that was hoisted to indicate that the target had been missed completely.

A practicing psychologist needs to be aware of social habits and local custom wherever he is. Even the mere home address of a client may tell something to a psychologist with a good knowledge of his community. And more is added by learning the client's church affiliation, social organizations, and recreational habits.

Problem 1. Answer the following questions about the city or community you know best.

1. Rank the various neighborhoods or suburbs in the order of their prestige within the community.

2. In what areas is living space likely to be inadequate?

3. What church is most likely to attract professional and managerial groups? What church has few managerial and professional people as members?

4. Is a girl who has her first date at the age of sixteen beginning to date early or late? Would attitudes on this matter be different in different parts of the community?

5. Is it considered respectable for young newlyweds to live for a while with the parents of one or the other?

6. If you moved to a new community, how could you find out the answers to the preceding questions about that community?

Familiarity with the Cultural Heritage. The professional clinician will be regarded as an educated person by his professional associates and by his community. And, especially if he is in private practice, many of his clients will be well-educated, intelligent people. They are likely to speak about art, music, drama, or current events with considerable familiarity. They may allude to a novel or a painting in order to explain their meaning. While clinicians cannot equal their clients in specialized backgrounds, they should have the fund of information that is commonly found among educated people. Clients may lose confidence in the professional competence of a clinician who appears poorly informed in general.

In *Brainstorm,* a novel by Carleton Brown, the central character describes an interview with a clinician after he had been admitted to a mental hospital. The patient says:

When he asked about some of the nonsense verses I had written, I said that I had been dabbling in a Joycean stream of fancy. "Joycean?" repeated Dr. Soup, with the expression of a man who has taken a doubtful oyster into his mouth and doesn't know what to do with it. "Yes," I said, "I'm an admirer of James Joyce and I was aping him in those verses." "This Joyce is a writer?" he asked superiorly.

I know, it seems almost inconceivable that such a conversation could have been held with a man presumably skilled in psychiatry, but held it was and a number of others like it. It would be too much to ask that every psychiatrist acquaint himself genuinely with the influences that mold the currents of thought of his age. . . . But it would be nice if he would read the papers (5, pp. 262 f).

THE CLINICIAN'S PERSONALITY

Clinical psychologists cannot work effectively if they are prone to become anxious in intimate interpersonal relationships. Within a single day, a clinician may meet open resentment, suspicion, and fear. He may be confronted by patients who insist he is their last hope and who threaten suicide. Relatives may condemn him because he is wrecking their loved one. Or cooperating specialists may doubt his conclusions. These and similar pressures can easily arouse defensive hostility or submissiveness on the part of the clinician, and if he is protecting his own pride he cannot face realistically the problems that confront him. He is likely to misinterpret the behavior of his clients. An even more serious consequence is that his own behavior may create new difficulties for the people he is trying to help.

It is certainly safe to say that the clinician should have "a reasonably well-adjusted and attractive personality" (1, p. 541). Although research evidence is lacking as to the specific personal qualifications needed by good clinicians, a number of suggestions have been put forward. Let us consider a few of those mentioned by the Committee on Training in Clinical Psychology of the American Psychological Association (1).

Interest in Persons without a Desire to Manipulate Them. Some students become interested in clinical work because they feel inadequate in dealing with people. Without realizing it, they wish to use psychological knowledge to dominate or control others. You can see this kind of desire in college students who attempt, without guidance and with too much success, to hypnotize their friends. Another example is furnished by students who use psychological terms to label their friends and family without thinking of the possibly harmful effects of such name-calling. Useful clinical work is carried on in a professional atmosphere by people who respect the rights of their clients. It cannot be done by those who build their self-esteem by manipulating individuals with emotional problems.

Insight into One's Own Personality. If you understand some of your own "sore spots" and fears, you are not likely to treat clients in a way that may harm them. A man who unwittingly regards all women as competitors will probably have trouble in helping female clients. Moreover, he will cooperate poorly with women who happen to be colleagues. Insight into his attitude may help him avoid serious trouble along these lines, and it may even help him change his attitude.

It is not easy to decide how to attain the needed insight. For some students, it is worth while to get psychotherapeutic help. But if they seek therapy merely out of an intellectual conviction that it is a good thing, they may not be able to alter their attitudes very much. For other people, the insight that comes with knowledge and maturity will be sufficient. If you know that you have trouble in human relationships or easily become anxious, probably you should plan to seek expert help early in your professional training.

Tolerance. At the very least, a tolerant attitude implies that one does not feel animosity toward specific racial, religious, or sectional groups. But the tolerance needed by a clinician must be even broader: he must be able to accept differences in values and ways of living among people. He ought to see that there are areas of legitimate disagreement about conduct without renouncing his convictions about the kind of life which is best for him. Actually, as you understand more about the causes of individual behavior you will find it easier to accept persons without requiring them to conform to your own standards.

Integrity and Self-control. The general public and the various professions certainly expect that a psychological consultant can be trusted. They expect him not only to keep promises and to be honest in his claims, but also to use his skill primarily for the welfare of his clients. Anything that savors of exploitation for personal gain cannot be countenanced within the profession. There are a thousand ways of misusing psychological knowledge; no code of ethics could list them all. Some specialists pretentiously claim to show clients how to be successful in marriage or business; others diagnose a patient's ills by mail; and some deliberately exaggerate the seriousness of a patient's condition in order to exact more money from him. Fortunately, such dishonesty is rare among professionally trained clinicians.

Outside his professional work, the psychologist should be worthy of respect and confidence. Public opinion will not apply one set of standards to the clinician's professional conduct and a very different set to his social conduct. Whether he likes it or not, the consultant is working within a social setting where ethical and moral judgments are expressed. If these judgments are unfavorable to the clinician, he is not likely to attract those who seek help. Generally, sexual escapades, excessive drinking, and a playboy attitude will make the members of the community feel that the clinician is unreliable and incompetent. If a clinician feels that the community standards are too stringent and unyielding, he had better move to a locality where he feels more at home. There are few places, however, that will welcome the opportunist, the notoriety seeker, the know-it-all, or the yes man.

People of integrity are presumed to have a set of mature convictions about important values and legitimate means for reaching them. Clients may not always agree with a psychologist's philosophy of living, but at least they know what to expect if he has one.

Other Qualifications. In order to complete the required training for a professional psychologist, a student needs superior academic ability, diligence, and interest in the subject matter. Few graduate schools will accept students who have earned only average grades during their college years. Ordinarily, a student must present a superior undergraduate record in order to be admitted to further work. Admission committees will also be interested in leadership, originality, and special proficiencies displayed in college. They attempt to admit students who will probably be successful in attaining the doctorate, but, of course, admission is no guarantee of successful completion.

Problem 2. Ed Stepak is in his last year of college. His grades have been better than average, and he stands in the upper quarter of his class. He is taking major work in psychology and minor work in biology. His single extracurricular interest in college has been choral singing. He has dated about three or four times a month in his last two years. Stepak is interested in becoming a clinical psychologist and hopes to go to graduate school.

Ed has some misgivings about his plans. His parents were born in the Balkan area and came to this country shortly before he was born. His father has been a foreman in an industrial plant for the last eight years, but the family of six has never been able to afford luxuries. Ed feels that his home did not help him develop social poise because of its foreign background and its economic level. His parents have helped him through college, but he has had to do some spare-time work each year. Around the campus he is liked, but is known as a rather quiet fellow, industrious, and serious. He wonders, in view of his background and seeming lack of social ease, whether he should try to become a clinician.

1. What are three or four specific things Stepak could do to help him decide?

2. Would there be other kinds of psychological work where his self-diagnosed handicaps would not hinder him? What are they?

3. What further information would you need about Stepak to help you decide what he should do?

4. Does the fact that Stepak doubts his own adequacy have any significance in judging his personality? Is it a favorable or unfavorable sign? Why?

PROFESSIONAL ETHICS

In order to protect the public against harmful or misleading psychological practices, psychologists have formulated ethical standards to govern their work. The most complete summary of a code of ethics has been published by the American Psychological Association (3). While these standards are meant primarily for professional psychologists, students who are in training for psychological work will be expected to observe them. When you begin the actual testing and interviewing of clients, you should familiarize yourself with the entire summary; for the present we shall consider only a few of the standards you should know about.

One of the most important statements in the code of ethics is this: "A cardinal obligation of the clinical or consulting psychologist is to respect the integrity and protect the welfare of the person with whom he is working. Vigilant regard for this principle should characterize all of the work of the psychologist and pervade all his professional relationships" (2, p. 49). While this is a very general and broad statement of the clinician's responsibility, its spirit and intent are clear. Psychologists must carefully inspect their methods of work, their relationships with the client, and their remarks to the client's family and friends, to ensure the welfare of the client. But more than this is involved; there must be a respect for the right of people to make important decisions for themselves. "Clinical services must not be imposed upon an individual, nor should a person be unduly urged to avail himself of such services" (2, p. 49). In some instances, of course, people may not be competent to make their own decisions; then the principle is applied to the parents or guardians of the person in question. Students, in particular, must not attempt to force their services on other people, even though they sincerely believe they can help.

Enthusiastic students who have discovered the value of clinical methods sometimes "oversell" psychology by implying that "it has all the answers." Actually, a psychologist cannot guarantee favorable results. "A considered and moderate description of probabilities . . . should be given when assessing for a client the likely outcome of clinical work" (2, p. 51).

Problem 3. At an informal social gathering, an advanced student of psychology mentioned that he had just completed a course dealing with tests of personality and emotional stability. Later, one of the guests asked the student privately if he would be willing to administer some of the tests to him. The guest indicated that he had been emotionally upset for the last year and thought the test could confirm his nervousness.

1. What line of action should the student follow?
2. What should the student tell the guest?
3. What harm, if any, could result from administering the kind of test requested by the guest?

In view of the intimate details which clinicians learn about the lives of their clients, psychologists insist that the information they gather about clients shall be kept confidential. Special problems, such as using clinical data for instructional and research purposes, require special principles. Students may use the following principle as their guide: "Information obtained in clinical or consulting relationships should be discussed only in professional settings and with professional persons clearly concerned with the case" (2, p. 56). If any doubt about this and other ethical standards should arise, you should consult your supervisor or instructor before taking any action. They will be able to inform you of specific local practice and the general principles which should apply to your problem.

In the course of working with people, as a student, you will be engaging in practice testing. While you may clearly understand that your work is practice only, your subject may be quite interested in his test scores or in your interpretation of the test results. Since your relationship with volunteer subjects is not professional in nature, it is usually wise to point out in advance that you are not qualified to release test information. Sometimes, with the advice of your supervisor, it is possible to make suggestions which will be helpful, however. You should be cautious in the matter, since communicating information to clients requires considerable skill. Without realizing it, you may arouse anxiety in a person by the language or tone of voice you use. If a volunteer should demand to know about his test results, talk the problem over with your instructor. In some cases, he may be willing to discuss the findings or their implications with your subject.

One final caution should be emphasized. Psychological tests are usually of no value when their scoring methods have been revealed. As a matter of professional pride, you should safeguard scoring keys and test materials that you use or own. "Demonstrations of tests and related devices . . . should be planned to illustrate the nature of the device (if this can be done without spoiling the test itself), but should avoid incidental or specific coaching in the use of the actual materials of the test or device" (2, p. 156).

Problem 4. Mr. Williamson is planning to apply for a position in a business firm which uses tests as part of its employee-selection program. He has been told that one of the tests is an intelligence test. Williamson goes to a friend of his, who is a psychologist and who is familiar with intelligence tests, requesting information about such tests. What kind of information could the psychologist ethically give Williamson?

Problem 5. Jim is an eighteen-year-old boy who has consulted a vocational counselor at his father's urging. Together, Jim and the counselor have arrived at some tentative vocational goals. One day Jim's father visits the counselor and asks to see Jim's test scores. He says that since he gave Jim the money to pay for counseling, and since he is the boy's father, he has a right to know the test results.

1. Should the counselor show the father Jim's test scores and discuss them with him?

2. Would it be ethical for the counselor to report to the father the general conclusions he had reached in his work with Jim?

REFERENCES

1. American Psychological Association, Committee on Training in Clinical Psychology. Report. *Amer. Psychologist,* 1947, **2,** 539–558.
2. American Psychological Association. *Ethical standards of psychologists.* Washington: Amer. Psychological Ass., 1953.
3. American Psychological Association. *Ethical standards of psychologists, a summary of ethical principles.* Washington: Amer. Psychological Ass., 1953.
4. Brotemarkle, R. A. Clinical psychology 1896–1946. *J. consult. Psychol.,* 1947, **11,** 1–4.
5. Brown, C. *Brainstorm.* New York: Farrar & Rinehart, 1944.
6. Lief, A. (Ed.) *The commonsense psychiatry of Dr. Adolph Meyer.* New York: McGraw-Hill, 1948.
7. Louttit, C. M. The nature of clinical psychology. *Psychol. Bull.,* 1939, **36,** 361–389.
8. Katz, S. (Ed.) *Freud: On war, sex, and neurosis.* New York: Arts & Science Press, 1947.
9. Reik, T. *Listening with the third ear.* New York: Farrar, Straus, 1948.
10. Shartle, C. L. Occupations in psychology. *Amer. Psychol.,* 1946, **1,** 559–582.
11. Stern, W. *General psychology from the personalistic standpoint.* New York: Macmillan, 1938.

CHAPTER 2

Prediction in Clinical Psychology

Studying persons in a clinical setting is an art or technology, not a scientific undertaking. This statement may sound derogatory because the term "scientific" carries prestige; and clinical psychology is new enough to want prestige. But there is no need to be apologetic about the position of clinicians as practitioners and appliers of knowledge. Studying and helping people requires just as much skill, training, and devotion to human welfare as scientific research does.

We are not saying that clinicians do not need to know scientific methods or a substantial body of scientific fact. Quite the contrary is true. The best clinical work demands this kind of background. With it clinicians can evaluate research reports and proposed methods better than they can without it. Training in scientific psychology produces a sharp awareness of the assumptions that lie behind measurement and prediction. Familiarity with psychological theory aids in recognizing fuzzy concepts and half-baked notions about human nature.

If clinicians must have scientific training and if they try to use scientific methods, how are they different from scientists? One difference is that clinicians must work within the limits of practical necessity. Pressures of time, expense, community attitudes, and administrative policy force them to use techniques that would not be scientifically acceptable. During World War II, for example, psychologists often had to use brief testing methods that were far from the best available. But there was an enormous number of men to be examined and time was short. What else was to be done? The clinicians invented and contrived tests as best they could, and their scientific training helped them contrive methods that were better than those used by practitioners who did not know scientific psychology.

In the second place, clinicians must fill gaps in scientific knowledge by guessing or overgeneralizing scientific findings. Faced with a person who wants help, they use available information even though it may not strictly apply to that particular case. Psychotherapy is a good example. Scientifically, very little is known about the therapeutic process. We are

23

not sure what variables are the most crucial nor exactly how to manipulate them. But the clinician does what he can, depending upon case reports, partly established theory, and his own experience for guides.

Another difference between scientific and clinical work is due to the uncontrolled and complex nature of "real life." Scientists control the conditions of observation and measurement; they can study the effects of one or two specific variables. Life situations come ready-made. Many variables have acted jointly to produce the personality we wish to study. We cannot be sure that we are picking out the most important variables to predict outcomes or to manipulate them so as to help our client. Even when sound scientific principles are at hand, we may be puzzled as to how they should be translated into action. The situation is illustrated by the following true story:

A young father tried to apply the principle of reward learning to the toilet training of his young son. The boy was rewarded with candy whenever he used the toilet, but somehow he could not learn to keep himself dry. "Good psychology" was not decreasing the size of the daily washing. Finally, the father consulted a clinical psychologist.

A brief conversation revealed that this only child was expected to meet standards of conduct that would have been high even for a four-year-old. Then too, although mother and son usually chatted freely with each other, mother became silent for some time after each toilet mistake. It must have been clear to the boy that this whole bathroom business was pretty important. Possibly the candy reward was changing a natural function into a technique for upsetting the parents. At any rate, the psychologist suggested discarding the reward and treating the whole matter more casually. Within a month the boy had learned to control himself satisfactorily.

In this example, the father erred by neglecting to consider the relationship of the candy reward to the complex family situation. Quite possibly the reward was effective in helping the child learn how to annoy the mother. The psychologist tried to take a broader view of the problem than the parents did, but can we be sure that his analysis was correct? Although his suggestion seems to have been helpful, we do not know that it alone was responsible for the change in the child's behavior. Perhaps the neuromuscular maturation that took place in a month was enough to produce the change. Or perhaps the outcome was due to a generally changed relationship between parents and child. The mere fact of a favorable outcome is no proof that the psychologist had advised correctly.

In the face of such uncertainties and limitations, the clinician must try to predict the outcomes of various lines of action. He must arrive at decisions about the future of his clients and the kind of help that will be beneficial. In this chapter we shall analyze the predictive process and its logic. As a beginning let us examine the kinds of decisions clinicians must make.

CLINICAL RECOMMENDATIONS

The end results of a long study of a single person are simple: a few paragraphs stating the clinician's recommendations. Usually the clinician writes a summary of his findings showing why he believes that his decision is correct. The important thing about the clinician's recommendations is that they always imply something to be done. He supports some course of action with reference to a client or he does not support it. Even though he works as a member of a team and does not make the final decision himself, the data he collects should have a bearing on the life of a person. He is not in the position of a writer or of a scientist; they are gathering data for the sake of art or the establishment of principles. The clinician gathers data for the sake of action. We may classify the kinds of action to be taken under three headings and consider each in turn.

Selection. In selection problems the question is: Given a number of persons and a limited number of positions or opportunities, which persons shall be permitted to fill the positions or have the opportunities? The clinician must arrive finally at a designation of the persons to be chosen or a list of the applicants in order of preference. In selecting executives, for example, the clinician may study three or four applicants. His recommendation may take the form of a listing of the applicants in the order of their estimated over-all ability, of their degree of emotional stability, or of some other particular trait. Many times he will be asked to report only on the personality of the applicants, while other specialists evaluate their technical background and skills. Pooling the information leads to a decision as to which persons to select.

A comparable problem exists when only a limited number of training opportunities are available. A professional school that can admit only fifty students will need to select that number from among several hundred applicants. The question is: Which persons will eventually make the best lawyers, physicians, architects, chemists, or teachers?

The point of view in selection emphasizes the requirements of the job or the opportunity. Obviously the clinician must be familiar with the job or training requirements. Then he seeks among the applicants for the characteristics that are needed. When there are large numbers of applicants, selection is ordinarily carried out by means of tests or scorable application blanks. If an applicant's score exceeds some predetermined value, he is considered suitable. Where there are few applicants and the position is important, some applicants will be eliminated on the basis of test scores or amount of experience, and the clinician will intensively study those remaining.

In selection work, the client may be a business, agency, school, or governmental unit, and the clinician has a primary responsibility to that client or employer. However, he must also consider the welfare of the applicants and decide what kind of information must remain confidential.

Disposition. The central question in disposition or placement problems is: Given a number of opportunities or jobs, which one best suits the requirements of this person? This kind of problem arises in connection with foster-home placements, vocational guidance, job assignments of prisoners, and dispositions made by courts. Usually there are alternative courses of action possible in attempting to settle a human problem, and the clinician helps to decide among the alternatives. In military work, for example, a clinician may recommend that a recruit be discharged, held for further study, sent to a hospital, placed on limited duty, or returned to regular duty.

As a clinician works in an agency, he comes to learn what dispositions are possible in that setting. Legal restrictions or agency policy may require or prevent certain kinds of action. Within these limits, however, the point of view in disposition problems is based on the requirements of the person being studied. What position, location, job, or opportunity will benefit him most?

Treatment. Given a variety of special methods for retraining or remedial work, which will benefit the client most? Among the possible alternative methods, the clinician seeks those which have the greatest probability of helping the client overcome his handicaps or increase his happiness. Methods may range from occupational therapy, remedial reading, and special schooling to intensive individual psychotherapy, lobotomy, or insulin shock treatment. We must consider the suitability of the client for the particular form of treatment and the probable success of the methods available.

Another task in connection with treatment is the evaluation of improvement. The psychologist may be requested to determine whether or not the patient has changed from his pretreatment status, and to describe the nature of these changes. The practical effect of this evaluation is to influence the decision to terminate treatment, continue it, or modify it.

Determinants of Recommendations. The chief determinant of a recommendation is the clinician's estimate of the probable success of a given course of action, whether or not it involves selection, disposition, or treatment. The accurate prediction of outcomes is thus a matter of prime importance, and we shall say more about it shortly. But there are special factors which modify recommendations so that they are not simply statements of predictions. These factors are practical limitations that must be taken into account, because no clinician works under ideal circumstances.

In the first place, a recommendation must take into account the facilities for disposition and treatment that are actually available. Psychotherapy may be impossible because of the lack of therapists. Agencies for training handicapped persons may be overcrowded, foster homes may be lacking, or particular jobs may not be open. A realistically oriented clinician must face these facts and will sometimes have to choose a course that is second-best. That would not prevent him from suggesting that another course of action would be preferable if it were possible.

Closely related to the matter of availability is the matter of cost. Many kinds of treatment or training are prohibitively expensive and thus, in effect, not available. Here again it may be necessary to recommend a course of action which is possible even though it may not be the most desirable. You should remember, however, that a client's objections to cost may sometimes mask other objections that are more fundamental. For example, a deep resentment against physicians may be the actual reason for refusing psychiatric treatment, but the expressed reason is that the fees are too high. Or parents may resist the recommendation of psychotherapy for their child, because they fear both a loss of status in the eyes of their friends and the revelations the child may make to the therapist. Objections to the cost of the treatment permit them to conceal the real reasons for their decision.

More rarely, a family is willing to sacrifice too heavily in order to follow a recommendation. Suppose that a family is informed that one of its members requires institutional care. Instead of accepting adequate public facilities, the family denies itself to the point of martyrdom in order to pay for private care. Such a decision can result from a fear of public opinion or from feelings of guilt over the way the relative has been treated. The family may not understand that when the patient is finally discharged from treatment, he may feel an oppressive sense of obligation. He may feel guilty because of the burden he has placed on his family.

Another factor to be considered in making recommendations is the risk involved in any proposed action. Suppose that two treatments have equal chances of helping a patient. One method is more hazardous than the other, however. In that case the less dangerous one would be recommended. This simple situation is rarely duplicated in real life. More dangerous treatments may offer greater chances for recovery. Brain operations, for example, sometimes produce a remarkable improvement in psychotic conditions; but sometimes they seem to destroy initiative, foresight, and good judgment. Occupational therapy, on the other hand, is safe but not likely to lead to recovery. In deciding to take risks, the values of patient, family, and clinician are crucial factors. Is life as a deluded psychotic preferable to life as a submissive invalid? Individual families will answer this question differently.

In view of the complex practical factors that enter into recommendations, clinicians should be wary of making important decisions alone. They should plan cooperatively with the client or his family for the best course of action. Clinicians can share their judgment of the probable outcomes of various lines of action and encourage the client or family to suggest their limitations and express their feelings. When the clinician explains his judgments, he provides clients with information they need. The final decision, jointly arrived at, can be accepted by the client or his family in such a way that they can give constructive help in following the course of action.

THE LOGIC OF PREDICTION

Although practical necessity influences selection, treatment, and disposition, the prime factor is the predicted outcome of the action to be taken. How can these predictions be made accurately? What do we need to do in order to forecast success on a job, in college, in marriage, in meeting the requirements and opportunities of the social environment? The answer to these questions is given in part by the logical and statistical analysis of prediction. Examining the logic of prediction will clarify the clinician's task. Probably the logical basis of a prediction is rarely made explicit in the daily work of the clinician. Familiarity with clinical material permits the experienced worker to leap quickly from observation to conclusion without laboring over the intervening steps. Often enough, however, he errs, and then the logical analysis must begin. Certainly, ignoring or deliberately violating logical principles will not result in good clinical work.

Defining a Logical Class. Suppose that we wish to separate a large group of people into subgroups on the basis of some attribute, say, hallucinations. We set up a standard or definition for determining whether hallucinatory behavior is present and apply it to each member of the group. When we finish studying each person, we should be able to form at least two subgroups: those who have hallucinations and those who don't. We pay no attention to age, sex, nationality, or any other characteristics in making the division. When the task is done, the subgroups contain representatives or samples of those who possess the attribute and those who do not.

Actually, this task of defining a class and assigning people to it is not as easy as it sounds. If we were to carry out the steps required to separate people into hallucinated and nonhallucinated groups, we should find some doubtful cases. What should be done with people who report having had an hallucination many years ago but have not had one since? What should be done with people whose statements are vague and indefinite? Probably we should end up with a "doubtful" class in addition to the two already defined. And the chances are, we should have to modify our original definition somewhat so as to be sure that the rules for assigning people to subgroups are clear and comprehensive.

You can probably think of dozens of attributes that could be used to form classes and assign people to them. Eye color, sex, location of residence, shoe size, ease of blushing, love of music, and sleepwalking are only a few possibilities. We could go further and define classes in terms of multiple attributes. We could define a class of "female visual hallucinators," another of "female auditory hallucinators," another of "female tactual hallucinators," and so on, with corresponding classes for males. It is easy to generate a large number of possible classes from a small number of attributes. If we consider only attributes that can be described as present or absent, we can form 128 possible classes from combinations of seven attributes. Adding one more attribute to the cluster would double the number of possible classes. Of making classes there is no end!

The crucial point to remember in connection with defining classes is that the basis for assigning people must be made clear and explicit. A class has no utility if we cannot decide which people possess the defining characteristics. Some classifications now in common use may not be valuable for precisely this reason. Ash (1) studied the diagnoses of three psychiatrists working in the same clinic. Thirty-five patients with clear pathology were studied through interviews and examinations performed jointly by the three specialists. Each psychiatrist made his own diagnosis independently, however. In one part of the investigation, patients were assigned to one of five classes: psychotic, neurotic, psychopathic, mentally defective, and normal. Ash found that all three psychiatrists agreed in their classification for only sixteen of the thirty-five patients. His finding certainly suggests that the criteria for these psychiatric groupings are not clear.

The Association of Attributes. By merely setting up classes, we have not gone very far toward prediction. But if we could discover that people assigned to a particular class regularly had distinctive characteristics in addition to those used in defining the class, we should have a basis for making predictions. In other words, we want to know whether one given attribute is frequently associated with another one.

We can do this by studying the members of groups assigned to various classes and recording the frequency with which various attributes occur. In practice we examine a large number of attributes at one time in order to be economical of time and money.

An example of this kind of investigation is furnished by Feldman and Maleski (7) who were studying men in an Army Special Training Unit. The men in this school were illiterate or unable to speak English. Feldman and Maleski wanted to find characteristics associated with having been absent without leave (AWOL) at least once. The defining attribute is thus any record of being AWOL. They studied a group of fifty men with this attribute and another of equal size without it. Both of these groups were similar in age, marital status, religion, learning ability, and size of home community. The data showed that the AWOL group contained more men with histories of aggressive acts against people, hatred for the Army, and various behavior disturbances. For example, 70 per cent of the AWOL group had been arrested at least once, but only 12 per cent of the non-AWOL group had been arrested. Clearly, the attribute "having been arrested" is associated with "having gone AWOL" among this kind of men.

Notice this: you cannot demonstrate association between two attributes by studying only people who possess one of them. Call the defining attribute X and the associated attribute Y. We find people who have X and others without X. To decide whether or not X is related to Y, we must find out how often Y occurs in *both* groups. If Y is just as common among people without X as it is among people with X, there is no association between X and Y. To find out whether beauty really is related to stupidity among women, you may want to begin by studying beautiful women. But remember: if you want to be logical you must study the homely ones, too!

Finding associations among attributes is what makes prediction possible. How do we know what classes to use so that significant attributes can be predicted? Only scientific investigation can tell us. We have to guess about important defining attributes and then test our guesses. One of the differences between mediocre and brilliant scientists is the ability to foresee what kinds of classifications will be useful. At one time it seemed absurd to suggest that people could be usefully classified on the basis of their reactions to ink blots; today it does not seem so absurd. You must have either immense insight or immense luck to make such a suggestion. There is no certain way to acquire either one.

The Most Probable Inference. Let us now see how you can base predictions on studies of the association of attributes. Suppose that you are called upon to study an illiterate soldier who has gone AWOL. Are you likely to find that the man has a record of arrest? Given the information found by Feldman and Maleski, the answer is yes. In any particular case, this prediction may be in error. The study showed that 70 per cent of the AWOL group had been previously arrested, and that leaves 30 per cent who had never been arrested. But, *in the absence of any further information* beyond the fact that the man went AWOL, no other prediction should be made. "The best method of prediction is defined to be that method which, if applied to all members of the population selected in random order, will yield the least amount of error for the population as a whole" (9, p. 258). If you choose some way of predicting other than to state the most probable outcome, you will accumulate more errors over a series of cases than if you used the correct method. Suppose in this instance that you decided to predict that every second AWOL soldier has a record of arrest, and that the others did not. How often would you be correct? A little calculation will show that you would be right half the time. On the other hand, if you had predicted a record of arrest in *all* cases, you would have predicted accurately 70 per cent of the time.

Let us take a more realistic example of a prediction problem. Feifel and Schwartz (6) studied the outcome of group psychotherapy in a hospital setting. Their experimental group received group therapy in addition to the usual routine of treatments used in the hospital (hydrotherapy, occupational therapy, recreation, etc.). The control group did not receive the additional group therapy. After three months, 71 per cent of the experimental group were rated as improved, but only 50 per cent of the control group received this rating. Could you properly say that new patients, assigned to group therapy, have a better chance of improving than those given only the usual hospital treatments? The data of Feifel and Schwartz indicate that the answer is yes, but there are several qualifications to be made.

In the first place, as the authors point out, we cannot be sure that the difference of 21 per cent between the incidence of improvement in the two groups is a dependable figure. Their statistical analysis shows that a difference of this size would be found by chance about 15 per cent of the time. That is, if they could repeat this identical experiment a large number of times with comparable subjects, about one out of every seven experiments would show at least this much difference between the two groups, even though group therapy had no effect at all.

In the next place, a clinician would note that the majority of the patients in this experiment were schizophrenic and that most of them were in their thirties. What could he predict about the outcome of group therapy with depressed patients in their forties? The best he could do, without further data, is to make a kind of "informed guess" that group treatment may be beneficial. He should not be surprised, however, if his prediction is wrong, because the older group he is considering is not comparable to the one in the published study.

Clinicians sometimes become discouraged because of predictive failures and do not remember that even under the best of conditions the most probable inference is, after all, only probable. When a treatment method that has worked well for some other clinician fails, they may accept almost any explanation of the failure. Sometimes they feel that the method is faulty or that they used it incorrectly. If a clinician dislikes his work, he may decide that the patients were unusually stubborn! The fact is that these difficulties crop up at almost every step in clinical work. The value of interviews, interpretations of tests, prognostic formulas, and counseling methods may change a good deal from situation to situation. All the clinician can do is to use his best judgment, keep an eye open for new evidence, and maintain a modest attitude about his predictions.

The Direction of Prediction. Scientists often conduct their investigations by forming groups that differ in some socially significant way and then finding other attributes that differentiate these groups. That is, they will compare happily and unhappily married couples, normals and neurotics, or successful and unsuccessful executives. This kind of investigation is useful in locating characteristics by which predictions can be made about the behavior of various persons. But such studies must be carefully interpreted by clinicians if they are to be used in prediction. Some peculiar quirks of probabilities turn up in practical situations, because the clinician must usually predict in a direction opposite to that of the scientist. Although the scientist tells us that 70 per cent of men who go AWOL have histories of arrest, the clinician wants to know what percentage of the men who have histories of arrest will go AWOL. The clinician's question is quite different and will ordinarily be answered differently. We can clarify this point by an example.

Table 1. *The Percentage of Normal and Psychiatrically Unfit Recruits Scoring High and Low on a Food-aversion Check List*

| | Aversion scores | | |
Group	Low	High	Total
Unfit	35	65	100
Normal	81	19	100

One published study concerns the relationship between food aversions and psychiatric unfitness for military service. The data from this investigation (16) clearly show that a larger percentage of men considered unfit for military service made high scores on a short food-aversion inventory than did normal recruits. Table 1 summarizes the essential data. You can see from this table that 65 per cent of the unfit men made high scores on the food-aversion list. On the other hand, only 19 per cent of the normal men made high scores. We could be fairly confident in predicting that an unfit man would have a high aversion score. But that is not the kind of prediction that interests the clinician. He wants to know whether the food-aversion score will pick out unfit men. His question is: "Of those with high aversion scores, how many will be unfit?" Table 2 contains the answer, but it requires some explanation.

Table 2. The Estimated Number of Normal and Unfit Recruits in a Sample of 500 Who Score High and Low on a Food-aversion Check List

| | | Aversion scores | |
Group	Low	High	Total
Unfit	17	33 (28%)	50 (10%)
Normal	364	86 (72%)	450 (90%)
Total	381	119 (100%)	500 (100%)

Table 2 shows the estimated numbers of fit and unfit men in a hypothetical sample of 500 recruits. It is based on the assumption that about 10 per cent of all recruits will be found unfit. (The correct figure may be somewhat larger or smaller without changing our argument.) The entries in Table 2 were computed by using the percentages of Table 1. That is, 35 per cent of the 50 unfit men are assigned to the low-scoring group, and 81 per cent of the 450 normal men are assigned to the low-scoring group.

Now notice what happens if you consider only those men who make high scores. About 72 per cent of the 119 men in that category are normal. If a clinician knows only that a man made a high score on the aversion list, he ought to predict that he would be normal. In this case, and there are many more like it, the clinician wants to predict *from* the test *to* the socially important attribute. In trying to estimate probabilities, it makes a good deal of difference whether you base your percentages on the row totals, as in Table 1, or on the column totals, as in Table 2. Your purpose determines which method is appropriate.

You have probably guessed by now that the crux of this problem lies in the fact that there are relatively few unfit men in the total population. Table 1 conceals this information, and a good many published studies conceal it, too. Whenever the attributes of normal and abnormal groups are being compared, and the groups are of approximately equal size, you will find that a correction is required if you wish to change the direction of the prediction. The correction consists of constructing a table in which the normal and abnormal groups are represented in the same proportions as they occur in the population. Since clinicians are usually dealing with the unusual or uncommon case, such corrections will be frequent. Without them, you will often arrive at over-optimistic estimates of probabilities.

Our analysis of the data from the food-aversion study does not mean that the check list is worthless. Notice in Table 2 that the chances of finding unfit men are much greater among high-scoring recruits than among the others. If the check list is used as a screening device, the clinician could select the 119 high-scoring men for further study. And his chances of finding unfit men in this group would be nearly three times as great as if he studied every one of the 500 men.

Problem 1. A psychological test for detecting cortical brain damage has been developed and applied to some patients in a mental hospital. Scores above a certain point are called "high scores." In a group of fifty patients with such brain damage, 90 per cent made high scores. In a group of fifty patients without known damage only 20 per cent made high scores. We want to estimate the effectiveness of such a test in a hospital setting. Of course, when the test is administered, we will not know which patients are damaged and which are not. That is why we plan to use the test. Assume that 10 per cent of all patients admitted to the hospital will eventually be found by neurological examination or autopsy to have this kind of brain damage. If the test works as well for new samples as it did for the author of the test, how would the following questions be answered?

1. Of 100 consecutive patients tested, about how many will have brain damage of the kind detected by the test?

2. How many of these damaged patients will make high scores?

3. About how many of the nondamaged people in this series of admissions will make high scores on the test?

4. Do you think the following statement is justified? "Patients who make high scores on this test probably have some brain damage." Explain your thinking.

5. If the clinician decided to use the test only with patients who, because of certain symptoms, were suspected of having brain damage, would the test be more useful? What further data are needed to answer this question?

Quantitative Prediction. Instead of classifying people on the basis of the presence or absence of some attribute, we often assign scores to them showing the *degree* to which the attribute is present. Scores may be based on the frequency with which a behavior appears, the intensity of the behavior, or the ease with which the behavior may be aroused. Thus when we describe people as "anxious" we may mean that they are frequently anxious, intensely anxious when aroused, or that normally ineffective stimuli arouse anxiety in them. Since all of these measures of a characteristic can be represented by numbers, we can use mathematical methods to show the association between various characteristics. The detailed study of these methods is properly placed in courses dealing with statistics, and we shall here only indicate several common methods.

When scores for two different characteristics have been found for each member of a group, it is usually possible to compute a correlation coefficient which describes the relationship between the two characteristics. Large positive coefficients, say between .50 and 1.00, indicate that one characteristic can be fairly well estimated from the other. Two well-constructed tests of intelligence will usually show a correlation of .80 or better. This means that there is a substantial association between the scores earned on the two tests. Not only can we say that people making high scores on one test will probably make high scores on the other, but, more generally, we know that any person's standing on one test will predict his approximate standing on the other. There are a good many precautions to be observed in using and interpreting correlation coefficients, but they are beyond the scope of this chapter.[1]

Multiple Correlation. Life is not so simple, of course, that very good predictions can be made on the basis of a single quantified attribute. A happy marriage or a favorable response to psychotherapy must be related to a number of factors. How can a number of attributes be combined in order to predict outcomes? One way of doing this is to use a statistical method known as multiple correlation. This method assigns weights (i.e., constant multipliers) to each predictor score and then adds the weighted scores together in order to obtain a composite prediction score. The weights are chosen so that the total score will be the best possible estimate of the outcome under the circumstances. Sometimes this procedure improves predictive accuracy a good deal; in other cases, the addition of more scores does very little to improve predictions. Multiple correlations are expressed by correlation coefficients having the same meaning as in the case of simple correlation.

A multiple correlation based on a single investigation can be impressively high and yet have little value for the practicing clinician. This circumstance is due to the fact that multiple correlations usually shrink in size when the prediction formula is applied to a new sample. A striking example of this shrinkage has occurred in efforts to predict whether patients will continue with psychotherapy once they have started it. Kotkov and Meadow (10) found that three scores derived from the Rorschach test could be used to predict which patients would continue treatment. Their method worked well enough to make correct predictions for 69

---

[1] If you need to review correlational methods, you will find them discussed in most textbooks on elementary statistics. Among many possible references are the books by Edwards (5) and by Peters and Van Voorhis (12).

per cent of their sample. Auld and Eron (2) applied the same method to thirty-three patients who received psychotherapy in a psychiatric out-patient clinic. They found that it classified only 52 per cent of the patients correctly—a result no better than chance would allow. Why did the formula fail to perform as expected?

Auld and Eron point out a number of possible reasons for this decrease in predictive power, but one is particularly important because it is due to the technique used in finding the weights assigned to the predictor scores. We pointed out that these weights are chosen so that they will yield the best prediction possible. But ordinarily this means the best prediction possible for the particular sample of patients being studied. If this sample does not really represent patients in general, or does not represent other samples where the prediction formula is to be used, then the weights will be in error. Special (but unknown) characteristics of patients studied in Ohio may result in emphasizing or heavily weighting certain predictor scores. These weights *are* the best for that particular sample. But when applied to a sample of patients in New York, the weights are grossly in error.

When you are a practicing clinician and discover that an investigator has found he can predict certain outcomes rather well, you will naturally want to use the prediction method yourself. But there are several questions you should ask if you want to be realistic: (1) Was the formula cross-validated by using it to predict outcomes in a second sample of patients *who were not used in finding the original weights?* (2) Are the patients I am working with similar enough to those studied by the investigator so that I can expect similar predictive accuracy? However you may answer these questions, if you decide to try the method, you should make an effort to find out how accurate the method is in your own work setting.

Subjective Prediction Formulas. It is obvious that clinicians cannot get much help from cross-validated multiple correlations in making many of the predictive statements they want to make. In a few situations such as estimating probable school success, adequacy in certain jobs, and marital adjustment, some combinations of predictor scores are known to be useful. But we do not have firmly grounded formulas for predicting the outcomes of psychotherapy, institutional placement, promotion to executive status, or even doing nothing at all for the person who wants help. And it is elaborating the obvious to point out that we know almost nothing about the effects of urging people to read books, find a hobby, change jobs, leave home, learn to dance, take a long vacation, and so on. For whom and under what conditions can we say that such activities will help or hinder?

Faced with the requirements of predicting in a specific case, the clinician probably uses some kind of subjective weights in combining his predictor measures. These subjective weights are based on his own experience, on his training, and on his confidence in his own ability. While these weights are not necessarily wrong, they are seldom made explicit enough to determine which ones are correct. It is a plausible guess, in the light of the difficulty of establishing validated prediction formulas, that these subjective formulas are not very accurate. That does not mean that we should stop predicting. It means that the study of persons is not yet far enough developed to be an engineering enterprise. It means that a huge amount of research still must be done.

Prediction and Richness of Data. Most of us assume that the more we know about a person the better we can predict what he is going to do. Certainly, when two people have lived together for a time, one of them can forecast the other's preferences, aversions, and moods with a good deal of accuracy. In such cases, generalizations are made on the basis of a large number of specific observations, and these generalizations work because people do not change their ways rapidly. On the other hand, even close friends occasionally surprise one another, and their long-term predictions about each other probably are not very accurate. The playboy does turn out to be a solid citizen often enough to make us cautious about forecasting.

A study of the logic involved in multiple correlation shows that adding more predictor scores does not necessarily increase accuracy of prediction. Additional predictors must contribute something unique to the equation if they are to be useful. If they substantially duplicate the kinds of measure already in the equation, they do not improve prediction. Actual empirical studies have often verified this proposition. But what we are most interested in is whether the rich data turned up by clinical study can improve prediction.

Sarbin (13) studied the ability of clinicians to predict college grades as compared with the predictive accuracy of a formula (called a multiple-regression equation) based on only two scores. The two scores used in the equation were based on a college-aptitude test and on the rank of students in their high-school graduating classes. It has been known for some time that these two scores are good predictors of college success, and Sarbin had a formula available that had already proved effective. In this study, five clinical counselors used various tests, individual records, and interviews to study 162 college freshmen. They also knew the results of the college-aptitude test and the high-school ranks. Predictions made by these counselors were correlated with the actual grades earned by the students at the end of one academic quarter's work. Sarbin's analysis shows that the predictions of the clinicians were no more accurate than predictions by formula, despite the additional data they used.

Apparently, when a fairly specific outcome is known to be predictable from a few well-known facts, additional clinical information does not add anything. Quite possibly, earning grades in college depends largely on ability and effective prior use of that ability; personality factors of a more subtle sort may not count for much in earning grades. If the students had been more homogeneous with respect to ability, then the clinicians' data might have been more valuable.[2] Something of this sort seems to have happened in a study reported by Bobbitt and Newman (3). They investigated predictions of academic success for about 1,900 men who were attending an officer-training school of the U. S. Coast Guard Reserve. These men were carefully selected for intelligence and were undoubtedly more homogeneous with respect to academic ability than freshman college students. The results of this study indicate that skilled clinical interviewers could add to the predictive power of the tests. This finding is less conclusive than it might have been, however, because the test scores were not combined in the most effective way. Thus, Bobbitt and Newman may have underestimated the predictive power of the tests alone.

Sarbin's (3) analysis of the role of the clinician leads him to believe that prediction by statistical means should replace the informal and intuitive method of predicting from a clinical case study. We must admit that both logical and empirical evidence support this conclusion. There are, however, several respects in which clinical data are of distinct value. We may remind ourselves that we are a long way from having the hundreds of regression equations that would be needed to make the predictions that clinicians must make. Faced with this situation, either the clinician must make a general assessment as best he can or else make no forecast at all. If he knows that certain traits or attributes are generally useful predictors, he can depend upon them to help him forecast even without an equation. Let us take the example of counseling a high-school student who wishes to go to college. Since the weights assigned to ability-test scores vary from college to college, there is no single equation for the clinician to use. Realizing, however, that intellectual-verbal ability is a good predictor, he makes use of the test score as a general guide. That is to say, his prediction is less accurate than it would be if he used the appropriate statistical equation, but it is better than nothing at all.

There is something more that a clinician may do by gathering extensive

[2] The homogeneity of a group influences the size of correlation coefficients. Suppose that variables X and Y are positively correlated in a certain sample. In another sample which is more homogeneous with respect to X (i.e., has a smaller standard deviation), the correlation between X and Y will be smaller. Thus, if only the most intelligent students are selected for training, the resulting group is quite homogeneous in ability, and the power to predict grades from intelligence is decreased. At the same time, however, the predictive value of nonability variables is increased. Study habits and motivation may become quite important under these conditions.

data: he may discover facts which should influence prediction in a particular case even though they can ordinarily be overlooked. For example, the counselor discovers that a prospective college student is seriously deficient in ability to write an acceptable term paper. If the student is otherwise acceptable, the counselor will suggest remedial training before entering college. Although ability to write does not appear in the usual formula, the counselor knows that it is necessary for college success. His counseling may actually increase the predictive power of the statistical equation! [3] Much of the clinician's work in gathering data on the individual consists of exploring attitudes, traits, and motives to find those which may cause difficulties in the future. The presence of psychotic trends or markedly hostile attitudes may cause us to revise a prediction made on purely statistical grounds.

Another reason why rich data may be needed is that certain predictive traits are not easily discoverable without extensive study. Let us take the prediction of homicidal attack as an example. At present we have no empirically determined prediction formulas to use. But we believe that the presence of delusions of persecution increases the probability of such attacks. In some cases, however, these delusions are not apparent and may be concealed by the patient. Then careful clinical study may be required to elicit evidence of the delusional structure.

The complex data collected by the clinician should also serve as a source of hypotheses about useful predictors. He is in a position to see possibilities that would otherwise go unnoticed. He can add to our useful knowledge by carefully formulating these hunches and hypotheses so that they may be tested. Then, as statistical formulas relieve the burden of examining many predictors, clinicians can devote more and more effort to the problems of disposition, remediation, and treatment.

[3] If you are familiar with regression equations, you may be interested in a note on this point. Think of a regression equation as composed of two sets of variables. First, there are those that actually appear in the published formula. Then there are those that do not appear because they have zero weights. Some of these unused variables are left out because they correlate with both the criterion and the other predictors. We could say that they are predictive but add nothing unique to the equation. Thus, writing ability, although related to college success, is usually related to intellectual ability or high school standing, and these are better predictors. An occasional person may deviate significantly from this general rule, however, and then the unused variable may be profitably considered. By advising remedial work, the counselor is helping the student fit the ordinary pattern of ability relationships that is assumed by the regression equation.

The crucial requirements for legitimately considering an unused variable are these: The variable must be related to the criterion and to the other predictors so that it normally receives zero weight. The individual in question must deviate significantly from the regression line relating the unused variable to the used predictors. Some variables are unused because they rarely occur. For example, epilepsy or psychosis is rare in college applicants. Yet the clinician must consider such conditions when he finds them.

THE CRITERION

We have talked rather generally about predicting "outcomes." We must now be more specific about what it is that we are trying to predict. In practical clinical work we want to predict some events that will have significance for the client or for the community. Some examples of such events are: performance in a job, satisfaction in following a chosen vocation, improvement in personal adjustment, leadership of some social group, committing criminal acts, recovering from schizophrenia, or acting in a reliable and trustworthy way. The intricate study of the person is directed toward the collection of data that will give such predictions more accuracy than would otherwise be possible. In order to decide whether predictions are right or wrong, we must specify in advance what should be measured or counted in order to verify the prediction. Such a specification is called a "criterion." It is some attribute or measurable characteristic of the person which we are trying to forecast. If the criterion cannot be observed or measured in some way that permits a prediction to be called true or false, we have no way of determining whether a clinician or a test is predicting accurately.

Vaguely Formulated Criteria. In order to verify a proposition about a person, the language of the proposition must be clear. If a prediction is vaguely stated, you cannot tell later on whether or not it was correct. Since ordinary language is often ambiguous, many propositions appear to be accurate predictions simply because they can be understood in several ways. Fortunetellers convert vagueness into a standard technique in order to make predictions that appear to be strikingly accurate. Suppose a palm reader says: "I see trouble for you in the future." What is the meaning of "trouble" and what is the duration of the "future"? Without further definition, "trouble" may be applied to everything unpleasant, from a minor illness to death, from the loss of a purse to the loss of a fortune. Try to evaluate such a prediction. It is impossible. Of course, if you are an ardent believer in the necromancer it will be easy to find instances to fit the vague words.

However, even experts can fall into this verbal trap. Consider the proposition "This man will benefit from psychotherapy." After the psychotherapy is finished, how shall we decide whether or not this prediction was correct? We can do it only if we have agreed in advance how we are to interpret "benefit." In other words, we must have a criterion that enables us to say whether the predicted outcome did or did not take place. In the case of therapy, it is a hard matter to arrive at a criterion for success. Shall we agree that the patient's own statements about improvement should serve as the criterion? That arrangement relies too heavily upon the patient's willingness and ability to be critical or approving. Shall we add the therapist's evaluation? But he may easily be biased in favor of his own work. How long must any kind of improvement last in order to qualify as improvement? If a patient is symptom-free for six months after therapy ends, would you say he has benefited from treatment? Or should he be symptom-free for several years? You can see how difficult the task is; yet if predictions are to be evaluated, some explicit criterion must be defined.

Specific, concrete predictions are easy to test, but it is hard to make successful ones. Suppose you say: "John, if paroled, will not be convicted of a crime within the next year." That proposition can be readily proved or disproved. On the other hand, if you say: "John will make an excellent adjustment on parole," no one really knows what kind of evidence is required to disprove the proposition. Of course, there are general statements that can be verified. The prediction "This man will make a suicidal effort within the next year" is capable of proof or disproof. We do not have to specify whether the attempt will be made by poison, gas, or jumping from a roof.

Clinicians often use abstract terms in predictive statements. Thus, they may say that Steve will continue to show aggressive trends or that Peggy is likely to become compulsive in time of stress. The practical value of these remarks depends mainly upon the definition of the terms "aggressive" and "compulsive." Grayson and Tolman (8) have shown that such concepts have considerable variation in meaning among experts. They asked psychologists and psychiatrists to write definitions of fifty terms that were frequently used in psychological reports at a neuropsychiatric hospital. They conclude: "The most striking finding of the study is the looseness and ambiguity of the definitions of many of these terms" (8, p. 229). The word "aggression" furnishes a good illustration. Many specialists in the Grayson and Tolman study defined aggression as destructive behavior. But definitions in terms of positive, forceful, assertive behavior (without destruction) were almost as popular.

This lack of agreement does not mean that clinical concepts are useless for descriptive and predictive statements. It may be very useful to say that Harold will continue to be hostile, even though we cannot say whether he will show it by sarcasm or stealing. We do need, however, to question ourselves as to just what we mean, and to define our concepts so that we are not misunderstood. Often you can use words that are more specific and less vague than much "clinical lingo."

Problem 2. Here are some sentences that use concepts of different degrees of vagueness. The vague concepts are italicized. For each one, write a clear definition and three or four actions to which the vague term, as you define it, could be appropriately applied. Then rewrite the sentences so that they are more precise.

1. John is unhappy unless someone *bolsters his ego*.
2. When Mary fails an examination, she becomes *defensively aggressive*.
3. For the first few days, Robert will be *upset*.
4. Anne tries to *play a masculine role*.

Vague Descriptions. Closely related to prediction is the problem of inferring traits, motives, and attitudes from test data or interviews. The logic involved is much the same in the two cases; the difference lies in the fact that prediction refers to the future, whereas the descriptive inference refers to some present state or potentiality of the person under study. Here, too, ambiguous or overgeneral statements give a spurious impression of accuracy. Consider this personality sketch: "You are a person of varied interests, although you pour most of your energy into a few activities that mean the most to you. In general, you show a well-balanced outlook and disposition, but when frustrated you can display temper. With those you know well you are spontaneous and expressive, but often you keep your feelings very much to yourself. You have a few defects in personality that you are aware of, particularly in connection with dealing with people. You are persistent enough, however, to achieve success in dealing with these faults. There are times when you worry too much. You will find that it suits you better to take things as they come and to show more confidence in your own future."

Does this describe you fairly well? Try it out on some other people and find out how well it describes them. Many people find it quite an acceptable picture. To complete the picture of pseudoanalysis, get samples of handwriting from a few people. Later, after "analyzing" the writing, read them this sketch. If you speak with confidence you will probably be able to convince them of your ability to "read character." Be sure to reveal the hoax when you are finished, otherwise you may find yourself with a reputation you don't want.

Actually, of course, the sketch says things that are true of most people who are educated and ambitious. And it is ambiguous enough to permit a variety of interpretations.

Similar language is sometimes used by clinicians who really think they are making inferences from data they have collected. Their remarks look more complex and sophisticated, but they contain the same errors. Look out for the glib use of phrases such as "operates effectively but with persistent visceral tension," "essentially a repressive personality," and "immature and emotionally underdeveloped." These concepts could refer to important characteristics, but they are usually pedantic smoke screens.

Refinement of Criteria. More attention has been paid to finding satisfactory criteria in industrial and educational situations than in the area of personal adjustment. One reason for this is the narrowness of the predictions needed for industrial and educational work. An industrial job requires a person to fit into a limited situation where highly specialized skills are essential. Many of the jobs involve activities that are not matters of common knowledge, and the surrounding conditions are quite different from those in "ordinary life." In emotional adjustment, on the other hand, the various activities (meeting people, worrying, getting angry, being criticized) are apparently matters of common knowledge, and the situations met by the person can be adequately dealt with in a number of ways. There are fewer ways to be a successful drill-press operator than there are to be a successful husband.

Moreover, clinicians have been primarily interested in deviates whose failure in ordinary life activities is so obvious that it can hardly escape notice. Relatively crude formulations of criteria, such as, "Is this man able to conduct his affairs with ordinary prudence?" have sufficed. Usually the student of persons is not concerned with those who are very happy or somewhat unhappy; he wants to predict who will be *extremely* unhappy or who will be *extremely* aggressive and so on. Under these conditions it has not seemed particularly necessary to build refined criterion measures. This state of affairs will not continue indefinitely, however, for as diagnostic methods grow in power and subtlety they may be able to predict unsatisfactory adjustment which is not extreme but is important. Then, too, reliable and objective criterion measures are requisite for the development of improved diagnostic methods.

Criterion measures of successful adjustment do not need to be limited to a single item. Probably, in setting up a criterion for improvement resulting from therapy, we should consider a number of things: ability to hold a job, absence of certain symptoms, expressed satisfaction of the patient's family, and the patient's own expressed satisfaction. How these should be combined and weighted is a complicated problem which will eventually require statistical methods of the kind used in dealing with industrial criteria.[4]

Analysis of Performance Requirements. One of the essentials for criterion construction is an analysis of the activity to be predicted. Formal analyses of performance requirements are almost completely lacking in many of the major areas that interest clinicians. For example, what are the basic performances required of a good parent, a satisfactory husband or wife, a socially useful citizen? Common knowledge suggests certain activities as minimum requirements: adequate functioning of physiologically based drives (for food, sex, sleep), knowledge and acceptance of social norms (language, clothing, social regulations), ability to acquire

[4] A more complete discussion of the general problem of criterion formulation will be found in *The Prediction of Personal Adjustment,* by Paul Horst (9). See especially Chapter 3.

basic necessities for living, realistic perception of the physical world, ability to give and accept affection. Even these specifics need to be more carefully defined, for we do not know from a mere listing what minimum is necessary for each performance.

It is obvious that these performance requirements are not independent of the social or economic status of the individual. Different social environments make quite different demands upon people. A person who is apparently happy and effective in a small community with homogeneous value attitudes may become distressed and ineffective in a large, heterogeneous community. People with poor abstract learning ability can function in a nondemanding, socially supportive environment but not in a social group organized around intellectual competitiveness. Sexual activity in marriage depends on two people, not on one alone.

Thus, there is no single criterion of a good parent, an adequate husband, or a successful executive. A criterion measure expresses the demands of a particular situation rather than of all situations. Bearing this in mind, we shall not place too much reliance on over-all formulations of "adjustment," "mental health," or "normality." We shall think of these as relative to the performance requirements of the client's own surroundings.

Problem 3. Two clinicians disagree as to the proper sequence of testing and interviewing. One believes that tests should be given first, and the results should be given to the interviewer. The other is convinced that the interview should precede the tests in order to establish good test-taking motivation on the part of the client. They decide to try out both methods systematically in order to find out which method is better. What possible criteria could be used in order to show the superiority of one method? What could these clinicians mean by "better"?

An Example of a Rating-scale Criterion. Changes in behavior can often be studied only by means of human observers. Their judgments can be used as a criterion, provided they are carefully instructed in methods of observing and reporting. An example of an attempt to improve measurement of behavior changes can be found in a study by Schrader and Robinson (14). They were interested in finding out the effects of prefrontal lobotomy in sixteen schizophrenic patients. Among other methods for evaluating the status of the patients, they made use of the Gardner Behavior Chart. The chart is essentially a rating scale for reporting judgments on fifteen kinds of behavior that can be observed in hospital wards. Such things as appetite, sleep, personal appearance, noisiness, and cooperativeness are rated according to the definitions provided. The authors admit that bias may decrease the accuracy of the chart, especially when ward attendants use it. But ratings of this kind are more useful than the vague criteria of "improved" or "much improved" that are so often used. The usefulness is not due simply to the fact that the chart yields a numerical score; the standard definitions and the specification of the concrete behavior to be observed are the significant features.

Schrader and Robinson found a statistically reliable improvement in ward behavior from the pre- to the postoperative periods. Furthermore, use of the chart permitted the investigators to discover the kinds of behavior which changed most. Had other investigators used such standard scales, we should be in a better position to predict the outcomes of lobotomy.

Problem 4. Personal counseling in industry presumably would aid workers to deal with their emotional problems, and this in turn should make more effective workers. Suppose that a firm is considering such a program. The president asks you to state what results you would expect if the plan works well. What kinds of predictions could you make? Can these predictions be verified? Is it possible that even though over-all production may not be increased, this kind of program could be advantageous for the firm?

DETERMINING PREDICTIVE SUCCESS

Merely making correct predictions does not show that one is a successful predictor, for some correct predictions may occur on a chance basis. In general, the success of a predictor may be measured by finding the ratio of the number of his correct predictions to the number of correct predictions expected by chance. You can apply this method either to a series of predictions about the same person or to predictions about a number of people. The problem in either case is to find a way of estimating chance expectancy. Let us consider first a situation where the characteristics of a selected group determine chance success:

A psychologist wishes to test the diagnostic effectiveness of a new test in the clinic where he works. He arranges to have the test administered to a large number of clients. Interpreting the test without any information about the persons tested save age and sex, he finds that, of all those eventually diagnosed as neurotic, he correctly predicted the diagnosis in 50 per cent of the cases. Since his best estimate of the incidence of neurosis in the general population is about 25 per cent, he assumes that his test is effective. That is, he uses 25 per cent as the figure indicating his success on a completely chance basis. Further study would show that the test is not really effective.

In this clinic, a final diagnosis of "neurosis" is given to about two-thirds of all cases studied. Within this restricted population—all those who come to this clinic—a prediction of neurosis will be correct about 66 per cent of the time. If the psychologist should simply call every client neurotic without any test, he could be correct in two-thirds of the cases. The new test, it seems, actually interferes with diagnosis.

Sometimes the problem is not that of estimating chance success, but rather of comparing the success of two methods. For example: A college has customarily accepted students if their grades placed them in the upper half of their high-school class. An eager admissions director decides to add a personal interview to the selection procedure. A small number of applicants are rejected on the basis of interview findings, and the director feels certain that the interview is valuable. In order to get factual evidence, however, he waits until the end of the year and makes a study of the success of students accepted under the new plan. When he finds that 90 per cent of the freshmen are passing in their work, he believes he has the evidence he has been seeking. An opponent of the interview method makes a study of his own. His results show that freshmen admitted under the old plan had the same proportion of successes. Since no change in grading standards has occurred, the only conclusion is that the new method does not aid correct prediction.

In some situations, there is little opportunity to estimate chance success. Consider a psychologist in private practice who developed a new method of psychotherapy. At the end of several years, he evaluated all cases treated, using an adequate criterion for improvement. He found that 80 per cent of his cases showed improvement. In the following two-year period, however, things did not go so well. Although he saw more patients, he found that more and more often his results were not satisfactory. A summary at the end of the second two-year period showed that only about 50 per cent of his cases were improved. Since it is unreasonable to suppose that he was becoming less skillful in the use of the new method, we must seek another explanation.

Let us proceed on the hypothesis that the new method was of no value at all. If, during his first two years of practice, he had received cases that were not very serious and in which the rate of spontaneous recovery was high, we could account for his initial success. Assume that this success added to his reputation. Then more difficult problems would be brought to him. People who had been unsuccessfully treated by other specialists would consult him. As the self-selected sample changed, the rate of spontaneous recovery changed—downward.

How are we to know whether the rate of spontaneous recovery really declined? Actually we cannot tell. Presumptive evidence favoring this explanation could be obtained by evaluating the kinds of cases that were treated in successive years, but a good estimate of the spontaneous recovery rate could not be made. One way to make such an estimate would be to require each patient to wait six months before treatment is begun.

The proportion of those who improve during the waiting period would afford a crude estimate of the rate. This procedure is clearly impractical. We shall probably never be quite sure, in private practice at least, how effective a given method of treatment is. Modesty is definitely in order for the clinician.[5]

The Value of Records. As we grow in knowledge and experience, we like to believe that our clinical predictions are increasingly accurate. This belief may be well founded, or it may not. It is easy for us to forget our failures and remember our successes, particularly if some of the successful predictions were dramatic. The neglect of our failures will give us a comfortable feeling, but it will not motivate us to search for ways of improving predictions.

One corrective for a sterile complacency about our ability is to make follow-up studies of predictions in actual clinical work. Such studies require record-keeping over a period of time, and the records must contain some kind of predictive statement or a recommendation which serves as a prediction. As records accumulate, we can find out whether the expected improvements, changes in attitude, or worsening of the life situation take place as predicted. Clinicians, then, should stimulate and encourage adequate record-keeping. They can initiate studies within their own work setting that will enable improvements to be made. Even rather simple statistical reports showing the disposition of incoming cases, changes in the nature of the clientele, or the number of various tests that were administered may give very useful information. And a logbook of one's own predictions would surely prove to be an interesting self-training device!

Effects of Unforeseen Circumstances. Although the calculation of actual predictive success requires knowledge of outcomes and estimation of chance success, another sort of information is needed, too, before we can say that a predictive method is good or poor. This information concerns the circumstances surrounding the person whose future is forecast. A change in the social surroundings may create pressures and demands unforeseen by the predictor. When the predictions fail, it is hard to say whether the methods were faulty or the changed conditions were to blame. Of course, there are times when things work out the other way: an ordinarily inaccurate prediction turns out to be correct because of special circumstances. Whether or not these opposite effects of unforeseen changes counterbalance each other over a series of cases, we do not know. But in evaluating our predictive methods, we can at least keep

[5] A change in self-selected groups of applicants has been observed in industry, following the installation of a testing program. Stromberg (15) suggests that when potentially low-scoring applicants learn that tests are being used they do not apply. It would be helpful to have comparable studies of groups coming to clinics and guidance agencies in the first few years after their founding.

alert to the part played by events beyond the control of both the clinician and the client.

The effect of unforeseen circumstances in decreasing predictive accuracy is graphically described in a report by the assessment staff of the Office of Strategic Services (1). They had the task of selecting men for a wide variety of special military assignments. Candidates were put through a number of test situations and were interviewed. Final judgments were based on staff conferences. Despite ingenious and penetrating methods of personality analysis and the careful formulation of written reports, many of the accepted candidates were placed in assignments other than those for which they were evaluated. Had the staff known the exact nature of the duty which each man would encounter, predictive accuracy undoubtedly would have improved. Even then, the accidents of circumstance would have limited the proportion of correct predictions. Two examples will demonstrate the difficulty:

A very hearty assessee, Stub, who was considered a rare "find" because he was intimately acquainted with many influential residents of a strategic occupied zone of coastal China, could not be rejected by assessment on the basis that he was a man of strong personal prejudices with whom some people would find it difficult to work harmoniously. He got on well with most of his associates at Station S and was eager for his proposed assignment, but, as luck would have it, when he arrived in China he was paired with an utterly incompatible person. Their tactical conceptions proved to be irreconcilable and they quarreled so violently that it became apparent that it would be impossible for these two to cooperate effectively in carrying out the hazardous project for which our assessee had been recruited. Since there was no qualified substitute, the plan was abandoned. . . . He was rated Unsatisfactory in the theater (11, p. 453 f).

In another case, completely extraneous circumstances, which were not directly connected with military life, altered an expected outcome:

. . . one high-ranking OSS officer, while operating abroad, received a letter from a friend of his in America informing him that his wife had run off with the local garageman, leaving no message or address. As a result the officer's morale, which had formerly been high, dropped to zero. The assessment staff could predict that a small percentage of men would have to cope with a profoundly depressing or disquieting event of this sort, but, again, it was not possible to guess which of the assessees would be thus afflicted (11, p. 454).

As a result of such considerations the staff concludes that "there is a certain inevitable and irreducible percentage of prediction errors ascribable to the fact that when it is a matter of deciding whether to accept or reject a candidate . . . only future events which are known to be probable . . . should be considered in making the decision, but in a certain proportion of cases, events which are improbable—and hence should not be included in the assessor's calculations—will actually occur" (11, p. 454). Fortunately, the conditions of civilian life in peacetime are more stable and better known to the clinician than the military exigencies that confronted the OSS.

THE EFFECTS OF PREDICTIONS

Predictions are made by human beings who wonder about the future. They are compounded out of the knowledge and experiences of the men who make them. Preferences, feelings, and beliefs enter into this human product in one way or another. Even the confirmed statistical psychologist, who would predict only by cross-validated multiple-regression equations, is expressing a preference for certain kinds of demonstrations. He feels a need for limiting the open expression of his fantasies and even for limiting the fantasies themselves. But his preferences do not guarantee and bind the future. He himself knows this and labels his guesses as guesses by attaching probabilities to them. There is always the possibility of the new treatment, of the change in circumstances, of the novel and creative event. When we use a prediction method that worked in 1950, we ought to be aware that we derive our prediction-fantasy about the future from a culture that was, not is.

Predictions as Stimuli. What you should not overlook is the fact that the forecast itself initiates changes and so modifies the outcome of the situation. It is not only the weather that influences people's choices of clothing; the predictions of the weather bureau affect them, too. In clinical work, the expectation of a favorable outcome may induce optimism and greater efforts in the relatives and friends of the client. Perhaps the client himself is stirred to a renewed attack upon his problems. If the status of the predictor is high and his logic convincing, other specialists—physicians, teachers, social workers, counselors—may take heart and search vigorously for ways to help.

Of course, unfavorable predictions may influence the social environment, too. Some persons are challenged and work harder when the odds are against them. More often, expectation of a dismal future leads to resignation and to apathy. When hope is nearly dead, small improvements in the client may go unnoticed; assistance may become perfunctory. The social supports of the distressed person become wobbly, and his own disintegration is hastened by the disintegrating hopes of people around him.

Even predictions that are not openly announced may affect treatment and outcomes. We may not tell anyone else about our forecast, but the formulation of it may end our concern and our further inquiry. Or, more seriously, we may misinterpret or fail to see data that conflict with our conclusion. As clinicians, counselors, and teachers we need not stop speculating about the futures of the people we see, but we should not file our speculations in the folder of established fact.

Clinical Predictions in Social Problem Solving. By now you may be thinking that we should base our predictions on their anticipated social effects instead of on the principles of probability. Perhaps our forecasts should be determined largely by their effectiveness in promoting social involvement with the client and his difficulties. That proposal is hardly defensible. Such a course would soon be found out, and then predictions would lose their power to motivate people. No, we must take predictions for what they are: the best estimate of the unknown future. They are important clinically because they modify our actions in connection with the present problem. But they should not blot out all the rest of the changing and rich reality surrounding us. Predictions ought not to freeze the relationship between client and clinician; they should contribute to the growth and change of the relationship.

Let us say that test results and scientific investigations permit us to predict with justifiable confidence that a boy will remain intellectually retarded—that he will never be able to complete the usual elementary school work. Does this mean that we and the boy's parents are done with the problem? Must we resign ourselves to the cheerless unfolding of an accurate prediction? Perhaps it would be better to conceal the bitter facts from the parents. "But knowledge of facts does not entail conformity and acquiescence. The contrary is the case. Perception of things as they are is but a stage in the process of making them different. They have already begun to be different in being known, for by that fact they enter into a different context, a context of foresight and judgment of better and worse" (4, p. 298).

The prediction, known, joins with our feelings and our other knowledge to aid the creation of a new set of relationships for the retarded boy. Changed attitudes and expectations of his parents, efforts to teach him in new ways, and a breaking of the old mold of his life bring about readjustment in ways not foreseen by the predictor.

Problem 5. Perhaps you can become aware of the present impact of predictions by pretending and imagining. Pretend that you have heard an expert predict that you will become a patient in a mental hospital six months from now. How does this make you feel? What do you want to do? Now consider these questions:

1. How could this prediction, once announced, increase its own chances of becoming true?

2. How could the announcement of this prediction decrease its chances of being true?

3. Should unpleasant predictions be withheld from clients and their relatives? Explain your point of view.

REFERENCES

1. Ash, P. The reliability of psychiatric diagnoses. *J. abnorm. soc. Psychol.*, 1949, **44**, 272–276.
2. Auld, F., Jr., & Eron, L. D. The use of Rorschach scores to predict whether patients will continue in psychotherapy. *J. consult. Psychol.*, 1953, **17**, 104–109.
3. Bobbitt, J. M., & Newman, S. H. Psychological activities at the United States Coast Guard Academy. *Psychol. Bull.*, 1944, **41**, 568–579.
4. Dewey, J. *Human nature and conduct.* New York: Holt, 1922.
5. Edwards, A. *Statistical analysis.* New York: Rinehart, 1946.
6. Feifel, H., & Schwartz, A. D. Group psychotherapy with acutely disturbed psychotic patients. *J. consult. Psychol.*, 1953, **17**, 113–121.
7. Feldman, H., & Maleski, A. A. Factors differentiating AWOL from non-AWOL trainees. *J. abnorm. soc. Psychol.*, 1948, **43**, 70–77.
8. Grayson, H. M., & Tolman, R. S. A semantic study of concepts of clinical psychologists and psychiatrists. *J. abnorm. soc. Psychol.*, 1950, **45**, 216–231.
9. Horst, P. *The prediction of personal adjustment.* New York: Social Science Research Council, 1941.
10. Kotkov, B., & Meadow, A. Rorschach criteria for predicting continuation in individual psychotherapy. *J. consult. Psychol.*, 1953, **17**, 16–20.
11. OSS Assessment Staff. *Assessment of men.* New York: Rinehart, 1948.
12. Peters, C. C., & Van Voorhis, W. R. *Statistical procedures and their mathematical bases.* New York: McGraw-Hill, 1940.
13. Sarbin, T. R. A contribution to the actuarial and individual methods of prediction. *Amer. J. Sociol.*, 1943, **48**, 593–602.
14. Schrader, P. J., & Robinson, M. F. An evaluation of prefrontal lobotomy through ward behavior. *J. abnorm. soc. Psychol.*, 1945, **40**, 61–69.
15. Stromberg, E. L. Testing programs draw better applicants. *Personnel Psychol.*, 1948, **1**, 21–29.
16. Wallen, R. Food aversions in behavior disorders. *J. consult. Psychol.*, 1948, **12**, 310–312.

CHAPTER 3

Clinical Sensitivity and Hypothesis Making

When students compare their appraisals of a person with those made by an experienced clinician, they are often amazed at their failure to seize upon significant observations and to make the proper inferences from them. Sometimes beginners feel that these "old hands" must have been born with intuitive powers. They forget the long history of training and contact with varied problems that the elder specialist has. This ability to note the significant features of behavior or of a history and to draw useful inferences we shall call "sensitivity." Dr. Stanley Cobb tells a good story to illustrate it:

I remember well, when acting as clinical clerk at Queen Square for Kinnier Wilson, I saw him present a new case to a group of students in the out-patient clinic. I was seated at the table taking notes; Wilson was standing, having just dismissed a patient, and there was an empty chair beside my table. Wilson rang for the next patient, the door opened and a man entered, followed by his wife. He walked across the fifteen feet of classroom, smiled at the students and at me and sat down. Wilson turned to me instantly and said, "Write down G.P.I. as the diagnosis." Probably my jaw dropped, for he went on, "Well, Cobb, what else could it be? Here is a middle-aged man coming to a nerve clinic. He enters the room smiling, pushes ahead of his wife, does not take off his hat, takes the only chair without asking and likes an audience!" Subsequent neurological and serological studies proved the correctness of the diagnosis (8, pp. 559 f).

Even though you criticize Wilson's dramatic performance as a hasty generalization, remember that his diagnosis of paresis (sometimes called G.P.I. or general paralysis of the insane) was based on well-known characteristics of the disease. The onset is typically in the fifth or sixth decade of life, and symptoms often include a disregard of social niceties and lack of inhibition. The diagnostician went beyond these things, however, and understood the significance of the simple fact that the patient had come to a neurological clinic. Perhaps further examination of the patient would not have supported Wilson's guess. Was he wrong, then, in making it? No, for the guess brought order into the available facts.

It served as a hypothesis to guide further observation and study. In order to teach sensitivity, Wilson announced his hypothesis sooner than is customary. But it is worth notice that further studies were done, despite the specialist's confidence in his conclusion.

Leaving aside the dramatic impact of being able to "smell a diagnosis," such sensitivity is of real value in the study of people. Many times clinicians must study people in settings that are not ideally suited for clinical investigation. Clinical work in industry, for example, requires the psychologist to be sensitive to the personalities of all the persons with whom he works: executives, supervisors, union leaders, employees. Often his only opportunity for assessing a person of key importance will come during a luncheon or a planning conference. If he is adept at picking up small cues and subtle meanings, he can learn a great deal without asking direct questions that would be inappropriate and would arouse opposition. In clinical interview situations, the psychologist has no time to meditate at length upon his next move. He must be able quickly to decide upon a line of questioning or whether to make another appointment. When heavy case loads allow only a little time for each client, the sensitivity of the experienced clinician is a great practical asset.

THE NATURE OF CLINICAL SENSITIVITY

In a broad sense, clinical sensitivity is awareness of significant internal and external events. When we say "significant" we mean the kind of events that help us understand people. The clinician cannot be aware of everything that is happening as he interacts with his client. The rumbling truck on the street or the dull hum of the office fan goes unnoticed, but a barely audible sigh commands the psychologist's interest. This happens because the specialist brings a framework of purposes and interests that accents particular details of his environment. This accenting is not mere vividness; it is vividness with meaning. That is to say, the vivid detail arouses tendencies to do something more than to attend to it. As he perceives, the clinician is already at work framing a question, making an inference, validating a conclusion, or reorienting himself to receive new data. The perceptual process could not be what it is without the motor readiness, nor could the motor process be released and smoothly guided without the sensory input. Clinical sensitivity, then, depends upon readiness to react in ways that are psychologically evaluational, diagnostic, and therapeutic.

Sensitivity to Actual Behavior Processes. A part of clinical sensitivity consists in being able to see and utilize the behavioral events in clients. The psychologist is aware of the shifting glance, the reddening cheeks, the tremulous voice. He notes the interlaced fingers, bitten nails, and hunched posture. He reacts to subtle changes without interposing a deliberate reasoning process. Smiles, for example, vary in ways that are hardly describable. There are smiles of friendly acceptance, of embarrassment, and of momentary triumph. And there are patronizing smiles and humble pleading smiles. Probably pictures of these facial patterns would show no stable differentiating features. Yet we can recognize them when we see their actual growth and fading in a context of social interaction.

You may think that these events are so obvious that no one could miss them. That is not the case. Some people do not even take a good look at those around them. And as for listening, the misunderstandings in most conversations testify to its intermittent character. Preoccupation with what he is going to say next or concern about the impression he is making often hinders the perceptual acuteness of the beginning clinician.

Problem 1. This exercise is meant to reveal the selectivity of interpersonal perceptions. Do not be misled by its apparent simplicity, for it can heighten your awareness of what you and others are perceiving.

In a casual situation, ask a friend to describe you. You may need to explain that you are doing a psychological exercise and need some help, but be careful not to influence his observation by what you say. Here are some neutral instructions: "Tell me what you notice about me." If he wants you to be more specific, simply say: "I'm not interested in any special things. Just tell me as much as you can about what you notice as you pay attention to me." As he observes, be casual and continue to move normally. Don't stiffen. At the end of the description, you may explain that you are trying to find out what people consider important as they watch other people.

As your friend describes you, notice how he does it. What does he pick out first? Does he note clothing, skin, hair, facial expression as he goes along? Does he mention actions? Does he describe his own feelings about you? Does he describe invisible qualities such as your traits, motives, and attitudes? At what point does he stop? Was his description rich or meager? Does he leave out items that often are avoided in polite conversation: facial blemishes, scuffed shoes, awkward posture, and the like?

Repeat this exercise with several other people, then answer these questions:

1. What kind of data is most commonly noted?
2. What kind of data is most often overlooked or neglected?
3. Summarize the chief differences you found among the observers.
4. Can you give any speculations or guesses as to the reasons for these differences?

In the second part of this exercise, you will try the more difficult task of noting your own observational method. Pick out a person on a bus, in a library, or at a lecture, and note your observations. Do this for several people.

1. Did you change your method or style of observing from one time to the next? How do you account for the changes, if any?

2. Were you aware of an unwillingness or a resistance to make any observations? Or of a preference for certain kinds of details? What were they?

3. Describe your way of noting things about people in these situations.[1]

Perception of Social Meanings. The behavioral events we have just mentioned tell very little to the clinician unless he understands them as part of a social event. If he knows that both general custom and personal interpretations of social relationships are at work, he will see richer meanings in the client's behavior. He can feel that the client is manipulating, entertaining, entreating, or fighting him. One person may, without asking, take a cigarette from his desk; another apologizes at length for a minor mishap. One woman may dress seductively for her interview; another appears in a house dress. These items cannot be understood without awareness of the social context. The nature of the consulting relationship, the circumstances that brought the client to the psychologist, the social formalities of the community—all provide a background for understanding the kind of relationship the client seeks to establish.

Most linguistic phenomena cannot be interpreted without familiarity with the techniques of expressing feeling. A sensitive clinician will be aware of evasion and of veiled meanings in language. He will hear a refusal to cooperate masked by polite speech forms. He will notice vulgarity, pedantry, euphemisms, and childishness in the choice of words. And he will note the pauses in the stream of speech and the topic under discussion when they occur.

The ability to note and interpret these social phenomena obviously depends on the life experience of the psychologist more than it does upon his reading. And among the experiences that count heavily, practice in psychotherapy ranks high. For there the circumstances make it possible to inquire directly into the meaning of the smallest events. Through long contact with a client, the therapist has an excellent opportunity to test the validity of hunches and guesses based on subtle cues.

Sensitivity to Data in the Client's History. There is another kind of clinical sensitivity that is quite different from those we have just mentioned. That is the ability to note and interpret details of a life history or symptom pattern. This ability comes only from familiarity with psychological

[1] The writer is indebted to Dr. Frederick Perls for the conceptions that led to this and some similar exercises in this book. Dr. Perls is concerned with the therapeutic use of such training; the present exercise has a different aim. Of course the writer assumes responsibility for his use of these conceptions.

diagnosis and personality development. As the client reports the events of his life, the clinician hears them in the light of his knowledge of other cases and his formal training. If the client describes a father who was "weak" and who "didn't mix well," the clinician has fantasies about the probable influence of a withdrawn parent. Rapidly, he speculates about the kind of model such a father would supply, about the father's ability to show affection for the client, and about the relationship between the parents. Another client may report that he is an only child, born to a mother who had given up hope of having children. Then the psychologist speculates about the amount of overindulgence such a mother may show and about her possible overprotective attitude.

Knowledge of psychopathology helps the clinician evaluate the seriousness of reported events in a way that is impossible for untrained people. A client may report quite casually that he has had several "spells where my words got mixed up, and I couldn't say what I had in mind to say." The clinician immediately thinks of the possibility of a transient aphasia and presses for a more complete description, but to the client this is only one of many puzzling events he has experienced. On the other hand, a client may attach pathological significance to facts which the clinician regards as essentially normal. For instance, a young woman may be deeply concerned about her occasional masturbation. The clinician, however, is thinking about her concern more than about her masturbation. He wonders about her sexual attitudes, relations with men, and her image of herself.

INDIVIDUAL DIFFERENCES IN SENSITIVITY

It is commonplace to say that there are wide differences in sensitivity among people. Two committee members or two party guests will perceive quite different happenings in their social groups, and these differences concern the unexpressed or partly revealed attitudes and motives of the people present. It is not simply that one person sees more than the other, although that often happens. The differences depend on the interpretive construction that is placed on what is seen and heard. Let us take a brief look at the basis for inferences or "intuitions" about the feelings of another person. How do people show us what they are not willing to tell us?

Any act is the result of more than one motive; usually there are many motives. Now these motives are not all equally strong, although they all may favor the action in question. Let us assume that they influence the action approximately in proportion to their respective strengths. The action is carried out in such a way as to satisfy the total motivational demand as much as possible, and this results in a particular course and manner of behavior. If the relative strengths are altered, the action will still occur, but there will be subtle changes due to the changed motivational pattern. Thus, two acts that are superficially similar betray differences in their motivational sources by differences in the style of the total act. We can illustrate these points by an oversimplified example.

Two clients are asked to take a test and both refuse. Let us suppose that they have identical motives for refusing: desire to talk about another problem, fear of the test, and hostility toward the clinician. The relative strengths of these motives for the first client are in the order given: desire, fear, hostility. For the second client, however, hostility is strongest, and desire to discuss something else is weakest. The second client is likely to use a sharper tone, to be more argumentative, to find fault with testing, and to be less willing to compromise. The bare fact of resistance to being tested is common to both clients, but by itself it tells us very little about the motives of the two people.

There is another thing that aids immensely in interpreting the emotional-motivational patterns lying behind various acts: seeing relationships between different events in the stream of social interaction, even though they are remote from one another. In the example we have just given, the clinician does not have to rely solely on the sharp tone and argumentative manner in order to guess the client's motives. He may also be aware that a few minutes earlier he openly disagreed with the client and that, at the opening of the interview, he refused to give the client certain confidential information. This background makes it easier for the clinician to realize the hostile character of the client's refusal to be tested. The clinician has already sensed that events were producing an increase in the strength of hostile feelings.

Development of Differences in Sensitivity. If the view we are proposing is correct, the insensitive person fails to take account of the style and timing of an act, and he fails to relate the events of a social interaction to one another. He takes behavior too much at its face value. The sensitive interpreter, on the other hand, does not abstract to such a degree. He neglects fewer details, and he tends less often to isolate events from one another. Why do these differences arise?

While we actually do not know the details of the process, people probably learn to be sensitive because it is useful to them. It enables them to adjust more effectively to social situations, to avoid unpleasantness, to satisfy more of their own needs. The learning must begin early in life when the young child learns to avoid the scowl and run toward the smile. As the developing individual becomes more practiced, he responds to less obvious changes in others. And the need for forecasting how family and friends will react to him leads him to seek consistencies in motives and attitudes. The result of this long learning process is that adults have "ready-made" reactions and appraisals—most of them without the deliberate use of logic or speculation.

Obviously, sensitivity does not always yield pleasant or satisfying outcomes. If awareness of subtleties in behavior continually reveals critical, rejecting, or contemptuous attitudes on the part of those around one, it could lead to chronic anxiety. One way of alleviating this anxiety is to shut off perceptions of subtleties—to act as if the disturbing information is not really present. And the same thing could happen when a person feels compelled to comply with the wishes of those around him. Acute perception then reveals a burden of requests on all sides. Better to blind oneself, at least in part. These and similar personality problems may end in producing defensively insensitive people—the withdrawn, negativistic, or contemptuous—who live in a world where the reactions of other people do not, indeed must not, matter.

The circumstances of family living, of course, vary widely in the opportunities they afford for observing and for validating our hunches. Persons with limited social contacts hardly have the chance or the need for much sensitivity. Families that express their feelings openly and strongly provide clear guides for the child. He can interpret social situations without resorting to minute behavior cues. And homes also differ in the amount of discussion and attention focused on the understanding of covert behavior. Consequently, children differ in their concern with such events.

Some people are excessively and inappropriately sensitive. Sometimes this is the outcome of living in a family where expression was cautious and guarded, and the control of children was accomplished by veiled rejection. These families produce the timid, dependent adults who habitually scan the social horizon for signs of disapproval or praise, but who see nothing more. Inappropriate sensitivity also occurs in suspicious, paranoid people. They read evil intentions into every smile, neglecting to consider the social setting of their observation. These instances show us that distorted personal development and coercive personal needs can interfere with accurate and sensitive social perception.

On the other hand, an intelligent adult with a fairly normal development, adequate social contacts, freedom from dogmatism, and a generally satisfying life may reasonably trust many of his reactions to people in face-to-face situations. To say this is not, however, to endorse snap judgments nor the glib, stereotyped interpretations of behavior made by socially dominant people who proudly announce their "knowledge of human nature."

Blunting. Of special concern to psychologists is the possibility that their training may decrease their sensitivity. It may be that the formal preparation in academic work robs a psychologist of a certain desirable naïveté in reacting to others, although it develops analytic and objective methods of thinking. For one thing, most formal training centers around the acquisition of knowledge by reading. Academic life encourages interaction with books rather than with people. Furthermore, the reward pattern in schools gives more benefits to the successful reader of books than to the successful reader of people. But we cannot condemn nor reject academic training simply because it may sometimes have these effects. Instead, we must seek experiences that take us beyond the lamp and the book.

Another characteristic of psychological training that can lead to blunting is the emphasis on the use of tests. For some unwary students, learning to use psychological tests produces an overdependence upon them. The trouble is not with the tests; it lies in the attitude of the tester. This attitude has been described by D. M. Levy in discussing the work of psychologists in military service:

A problem that seemed a special addiction of psychologists, as revealed in a number of their interviews, was failure to recognize the importance of their own findings—a type of shyness quite unlike the feeling of confidence they had with data derived from tests. Their underemphasis of frequently excellent perceptions of personality difficulties was due, I assume, to inadequate background of clinical experience, especially of psychopathology. Hence they missed those strengthening elements in clinical vision derived from exposure to a large variety of psychiatric patients and were unable to stand by their more subtle observations. That may explain the curious phenomenon when a person was discharged from service for the very reasons the psychologist had recorded in the original examination, but whom he had recommended nevertheless (10, pp. 97 f).

Probably the "curious phenomenon" described by Levy is due not only to lack of clinical experience but also to excessive reliance upon test data. Good psychological tests are as revealing in the study of persons as X rays are in the study of organs, but much pathology escapes both methods.

Another contributor to the blunting of sensitivity is an extremely analytic observational attitude. There is some evidence that deliberate efforts to analyze your own observations interfere with correct judgments. To some unknown extent, then, academic emphasis upon analytic methods of thinking may decrease the usefulness of your direct reactions to the people you study.

OBSERVATIONAL ATTITUDES

Analytic Observation. The attitudes of the clinical observer vary from a deliberate focusing of attention upon specific aspects of the client's behavior to a rather drifting, global, and diffuse receptive set. We shall

call this latter kind of observation "free-ranging" as opposed to "analytic."
Extremely analytic observation is frequently used in research studies.
Certain aspects of speech, gesture, or general motility may be watched
and tallied. In clinical observation, an analytic attitude may be adopted
by a clinician who has certain hypotheses about his client and is seeking further evidence. For example, he may believe that the client is
excessively anxious about sexual matters; for a time, then, he is particularly intent upon the client's reactions during the discussion of sexual
topics. Or, early in a diagnostic interview, the clinician tries to acquire
information rapidly by focusing on specific features of behavior: voice,
facial expression, manual and postural activity. This deliberate shifting
of observational set is continued until the clinician has covered most
of the observable features of behavior.

Probably no one in clinical work is continuously analytic in a rigid,
completely systematic way. Some people approach it more closely than
others, however. Usually, using a systematic survey outline, such as
a standardized interview blank, results in more analytic observation.
Such blanks are meant to keep the clinician from overlooking significant
aspects of behavior. For example, forms for recording the data from
psychiatric observation include mood, general appearance, stream of
speech, condition of the sensorium, recent and remote memory, spatial
and temporal orientation, and so on. Some systematic outline is helpful
to beginners, although they will probably use it quite flexibly as they
become more experienced.

Analytic observation leads to data that are readily communicated.
Fairly clear descriptions of events can be recorded, and these aid efforts
to make formal inferences. Perhaps that is why we find the analytic
attitude so frequently in the psychological laboratory.

Free-ranging Observation. In this kind of observation the clinician
allows himself to be carried along by the client, and attempts to be
sensitive both to his own reactions and to those of the client. As the
interview continues, certain impressions emerge without deliberate effort.
This kind of attitude probably increases the chances that the clinician
will react to minimal cues (perhaps even subliminal ones) and will
reach judgments that have a "global" character. This diffuse form of
observation is more often found in therapeutic interviews than in diagnostic sessions. In the former, the intimate acquaintance of the clinician
with his client enhances the opportunities for correct judgments, just
as is the case with friends who know each other well. Then, too, therapy
more easily allows the clinician to lapse into the passivity required in
free-ranging observation; he does not have to pay attention to directing
the session.

Free-ranging observation seems to depend for its value on the emergence of "natural" or spontaneously formed perceptual units. The impressions of the clinician are successive figures that form against the general background of the flow of behavior. Probably the principles used by gestalt psychologists to account for visual-figure formation operate in this more complex situation: proximity, similarity, simplicity, good continuation, and closure. As the psychologist observes, he is struck by repetitions, by an ordering of the client's actions, by gaps and deviations. He does not begin by intending to discover such things; they impress themselves upon him. If these impressions are to form spontaneously, it is important for the clinician to refrain from forcing his observational data into a pattern. He needs to let himself experience the fluidity and unstructured character of his early impressions, and to wait until some impression intrudes upon the jumble of events. The patterns of observation form themselves.

In this kind of attitude, it is essential that the clinician be aware of his own feelings. We mean this quite literally. He must know what is occurring inside him, what he is doing, wanting, and sensing as the client stimulates him. These inside events are part of the data that tell us what the client is doing just as surely as his actions show us. For the clinician, too, is a person, and in a social interchange his own reactions have meaning. The process of using one's own reactions as data has been called "recipathy" by Murray (13). He contrasts this process with "empathy" in which the clinician feels something akin to the feelings of the client. In the writer's opinion, recipathy is the more important of the two processes; empathy is always one's own feeling in the last analysis, anyway, and should be recognized as such. There is, of course, no reason why the data supplied by one's own feelings cannot be used in all observation, but it seems easier to be aware of them under conditions of free-ranging observation.

Several examples will help to show you how recipathy can be used. Here is an instance from the writer's experience:

Early in my clinical work, I was trying to understand the occupational history of a nineteen-year-old boy. I could not grasp the chronology of events nor his reasons for changing jobs. As we talked, I became increasingly aware of my confusion. At first, I attributed my feelings to a lack of interviewing ability. Only after the interview did the real significance of my mixed-up state dawn on me. I realized that usually I did comprehend the chronology and the reported motives of the people I talked with. My own confusion must be a reflection of the confusion in the boy. Later, testing and study by other clinicians proved he was, indeed, a mixed-up, schizoid personality.

The second example is from Reik's experience:

At the beginning of her analysis, a young woman doctor described her feelings during sexual intercourse in a quiet objective manner. In doing so she spoke of sensations at the *"orificium uteri,"* the *"mons Veneris,"* etc. As I listened I felt a slight touch of astonishment. It was quickly suppressed. Why should not a doctor use these Latin terms? They are familiar to her. The subsequent course of the analysis proved my reasonable reflection to have been misplaced, and my fleeting sense of astonishment to have been psychologically justified. Her markedly objective manner of speaking about sexual matters proved to be mental camouflage. At a later stage it was easy to ascertain that the young doctor's apparent lack of embarrassment in speaking on the subject of sex concealed a strong inhibition (14, p. 223).

Often the clinician's reactions to the client will be similar to the reactions of other people. If he is annoyed, repulsed, or made to feel protective, it is probable that other people often react the same way. Of course, we must always allow for individual tendencies and biases in the clinician. If he is moody, easily irritated, or moved to sympathy, he ought to know it and to modify his interpretation of his own feeling responses to a client.

It is difficult to explain the reasons for judgments made under free-ranging conditions. Impressions tend to be general and without obvious and clear-cut external basis. We may describe a person as "warm," "sly," or "patronizing," without being able to point to the specific acts that produced this impression. In part this is because the observer is not set to recall details. But it is probably also due to the fact that the clinician does not mull over a list of observed details in arriving at a conclusion. His judgments are as immediate as those of a lover who realizes in a flash that the affections of his beloved have cooled. The realization comes to him *before* he starts the search for detailed evidence.

Since the outcomes of free-ranging observation depend on the cumulative (but probably nonadditive) effects of subtle cues, the observer cannot recount the steps by which he reached a conclusion. This fact, in addition to the difficulty of communicating the external events on which the impression is based, has given this kind of observation a bad name in some scientific circles. Yet that is hardly enough to condemn it as a useful clinical method. For at the very least it can serve as a source of hypotheses. At the best it can lead to impressions that could be obtained in no other way. There is some evidence that it has value.

Attitudes in Observing Simple Performances. Estes (7) prepared a series of silent films showing fifteen subjects doing simple tasks. This film ran about two minutes for each subject and showed him doing such things as building a house of playing cards, holding a lighted match until it burned out, or pushing another person off balance. Various groups of people were asked to view the films and estimate certain personality characteristics of the subjects. The fifteen subjects had been studied intensively in a cooperative research project, so that Estes had adequate criterion data for use in checking the accuracy of the judges. Among other things, Estes found that judges who had interests in dramatics or in the graphic arts were more accurate than judges whose main interests lay in the sciences and philosophy. Furthermore, the thirteen best judges did not use a deliberate analytical method of observation and inference. They made use of what we have called "free-ranging" observation. On the other hand, some judges, from college faculties, were consciously analytical and logical. They did poorly in sizing up the personalities of the subjects.

While the conditions of this experiment were quite restrictive in terms of the amount of cues offered, the results suggest that free-ranging observation may have some merit. They also suggest that deliberate logical analysis of behavior may not always be the most useful method for clinical observers.

Value of Both Methods. Probably beginners in the study of people can do little else than adopt an analytic attitude. Gradually habits of noting significant aspects of a client's dress and behavior will be formed and become automatic. And, presumably, they will then find it easier to utilize a less deliberate procedure. Undoubtedly some of you have personalities that make analytic methods of thought and observation so congenial that you will find no point in trying to do anything else. And a few will find the same methods nothing but dull impediments. Perhaps most of you can attain a certain flexibility, veering now toward one, now toward the other method. As Murray sums it up: "We hold no brief for uncontrolled, free-floating intuition. But we do maintain that critical emotional participation (empathy and recipathy) may be cultivated to advantage and, when corrected by all other means at our disposal, is the best instrument that we possess for exploring the 'depths' of personality" (13, p. 249).

As we go on in this chapter, then, we shall run the risk of making you overanalytical by pointing out certain things to look at and to hear. These will be for the most part commonplace things. But they have their place in helping to develop sensitivity.

PRACTICE IN OBSERVATION

Problem 2. For a start in looking carefully at a person, try observing arm and hand movement. Seat yourself in a library, streetcar, restaurant, or in an auditorium and pick out a person whom you can watch inconspicuously. Pay attention to movements of arms and hands alone for about five minutes. If you can, use a pad to record notes or diagrams. At the end of your period of observation you should be able to answer the following questions:

1. Did the person make many or few movements?
2. Was one arm used more often than the other?
3. Were the gestures generally rapid or slow?
4. Were the movements small or large in the area of space covered?
5. Were particular movement patterns repeated or were all gestures different from one another?

If you observe the gestures of four or five different people, you will begin to develop a set of rough norms as to frequency, rapidity, and extent of movement. You will also find that the circumstances under which the observations were made affect your findings. Observation of the gestural patterns of three people under similar circumstances (for example, during library study) will soon convince you of the marked individual differences to be found in even these simple patterns.

Naturally, you will notice features of the gestures which are not covered by the five questions in Problem 2. There are differences in gracefulness, jerkiness, and forcefulness of movement. Certain body parts may be favored as targets of the gesture: the hair, eyes, nose, or chin may be touched or rubbed repeatedly. The position of the fingers will vary from outspread hand to clenched fist. And objects such as pencils, books, theater programs, and rings may be handled in characteristic ways.

As you become more skillful in observing, you should be able to incorporate more of the context of the gesture into your formulation of what you see. Thus, you may be able to notice, during a conversation, that your subject's hands increase their activity during the discussion of certain kinds of topics. Or you may find that a special pattern is repeated under similar motivational and emotional conditions. One such pattern is the drumming of fingers on desks by students who are impatient for a class to end.

Other Bodily Gestures. Although the arms and hands are mobile body parts and easily observed, your observation must eventually include the whole body. For instance, the head may incline forward slightly in a submissive gesture or tilt back as in aversion or surprise. The shoulders do not remain motionless. You can easily notice shrugging, slumping, straightening. The feet and legs sometimes yield useful cues. Thus, impatient drumming of the fingers has its counterpart in restless tapping of the feet. Or people who are ready to rise from a seated position will often assume an anticipatory posture, drawing the feet back and keeping them flat against the floor.

Movements of the face are particularly important in the study of people. Faces show such a rich variety of patterns and rapid transitions, however, that it is not easy to formulate clear statements about what the observer has seen. Ordinarily we do not describe the actual facial pattern but state the inferences we have made. Thus we say, "He didn't like my remark," instead of reporting that he frowned or tightened his lips. In most cases, such inferences are not based on facial movement alone but on our understanding of the whole immediate situation. Even without the frown, we suspect that our remark would arouse opposition in this individual. If the frown actually occurs, it tends to reinforce our belief in the correctness of the guess.

As with other body movements, people show wide individual differences in the degree of facial mobility. Some maintain an almost motionless face for an entire interview (think of the experienced poker player), while others continuously change expression in response to the affective shifts in conversation. A few people will strike you as deliberately acting or striking poses intended to impress you. Examples can easily be found among intellectual posers who knit their brows into deep furrows when asked a question. They want you to realize how deeply they consider each precious thought.

Changes in the eyes are instructive. Careful observation will show an increased shine or glisten of the eyeball, the result of a slight increase in tears. Sometimes tears accumulate along the edge of the lower lid, even when the person appears otherwise well controlled. Such changes can often be noticed a minute or so in advance of actual crying. Sometimes people resort to rubbing the eyes or nose blowing; they want to remove accumulated tears without appearing to do so.

Eyelids may be lowered or completely closed as part of an emotional reaction. Sometimes partial closing is a way of avoiding the examiner's gaze. Relaxation or attempts to concentrate on thinking often include eyelid closing. But always the lowered lids show withdrawal from the immediate social contact.

Shifting fixation of the eyes to avoid looking at the examiner is frequently found, but it has no single meaning. An early study by Moore and Gilliland (12) suggests that nondominant men are less able to keep a fixed gaze directed at the examiner's eyes than dominant men, but more evidence is needed on this point. It is fairly common for persons to report in counseling interviews that they feel others can "see through" them by looking them in the eye. Some such attitude often lies behind the lowered eyes that betray a sense of guilt or shame.

SIGNIFICANCE OF GESTURES

Movement and Expression. At one time, psychologists tended to view bodily gestures as expressions of "psychic" or "mental" states. One of the important problems for investigation was to discover the bodily correlates of particular "states of consciousness." Work on this problem developed useful methods and resulted in a good-sized body of fact, but the problem has never been really solved. When it was possible to take a naturalistic view of human behavior and to give up the "mind-body" notion, it became clear that there was no such thing as a movement which "expressed" a state of consciousness. The "expressive movements" could be understood as overt portions of a total reaction pattern. Although we retain the phrase today, we use it to refer to movements which have symptomatic value, which permit inferences about the covert side of responses, and which may indicate something of the person's personality patterns.

The gesture of a body part must be initiated by some motivational state. Thus, fatigue resulting from a fixed position brings changes in posture or arm position. Local irritation, caused by a mosquito bite or by perspiration, may lead to scratching or rubbing. The requirements of communication favor the appearance of waving, pointing nodding, and so on. Certain gestures are part of a more general avoidance or approach pattern. Some clients, for example, may place a piece of test equipment on the desk with a quick shove that clearly shows they want to be rid of it.

One of the motive states that particularly interests clinicians is anxiety. Anxiety usually involves increased tension in the striped musculature as well as altered visceral action. Common covert reactions include: motility changes in the gastrointestinal tract, rising blood pressure, and glandular secretion (as in crying and sweating). During anxiety the rate of movement and the total number of movements usually increase. Often the movements appear jerky and clumsy. These indicators of anxiety are important for they are sometimes the first sign of the patient's reaction to topics with personal significance.

Style of Movement. Although the specific goal of a gesture depends on the person's motives, the "style" of movement is partially independent of the motive involved. Style may reflect more general characteristics, such as social role or status. Efron and Foley (5) were able to demonstrate this fact in a study of differences between the common gesticulations of "traditional" Italians and "traditional" Jews. They also found that assimilated Jews showed gesture patterns unlike either of the "traditional" groups, although they resembled the gestures of the non-Jews in their own social environment. Of course, individual differences were evident, even within the same social group.

Some gestures originate in the unique personal history of an individual and may have symbolic significance. Allport gives this example:

Another young man has a peculiar habit of jerking his arms whenever he thinks of embarrassing things. This habit has been traced back to a time when he had unpleasant compulsive thoughts of striking people on the street. At such times he would jerk his arms to throw off the impulse. With time this habit came to be used on other occasions where freedom from unpleasant thought was desired. Though freed from the initial compulsion, the gesture remained, and finally came to express and symbolize new conflicts (1, p. 473).

Probably the most intensive studies of this kind of gesture have been made by Krout (9), who calls them autistic gestures. His definition of these responses implies a useful theoretical framework: "When an individual, inhibiting his direct responses to an external situation, responds to subsequent internal stimulation explicitly, we have what we may call autistic gestures" (9, p. 18). This statement suggests that, were it not for certain inhibitory responses, the gesture would not appear but would be replaced by a complete action or statement. And it is true that such replacement does seem to occur in a very permissive therapeutic situation.

The role of inhibition in movement is not confined to autistic gestures, however. As a general rule, overt responses are restrained in mild anxiety-producing situations. For example, conversational gestures are somewhat less expansive and frequent in the early part of an interview than later when rapport has been established. The experienced examiner therefore attaches more importance to inhibition in the latter part of the session. He is also partially dependent upon gestures to indicate the rapidity with which the initial anxiety is overcome. Since inhibition due to anxiety results from the patient's own characteristics as well as from the social situation, some people will exhibit very little movement even in a permissive interview. They appear stiff and hesitant despite their effort to seem calm, allowing the examiner to make a fair guess about the strain they feel.

Movement Style and Personality. Some stylistic features of gesture indicate fairly general personality characteristics. We do not think of the person who habitually makes slow and sweeping arm gestures as a sour, embittered pessimist. And friends whom we find warm and accepting are rarely tense, rapid, and contracted in their movement patterns. While we do not want to yield to common stereotypes in this matter, we must realize that some evidence points to relationships between movement and personality. The problem is by no means a simple one, as the studies of Allport and Vernon (2) show. In an effort to measure consistency of movement patterns, they found it necessary to take account of patterns which appeared statistically contradictory but which were congruent with one another when viewed in the light of the individual personality.

In one of the case studies presented by Allport and Vernon (2), a forceful, decisive man ranked fairly high in walking speed but quite low in strolling speed. Considered only from the point of view of speed, these findings appear inconsistent. If you know more about the conditions of measurement, a plausible explanation is possible. Walking speeds were measured as the subject left the laboratory, i.e., the subject had some fairly definite goal. Strolling speeds were measured under instructions to walk as if meditating. In the light of other information about this subject, the discrepancy in the two measures could indicate his ability to adapt quickly to the demands of the immediate situation.[2]

A study reported by D. W. MacKinnon (13) shows a different aspect of the relation of gesture to personality. As part of an experimental investigation of repression, subjects were required to solve problems in a room by themselves. Booklets on the table where the subject worked contained solutions to the problems, but the experimenter gave the subject permission to look at only certain solutions. The experimenter left the subject alone but continued to observe him through a one-way screen. About half the subjects violated the instructions not to look at certain solutions. The part of MacKinnon's data most relevant to our present discussion concerns the kinds and amount of gestural activity which the subjects showed when they could not solve the problems readily.

Subjects who violated the experimenter's prohibitions showed aggressive, restless behavior more often than did the nonviolators. They pounded their fists, kicked the table, and stamped back and forth across the room. The nonviolators fidgeted and showed restlessness but in a nonaggressive way. Gestures directed toward the nose and mouth (such as fingernail biting, nose-picking, smelling a part of the body, and licking the hand) were a good deal more frequent among the nonviolators. The aggressive actions of the violators were, of course, directed toward external objects—a neat parallel to their rejection of the authority of the experimenter. The nonviolators, on the other hand, showed their generally anxious state without an externally directed aggressiveness. Later questioning indicated that these nonviolators tended to feel guilty more often than violators (13, pp. 491–501).

At the risk of overgeneralizing, we think it should be pointed out that these data support the usefulness of observing gestures in arriving at a picture of personality. There may well be wide differences between the life-style of the client who pounds the chair and of the one who rubs his face and bows his head.

Be suspicious, however, of the easy assumption that certain movement patterns are invariably connected with the same personality traits

[2] This interpretation differs from that of Allport and Vernon, and no claim is made for its accuracy.

or emotional reactions. There is a kind of "functional equivalence" of movements, so that different movements may go along with similar traits in different people or even in the same person seen at different times. Expressive action must be considered in the light of all the information you have about a particular person and the circumstances of the observation. This view has been clearly stated in a summary of the experimental work on emotional expression by Cole:

And while common sense may insist that we do read emotional expressions . . . the experimental findings would seem to indicate that the signs are likely to be individual affairs, that we should not expect to be able to identify fixed biological patterns of facial expression in social situations, and that in all probability our success (and there is reason to doubt this, frequently enough) is dependent upon a total impression involving the whole posture, and even more, the entire situation and sequence of events leading up to the moment of judgment. We read situations rather than faces, or at least when we do not have this matrix we have lost the key to the facial puzzle (3, p. 279).

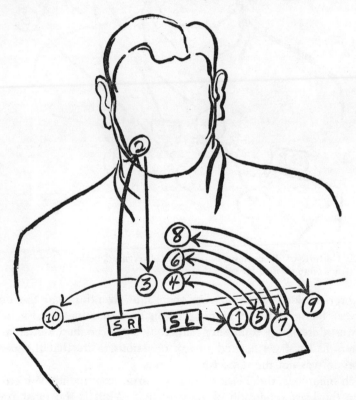

Figure 1. Gestures of "A" during a ten-minute observation period. For movements 1 through 9 his elbows rested on the table. At positions 4, 6, and 8, the right hand clasped the left.

Problem 3. Figures 1, 2, and 3 show diagrams of actual gesture patterns observed under comparable conditions. The numbers in the circles show the successive positions assumed by the hands. At the beginning of the observation, the right hand was in the position shown as S_R and the left hand was at S_L. There is no indication of the speed of the movements, but you can get an idea of the frequency, extent, location, and pattern of movements from the diagram.

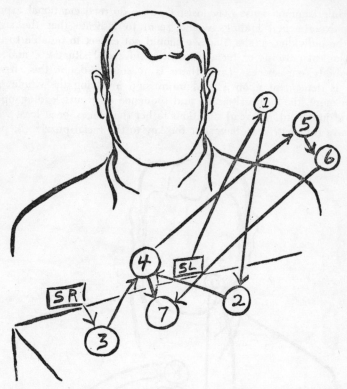

Figure 2. Gestures of "B" during a two-minute observation period. At positions 4 and 7, the two hands were clasped for several seconds.

All three subjects were men in their late twenties, and the observations were made at the beginning of an oral examination. Each of the three was describing some experimental work he had done, and the examiners had not yet started to ask questions. Note that the period of observation was not the same for all three.

Which man has the highest rate of arm movement? Which seems to show the least repetition of movements? What is the most probable explanation for the frequent use of the left hand by A?

Which man was most calm during the examination? Could you speculate about any personality traits that these men may show? At the end of this chapter you will find brief descriptions which you can compare with your own guesses.

It would be very worthwhile for you to construct similar diagrams on the basis of your own observations. Try to observe a person twice on the same day, once in the morning and once in the evening when he

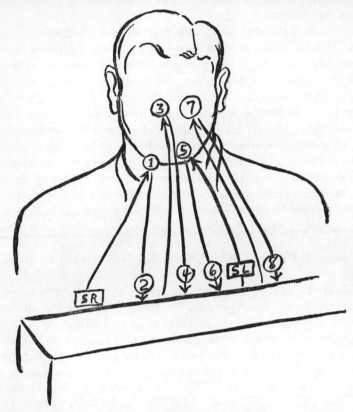

Figure 3. Gestures of "C" during a twelve-minute observation period. In addition to the movements shown, many small ones were made while the hands were lying in the lap.

is tired. The social situation and physical surroundings of the two observations should be similar. What changes in gestural behavior appear to be due to fatigue?

LEARNING TO MAKE RELEVANT OBSERVATIONS

Selective Sensitivity. Expert observers do a great deal more than record details accurately. They show a nearly automatic selectivity in the kind of things they attend to, for they have learned that some events are unimportant for their purposes while other data suggest worthwhile generalizations or fruitful lines of inquiry. Counting the buttons on a dress or the number of blinks in five minutes is not likely to be rewarding in the clinical interview. There is no point in being sensitive to everything at once. Facts which bear heavily upon the problem at hand may be neglected by an unfortunate observer who is intent upon noting every small detail.

It is not easy, though, to specify just what to look for in studying persons. The relevance of data depends upon the purposes of the observation, and these purposes change as the requirements of the situation change. For example, an employment interviewer who fails to notice the bitten nails of a woman applying for a job as a punch-press operator is not making a mistake. He is quite properly more interested in her manual dexterity, intelligence, and reasons for wanting the job. But an interviewer who overlooked the bitten nails of an applicant for a job as model in a dress shop would be guilty of a real oversight. It is good practice to understand clearly what you expect to accomplish during an observation period or examination. Do you wish to decide whether psychotic trends are present, whether a person is honest, whether a junior executive is promotable; or are you interested in a broad understanding of the major needs and adjustive techniques of an unhappy patient? Different selectivity is needed in each of these situations.

The ability to select significant data probably requires practice, intelligence, familiarity with personality theory, knowledge of common syndromes, and wisdom. None of these is to be had for the asking! Part of the genius of great scientists, clinicians, and masters of literature lies in seeing the possible importance of actions and events that could be considered trifles. Freud's *Psychopathology of Everyday Life* is a brilliant record of such sensitivity. Then, too, as we suggested at the beginning of this chapter, experience and familiarity with certain kinds of human problems contribute enormously to skill in selecting relevant data. Beginners are severely limited by their lack of experience. Despite these difficulties, there are a few ideas that may help you.

Deviations from a Group Norm. When actions, speech, dress, or biographical details differ markedly from what you usually observe in a given setting, they should be regarded as probably significant. You may not know why they are significant at the time, but you can remember them for future reference. In routine testing and interviewing, the behavior of clients tends to fall within certain limits. This "range of expected behavior" depends upon the examining situation (vocational guidance, employment, college admissions, mental-hygiene clinic, social agency), the kinds of people who ordinarily come for examination, and the personal qualities of the examiner. After some experience in a particular setting you will know about what to expect. Deviations from this roughly defined range are worth thinking about.

Suppose a college counselor discovers that most men students adopt an easy informal manner with him after a few minutes of conversation. A student who persists in saying "sir" throughout the interview is deviating from this rough norm, and the word may prove to be a valuable cue to certain attitudes. On the other hand, where "sir" is common practice, failure to use it is an equally important cue.

Deviations from norms of region, community, or neighborhood are also significant. In a particular locale, special ways of acting or dressing may be common practice in a whole community. Fads may rise and fall, and local events may temporarily affect speech habits, conversational content, and even gestures. A clinician who is in touch with his community is able to evaluate more accurately what he sees and hears in the consulting room than one who is indifferent to the social context in which he works.

Here is an actual example of a deviation from a pattern which is standard throughout much of the United States:

A young man came to consult a psychologist about his inability to decide to separate from his wife. In the course of the interviews, the psychologist noticed that the man wore a wedding ring on the little finger of his left hand. This deviation from a common custom prompted the psychologist to ask, at an appropriate time, whether he usually wore his ring on that finger. The indecisive husband replied that he did, and added, "But I haven't always worn it there. When I was first married, I wore it on my right hand." It was no surprise to find that he felt he had been pushed into marriage by his wife and that he had avoided sexual relations with her as much as possible. The more interesting question is why he wore a wedding ring at all. The culture pattern permits but does not require husbands to wear wedding rings. Apparently this man's deviant behavior is related to his general ambivalence about the whole marital situation. He was able neither to accept his marital status completely nor to move toward changing it.

Obviously, as the clinician grows more familiar with the common behavior of the group he works with, subtle deviations will be more easily noticed. But if his work changes so that he meets people from a different subculture, or people with a different kind of problem, or if his contact with them involves a different relationship (as in shifting from a mental-hygiene clinic to an industrial-counseling service) he will need to establish new norms. During the initial phases of readjustment he is likely to find himself handicapped by unfamiliarity with prevailing patterns or by incorrect inferences based on his earlier experience.

Some years ago Stanley Hyman in *The New Yorker* [3] recognized the effects of unfamiliarity with the culture pattern in the following paragraph:

Psychoanalysis seems to be here to stay, but one of the bugs that will have to be ironed out sooner or later is the problem of the foreign-speaking psychoanalyst and the English idiom. We know a girl, now in the process of being psyched, who mentioned to her analyst, a recent arrival from Zurich, that she had had a dream involving a desk with pigeonholes. She heard him draw in his breath sharply, and the direction of his inquiry changed. It wasn't until six months later that she discovered he had built an entire theory of her personality around the assumption that her dream desk included accommodations for birds (15).

Deviations from a Prior Pattern. When it is clear that a person has shifted from a previous pattern of behavior, the kind of change, its rapidity, and its extent should be carefully examined. Ordinarily we expect people to continue doing about what they have been doing, with perhaps gradual changes in interests, attitudes, and traits. Rapid and extreme alterations in a customary pattern indicate powerful environmental pressures or serious personality disturbances. Minimal but rapid changes are usually less important as warning signs, but they often point to significant attitudinal shifts.

Miss Johnson was a nurse in her late forties and had been having weekly consultations with a psychologist for several months. One day she told him that she had made an appointment for a permanent wave but had broken it. Two weeks later she appeared with curly hair! Her action, while not unusual for women in her group, deviated from her own prior pattern. She had consistently refused to spend money on herself for things she described as "worldly"—movies, cosmetics, and dress-up clothes. Her new permanent wave was part of a shift toward increased acceptance of herself and more spontaneity.

It is not uncommon for severe behavior disorders to be preceded by marked changes in a person's usual actions, although his changed behavior may still be within the limits of group norms. Agitation, long silences, talkativeness, listlessness, exuberance, pessimism, and so on may suddenly occur without apparent cause. Thus, one student annoyed a college class by talking persistently out of turn and trying to dominate the discussion. His behavior surprised the class, because he rarely recited and was usually quiet. A few days later, after continuing his restless, talkative, and dominating behavior at home, he was admitted to a hospital with a diagnosis of schizophrenia.

Since clinicians are not familiar with the customary actions of the patients they see, they must frequently rely on the testimony of friends

[3] By permission. Copyright 1945 The New Yorker Magazine, Inc.

or relatives about changes that have occurred. Except in instances of extreme changes, the clinician will need to question these informants carefully. They are not sensitized to the significance of shifts in behavior patterns and are likely to forget what they have noticed or to dismiss their observations as unimportant. It is also important to determine whether environmental changes have taken place—changes which could be related to behavior shifts. Moving to a new home, starting a new job, the arrival of a new baby, a death in the family, the lengthy absence of a parent, or a long illness, all present psychological problems that must be met somehow. Many times the onset of symptoms coincides with or shortly follows events such as these.

Inconsistencies. Another significant datum is one which is inconsistent with other observations or knowledge about a person. One of the commonest places to find inconsistency is in biographical details. Dates or times of certain events should fit in with the remainder of the story. Occasionally you will find that in retelling a story a patient makes changes that are inconsistent with an earlier version. These incompatible versions may raise questions about the memory of the patient, about possible motives for distortion, or about the influence of the circumstances in which the story is told.

Inconsistencies in grammar and vocabulary sometimes point toward posing or toward the effects of an early background which the client is trying to overcome. Then, in the midst of a flow of polysyllabic words, you may hear several mispronunciations or incorrect usages which you would not have expected from the speaker. An interesting example of the opposite kind is furnished by people with average educational backgrounds who have anxiously read medical articles and books for a long time: ordinary speech becomes interlaced with unexpected technical words whenever medical topics are discussed.

In testing, other kinds of inconsistencies are found. Easy items on an information test may be missed although a number of difficult items are passed. Sometimes this suggests marked initial anxiety, sometimes confusion, sometimes a deliberate attempt to deceive the examiner. Several interest tests for the same person may show conflicting patterns of scores which cannot be explained on the basis of differences in type of test. They may point to general attitudes of uncertainty, to resistiveness, or simply to failure to comprehend the task.

Problem 4. Each of the following descriptions tells of a change in a person's behavior. Give several plausible explanations for each change. Also tell which explanation seems most likely to be correct and why you favor it.

1. A businessman in his late forties has recently started to act boisterously in informal social gatherings. He also has begun to tell "dirty

stories" in mixed company. His family is surprised and somewhat shocked by this behavior, for he has usually been much more restrained in such situations. In the past he confined his off-color jokes to meetings with other men. The family knows of no events that could account for this change.

2. A bright young man in college has become interested in occult phenomena, spiritualism, trance states, and the like. What surprises his friends is that he accepts uncritically many ideas he reads, although he has been a strong advocate of scientific method. Then, too, he has become something of a pest by introducing his occult ideas frequently and somewhat inappropriately into conversations.

3. The family of a girl in her late teens noticed that she had stopped accepting dates from young men. She had usually dated three to five times a month. When her mother inquired about this matter, she said that she had lost interest in men and that they were generally boring. She still sees her girl friends, however, and occasionally goes shopping, to the movies, or plays cards with them.

INTERPRETING OBSERVATIONS

Clinical observation is useless unless it leads to significant ideas about the client. To report a list of the things that happened in the interview is not the aim of an expert clinician. He wants to go beyond what he sees and hears in the consultation room to understand the motives, conflicts, and emotions of the client. The psychologist who studies people is a fertile hypothesis maker. He is forever wondering about the meaning of this and the significance of that. Many of his guesses turn out to be poor ones. Some suggest interesting lines of thought and nothing more. But a few result in the discovery of the main trends in a personality. The clinician cannot afford to stop speculating about what lies behind his data, even at the risk of following false leads. Despite the bad features of overinterpretation, a refusal to make any guesses about the significance of data is even worse. That leads to sterile neutrality.

People who won't consider the implications of their observations begin by insisting that everything be taken for granted. If they learn that a previously happy couple has quarreled, they say, "Well, everybody fights once in a while." When a woman who has usually dressed somberly appears in vivid clothes, they comment, "Women always have to have a change, you know." The fact that a woman misses the arrival of her husband because she forgot the time the train was due simply means, "She probably had so many things on her mind that she couldn't remember. After all, no one is perfect." Presumably these matter-of-fact souls could face a vacuous hebephrenic smile for half an hour and decide that "it is just wonderful how cheerful some people can be!" This intellectual myopia is the early phase of a more serious disease: complete inability to see and hear anything significant.

Tentative Generalization. Students who have been well trained in the use of scientific method in psychology develop a mistrust of conclusions based on insufficient data. Their familiarity with the history of psychology, with actual laboratory studies of people, and with controversies in psychological literature helps them maintain an attitude of suspended judgment. They know that experiments do not always support the interpretation put forward by the experimenter. Consequently they emphasize the need for a respectable number of cases, correct statistical analysis, control of relevant variables, and methods that are objective and repeatable.

This skeptical attitude is desirable, and there is no necessity for giving it up in clinical work. But it can lead to a habit which is quite likely to be damaging to clinical insight. This habit consists of an unwillingness even to consider possible generalizations and to explore their consequences on a tentative basis. Then, instead of having a number of integrating hypotheses available, these factual-minded people have only a few, and they run the risk of overlooking the significance of the observations they do make. Sometimes it almost seems that overcautious scientists refuse even to *think* some kinds of thoughts. And yet there is nothing unscientific in entertaining several possible interpretations of the same data.

Let us consider how several interpretations of clinical observations work out. A young, single woman undertook a series of interviews for the purpose of overcoming a fear of riding in closed vehicles. Upon arriving for the first interview she discovered that she had forgotten her cigarettes and asked the psychologist if she might smoke his. The same thing happened at the second session a week later, but she brought her own at the third meeting. Now, there is no particular reason for generalizing about these episodes. It is perfectly conceivable that understanding her forgetting would not change anything in the psychologist's opinion or method. And it is equally true that so far as diagnosis or treatment was concerned no damage would result from overlooking the lapse of memory. Clinical sensitivity is built by attention to such details, however, as the story by Stanley Cobb illustrates. It is by the accretion of information drawn from such subtle sources that larger trends and broader hypotheses can be substantiated. If you insist that speculation about such events is nothing but wasted time, then your attitude will be the same toward a thousand other details. Large amounts of clinical material will merit the same indictment, and you will have relatively little left to use.

Let us list some of the possible generalizations from the fact that the client forgot her cigarettes:

1. She is forgetful; has a poor memory.
2. She likes to take cigarettes from other people.
3. She likes to receive things from other people.
4. When faced with a psychologist, she wants to receive cigarettes.
5. When faced with a psychologist, she wants to receive something.
6. When faced with a new social situation, she wants to receive cigarettes.
7. When faced with a new social situation, she wants to receive something.
8. When she is anxious and upset, she forgets things—assuming that visits to a psychologist upset her.

None of these generalizations has much to support it. On the other hand, there are none of them demonstrably false. They are just possibilities. With more evidence we could begin deciding that some were more likely to be true than others.

The content of the first interview sheds some light on the problem. After describing her complaints, the client said that she had been to see two psychiatrists in the past several years. Both had a psychoanalytic point of view, and, according to her story, both had begun probing into her sexual history in the first interview. With scorn, she expressed her lack of confidence in their methods and in the doctors themselves. She proceeded to tell the psychologist that she had no patience with probing into childhood happenings, and that sex had nothing to do with her problem. Clearly, at this point she was antagonistic toward any specialist who would presume to help her.

The fact that she forgot her cigarettes for the second interview has weight in eliminating a hypothesis which emphasizes the part played by the novelty of the situation. In most cases clients do not forget their cigarettes twice in succession; it is rare for them to forget even once. This fact suggests that either the forgetting is motivated or that a genuine memory defect exists. This client complained of no particular memory defect and the content of her conversation did not show it. Could it be that her antagonism toward psychological interviews had something to do with the memory lapse? We could fit the two together if we assumed that she wanted to be sure she would get something, even if only cigarettes, from this consultation.

The third interview brought a remarkable change in her manner. She said, quite spontaneously, that she felt that she would be able to work with the clinician, that she felt he understood her case, and that she was willing to do what she could to help. She came to this interview with her own cigarettes! Furthermore she insisted that the clinician accept some of hers as repayment for those she had already taken. Certainly the notion that she wants to receive something (help) from a psychologist begins to appear plausible. When she does not expect help, she will take something else.

Now the findings do not conclusively establish the inference just stated. Perhaps there is no way that it can ever be established, for even if she agreed that her forgetting was motivated in just this way, that would hardly be final evidence. Yet it is a fairly probable interpretation and certainly a useful one in forwarding the organization of new observations. If we take a leap to an even broader generalization we may believe that the cigarette incident is only part of a pattern due to an intense need for acceptance. "If you don't want me and won't help me, I'll take whatever I can get." In the year that followed the initial interviews, the psychologist found a great deal to support this more general view of the case. As an example, the woman paid only a small part of the fees which she allowed to accumulate during the first year. It was not until much later that she made arrangements with the clinician to pay more regularly. The delay was not due to her lack of funds alone.

Problem 5. In thinking about the forgetting of the cigarettes, what would be your opinion of this statement: "Since cigarettes may serve as symbols of the male sex organ, the forgetting of her own cigarettes and the taking of the therapist's suggests deep needs for sexual relations." What kind of data would be needed in order to make such an interpretation plausible?

It is true, of course, that you can become addicted to overinterpretation. By using hazardous assumptions about symbolism and neglecting the complex relation of causal factors, it is possible to make anything stand for something else and produce weird interpretations of factual data. Specialists who create esoteric explanations appear to suffer from an inability to generate a variety of hypotheses. They tend to rely on standardized types of explanations, usually based on single motives such as sex or status, and on oversimplified theories of development.

Generalizing about Personal Characteristics. Some psychologists believe that observing a person in one situation affords little basis for making general statements about his personal characteristics. They point out, quite properly, that different situations make different demands. A person may behave so differently at church, at a party, and at a business conference that an observer who saw him in only one situation would come to erroneous conclusions. But these situations are somewhat more socially standardized than diagnostic interviews, and, except at a party, do not allow for great individual differences in behavior. Furthermore, it may very well turn out that timid people behave differently from bold people both in church and at a party, even though the timid may become bolder at the party.

If the diagnostic interview situation is well understood and due allowance is made for effects that are attributable to its special nature, the experience of many clinicians suggests that valid generalizations may frequently be made from the person's behavior in that one situation. It is easier to generalize about some characteristics than others; and neurotic persons who have fairly rigid adjustment patterns are easier to generalize about than are more flexible people. Allport (1, pp. 500–509) cites several studies indicating that ascendance-submission, degree of emotionality, and impulsiveness-inhibition can probably be judged fairly well. Wolf and Murray (13, p. 271) found that, among the variables rated by their judges, the most easily rated were anxiety, emotionality, impulsion, and aggression. Eisenberg (6) showed that students who scored high on a dominance questionnaire acted differently in the interview from those who scored low. These latter tended to blush, stammer, apologize when late, but students who felt dominant in many circumstances did not generally act this way. Their behavior was more often of the kind that is commonly called "self-assured."

CONSTRUCTING HYPOTHESES

Searching for Causes. In present-day Western culture people are expected to account for their actions on the grounds of their desires and the circumstances which they face. Generally speaking, explanations involving ghosts, possession by demons, control by telepathy, curses, spells, and incantations are not considered valid. But, although civilized children are taught to explain their behavior in more naturalistic terms than primitive children it does not follow that their explanations are always correct. For at the same time that the child is learning to make certain kinds of explanations, he is also learning that certain desires are not approved. By the time he reaches adulthood, he has become fairly expert at assigning socially acceptable motives as the causes of his actions (rationalization). Sometimes he is unable to give any reason for his actions (repression). Furthermore, people are not usually trained to inspect their histories for cause-and-effect relationships, so that even when they know they will not be condemned they may not be able to explain their behavior.

The clinician is thus forced to construct explanations on the basis of inferences. Confronted with a particular event, he seeks plausible hypotheses about the causes of that event by working backward. For example, in trying to find the basis of an amnesia, he would try to discover what had happened to the patient on the day the amnesia began and to locate disturbing events in the weeks prior to that time. These, in turn, would be related to what the clinician could find out about the personal characteristics of the patient—his attitudes, hopes, fears, and desires.

Developing Explanations. How can you learn to develop explanations? The first thing you can do is to try deliberately to think of alternate, even opposite, explanations. Too often we stop with one formula—the one that seems clearest to us. If you frame several explanations, you can be much more sensitive in inspecting further information about the person you are studying. Trying to think of alternative explanations will soon become habitual, and you will gain in flexibility of interpretation. An aid in developing alternative explanations is familiarity with several theoretical approaches to personality. It is good practice to formulate a problem as it might appear to an orthodox psychoanalyst, a neo-Freudian, a Lewinian, or a neo-behaviorist. In many instances these points of view may converge on a single explanation; more often each new way of looking at things forces you to emphasize hitherto unnoticed matters and to reorganize your interpretation.

When you are deciding what a given behavior sequence means, you are trying to answer this question: *What conditions are required to produce and maintain these actions?* This question is deceptive because it appears so simple. Actually, to answer it you must consider motives, past learning, family and cultural patterns, physiological conditions, and immediately preceding stimulus situations. What you try to decide is this: What kind of person would do these things and what circumstances would be required for them to appear? If you can generate several sets of answers, you can test each answer to see which one best fits the facts.

As you consider a person's action you draw on a fund of information about cause-and-effect sequences. Some of this information comes from your knowledge of the people you have lived with, some from stories, plays, and gossip, and some from the technical literature of psychology. You know that hungry people try to get food, that people who are insulted tend to retaliate, that adolescents usually feel guilty about masturbation, and that women are usually interested in their appearance. On a somewhat more sophisticated level you may know that people avoid talking of topics that arouse anxiety, that inability to obtain real satisfactions may lead to daydreaming, and that submissive people may rule a household. This store of information forms a catalogue of normal cause-and-effect sequences that you constantly use in understanding what people do. It is no surprise when a woman says she would like to have a new dress; you infer a normal feminine interest. But a woman who pays no attention to her appearance poses a problem. Again, people angered by insults are usual; you sense a problem when repeated insults arouse no retaliatory action.

Our notice is attracted to these deviations because we commonly assume that certain causes *should* produce certain effects. Again and again the clinician uses this assumption as he tries to reconstruct the background that led up to an action. Why does the death of a mother occasion no grief in her son? The only reason for asking is that our expectation is so different from what actually happened. The process of explanation then proceeds by assuming that, like others, he would have felt grief had not special events taken place. When a woman shows no interest in clothes, we assume that, like others, she would be interested were it not that special circumstances or attitudes have disrupted the expected course of development.

During psychotherapy, patients often behave inappropriately toward a therapist. They may become angry or fearful, without apparent cause. The therapist spots these "transference phenomena" because they are clearly deviations from the usual cause-and-effect sequences. Behavior of this kind is quite important to the clinician since it permits him to make inferences about certain events that must have taken place in the life of the patient. He begins by assuming that this behavior was probably part of an understandable cause-and-effect sequence when it was learned. Then he examines the relationship between himself and the patient at the time the inappropriate behavior occurred. Finally, he tries to find any similarity between this relationship and possible earlier relationships that the patient had with his family:

As the transferred responses unroll in the course of therapeutic work, they show what the patient has learned in his past experience. The patient can make only those responses which he has learned, and has to produce them when the stimuli are appropriate. . . . They can therefore provide a basis for inferences about what the earliest conditions of the patient's life actually were. He who fears "never getting enough" must have learned this painful attitude in a situation of privation. The man who reacts with immediate defiance to any type of authoritarian control must have adopted this attitude as a defense against the excesses of force and authority. He who is eternally suspicious must have been betrayed. If the patient fears to make the sentences denoting sexual acts, he must have been punished for such thoughts and expressions (4, p. 277).

These remarks apply equally well to inappropriate actions outside of therapy, except that there it is harder to decide when a normally adequate cause is missing.

The Adaptive Hypothesis. In building explanations, most specialists make use of a general principle which we may call the "adaptive hypothesis." Although it may be stated in various ways and with qualifications, this principle is essentially that patterns of behavior are due to the efforts of the individual to satisfy his needs within the framework of the opportunities available to him. Specific symptoms such as amnesia, fatigue, or daydreaming, and broad traits such as submissiveness or seclusiveness, are seen as ways of decreasing the strength of drives, primary and secondary. Since there are a number of drives present and since the activity of reducing some may interfere with the reduction of others, the behavior patterns finally acquired represent a kind of compromise.

One of the most important drives is that of anxiety reduction. Anxiety is easily aroused by a wide variety of situations, and the activity required for reducing it often interferes with the reduction of other drives. Anxiety is a concept of central importance in the study of persons, for much behavior that would otherwise be incomprehensible can be understood as adaptive in the sense that it is anxiety-reducing. Even in people who show no signs of present anxiety, interference with their customary methods for preventing its arousal will sometimes release objective signs of it. The so-called "Sunday neurosis," for example, consists of restlessness, tenseness, and perhaps worry or irritability which occurs on days of vacation, holiday, or on release from work. Once the fidgety victims resume work (a necessity for holding anxiety at a low level) the temporary symptoms disappear.

Adaptive and Expressive Symptoms. In applying the adaptive hypothesis, you should remember certain cautions. For one thing, there are some symptoms that are the direct outcomes of anxiety rather than techniques of anxiety reduction. Sweating and a rapid pulse are part of the anxiety pattern, and attempts to theorize them into techniques for reducing need conflicts are likely to end in dark confusion. Other parts of the anxiety reaction, such as vomiting or tremulousness, may be either direct symptoms of physiological disturbance (as in anxiety neurosis) or conflict-reduction devices (as in hysterical vomiting). A differentiation can usually be made on the basis of whether or not other signs of anxiety accompany the symptom in question. Sometimes the circumstances in which the symptom appears will indicate whether it is an adaptive or an expressive symptom. Complaints of an upset stomach by a child who has just been severely ridiculed at the dinner table are probably rooted in the physiological changes due to anxiety. If he voiced similar complaints when presented with a disliked food, we would regard them as a way of resolving a conflict.

Keeping this distinction in mind will help you guard against overinterpretation when you cannot decide in favor of one or the other alternative. Consider this case: A man, driving his auto to work in the morning, is involved in a traffic accident because he failed to stop for a red traffic signal. He is shaken up and bruised a bit, and the car is damaged slightly. He returns home, rests the remainder of the day, and receives the sympathetic attentions of his wife. A psychologist, discovering that the couple had quarreled at breakfast, may work out an explanation stressing the adaptive nature of the accident. He may infer that the husband felt rejected by the wife's attitude and that the accident served to reassure him of her affection. But it is at least as plausible to assume that the anxiety aroused by the quarrel resulted in poor coordination and in preoccupation with what had happened at home. The accident could be seen, then, as the outcome of lowered driving efficiency due to the emotional disturbance. This example also shows a second caution that should be observed in applying the adaptive hypothesis: do not assume that, merely because events satisfy certain needs, these needs spurred the person to seek or create those events. The fact that the wife was sympathetic after the accident is not sufficient evidence for thinking that the accident was part of an unconscious plan to get sympathy. If we knew that the man got sympathy only when he was injured or ill, we would have stronger evidence for the purposive nature of the accident. If we found that his demands for tender care were out of proportion to the severity of his injuries, our belief would be intensified. But even then we should remember that people with measles and mumps also get tender care, although the desire for the care doesn't produce the disease. Life occasionally yields dividends we are not striving to get!

Our discussion of adaptive and expressive symptoms is based on the distinction made by Maslow (11). He, too, points out the need for caution in assuming that unconscious purposes can be found to explain all human events: A married man in psychoanalysis had severe guilt reactions over his secret sexual relations with his mistress. After each visit with the woman, he developed a skin rash. Some eager interpreters of psychosomatic ills would call the rash a self-punishing reaction, an unconscious effort to relieve guilt feelings. "Examination, however, brought to light a much less esoteric explanation. It turned out that the bed of the patient's mistress was infested with bedbugs" (11, p. 271).

Four Kinds of Causal Variables. Complete explanations require more than a list of the needs and motives that instigate and sustain behavior. They must include other conditions that modify and set limits on action. The clinician in search of hypotheses should investigate four broad areas:

1. The client's environment, physical and social. The clinician may note the effects of rural living, crowded living quarters, membership in a minority group, or a nagging mother.

2. The client's physiological condition. Here we would be alert to fatigue, endocrine dysfunction, eating habits and nutritional status, dis-

eases, bodily handicaps, and chronic use of drugs, patent medicines, and laxatives.

3. The client's acquired and relatively enduring predispositions: needs, attitudes, interests, values, and traits.

4. The client's capacities and abilities. Here we think of intelligence, strength, manual dexterity, and special aptitudes for music, art, or mechanical work. We must also consider how the client's capacities have been developed into skills and knowledge.

Although notions about motivation are central in most of our clinical descriptions of personality, we must not lose sight of the other factors. It may be true that a young man turned to music because he was socially withdrawn and feared direct emotional contact with others; but the fact that his parents had musical interests, that lessons were easily available, and that he had at least some talent are also significant.

The person in action is laying hold of his environment, using it, destroying and assimilating it as needs and desires direct. This coming to grips with things is always bounded by the limits of physiological functioning and ability level. Poor metabolism hardly permits unsparing investment of energy in living, and poor intellect weakens the tools for extracting satisfaction from a competitive society.

BRIEF DESCRIPTIONS OF SUBJECTS USED IN PROBLEM 3

A. This man invariably gives the impression of being relaxed and easygoing. He speaks slowly and moves slowly. Some people think he is lazy, but topics of special interest to him are likely to call forth considerable effort. He was shifted from left- to right-handedness early in life, he recalls. He reports that he is more ambidextrous than most people. He is happily married but has no children.

B. This man is considered tense, brilliant, erratic, and excessively concerned with detail. His thesis was probably the poorest of the three, although he is probably the most brilliant of the three men. Its deficiencies were due mainly to lack of careful planning and organization. He is married and has one child, but his remarks about his family do not convey satisfaction and contentment. Rather, there is frequent friction between him and his wife.

C. This man is younger than the other two and is unmarried. He gives people the impression of social awkwardness. He seems eager to gain acceptance and is probably less independent than the other two men. He is under psychotherapeutic treatment for anxiety neurosis. Of the three men, he was probably the least confident about the outcome of his examination.

REFERENCES

1. Allport, G. W. *Personality*. New York: Holt, 1937.
2. Allport, G. W., & Vernon, P. E. *Studies in expressive movement*. New York: Macmillan, 1933.
3. Cole, L. E. *General psychology*. New York: McGraw-Hill, 1939.
4. Dollard, J., & Miller, N. E. *Personality and psychotherapy*. New York: McGraw-Hill, 1950.
5. Efron, D., & Foley, J. P., Jr. A comparative investigation of gestural behavior patterns in Italian and Jewish groups under different as well as similar environmental conditions. *Z. Sozialforsch.*, 1937, 6, 151–159.
6. Eisenberg, P. Expressive movements related to feeling of dominance. *Arch. Psychol.*, 1937, No. 211.
7. Estes, S. G. Judging personality from expressive behavior. *J. abnorm. soc. Psychol.*, 1938, 33, 217–236.
8. Hunt, J. McV. (Ed.) *Personality and the behavior disorders*. Vol. 1. New York: Ronald, 1944.
9. Krout, M. H. Autistic gestures: an experimental study in symbolic movement. *Psychol. Monogr.*, 1935, No. 208.
10. Levy, D. M. *New fields of psychiatry*. New York: Norton, 1947.
11. Maslow, A. H. The expressive component of behavior. *Psychol. Rev.*, 1949, 56, 261–272.
12. Moore, H. T., & Gilliland, A. R. The measurement of aggressiveness. *J. appl. Psychol.*, 1921, 5, 97–118.
13. Murray, H. A. *Explorations in personality*. New York: Oxford, 1938.
14. Reik, T. *Listening with the third ear*. New York: Farrar, Straus, 1948.
15. Hyman, S. The Talk of the Town, *The New Yorker*, June 30, 1945.

CHAPTER 4

The First Meeting: Expectations and Orientation

Meeting somebody for the first time is an adventure. We never are quite sure what will happen nor how it will happen. This uncertainty is bothersome to many of us, but there are others who are excited by it. First meetings are interesting to analyze because there are so many feelings that are hidden behind the formal and careful approach of the two people toward each other. As a prelude to this chapter, let us look at the story of a meeting outside a clinical setting.

Sam Williams pulled the crisp envelope from his campus mailbox. In the upper left corner he saw "Office of the President." Fumbling in his eagerness, he ripped the envelope open. Inside he found a note requesting him to appear in the office of the President of the university at four o'clock that afternoon. What did it mean? What did the President want? Sam ran through the possibilities: "Grades are O.K. Semester bills? No, they're paid. Maybe I was too intense in that disagreement with the history prof last Tuesday. Hardly that. You wouldn't think the President would bother about a classroom argument."

Sam had seen the President but had never met him. Tall and slender. A lot of people said he was efficient and business-like. Sam had heard that he was inclined to be domineering. "Still, he's got nothing against me. I wonder what he wants. Doesn't call students in just to get acquainted. Maybe it'll be interesting anyway. Wonder what he wants."

When Sam appeared that afternoon, the President did not suspect that the interview with Sam had been going on for four hours already—inside Sam. To him, the meeting was a chance to talk briefly to a student and to get a bit of help. He did not guess, indeed did not even think of guessing, that Sam had rejected his sports jacket and slacks in favor of the plain business suit he wore. The young man responded to the President's greeting hesitantly, and waited.

What is the psychological situation here? The President knew the reason for the meeting; Sam did not. Moreover, Sam was complying with a request from a person with higher social status and more power than he had. The control of the meeting rested almost entirely with the older man. The circumstances of the interview created quite a different and more anxiety-provoking problem for Sam than they did for the President.

When the President asked Sam to be one of several students who would represent the university at nearby high schools, Sam's manner changed. He was enthusiastic. The argument in history class faded from his thoughts, once the purpose of the meeting was clear.

The initial meeting between two people is always a novel event. What happens in the meeting depends not only on the actual behavior of the two people but also on the backgrounds from which they come and the social context of the meeting. Meetings with clinicians are likely to pose special problems for clients because of the clients' expectations and attitudes. At the same time, the clinician wants to learn about his client as rapidly as he can. If he is to function effectively in his first contact with his client, he should understand what it means to the client.

The first part of this chapter explores the social setting in which clinical contacts occur. It presents some of the attitudes that may affect the initial meeting and suggests how the clinician should define his role. In the second part of the chapter, you will see how the clinician can orient himself toward his client by viewing him in relation to the culture and the community. We shall try to show how simple data can guide the clinician toward his first tentative inferences.

RAPPORT

The most important task that the clinician must undertake in the first meeting is establishing rapport (14, pp. 93 ff). This term refers to a harmonious, cooperative, and friendly relationship between client and clinician. It implies that they share a common understanding about the kind of work to be done and a willingness to get on with it. If rapport can be established, it will make the further study of the person a much easier task. Consequently, the experienced clinician is more concerned with the quality of his relationship with the client in the first meeting than he is with the amount of factual data he obtains.

On the side of the client, there are two essential components of rapport. One of these is the absence of anxiety about the relationship and its consequences. The other is a belief that the clinician can help relieve his distress or aid in reaching important goals. If these two conditions can be created, the client can talk freely, cooperate in taking tests he doesn't understand, and contribute actively to joint planning.

It is not a simple matter to create rapport; there is no single rule to follow. Sometimes clinicians are advised to adopt a bluff and hearty manner, to joke with the client, or to have some interesting incident ready to start the conversation. With some clients, these things may help, but they will alienate others. Of course, comfortable informality and courtesy are seldom out of place. In the long run, rapport is probably created as the client comes to see that the clinician is really interested in him and at the same time is not likely to shove him around or smother him with help.

Some elementary errors can be pointed out for you to avoid. Don't try to create a belief in your own competence by telling about cases that you have helped or about the important people who refer cases to you. Information of this kind may increase the client's faith in you, but not if you are the one who tells him how good you are. Don't be flippant or sarcastic about events and facts reported by the client. They may seem funny or stupid to you, but they probably don't to the client. Don't act busy. Reading your mail, glancing at memos, and taking phone calls may convince him that you are much in demand, but they may also convince him that you don't have time to be interested in him. Don't lecture the client by telling him that he should have sought help sooner, or by telling him how wise he is to have come so soon. Don't try to make him feel comfortable by saying you have troubles and worries, too. There is a time in some clinical relationships where this is appropriate; the first meeting is not that time.

One powerful aid in creating rapport is the knowledge that you will keep the information given you confidential. If you and your agency have a reputation for being close-mouthed about case data, clients will have one common source of anxiety removed. In order to do the extremely delicate job of taking sexual histories, Kinsey and his associates (6, pp. 44 f) developed the most elaborate safeguards for security of information that have ever been used in research studies. As people learned of these precautions and found that the precautions were observed, they were more willing to volunteer as subjects.

Knowing how various clients feel about consulting a psychologist will help you understand the differences in their reactions to the first meeting. Awareness of possible expectations makes it easier to spot the attitudes of a client and to establish rapport.

ANTECEDENTS OF THE FIRST MEETING

People who visit psychologists rarely do it on a spur-of-the-moment impulse. Usually they have wondered for some time whether the visit is really needed and whether it will be helpful. After a clear decision has been reached, they must ordinarily wait a while before they can see the clinician. Sometimes this waiting period is four to six weeks long because of the heavy case load of an agency. Knowing that a meeting will take place, people are likely to speculate about it and to anticipate what will happen. Some people habitually engage in this "inner rehearsal" more than others, but the fact that they are meeting with a psychologist is partly responsible for these fantasies. Clients have heard or read accounts of other people who visited psychologists, and they may wonder what dark secrets they themselves will reveal. Sometimes the client is summoned to appear before the clinician (as in prison, school, and hospital settings): then he may search his memory for misdeeds, fights, or other offenses that may be judged unfavorably. If the clinician is reputed to have power or influence, the pre-meeting fantasies may center around methods for getting his favor and help.

In understanding how clients may feel about the first meeting, the clinician relies on several kinds of information. In the first place, he knows something about his own relationship to the community where he works. Secondly, he has heard other clinicians or clients tell about the expectations that people commonly have in his community. Finally, he listens to what his own client has to say about his reasons for coming. Let us see what some of these expectations may be.

Clinician and Community. Most professional workers are attached to agencies which render special and limited kinds of services. Thus, we find "Vocational Guidance," "Family Service," "Marriage Counseling," and "Mental Health" in the titles of various agencies. These names have been chosen partly to designate the agency's function and partly to allay anxiety among prospective clients. A psychological clinic may be called "Personnel Counseling Service" because of a fear that students would avoid coming to a "Psychological Clinic." Some experts question the desirability of these evasive tactics. They feel that psychological and psychiatric services are part of the reality in our society, and that a euphemistic name contributes to the feeling that a stigma is attached to using these services.

To supplement the information carried by the name, agencies often prepare announcements or brochures describing their services. These announcements probably do not really shape the client's expectations, but they provide him with some basis for selecting an agency. However, the client is usually left in doubt about what will happen when he walks in the door.

Problem 1. Assume you are employed to write a brochure for a marriage-counseling agency. The agency is partially supported by contributions but makes a charge of $10 for each couple. Clientele is limited to engaged couples and couples who have been married less than a year. Counseling interviews and a few tests are the chief methods used. The brochure is to be printed in quantity and distributed to the general public through various community and social organizations. Prepare about 300 words of copy, then answer these questions:

1. What further information would have enabled you to write a better description?

2. What assumptions do you make about your readers, their abilities, and their attitudes?

3. What kind of appeals did you use in order to make people want this service? How did you decide what appeals would be effective?

Clients are strongly influenced in their attitudes toward an agency by the attitudes of their social groups. Suppose an agency has been involved in the commitment of several people to a mental hospital. Friends of a prospective client may talk about the psychotic patients without mentioning the fact that many "average people" also use the agency. Such remarks from acquaintances and friends are likely to outweigh printed pamphlets about the agency in shaping the client's expectations. On the other hand, a middle-class mother may belong to groups that value and stress "modern methods" of child rearing. This mother may readily seek the help of a child psychologist because her friends would approve her action.

In a military setting, a psychologist or psychiatrist may find that he is regarded mainly as a gateway out of military service. Recruits who are fearful of or dissatisfied with military life will approach the first meeting hoping to impress the clinician with their unfitness. Others, who have personal reasons for fearing discharge, will be reticent about real handicaps. The writer has seen many men try to conceal symptoms because they hoped that military service would prove their adequacy. Some men feel that there is a stigma attached to a discharge granted on psychiatric grounds; they are likely to emphasize medical handicaps and to resist psychological study.

Clinicians who are aware of the common attitudes toward their work will be prepared to deal with these attitudes in their clients. Fear of the clinician due to community misconceptions can be distinguished from fear due to personality dynamics. Resistance to treatment stemming from misinformation can be recognized for what it is and diminished.

Expectations about Treatment. Many clients come to the psychologist with specific but erroneous ideas about the kind of treatment they will receive (10, pp. 4 f). Their expectations are formed by the name of the agency, by their own educational background, prior experiences with social agencies, and the dramatic stories in movies and Sunday supplements. Relatively few people know what kinds of treatment are available in their own locality or what agencies use certain forms of treatment.

One of the most common expectations about psychological service confuses it with medical prescription. We may paraphrase the client's anticipation this way: "If you feel bad or there is something wrong with you, go to a doctor. He will find out what is wrong and give you something to fix you up." The notion that a doctor will "give you something" is so firmly rooted that many people are disappointed or resentful when their physician does not give them pills, salves, or shots. Moreover, the conception of the physician's role includes ideas about the kinds of symptoms he is interested in and the kinds of questions he will ask. Most people, for example, would be surprised to find a physician encouraging them to discuss their religious convictions. Since clients do not usually distinguish among the various professional groups interested in the study of persons, they often expect about the same treatment from social workers or psychologists that they expect from physicians. This tendency to put all specialists in one class is more likely to occur when an agency has a medical name and a medical atmosphere.

An illustration of the way in which this kind of problem may be handled has been given by Curran (1). The staff of an allergy clinic wanted an evaluation of the emotional status of patients with multiple complaints. It was felt that getting the usual medical history and performing allergy tests probably made such patients resistive to a psychologically oriented interview. Therefore the staff decided that the psychological interview should precede the medical examination. The areas covered by the interview were broadened beyond purely physical complaints. This procedure seemed to make it easier to establish a counseling relationship and provided more information about the clients' emotional problems than the customary sequence of examinations. In addition, Curran believes that the new procedure helped clients to change their treatment expectations and to accept counseling instead of medication alone.

Even when people know there are differences between physicians and psychologists, they may still have erroneous conceptions about what the psychologist will do to and for them. Because of the wide use of psychological tests and the publicity given them, people have come to expect that a psychologist will administer tests whenever he is consulted. A widely used book on child care (13) fosters this belief by referring to child psychologists as people trained in giving intelligence tests and in treating learning difficulties in school. Some clients talk about tests as if they believe that the mere administration and interpretation of a test would solve their problems of adjustment. The writer has been approached many times by people requesting the administration of a particular test; further conversation nearly always revealed that these people were actually concerned about problems in living. They wanted to be tested because they thought that was the way psychologists helped people. Of course, clients who are fairly sophisticated about psychological work will sometimes request testing without really expecting it. For them, the discussion of tests provides an opening for bringing up the problems that really concern them.

The belief that a psychologist ought to give advice to a client is found as often as the belief that he ought to give tests. Instances of the hope for advice are especially easy to find among the interviews reported by client-centered (or nondirective) counselors (12). Since these counselors are committed to a definite policy of avoiding giving advice, their interviews reveal with considerable clarity the frequency of such expectations. One of the chief reasons why clients think that psychologists will advise them is that they regard a psychological consultation as analogous to a medical consultation. Advice-giving is to them the psychological equivalent of pill-giving. Although lack of information about psychological methods is partly responsible for the belief that advice will be given, it also has other sources. A continued demand for advice suggests that the client resists making his own decisions. This fact, in turn, may indicate lack of confidence, dependence upon authority, and inability to assume responsibility for his own problems of living.

Occasionally clients will expect and request hypnosis. They have usually read reports of the ease with which a hypnotist can improve concentration, assuage pain, or banish bad habits. Hypnotic treatment seems to them an effortless way of improving personality and even of attaining success. We can understand how attractive hypnosis appears to a person who is fearful of what he would find if he tried to understand himself. He sees a chance to clear up his difficulties without any real personal involvement. On the other hand, it is clear that some people seek hypnosis in order to prove that even such a mysterious and drastic treatment will not help their case. If hypnosis is tried and found wanting, the client may be able to give up further efforts to change his behavior, without any sense of guilt. If the desire for treatment is weak to start with, such an outcome is quite likely. The client has, in the eyes of his immediate social group, done his best to get help. Friends and family can only regard him as a pathetic person beyond the help of "science." And, of course, he can hardly be blamed for seeing himself in the same light.

What is the clinician to do about clients who want a kind of treatment that he does not favor or does not offer? Perhaps the simplest answer is that the clinician should explain what he is prepared to do and what he cannot do. That is, he should clarify and define his role and the agency's function. But such explanations may easily appear blunt and inconsiderate. Some clients may feel ashamed of their ignorance, and others will become antagonistic toward the agency or the clinician. If this happens, it will be difficult for the clinician to help the client accept the kind of assistance he needs.

Often a client indicates fairly early in the first interview that he expects treatment the clinician cannot give. Then it is wise to defer any definition of the clinician's role until the client has told a more complete story. The psychologist should ask for a more detailed description of the complaints, for other difficulties, and for the reasons why the client thought a particular form of treatment would help. This additional information accomplishes two things: it enables the client to feel that an effort has been made to understand him; and it gives the clinician a chance to understand the motives and beliefs which led the client to want a certain kind of treatment. Then the psychologist can explain the services he does offer in terms that relate to the specific attitudes of the client.

An example will make this approach clearer. A young woman came to a psychologist requesting some vocational tests to determine what kind of work she ought to be doing. He asked her to explain more fully what use she would like to make of the test results. She replied that she had been working as a stenographer in a business firm, and that recently she had become dissatisfied with her job and wanted to change. She hoped the test results would help her decide what kind of job to seek. The psychologist told her that it would be helpful to know more about the kind of dissatisfaction she felt before he could evaluate the usefulness of the tests he had available. The stenographer went ahead to tell of her restlessness and feelings of tension at work and ended by saying that she really liked her job. The main trouble, she thought, was that she had fallen in love with her boss, who was a married man. He had already asked her to go out with him, and she had refused. But she feared that she would eventually accept a date with him and thus create a social situation that could lead to serious trouble. The psychologist pointed out that any tests he had would be of little value, since the major difficulty did not lie in the area of job satisfaction but centered around personal relationships. He suggested that it would be more worth while to continue discussing her feelings toward her boss. She accepted the suggestion and did not repeat her request for testing.

Problem 2. Assume that a mother has asked you to give an intelligence test to her seven-year-old son. Without refusing her request, you have asked her to explain in more detail the situation that led her to request the testing. She tells you that her husband has been dissatisfied with the boy's schoolwork, although his grades have been average. Her husband wants to make strict rules about home study so that the son can get higher grades. She is satisfied with the boy's progress and reports that his teacher told her that the boy was getting along well. The mother feels, however, that if her son is really capable of better work she would agree to her husband's demands for study periods at home and for restricting the boy's privileges until the grades improved. She would like to have the boy tested to find out whether he is capable of better work.

1. Do you feel that this explanation is sufficient grounds for administering the test to the boy?

2. Write a paragraph telling what you would say to the mother at this point in order to explain your position about this problem.

THE CLIENT'S VIEW OF THE CLINICIAN

The decision to seek professional help depends upon the balance of the motives favoring and opposing such an action. We may assume that the client cannot actually visit the clinician until the motives for seeing him are stronger than those for remaining away. But even though the client has actually arrived, strong motives for avoiding psychological assistance may still be present. When this is true, we may expect to find that rapport is hard to establish, and that evasiveness or open resentment will appear. Merely because the motive balance favors visiting the clinician, we cannot infer that it also favors a cooperative relationship with him.

The Clinician Viewed as a Threat. In some instances, external coercion forces a person to visit a psychologist, but he cooperates poorly because he thinks the psychologist's activities may be harmful. A clear case of this kind occurs in prison settings. Some of the problems faced by a psychologist in prison work have been described by Farber:

. . . If the investigator is a staff psychiatrist or psychologist he is often seen by the inmates as the dreaded "bug doctor" who might, by an interview or test, find a man insane or feebleminded and commit him to a stigmatized institution. The fear and apprehension engendered in the inmate by a summons from the "bug doctor" will profoundly influence the experimental or interview situation. Finally, it must be kept in mind that in any situation where an inmate is faced by an official who has it within his power, or is thought to have it in his power, to help or hurt that inmate, then the inmate will be on his best behavior, his responses shaped and colored by his desire to make a favorable impression (4, pp. 298 f).

What Farber has said about the clinician's power holds true in many settings. A psychologist in military service or in industry must be prepared to find that clients will be uncommunicative if they think his decisions could hurt them. And, it must be admitted, clinicians sometimes do have positions carrying a good deal of influence.

Some people regard a decision to seek psychological help as an admission of weakness and so feel threatened by the consulting relationship. If a person is proud of independence and detachment from others, he is likely to steer clear of professional helpers. But the imminent loss of his job or the breakup of his marriage may motivate him sufficiently to visit a psychologist. After arriving, however, he may be defensive because he feels he has given up some control over his own life. In a series of counseling contacts reported by Muench, a client makes this point clear in the sixth interview. He says: "But I was bothered to come here in the first place. It was a real battle to come and admit that I wasn't complete master of my fate; that by myself I haven't mapped out an adequate course" (12, p. 226). Attitudes of this kind are quite likely to occur in men who have achieved high status and have authority over others.

Another group of people who are likely to see accepting help as a weakness are those who set great store by reason and logic in solving the problems of living. For them, the seeking of help indicates a lack of intellectual mastery or of intelligence. Efforts to restore some sense of their intellectual ability may take the form of veiled criticism of the psychologist's methods, of displaying knowledge about psychology, of detailed questioning about the scientific basis of tests, or of hinting that the clinician's "techniques" are obvious and transparent.

Since psychologists and psychiatrists are commonly thought to have unusual ability to "see through" people, they appear threatening to clients who do not want to think about, or openly admit, certain feelings or acts. Thus, a man who is desperately trying to avoid recognizing his hostility toward his father may fear the consulting relationship because he fears that he cannot hide his feeling from the psychologist. Or a woman, deeply ashamed of some sexual misdeed, may feel that it will surely be revealed. Such people, afraid of half-recognized feelings, may violently reject the idea of psychological consultation. For example, here is the way an eighteen-year-old girl began her first interview: "Well, here I am. This is all perfectly silly, but the doctor insisted that I come in and see you. I promised the doctor that I would come for one hour and here I am. . . . The doctor says there isn't anything wrong with me physically—that all my symptoms are because I am emotionally disturbed about things. Well, that's a lie. I'm not emotionally upset about anything" (12, pp. 312 f). But in the following hour this girl wept and expressed a good deal of hatred for her mother. The psychologist had appeared as a threat to her control over her resentment and guilt.

The Clinician Viewed as Miracle Worker. Some people overvalue psychological help; they assume that the psychologist can change them by some subtle means so that they will be successful, happy, or lovable. This attitude is often not openly expressed in the first contact of clinician and client, but therapists find evidence of it in comments made during therapy. A clear statement of the "miracle worker" attitude appears in the fourth interview of a case reported by Rogers: "And I had a sort of mystical faith in psychoanalysis. I imagined I wanted the same there— in other words, I wanted the psychoanalyst to turn the key for me, rather than do it myself. . . . But I'm to the point now where if the analyst would flash the light upon a key I believe that I could turn it myself. Or maybe there isn't any key—maybe it's—that is maybe the key and the turning are one psychologically" (11, p. 357). Here the client contrasts his initial expectation with his new insight into the nature of the therapeutic relationship.

This kind of attitude seems to be found most often in people who have difficulty in taking responsibility for their own lives. As their history unfolds, it becomes obvious that they have continually turned to the dominant and authoritative people in their social environment for advice, help, justification, and protection. If they have been acutely distressed before seeking psychological help, they may overvalue such help as a way of relief. Some clients will say: "I have done everything I could, but it didn't help. Nobody that I have consulted could find out what was wrong. I have heard people say such complimentary things about your work that I'm sure you can help me. I just feel that you're my last hope, because I don't know what I'm going to do if you don't help me." These remarks, while arising out of despair, imply that the psychologist must assume the responsibility if the desired improvement fails to occur. And it is a fair guess that such clients have put the same kind of pressure on other people, both lay and professional.

People who regard the psychologist as a miracle worker easily come to see him as a threat. Indeed, the great power which must be attributed to him if he is to perform wonders is in itself threatening. The possession of unusual abilities is no guarantee that they will be used to help instead of hurt; this guarantee must come from the client's faith in the kindness and good intentions of the clinician. Consequently, clients who endow clinicians with magical powers must also reassure themselves of his kindness. They will be alert for signs that he likes them and will be over-sensitive to indications of the clinician's possible insincerity or lack of sympathy. Unrealistic vigilance of this kind can easily lead them to misinterpret the clinician's speech and behavior. So it comes about that people who exaggerate the power of psychological services may be frightened by them and display ambivalent attitudes toward the psychologist.

The Clinician Viewed as Intercessor. Sometimes people seek psychological services in order to manipulate a specific person in their environment. In these instances, the clinician is seen as an authority whose pronouncements can change opinions that the client has been unable to alter. For example, a young man wishing to dissuade his parents from sending him to medical school may request vocational guidance. Actually he is not interested in guidance; he hopes that the psychologist's findings will alter his parents' attitude. He may want copies of the test scores sent to his parents or may ask the psychologist to see them personally after the test is finished. Under these conditions, the vocational counselor will probably doubt the validity of the test scores. The client's special interest in the outcome introduces an unknown amount of distortion into the results.

The basic pattern of "using" the clinician can be varied in many ways. Occasionally the clinician is requested to talk to other people in an effort to get favors for the client. Thus students will sometimes ask an educational counselor to speak to their professors, hoping that they will be given special consideration. A different and more subtle use of the clinician occurs when a client repeats the clinician's judgments in order to criticize another person. For example, a man wants to discuss his failing marriage but continually makes it clear that his wife is the one at fault. If he succeeds in getting the clinician to give diagnostic names to his wife's behavior, we may suspect that the husband will condemn her with these psychological labels. By quoting the clinician as the source of these judgments, the husband adds weight to the condemnation and justifies his own attitudes.

A counselor can withstand pressure to act as an intercessor fairly easily if he has a therapeutic relationship with a client. Then special requests become questions for exploration, discussion, and interpretation, as with any other therapeutic material. When the relationship is largely for diagnostic purposes or when it is confined to a single interview, the clinician needs a clear conception of his role and the ways in which he can give help. In general, it is wise to follow the rule that the clinician is a consultant, and that the client must assume responsibility for his own actions. This principle does not prevent the clinician from reporting his findings to other specialists concerned, nor from preparing special reports setting forth his judgments about the client. Thus, a neurotic man may request a psychologist to examine him and send a report of his findings to an Armed Forces induction station. The neurotic hopes that such a statement will help to disqualify him for service. If the psychologist is willing to grant this request, he should make it clear that his report will include his opinion about the client but will not include a request for specific disposition nor for exemption.

An example of excellent handling of a request for intercession is given by Greving and Rockmore (5):

A soldier came to an army mental-hygiene unit and asked the unit to obtain an emergency furlough for him. He threatened to go AWOL if the unit did not comply with this request. The intake worker pointed out that all such requests must be initiated through the commanding officer and that the unit could not help him. The worker suggested that if the soldier had a legitimate reason for a furlough, he would not need anyone else to intercede. The soldier then requested the furlough through his commanding officer. The request was denied, but the soldier was referred to the mental-hygiene unit. When he returned to the unit, both the soldier and the worker were prepared for a full discussion of the problem. It turned out that the soldier was nearly failing in radio operators' school and that his fiancée was putting considerable pressure on him to get married at once. These problems were discussed in a series of interviews. The soldier finally decided to try explaining the situation to his fiancée and to wait until his radio training was finished before getting married. He was successful in persuading his fiancée to wait. When he finished his training, he was granted the furlough and was married.

In this case, the caseworker understood the limits of the service which the mental-hygiene unit could offer and refused to go beyond them. On the other hand, the worker was able to show the soldier how the unit could be of use to him. Obviously, it requires a great deal of skill to refuse requests without appearing unsympathetic. In addition to the skill needed, however, it is important for the clinician to remain undisturbed by the direct or disguised threats of the client. If the caseworker had been upset by the soldier's threat to go AWOL, he might have become defensive and resorted to counterthreats or to coaxing. In either case his effectiveness would have been impaired. The fact that the worker was clear about his own role and his relationship to the client enabled him to resist the temptation to appear as a goodhearted intercessor.

We may now review some of the implications for the study of persons that have been suggested in our discussion of the initial contact:

1. The client's behavior in the first meeting is influenced by the circumstances of the meeting, the reputed activities of the clinician, and his power and prestige.

2. Anxiousness, resentment, or demands for special treatment may arise from misinformation or inaccurate stereotypes of the clinician.

3. Generally, the clinician should not explain his function and services early in the first meeting. After the client has told the story of his complaints and his distress, it is easier to structure the clinical relationship.

4. The clinician's explanation of his function may easily appear as a rejection or as a threat to the client. It should be given calmly and considerately. The language should be simple and nontechnical. Usually it is possible to couch the explanation in terms that relate to the client's own circumstances and desires.

5. Persistence of unrealistic expectations about the clinician after he has explained his services and limitations usually indicates important motive patterns in the client. Often these expectations reflect the client's demands upon other people in his life who possess power or authority.

6. The clinician should ordinarily regard himself as a consultant. He is able to offer a special kind of help because of his training and the

setting in which he works; but he cannot assume responsibilities appropriate for relatives, friends, lawyers, and so on. If he understands his unique relationship to his client, it is easier to refuse inappropriate requests without being defensive.

ORIENTATION DATA

Before a clinician begins the intensive study of a person he usually has information about the client's age, sex, marital status, education, and occupation. Facts of this kind we shall call "orientation data." There is no hard and fast rule about what information is classed under this rubric, but it is usually limited to easily available data that roughly establish the client's position in the community. Sometimes orientational information includes religious affiliation, nationality or ethnic-group membership, leisure-time activities, and membership in clubs and social organizations. These data are often written down on a standard form at the time the client is first seen. In educational and vocational guidance agencies, clients usually fill out the form themselves. In other agencies this information is obtained by an intake interviewer or even by a trained receptionist.

In organizing a standard form for recording orientation data, three general requirements should be met. In the first place it should contain the client's full name and address. If he can be reached by phone, the number should be given. This information is needed in case special appointments are to be made or broken; but other kinds of unforeseen conditions also arise that require mail or phone contact with the client. The second general requirement for orientation-data sheets is that they should request information which is not likely to make the client embarrassed or resentful. Asking for data about occupation, education, and marital status is usually taken for granted; but requests for religious affiliation or ethnic-group membership may produce suspicion. More intimate questions, such as those concerning sexual activity or criminal offenses, have no place on orientation-data sheets except under unusual circumstances.

Questions about health, physical defects, and medical history are often included on standard forms, but they usually cover only the superficial aspects of such information. The third requirement for developing an orientation-data sheet is that the information sought should be relevant and potentially significant. This is to say that there should be some reason for the inclusion of each question on the sheet. Since the services offered by various agencies differ, the decision as to what is relevant information will vary according to the requirements of the agency and the clinician. Questions about the amount of life insurance held by a client, for example, would ordinarily not be worth including, but it is possible that it would be useful in some special instances. As another illustration, the amount of detail requested about occupational history would vary depending upon the goals of the clinical agency. The data sheet should be kept fairly short, so that only fifteen or twenty minutes is needed to record the information. It is not meant to serve as a substitute for the interview but to provide a frame of reference for the clinician.

A short data sheet is shown in Figure 4. This sheet was not constructed for any particular kind of agency, but it suggests how a form could be organized. It is important to leave ample space for writing in the information, since some people have a large handwriting. Note that both age and birth date are requested. This may seem to be a needless duplication, but it provides a double check on this point. The item about persons in the household gives some idea of possible interpersonal frictions and economic status. Asking for year of graduation permits the clinician to find out whether school progress was regular or whether it was retarded by illness or failure. The items about parents permit inferences about the socioeconomic status of the client's family. The question about organizational membership yields a rough framework for evaluating the social contacts of the client.

Answers to the last item may not necessarily reveal the most important reason for seeking help, but they provide a convenient starting place for an interview. Sometimes they reveal an unwillingness to assume responsibility for wanting an appointment. For example, a client may write: "My doctor told me to come." Or there may be a plea for assistance without concrete details: "I hoped you could help me." Another client may disclose his sophistication: "To see about getting psychotherapy." The question is deliberately framed to permit these variations in interpretation. Another item of this kind that could be added to the sheet is: "How did you happen to seek an appointment at this particular time?" Answers to this question may yield further cues as to motivation and attitudes toward the agency or the clinician.

A Rationale for the Use of Orienting Data. In Chapter 3, we pointed out that the clinician must be sensitive to the possible significance of fairly minute details of the client's behavior. Orienting data provide a framework of broad hypothesis within which these more minute details must be placed. This orientational framework is possible because a given culture pattern tends to produce fairly homogeneous results among the persons exposed to it. That is, the social structure tends to force people to develop so that if they have characteristic A, they will also have certain other characteristics X and Y. A simple example will help you understand this principle:

Suppose you know only three facts about a person, namely, that she is an eighteen-year-old girl who has epileptic convulsions two or three times a year. Can you answer the following questions about her with any probability of being right? Is she glad that she has epilepsy? Does she worry about her chances for marriage? Does she feel that she is a burden or liability to her family? If you answered yes to these questions, it is because you assumed a fourth fact—that she was reared in recent United States culture or something similar to it. If you knew that she lived in a society where epileptic seizures were regarded as divine visitations and the afflicted people were thought of as holy persons, you would probably answer in quite a different way. Knowing the widespread attitudes of a social group, you predict that a given person's attitudes will be congruent with those of the group.

The principle of the socially determined association of personal characteristics can be seen most clearly in connection with systems of social roles (8). A role may be defined as the pattern of attitudes, motives, and actions that the members of a group expect of persons who occupy a given position. In our own society, for example, women are expected to wear their hair longer than men, to be prepared to do domestic tasks, and to let men take the initiative in courtship. The role of adult female includes many other characteristics, of course, nearly all of which are socially determined. The cluster of motives, attitudes, and acts which we label "feminine" are found associated together, not because they are biologically related, but because they are associated in the norms of a group. It is as if a community, finding in its midst a female child, set itself the task of continuously teaching that child to be domestic, interested in adornment, unaggressive, and so on.

The most important characteristics for defining what role pattern shall be learned by the individual are sex, age, kinship position, marital status, and occupation. In our own culture, socioeconomic status and race must be added to this list. A combination of these characteristics defines the individual's role with sufficient precision to allow for a considerable amount of success in making predictions about a given person's motives, attitudes, and actions. You can see that one of the chief uses of orientation data is to enable us to specify the main roles of the client. If our knowledge of the social norms surrounding the client is full and accurate, many inferences can be drawn about him. They serve to rough out the broad outlines of a life and to suggest certain lines of inquiry to the clinician.

Age and Sex Roles. As examples of the kind of norms provided by roles, let us briefly inspect two kinds of ascribed roles, age and sex roles. In general, these patterns are not optional for the individual; he may not take them or leave them as he chooses. Rather, he is expected to show certain characteristics appropriate to his age and sex. In United States middle-class urban society, for example, children are expected to conform to parental demands, and are expected to be dependent upon their par-

Name (in full) _____

Address _____

Phone number _____ Today's date _____

Age last birthday _____ Date of birth _____

Are you single, married, divorced, separated? _____

If married, give date of marriage _____ Number of children _____

What persons besides yourself now live in your household (such as father, wife,

son, etc.)? _____

_____

What was the last grade in school you finished? _____

If a high-school graduate, give year of graduation _____

What is your present job? _____

How long have you worked for your present employer? _____

What other jobs have you had? _____

_____

Is your father living? _____ Father's occupation _____

Is your mother living? _____ Mother's occupation _____

Father's schooling _____ Mother's schooling _____

What organizations do you belong to (such as church, clubs, lodge, choir, etc.)?

_____

How is your health? _____

_____

Are you physically below par or handicapped? _____

_____

What is your reason for wanting an appointment? _____

_____

Figure 4. A Sample Form for Orienting Data

ents but not upon other adults. They are supposed to attend school and to value the learning of verbal skills. Adolescents are expected to show most of this pattern, but they are often permitted wider limits than children as to travel and hours of arriving home. They are expected to be serious about their future vocational and marital plans, and these plans are supposed to conform to parental wishes. The adolescent is close to the world of the adult, sees its apparent freedom and satisfactions, is told that he will soon take a place in that world, but, for a few years at least, he is reminded that he is not really adult after all.

Somehow, at an indefinite time, the adolescent becomes the young adult. The high-school fads, so highly valued only a few years earlier, become old hat. Effort is now directed toward establishing a place in the competitive adult world. Marriage, money, and status become primary concerns, and the choice of occupational role is intimately related to all three. The third decade of life is expected to include the establishment of a home and family; and the fourth decade presents the problem of the consolidation of the family position and the establishment of contacts with community groups. The PTA, the Sunday school, the bridge club, the men's service clubs now become important modes of affiliation with the social environment.

By the fifth decade, the status of the individual is generally fixed, and the possibility of movement upward is decreasing. The children in the family have reached adolescence, and the parents find themselves regarded in a new light by their children. Social norms for this age level do not include sexual attractiveness as a basis for personal relationships; sexual "adventures" and rowdy parties are considerably less acceptable than for people in their twenties. People in their forties are also expected to assume responsibility for their own elderly parents if they need assistance. Often, therefore, a change in the membership of the household takes place, and the adult in his forties is faced with significant alterations in his relationship to both his children and his parents.

This sketch of the successive age roles in one segment of society is all too brief, but it suggests patterns of living that will be seen by the psychologist. Intertwined with these age roles are the patterns that are ascribed to the two sexes. The male is expected to be more competitive and aggressive, more oriented toward occupation and earning income than the female. Sexual exploration in the second and third decades of life, while not prescribed for the male role, seems to be among permitted activities. This is much less true for the female role. On the other hand, it is expected that females will exploit physical appearance as a basis for personal relationships with males.

The achievement of motherhood brings with it a host of prescribed characteristics that include appropriate thoughts and feelings about children as well as certain kinds of overt behavior toward them. The burden placed upon women in a mother role is heightened rather than alleviated by the idealization of this role presented during celebrations of Christmas and Mother's Day. Nothing comparable to these specifications has been prescribed for fathers.

Middle-class fathers, of course, must bear the brunt of establishing status for themselves and for their families. Social norms for this role emphasize ability as "good providers" first, and assign secondary importance to mutual emotional relationships between the father and the family. It should be noted that the intense economic activity of men in this position, although it is described as "earning a living," is actually devoted to the conservation and improvement of the socioeconomic status of the family. Failure of fathers to accomplish this improvement brings condemnation not only from the family but from themselves as well.

Clinical Use of Social Norms. Information as to age, sex, and class status leads the clinician to form certain expectations about the motives, attitudes, and behavior of individuals. His knowledge of the role behavior prescribed and permitted within a community enables him to construct an approximate picture of the characteristics that a given person probably has. When the clinician also uses other orienting data such as educational level, occupation, religious affiliation, race or nationality origin, and membership in organizations, he can construct a more detailed picture of the motives and attitudes of his client.

These expectations are used by clinicians much as they use achievement test norms. The norms furnished with tests of reading, arithmetic, or chemistry are based on groups of people who have had certain opportunities to learn the material covered by the test. When we test a client for the first time, we compare his score with the norms to find out how well he has succeeded. If a marked deficiency is found, we seek further information about the client, hoping to find reasons for his poor showing. So too, social-role prescriptions are standards against which the clinician first measures his client in order to discover gross deviations. They are not expressed in numerical terms as test norms are, and clinicians do not usually state what social norms they are using. Despite their crudity, however, these expectations form a base line for important parts of every clinical evaluation. No formal test battery covers such broad and significant areas of personal development and permits such a rapid and inexpensive appraisal.

An Example of Implicit Norms. To show how simple orienting data arouse expectations, the writer asked a group of graduate students in psychology to rate certain personality traits for a subject they had never met. Prior to making their ratings the students were informed that the subject was a single female college graduate who was twenty-six years old. They knew also that this woman had been studied clinically, but they did not know why this study had been undertaken. The average ratings are shown by the solid line in Figure 5. The scales are shown here in condensed form; actually, the traits and the points on the scales were defined more fully for the student raters. In Figure 5 only the end points of the scales are defined, but in every case an average rating would be indicated by 5. You will notice that, although the averages of the ratings lie close to the center of the scales, it would not be correct to say that the raters regarded her as an "average woman." They think of her as fairly talkative, more anxious and cautious than the average person, tending toward conventional morality, somewhat worried about sexual matters, and definitely more ambitious than average. They guess that her home was about as harmonious as the usual household but think that she may feel somewhat deprived of love and affection.

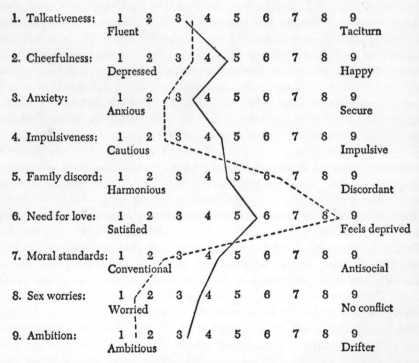

Figure 5. Personality Ratings of One Person. Solid line shows average of ratings based on very limited information. Dotted line shows ratings based on extensive test and interview data.

The dotted line in the figure shows the average ratings made by two psychologists who had access to a considerable amount of test and interview data for this woman. Their ratings are more extreme than the students' ratings on nearly every scale. It is worth noting, however, that on eight of the nine scales the students' guess lies on the same side of the center point as the judgment of the psychologists. Although the students were wrong in their guesses, the guesses were not completely foolish nor random. How can we account for this finding?

The orienting data about age, sex, marital status, and educational level must have permitted some inferences about other characteristics. Fortunately, the subject who was being rated came from the same section of the country and belonged to about the same socioeconomic stratum as the raters, although they did not know this. The raters, acting on their own knowledge of college students and single women, arrived at conclusions that seemed probably true. They must have believed, for example, that an unconventional, unambitious girl would not have finished college successfully. Moreover, a single woman in our culture would probably feel some need for love and affection; and it is safer to assume that she would be worried about sexual matters than to assume otherwise. Of course, individual raters varied widely in their guesses, depending on their experience and the additional assumptions they made. Some raters assumed that the woman had sought psychological assistance for her personal problems; they imagined that she would be quite anxious, worried about sex, and feel lack of affection strongly.

Accuracy of Inferences from Orienting Data. As part of a larger investigation, Kostlan (7) studied the ability of twenty clinical psychologists to make inferences from orienting data. He first constructed a true-false test based on sentences actually found in reports of psychological diagnosis and psychotherapeutic progress. The next step was to have eight expert clinicians study the complete case data for five patients. Then they marked the true-false items separately for each patient. When six of the eight experts agreed on how an item should be marked for a patient, their choice became the "correct" answer. Thus, Kostlan constructed a scoring key for each patient. The test could now be used to measure the accuracy with which clinicians could make inferences about each case, given various amounts of information.

The twenty clinicians were asked to study the case data when certain information had been systematically deleted. Then they answered the true-false test. Under the "minimal information" condition, the clinicians were told that the patients were white male veterans who were patients at a mental-hygiene clinic. They were also told the age, marital status, occupation, educational level, and referring source for each of the five patients. Due to the experimental design, only four psychologists answered the test for any one patient under these conditions. All twenty participated in this part of the study, however.

Kostlan's data show that, with only this minimal information, the clinicians made more correct inferences than would be expected on a chance basis. More surprising is the finding that the average number of correct inferences did not increase reliably when the clinicians used both minimal information and test data.[1] Giving them social-history information, however, did produce a reliable increase in correct inferences. It is possible, of course, that the true-false test did not permit the most effective use of the test data. But the study does show that orienting data can aid clinical inference.

Problem 3. Part *A.* A twenty-four-year-old man is married and has no children. He is a high-school graduate, is employed as clerk in the meat department of a large market, and lives in a rented furnished apartment. He is located in a city with a population of about 30,000 in the Middle West. On the basis of this limited information, how would you answer the following questions?

1. How intelligent is he?
2. How well does he like his job?
3. Do he and his wife get along well together?
4. What kinds of recreation does he enjoy?
5. Is he generally optimistic or pessimistic in his outlook?

Part *B.* Now answer the same questions for another man. All the information given in Part *A* remains the same except the age. Assume that this man is thirty-eight years old.

Part *C.* On what basis did you arrive at your answers for the two men? What kinds of assumptions are you making about typical motives in Middle Western culture? Can you trace the source of any of these assumptions to specific reading or experiences?

Using Inappropriate Norms. One of the elementary precautions you must observe when interpreting psychological tests is to use the proper set of norms in evaluating the client's scores. You would probably not compare the spelling achievement of an eighth grader with the expected score of a college freshman except for very special reasons. This kind of error can very easily occur when you interpret orientation data. The use of inappropriate social norms can occur in two ways.

The first kind of error is a failure to take into account local or subcultural variations in social-role prescriptions. The United States is culturally less homogeneous than you may suppose. Not only do role prescriptions vary slightly from region to region, but even within a given region subgroups may have standards of attitude and conduct that are peculiar to themselves. This local variation is easily noticed in urban areas where many immigrants have settled. In cities with Polish, Italian, German, or Hungarian areas, you will find different expectations in the

---

[1] The tests were the Rorschach, the Minnesota Multiphasic Personality Inventory, and a sentence completion test.

different nationality groups. In evaluating persons from these groups, the clinician must reckon with the distinctive standards of the subgroup, and he must also recognize that group members have come into contact with what has been called "the American core-culture." Here, he must evaluate the conflict among the expectations of several different groups.

The second kind of error is failure to recognize the differences in social norms among the various status levels in a community. Davis (15) has pointed out that underprivileged workers lack interest in the social rewards which appeal to middle-class workers. Nor are the same fears present in these two groups. The lower-class worker who has been fired is not likely to lose status with his kinship group. He will feel less anxious about "bunking in" with relatives for a while than a middle-class worker would. Furthermore, Davis and his coworkers (2) have shown that middle-class parents differ from lower-class parents in the role they assign to children in the family. Middle-class families are likely to have more exacting standards of conduct for their children and to try to accelerate their development toward adult standards. Lower-class families are often more permissive, sometimes to the point of negligence. Even the norms for sexual behavior and attitudes differ among various status levels, according to Kinsey (6). His data indicate that religiously inclined males and upper-level males engage in sexual intercourse less frequently during marriage than do males in the lower educational levels. Upper and lower educational levels also show differences in the incidence of premarital coitus.

Since a majority of clinicians have probably been exposed to the norms of the middle class in the locality where they were reared, it would be easy for them to use these norms as a base line for evaluating clients. Then they would mistakenly interpret many of the motives and practices of lower-class or upper-class clients as deviations.

Stereotypes and Social Roles. The suggestions that have been made about the use of orienting data may make you think that we are encouraging the clinician to rely on stereotypes. It would be a mistake, of course, if clinicians actually did make snap judgments of people on the basis of false ideas about the association of various attitudes and traits. Notions that Germans as a group are scientifically minded and methodical, or that Jews as a group are shrewd and grasping are good examples of common stereotypes that are misleading. But the proper use of social norms about roles should prevent the error of prejudging a person because of his national origin or race. Thinking in terms of the social influences that probably acted on a person forces the clinician to ask himself about the basis for his judgment, and he is continually reminded that his first ideas about a client are only *probably* true. If you believe that "Southerners hate Negroes" and assume that each client from that region will show that hatred, you are reacting on the basis of a stereotype. But if you know that the norms in the South prescribe certain relationships between colored and white people and that variations in attitude may occur depending on locality, travel, education, age, and social-class membership, you will react on the basis of social reality. You would be correct in assuming that a person who was reared in the South probably favored segregated schooling, but you would also be prepared to find that your assumption was wrong in a given case. And if you did find that you were wrong, you would then have to ask, "Why, if the prevalent attitude in this client's social environment favored segregation, did he develop a different one?" A potentially worthwhile line of investigation would be opened.

Roles and Social Learning. The particular roles that a group associates with age, sex, occupation, or parenthood should be regarded as standards toward which the group pushes each person. These standards are only approximated in actual behavior, however, for a variety of reasons. In the first place, the conception of the appropriate characteristics for each role allows for some variation. Mothers, for example, are supposed to see that their children are fed and clothed, but there is some latitude as to what is served and what styles are chosen.

More important for the clinician's purpose is the fact that learning social roles takes place under unique circumstances for each person. The child learns what it means to be a male or a female in terms of his parents' conceptions of sex roles, and these conceptions will emphasize some features of the role more than others. Furthermore, families will vary in the degree to which children are motivated to learn various roles. In some families, a good deal of praise is given for learning the role of "democratic citizen," while in other homes it will be barely mentioned. Many times, children learn fairly accurately what a role is but hear it devalued. One instance of this combination occurs when a wife is contemptuous of her husband. Her son may learn to know his father's occupational role and at the same time regard it as undesirable.

It is precisely because of the importance of the unique circumstances of role learning that the clinician needs a base line or standard of comparison. Without a knowledge of the common directions in which individuals are being led, he is insensitive to the unique modifications his client may show. With a knowledge of the social norms surrounding his client, he must account for the success or failure of the client in learning them. To learn that a man customarily sells articles made by his wife and returns the proceeds of the sale to her may mean much or little depending upon the social norms of his society. Among the Tchambuli of New Guinea these actions are part of the expected male role. If a clinician learned that his twenty-five-year-old male client in Chicago behaved this way he would think of a good many questions.

SOCIAL NORMS AND UNCONSCIOUS MOTIVATION

Toward the close of Chapter 3 we saw how clinicians seek to reconstruct the motives that produce behavior sequences. We are now ready to examine a special problem in clinical work: making inferences about unconscious motives. These inferences pose a difficult problem because we cannot verify them by direct statements from the client. Many inferences about motives can be checked by the client's own report, once he finds he can talk without fear of criticism. But the chief characteristic of unconscious motives is that they cannot be reported even by a sincere and willing person in a permissive atmosphere. Despite this fact, such motives do influence behavior; in fact, we cannot understand some of the puzzling things that people do without assuming the existence of unreportable motives. At the same time, the clinician has no license to invent unconscious motives whenever he finds it convenient.

To justify an inference that an unconscious motive exists, he must be able to establish at least the following:

1. Reportable motives do not sufficiently account for the existence or the extreme intensity of certain actions.

2. The person has had opportunity and encouragement to acquire a motive or motives which could account for behavior in question.

3. Conditions favoring repression of the assumed motive exist.

The argument we want to develop is simply that social norms provide conditions favoring the repression of certain motives. The clinician's familiarity with the group norms of his client enables him to make some plausible inferences about the nature of these motives.

Repressive processes must be motivated, just as is true of any other human action.[2] The most important motive sustaining repression is the need to reduce anxiety connected with unfavorable judgments of one's value or "goodness." As long as we do not know that we have unacceptable feelings or motives, we can remain relatively free from anxiety about our personal worth.

[2] The exact nature of the repressive processes is only partially understood. We feel sure that one of them consists of "mislabeling" (3, pp. 211 ff). A person may call his fear "anger." Or criticism meant to hurt another person may be described as "telling him something for his own good." Another kind of process may consist of muscular contractions that oppose incipient action tendencies. A motor readiness to swear may be automatically opposed by tensing the muscles in the jaw (9, pp. 146 ff). The proprioceptive pattern associated with "I want to swear" is thereby altered. The original motive cannot be identified and hence cannot be named. It is repressed.

Social Norms Determine Acceptability. The standards or prescriptions of the social group apply to covert as well as to overt behavior. By general agreement, some impulses are defined as "good," others as "bad." Thus, hatred of parents, homosexual impulses, and the desire for extramarital sexual relations are commonly condemned in our culture. The "badness" of a motive is determined by how much anxiety is attached to it during the training of the individual. As the child grows, he learns that "as a man thinketh in his heart, so is he," and he learns to be anxious when he thinks the proscribed thoughts. He comes to share the condemnatory standards of his group and to apply them to his own behavior. For example, anti-Semitic feelings in a Jew are especially abhorrent to the Jewish community.

Social norms also prescribe the acceptability of various kinds of actions as means for motive satisfaction. It is entirely proper, in the middle class, to want money and perfectly correct to desire marriage. But it is not respectable to marry in order to acquire wealth. Joining a church is a good thing, but it should not be done in order to enhance one's social status. A man may take a job involving travel because it pays well; he should not take it in order to avoid spending time with his wife.

The socially disapproved impulses and explanations are, of course, the very ones that are most likely to be repressed. Since there are multiple motives behind most actions, it is not hard to believe that we are activated only by those which are "good" and to repress the others. The clinician's knowledge of social norms thus helps him guess which motives will be unconscious. Of course, many other motives, not specifically denounced by general social norms, may be repressed because they are disapproved by families or other small primary groups. As the clinician learns more about the social environment of his client, he can be more precise in locating motives that are probably repressed.

Common Values and Needs. Knowing that a motive arouses anxiety is a necessary but not a sufficient condition for inferring that it is repressed. We must also know that the motive exists, that is, that the person is capable of being stimulated to want certain goals. For some kinds of motives (sex, food, rest, etc.) we infer the existence of the need from the common physiological structure of human beings. But the probable existence of other kinds of motives is inferred from the presence of group norms about what people should want. A culture emphasizes certain values, and adults teach children to accept them as their own. This homogenizing effort is furthered by social arrangements for rewarding those with the approved set of values. Adults, then, come to have a number of motives in common. In our own culture, we find widespread agreement on the desirability of social status, the acquisition of money, self-improvement by education, marriage, and so on.

When a clinician finds a person who was exposed to the customary value training but who denies having the customary value, he suspects that repression has taken place. Thus, in view of the cultural machinery for inculcating an interest in marriage, we expect single women in their twenties to want marriage. A woman who denies any such desire is usually assumed to be repressing it.

The soundness of such an inference depends on establishing the fact that the typical social pressures were actually operating in a given case. Not every single woman who denies wanting marriage is repressing. Peculiarities of family attitudes or seriously inadequate chances for contact with social norms may prevent the acquisition of the typical motive. Then, too, inconsistencies in cultural manipulations of rewards may hinder the establishment of the standard motive. Detailed knowledge of the life history usually enables us to decide whether the client really had a chance to learn the typical motives.

An Example of Repression. To illustrate how social norms function as a context in which the clinician evaluates a client's remarks, we shall give some excerpts from a recording of an initial interview. The client, Hal, is talking about his financial responsibilities to his mother:

She does have a few dollars and they might last for two years or three years if I don't contribute to her support. But at the end of that time I'll have to be in a position where I can not only, uh, support her, but myself and my fiancée. Became engaged last Christmas. Strangely enough, the fact that I'm engaged doesn't bother me as much as it probably should. I don't worry about that relationship at all. The fact that I'm not getting married—I'd like to get married, but I don't feel any pressure there at all. I do feel pressure to go to college and study.

The interesting point in these remarks is the lack of concern about the engagement. It probably would have gone unnoticed had it not been that Hal himself called attention to it. He used the phrase "strangely enough," and then indicated that he should be more bothered about the engagement. Hal and the clinician were both aware that engaged men usually want to get married and that they are usually thinking about plans, financial arrangements, and so on. At this point, Hal makes an outright slip of the tongue: "The fact that I'm *not* getting married . . ." His attitude is exactly the reverse of what we expect to find (on the basis of social norms) in an engaged and eager man. He corrects his unintentional error: "I'd like to get married"—and then proceeds to deny this desire indirectly—"but I don't feel any pressure there at all." Could it be that Hal actually does not want to get married, at least not in the near future? If this is the case, there is good reason for repressing his desire to avoid marriage. The social standards of Hal's community do not approve of men who become engaged and then try to escape the commitment. And Hal does not approve either. Since this client had a series of therapeutic sessions we can check up on the speculations made during the first interview.

Three weeks later the following conversation occurred:

HAL: It's so easy for me to disassociate her from my thoughts completely that I don't see how it can be possible.

CLINICIAN: How do you mean, it's so easy to disassociate her from your thoughts?

HAL: Well, I can see her. . . . Like I'm downtown calling on somebody, so I stop up to the office and I talk to her and I'm in her company and I become excited. And I leave her company and, uh, I can read something, I can write something, and just forget all about her. That is, I *think* that I forget all about her. I don't know whether in the back of my mind someplace I do. *I don't.*

CLINICIAN: But it seems to you that actually once she's gone, she's gone. Just like that?

HAL: Yeah, that's right. If I'm talking to her on the phone, I'm, of course, I'm very conscious of her on the other end of the line. But when I hang up the phone and I start reading, I just become, just get away from her. I daydream a lot. I don't say I become immersed in what I'm reading, but my thoughts don't jump over to her. They jump to other things. That worries me, too. I mean either it's a question whether I am, really, in love with her. . . . Sometimes I try to figure out whether I became engaged to her or she became engaged to me. I, I, I, it's a terrible thing to say, but now I'm beginning to think that she became engaged to me. I'll have to ask her about it and see what happens. . . . I'm almost positive when I think about it that I didn't apply any pressure in the—in the action.

CLINICIAN: You're not even sure whether you want to be engaged?

HAL: Yeah, that's right. I've only been three months. Three months next week. [*Sighs.*] Quite a situation. If people, if I ask myself if I'm in love, I say yes. And I say, am I? And I start thinking about it.

Hal's expressed attitude toward his engagement has changed considerably from the "no pressure" attitude he showed three weeks earlier. Actually Hal had been unaware of his desire to avoid marriage. But the peculiar way he discussed his feelings did not coincide with the clinician's perception of the social norms for engaged men. Moreover, the desire to avoid marrying the girl is a socially unacceptable one and therefore prone to be repressed. In the latter excerpt, we see the weakening of the repressive forces and a fuller description of the conflict. Notice that the beginning of correct labeling was accompanied by open self-criticism: "It's a terrible thing to say." Statements of this kind are common when repressed impulses are being experienced.

REFERENCES

1. Curran, C. A. Nondirective counseling in allergic complaints. *J. abnorm. soc. Psychol.*, 1948, **43**, 442–451.
2. Davis, A., & Havighurst, R. J. Social class and color differences in child rearing. *Amer. sociol. Rev.*, 1946, **11**, 698–710.
3. Dollard, J., & Miller, N. E. *Personality and psychotherapy.* New York: McGraw-Hill, 1950.
4. Farber, M. L. Prison research: techniques and methods. *J. soc. Psychol.*, 1941, **14**, 295–310.
5. Greving, F. T., & Rockmore, M. J. Psychiatric case-work as a military service. *Ment. Hyg.*, 1945, **29**, 1–72.
6. Kinsey, A. C., Pomeroy, W. B., & Martin, C. E. *Sexual behavior in the human male.* Philadelphia: Saunders, 1948.
7. Kostlan, A. A method for the empirical study of psychodiagnosis. *J. consult. Psychol.*, 1954, **18**, 83–88.
8. Newcomb, T. M. *Social psychology.* New York: Dryden, 1950.
9. Perls, F. S., Hefferline, R. F., & Goodman, P. *Gestalt therapy.* New York: Julian Press, 1951.
10. Richards, T. W. *Modern clinical psychology.* New York: McGraw-Hill, 1946.
11. Rogers, C. R. *Counseling and psychotherapy.* New York: Houghton Mifflin, 1942.
12. Snyder, W. U. *Casebook of non-directive counseling.* New York: Houghton Mifflin, 1947.
13. Spock, B. *The pocket book of baby and child care.* New York: Pocket Books, 1946.
14. Watson, R. I. *The clinical method in psychology.* New York: Harper, 1951.
15. Whyte, W. F. (Ed.) *Industry and society.* New York: McGraw-Hill, 1946.

CHAPTER 5

Interviewing: Observational Data

Of all the ways for studying persons, interviewing is probably the most important. It can provide richness of data and precision in communication unmatched by most other methods. Since no special equipment is needed, it is always available to the clinician. Furthermore, it is a rapid method for collecting information. When the time for studying a person is sharply limited, interviewing is likely to be the best method to use.

It is true, of course, that interviewing has serious defects. Interviewers rarely can make judgments of intelligence, interest patterns, or aptitude that are as precise as those based on well-constructed tests. And there is always the possibility of being given misleading or false information in an interview. What can be done in an interview is to get information about aspects of the client's life that are not subject to testing, and to form a general notion about his main characteristics and the important influences on his development.

What you see and hear in an interview is not very valuable until you interpret it, and it is at this point that some of the most glaring mistakes in interviewing can be made. You are at the mercy of your own stereotypes, biases, preconceived ideas of human nature, and your own tendencies to be harsh or charitable, cautious or impulsive in judgment. The improvement of interviewing seems to be a matter of improving the interviewer's skill in making inferences and interpretations, more than developing his skill in conducting an interview. For there is little point in being able to draw out information unless you can make use of it.

The main purpose of this chapter is to help you think more effectively about interview material. We shall point out some of the observations that can be made during interviewing and some possible interpretations of these observations. Most people who are interviewed believe that the interviewer is interested only in what they are saying, that is, in the reporting aspect of interviewing. Skilled interviewers, however, are interested not only in the report but in how it is given, how the client is behaving, and how he is meeting the social situation of the interview itself. In order to stress the importance of these latter items, we begin the study of interviewing by discussing the data of observation.

116

OBSERVING GENERAL APPEARANCE

The first thing that an interviewer does as his client walks in and sits down is to take a good look at him. What he sees may suggest lines of inquiry to be followed up later or may reinforce some impression gained from the client's story. Sometimes a striking physical characteristic or mannerism may start the interviewer guessing about the self-attitudes or motives of the client.

Physical Appearance. The height, weight, and body structure of people create a kind of global impression; and we try to sum it up in words like "hulking," "petite," "frail," and "plump." Probably the impression that the client makes on the interviewer is similar to the impression he makes on other people. He may appear well constructed and physically adequate to meet the demands of living, or he may appear inadequate, with few physical resources. Whether or not he is in fact adequate or inadequate, it is likely that the impression he creates affects his relationships with people. A person who appears physically adequate, for example, may actually have physical deficiencies which prevent him from living up to the expectations of those around him. When he fails to perform in the expected way, they may decide he is lazy or a coward not worthy of sympathy. Such judgments may lead to social rejection and the loss of self-esteem. On the other hand, a person with a slender physique may arouse sympathy and even overconcern for his health among his family. As a consequence, he may develop excessive concern for himself; or he may react against the family attitude and "harden" himself to prove his physiological adequacy.

Among men, tallness and masculine build are valued. Consequently, a man's attitude toward himself may be related to his physical characteristics. One study (5) has shown that height, shoulder width, and circumference of the biceps muscle have significant correlations with favorable attitudes toward these body parts. Favorable attitudes toward one's weight, however, are not related to actual weight. It is generally believed that men also value genitals that are large and adequate in appearance, but systematic evidence on this point is not available. A favorable attitude toward one's body is likely to indicate a favorable attitude toward other aspects of the self-concept and is also slightly related to feelings of personal security (12).

Since physical appearance favors or hinders the social acceptance of women in the United States, we should expect to find it related to their own self-evaluations. Evidence supporting this expectation has been provided by Rokeach (8). He showed that ratings of the beauty of young women have a positive correlation with their feelings of dominance and of security. One curious feature of Rokeach's findings is that beauty ratings made by men were more closely related to dominance and security feelings in a woman than were ratings made by other women. Perhaps similarity to the masculine ideal facilitates masculine social acceptance, and this contributes more to feminine security than feminine acceptance. You should not generalize too far from these findings, however, for the correspondence between beauty and security feelings was far from perfect. Appearance is not the only personal characteristic making for a sense of security and may not even be the crucial one.

Deviations from a normally proportioned physique suggest glandular abnormalities. For example, malfunctioning of the pituitary gland causes abnormalities of bony growth. One characteristic often found in such cases is a peculiar facial appearance due to a large jaw and pronounced ridge above the eyes. Obesity, too, may be the result of endocrine disturbances, although emotional factors are often more significant. Other deviations in physique are due to injuries and their sequelae. Thus, a broken nose that did not receive proper treatment may have resulted in an odd-looking face.

The clinician also notes the color, texture, and firmness of the skin. These qualities often change because of disease, glandular disorder, or malnutrition. Deficiency of vitamin B_2 may produce marked chapping of the lips, angular fissures at the corners of the mouth, and inflammation of the adjacent skin. Skin changes also occur in pellagra, due to a deficiency of niacin. In this disorder there will be redness or crusting of the skin; sometimes a thickened, inelastic skin occurs at pressure points. These deficiencies are only two of the many possible causes of skin changes; whether the clinician is familiar with skin disorders or not, he can at least note outstanding symptoms. A tanned skin is currently popular, partly because of its association with those social groups that have a good deal of leisure. But people with status aspirations may resort to sun lamps! Frequently persons who are seclusive and asocial have pale skins. Probably they are prone to stay indoors and to avoid outdoor group recreation.

There are three kinds of hypotheses that a clinician considers when thinking about deviant physical appearance:

1. Hypotheses about the physiological origins and significance of the physical peculiarity
2. Hypotheses about the kind of attitudes, motives, and behavior that may have produced the peculiarity
3. Hypotheses about the effect of the peculiarity on the client and his social group

When we see an obese twenty-year-old girl, for example, we may wonder whether glandular trouble is an important causal factor, whether she has the normal dating and social pattern for this age, and whether she uses excessive eating to control her anxiety. A young man with marked development of the muscles of the arms and shoulders may make us note his undersized physique and speculate about his attitudes toward his own adequacy, his compensatory efforts at physical exercise, and the kind of status he has achieved among his age mates.

As a final example of the interrelation of physical, personal, and social factors, consider the problems stemming from early physical maturity in a fourteen-year-old girl. Her adult appearance makes her a sexual object attractive to males a half-dozen years older. Her immature friends envy and resent her. Her attitudes toward herself are confused. And her parents, aware of her new status, become overanxious and restrictive. All these are possibilities for the interviewer to explore, and he may think of all of them before a word has been exchanged.

Clothing. Even more apparent than physique is dress. The clothing that a person wears is always in some sense an expression of his relationship to his social environment and of his perception of himself. True, his funds may place limitations on what he can buy, but there are discernible variations in the dress of people in the same income bracket. Looked at from the standpoint of social psychology, clothing has a good deal of similarity to language. Both are taken from the surrounding culture and are subject to the limitations imposed by the social group. Both permit individual, stylistic variations while holding the user to the common norm. Both may convey messages, and both call attention to oneself.

It is commonly understood that sex and status are communicated by clothing. Consequently, it is easy to use clothing to indicate attitudes or aspirations in these areas. People who hope to be identified with a social class they consider higher in status will adopt clothing as nearly appropriate to that class as they can. (Here you may be reminded of the eagerness of adolescent girls to get into "glamour" clothes.) And some homosexuals, hoping to deny their biologically given sex, turn to dress appropriate to the opposite sex. Of course, clothing can be used to enhance one's body as a sexual object; and those who fear they lack sexual attractiveness may go to extremes in order to invite attention. We may see women in the middle years clinging to "youthful" dress, and perhaps their efforts are directed as much toward reassuring themselves as toward impressing their peers.

Clothing can be used to compensate for a number of kinds of deficiencies other than low status. The simplest case of this is the woman who dresses to "bring out her good points." Somewhat more compensatory is the loud or "snappy" dress of short men who are bothered by their stature. The extreme of this showy clothing is found among the "zoot suit" crowd—adolescents in minority groups who affect exaggerations in the length, color, and cut of their clothing.

Among young men of the professional and managerial groups cautious, conforming dress is often observed. They choose ties that are unobtrusive in color and design. Their suits are often dark gray or blue. They are well aware of the "importance of making a good impression," and a good impression means restraint and deference.

What we have said so far about dress implies that the person is aware of customs—is in contact with his group. But what about the relatively unsocialized person who is indifferent to his group? There is some evidence that such people are indifferent to dress, or at least they are not motivated to put what knowledge they have into practice. Janney (4) made a study of clothing fads over a two-year period in a Middle Western college for women. He found a group of about twenty women who generally were behind the others in the style of their clothing, even with newly purchased items. Moreover, their clothing often did not fit well. These "obsolescent faddists" did not belong to cliques on the campus, had trouble finding roommates, and rarely attended teas and receptions. As could be expected, they had few dates. Only one of the twenty used cosmetics. Janney points out that their insensitivity to the campus patterns of dress matched their general lack of awareness and skill in social situations. Other women on the campus who showed interest in and awareness of dress were less solitary and more active socially. Investigation of the intelligence, health, and financial status of these college women showed that these factors did not account for their patterns of dress.

Observations during psychotherapy support Janney's findings. It is not uncommon to see women who are dowdy or who are given to somber clothing begin to attend to their appearance or to choose more colorful clothing as therapy progresses. This change seems to parallel changes in the direction of greater self-confidence and greater interest in the relationships between themselves and others.

The acts of choosing clothing and of putting it on are acts that center around one's own body. There is, therefore, an element of self-interest present in such actions. Sometimes clothing reflects excessive self-interest. Such narcissistic patterns of dress are revealed not only by the kind of clothing worn, but by perfection of detail—a kind of fashion-plate quality which is usually achieved only with considerable effort and time. It must take a good deal of self-love to spend hours every day attaining faultless dress and grooming.

Our comments on the attitudes and motives behind patterns of dress are meant to suggest hypotheses to the clinician; they are not intended as prefabricated interpretations to be made uncritically. In thinking about the significance of clothing, you should keep several cautions in mind. In the first place, a single interview provides only a single sample of the client's dress. This sample may not be representative of his typical dress. Since it is fairly common for people to "dress up" for visits to specialists, you may be seeing only the client's conception of "dressing up." While this kind of dress may reveal something of the person's taste or the importance the interview has for him, it is not a very good basis for understanding how the person uses clothing in establishing contact with his social environment. Additional interviews provide a chance to test hunches arising in the initial interview and to study the client's range of variation in dress.

A second limitation on inferences based on dress comes from the difficulty of knowing the norms of the client and of his social group. For example, a counselor notes that Frank arrives for an interview wearing a sweater. Since most clients wear suits to their first interview, the counselor imagines that Frank did not "dress up" for his visit. On this basis, he guesses that the young man thinks the interview is unimportant. He may even find apparent confirmation of his guess when he finds that his client does not talk very freely. What the counselor does not know is that Frank actually made a special effort to "dress up." He decided to wear a new sweater—his best clothing for such special occasions. The counselor, however, errs by not allowing for the difference between his own standards of dress and those of his client.

Hair Style. The arrangement of the hair seems to have a psychological significance similar to that of clothing. Usually, however, hair style is not changed as often as clothing. Among men, particularly, one way of arranging the hair may persist for many years. Although hair does not lend itself to social communication and expression of the self-concept as well as clothing, we may point out a few of the ways in which these two functions are carried out. An obvious lack of attention to one's hair may indicate the same lack of contact with the social environment as does obvious lack of attention to clothing. While this interpretation is probably more true of women than of men, it sometimes applies to men, too. Men who are very much concerned with ideas or things, but less concerned about people, may allow their hair to grow fairly long between visits to the barber shop. Then, when they do get a haircut they want it cut rather short. This behavior could easily stem from a pattern of values that relegates human interaction to a minor position. But it could be due to scanty funds!

Bleaching or dyeing hair is often motivated by a desire for social acceptance and admiration. This desire is heightened by dissatisfaction with one's personal qualities and fear of social competition. In one case known to the writer, a young woman in psychotherapy spontaneously decided to stop bleaching her hair. Discussing this change with the therapist, she said that it was part of a general effort to "get honest with myself." Apparently, as she began to feel that she was a worthwhile person, the need to make special efforts to attract others decreased.

In some persons, high standards of personal conduct along with caution and meticulousness will affect hair arrangement. Here we may find hairdos that are tight, close to the head, and firmly held in place. One would imagine that women who customarily arrange their hair this way are not likely to adopt, or even consider adopting, fads in hair style.

The clinician should also be aware of the sexual implications of hair, especially among women. In United States and European culture there is a sharp distinction between the hair arrangements prescribed for the two sexes. Certain treatments of the hair thus become associated with femininity and may be used to express that complex of motives and attitudes. Rejection of the feminine role can be communicated by rejecting "typical" feminine hair styles. Hair is also commonly regarded as enhancing the sexual attractiveness of women, and willingness to spend time on its care and arrangement will often reflect an acceptance of sexual feelings. For some women, hair may come to have a direct symbolic relationship with sexuality, so that excessive concern with its arrangement may indicate a corresponding concern with their own sexual feelings. Ordinarily, of course, any symbolic meaning of hair would have to be discovered during a detailed and prolonged study of the person.

Problem 1. Part A. Teen-age girls sometimes try to appear "glamorous." What kind of clothing and hair style could express this aim? What significance do such efforts have, that is, what motives are involved?

Part B. Although urban culture in the United States includes a standard of clean-shaven faces for men, mustaches are permissible. List three or four possible motives that could lead a man to wear a mustache. Are any of these motives not likely to be admitted by the wearer?

OBSERVING EMOTIONAL REACTIONS

An interview is considerably more than an exchange of information or a question-and-answer period. It is a social relationship, and, like all social relationships, it is grounded in the emotional stimulation and emotional response of both participants. An interviewer who does not push the interaction in a particular direction will find that distinctive "emotional climates" emerge with different clients. Sometimes the whole relationship is flavored with good-humored joking, while with other clients the interviews are marked by tenseness or by half-concealed hostility. If these climates are to aid us in understanding the client, we must be certain that our own emotions have not produced them. If our own preferences for a certain kind of emotional atmosphere dominate the interview, we may be able to make some inferences about ourselves but not about the person we are studying.

It is easy to establish a social norm early in the interview that may prevent even mild forms of emotional reactions from being expressed. An educational counselor who tries to create an atmosphere of goodfellowship by taking an "I'm just a boy myself" attitude may check expressions of serious concern on the part of his counselee. So too, the brisk efficiency of the "I'm all business" psychologist defines an atmosphere that makes crying seem silly. On the other hand, a clinician with no standardized conception of the emotional climate in interviewing is likely to be sensitive to his client's feeling and to permit him to define the emotional relationship.

Generally, interviews begin like any other unclear social relationship. The client is tense, uncertain, and hesitant. He may handle this by joking to cover his uncertainty, but more often he reveals his feelings by hesitant speech and rigid posture. After ten to twenty minutes, he speaks more easily, using colloquialisms and slang, and leaning back or slouching in his chair. The time required for this relaxation to appear will vary with the interviewer's skill and, of course, with the client. After a number of interviews with different people, a clinician will know about how long the average person requires to become at ease with him. Persistence of tenseness and discomfort beyond this period will probably indicate a chronically anxious person whose tension originates in sources outside the interview.

Tension Indicators. As the interview progresses, some of the topics will provoke anxiety. These topics interest the interviewer, because they indicate problem areas in the client's life. Although the signs of anxiety may be minimal and fleeting, they show the clinician that the topic has special significance for the client. It may be useful, therefore, to review common manifestations of tension in the interview. For the most part these signs arise from activity of the sympathetic nervous system. Some of them depend upon glandular activity, some reflect smooth muscle changes, and some result from increased tension in the striped muscles.

One observable product of glandular activity is tears. It is not necessary for the client to weep, however, in order for the clinician to observe increased tear production. When the eyes glisten more brightly at some points in the discussion than at others, it is safe to assume that a change in tear-gland activity is responsible. The drainage of excess tears into the nasal passages starts some persons dabbing at their noses with a handkerchief or sniffing frequently. It hardly needs to be added that these indicators cannot be used when the client has a cold.

Perspiration is another common sign of emotional arousal and may be observed directly on the forehead. Palmar sweating is more difficult to observe and is usually discovered when shaking hands with the client at the end of the interview. But sometimes it can be noted when clients wipe their hands on handkerchiefs or clothing.

Salivary secretion ordinarily decreases in fear and anxiety, and this results in drying the mouth and lips. Under these conditions the interviewer will note frequent moistening of the lips or requests for a drink of water. While other glandular changes occur during emotional arousal, those we have mentioned are the ones most often seen in interviews.

Changes in smooth muscle taking place during emotion are difficult to observe. Perhaps the most pronounced effects are the blushing or paling of the face due to dilation or constriction of blood vessels. Increased size of the pupils may also occur in anxiety, although it is not easy to see.

Increased tension in the striped muscles provides a number of obvious indicators. There is the fine rapid tremor of the fingers and of the lips against a background of tense, vigilant posture. And you are already familiar with restlessness, frequent shifts in position, and drumming or tapping with feet or fingers. Rapid respiration also often occurs. The pitch of the voice may rise. The anxious client may literally sit on the edge of his chair throughout the entire interview. The generally high level of muscle tension facilitates startle responses, and the sudden slam of a door or sound of an auto horn may make him jump. Some people discharge muscle tension by way of fairly well-organized actions such as laughing, smoking, pacing, or doodling with a pencil. The frequency and intensity of these actions betray the general tension motivating them.

On the other hand, some people react to anxiety by adopting an air of calmness and deliberateness. They will sit quietly, speak slowly, gesture very little, and take on a formal manner. Superficially they appear undisturbed, but it is often possible to show that they are in a state of heightened muscular tension. They can be distinguished from people who are genuinely relaxed by the fact that their behavior is more extreme and inflexible. The person who is really at ease smiles more spontaneously and changes positions more frequently than the tensely controlled person.

Mood. It is easy to see that interviewees differ from one another in the general mood they display during the conversation. Some will appear optimistic and cheerful, while others will be sober and pessimistic. Despite these differences, however, the normal person will be able to follow the changing emotional qualities of the discussion. If you watch the facial expression of a person during conversation, you will see that he responds continuously to the flow of topics. He nods agreement, shakes his head with disbelief, frowns as he considers a point, smiles at some bit of humor. Even the optimist will look serious for a moment when some distressing experience or problem enters the talk. We are so accustomed to these conversational accompaniments that we rarely attend to them explicitly. Yet they impart warmth and feeling to speech, and they show the attentiveness of the other person. You can sensitize yourself to the quantity and communicative value of these actions by watching people talking on a television screen when you have turned off the sound.

In serious disorders of behavior this flexibility of emotional responsiveness is often missing. In depressed conditions, for instance, patients talk slowly, almost inaudibly, and sadly about every topic. Facial expression is constantly perplexed or blank, and the posture conveys the impression of sagging, inert muscles. An effort to inject humor into the conversation meets only a questioning look. This same inflexibility of mood occurs in the pathologically elated person, who is unable to restrain his buoyancy long enough to consider a pressing problem. Boastful statements and grandiose plans will be loudly voiced, often with a good deal of gesticulation. Among the schizophrenic reactions, inappropriate mood and emotional responsiveness are often seen. Here, you will sometimes notice silly smiles that have no relationship to the conversation. Or the patient may take a matter-of-fact tone while discussing some frightening experience.

OBSERVING SPEECH

Of all the behavior observed in interviewing, linguistic behavior is probably the most adequately sampled. We have pointed out that only limited samples of dress and of emotional reactions are available in a single interview, but an hour's discussion permits fairly adequate opportunities for judgments of speech. And since talking is intimately linked with thinking, we can often arrive at some conclusions about the way the client thinks.

Speaking requires fine motor coordinations. The ability to produce adequate speech rests on the soundness of the organs involved in talking, including the central nervous system, and on the general state of the organism. Extreme fatigue, drowsiness, or emotional arousal produce defective enunciation, misuse of words, and inability to organize and develop ideas. Drugs and alcohol have similar effects. The physiological state of the individual also affects the selective process required in speaking. To communicate coherently, the speaker must inhibit tendencies to talk about irrelevant material such as his own marginal associations and private preoccupations. For this inhibition to operate smoothly, the speaker needs to be adequately motivated and to have available the energy required. When these conditions are not met, as is often the case in fatigue, illness, and senility, speech may be rambling, repetitive, and irrelevant.

Language is a highly standardized form of social behavior, and its effectiveness as communication demands observing commonly recognized conventions and rules. Obviously, then, the conditions under which the learning occurred will determine the more formal aspects of speaking. Some persons grow up in families that provide good "speech models" and value proper grammar and a large vocabulary. Others are exposed to barren speech environments where attention is paid only to the most elementary conventions of expression. Formal education, of course, can equalize opportunities for language learning and may even help establish correct speech as valuable. Grammatical speech, a large vocabulary, and a modulated voice are also status indicators, and they may be deliberately cultivated by persons with status ambitions.

Even within the framework of speech conventions, however, there is ample room for variation in the style of expression. Thus Sanford (10) was able to show that one of his subjects used many complex sentences, parenthetical clauses, and long sentences. This subject rephrased his thoughts frequently and was explicit and explanatory about his meaning. Sanford describes his style as complex, perseverative, thorough, and cautious. Another subject's style could be characterized as colorful, emphatic, direct, and active. Although we are not told how these styles were related to other personality characteristics of the subjects, we may be sure that they were related. Speech is not only a way of telling things to others; it is a way of establishing emotional relationships. And we may whine, assert, or soothe with our voices, depending upon who we think we are and how we perceive our personal relationships.

Pathological Speech. Striking deviations from the normal way of speaking are always significant and immediately suggest that the speaker is disturbed in nonlinguistic activities. Sometimes the deviation is largely a matter of enunciation or articulation. Sometimes the content of the stream of talk is unusual although the production of the words is satisfactory. The most commonly observed abnormality in the former category is stuttering. The importance of neurological factors in causing stuttering has not been clearly demonstrated, but there is considerable evidence that stutterers often have emotional problems. Even on the assumption that emotional problems do not cause stuttering, the defect itself could easily produce social and emotional difficulties. The stutterer is handicapped in ordinary social interactions and is often marked for pity or ridicule. Consequently the clinician will be alert to see how the defect has affected the self-concept and the social relationships of the patient. Some evidence indicates that investigation of the family background will be rewarding also. Wood (15) obtained evidence that the parents of children with defective speech tended to be emotionally maladjusted. Since her sample did not include cases in which the defect was due to organic factors or to low intelligence, we may assume that the maladjustment of the parents was somehow instrumental in the acquisition of the speech handicap. Rotter's (9) view is more specific as to the nature of the parent-child relationship. Intensive study of stutterers leads him to believe that pampering, with consequent emotional dependence, will be regularly found in their background.

Lisping is a speech defect which is confined largely to the incorrect production of the sounds *s, z,* and *sh.* It may be due to structural defects of the tongue, teeth, jaw, and palatal arch or to faulty speech habits. If the structures involved in speaking are normal, there is a possibility that the lisping may be part of a neurotic pattern (11). In studying a child who lisped the clinician would probably want to determine whether or not the speech defect was connected with an attempt to cling to an infantile status.

Another defect which is easily noted in an interview is slurred speech. It consists of omitting or slurring over consonant sounds such as *s, t, l,* and *r,* giving the speech a "thick" quality. For many years, the test phrases "truly rural" and "Methodist Episcopal" have been used to demonstrate the presence of this defect. Slurred speech is caused by the speaker's inability to make the fine muscular movements required in clear enunciation. The most common condition in which slurring is noticed is paresis, where syphilis has interfered with the normal functioning of the cerebral cortex. Sometimes this defect is the result of a cerebral tumor. While other symptoms will usually be found along with slurred speech, its presence is enough to indicate the need for a neurological examination.

Brain damage may result in aphasic conditions which interfere with speech. Sometimes the patient has great difficulty in finding the correct word to use in a sentence. Often there is an inability to name simple objects. In some cases parts of words may be interchanged, or words may be spoken in the wrong order so that speech is meaningless. Occasionally an aphasic will choose words that are related to those he would like to use, but they convey quite a different meaning. For example, the patient may say, "I went to the cellar yesterday," meaning that he went downstairs this morning. The location word refers to "below" and the time is expressed as past, but ordinary precision is lost. In other kinds of aphasia, speech may not be disturbed, but defects will appear in reading, writing, or comprehension of spoken language. Neurological examination and special psychological testing methods are required for the satisfactory study of the aphasic patient.

Severe disturbances in the content of speech are often found in psychotic conditions and will be apparent even to an untrained observer. Jumbled, senseless speech (word salad) or bizarre topics characterize the talk of some schizophrenics. Rapid shifts in topic, rhyming associations, and frequent punning on single words are found in manic patients. Senile patients may go into endless explanatory detail while still holding to the central point of their story (circumstantial speech), or they may ramble from detail to detail without any continuity. Their difficulties in remembering what has been said may lead to repetition of stories or questions that they used only a short time before.

Speech Style and Personality. Even in the absence of obvious pathology, speech and personality are related. The investigations of Allport and Cantril (1) and of Wolff (16) show that voices can be matched with personality sketches better than would be expected on a chance basis. Moore (6) found that students with breathy voices tended to score toward the introvertive, submissive, and neurotic ends of the Bernreuter scales. But these investigations are concerned with only limited aspects of speaking. In interviewing, the clinician is able to react to the whole flavor of the client's talk, noting word choice, pauses, mispronunciations, emphasis, and sequence of topics as well as voice quality. While there is still much to be learned about the precise connection between speech style and other personal characteristics, it is worth while to point out some possible relationships.

One promising lead can be found in the work of Balken and Masserman (2). They analyzed the language used by patients in telling stories about the Thematic Apperception Test pictures. The patients were all neurotic and could be classified as cases of conversion hysteria, anxiety state, or obsessive-compulsive neurosis. Analysis of the language used in telling the stories showed that the hysterics did not often qualify their statements by indicating some limitation or reservation. But qualification was frequent among the obsessive-compulsive group. The hysterics used many more expressions indicating certainty ("sure," "no question") than expressions of uncertainty ("don't know," "afraid to say"). This relationship was reversed for the obsessives. Anxiety cases showed more vagueness and hesitation in their language than either of the other two groups. These findings seem to fit the known personality characteristics of these neurotic types and express the adjustive mechanisms commonly found in each one. The promising lead that Balken and Masserman give us is that speech style may be partly the result of the individual's efforts to cope with anxiety. While this interpretation of their findings is incomplete, let us see how it can illuminate some of the forms of speech observed in the interview.

Occasionally you will see a person who continually engages in justification and explanation. If he arrives a few minutes late for the interview, he goes into detail explaining just how it happened and ends with profuse apologies. If he knocks over an ashtray, he tells how clumsy he is, how he wishes he were more graceful, and how sorry he is to have caused this inconvenience. It seems that he is unable to say simply, "I'm sorry," and do what he can to remedy the mistake. If we assume that this person is anxious about his acceptance by others and has learned to decrease this anxiety by explanation and self-abasement, the meaning of his speech style becomes clearer. If we find also that he is vague in his descriptions of unpleasant social situations, we may infer that he hesitates to criticize other people. His vagueness avoids the risk of endangering his acceptability by open criticism. At the same time he conforms to the demands of the interview situation by saying something.

Some people weave their excuses into nearly every sentence. They condemn themselves for their remarks and so appear deferential and humble. They say: "I'm probably wrong, but I think Jones will lose." Or, "I shouldn't say this, but Emma is really too fat." Or, "This sounds stupid, but who is Bartok?" The beginning clauses here are efforts to forestall criticism. But why does the speaker continually assume he will be attacked? Is it that he is frightened? Or could it be that he makes harsh judgments about other people's remarks? Of course, people who habitually use these expressions are only dimly aware of them and do not really take them seriously. Imagine what would happen if you agreed with someone who says, "I suppose I'm being silly, but . . . !"

Other people say very little, seem to swallow their words, and hardly move their lips enough for clear enunciation. The interviewer gets the impression that their speech is like an object that they are unwilling to project into their environment. Is this withdrawal of language an anxiety-control device comparable to the physical withdrawal of sitting in a corner? It often seems so. Withdrawal of speech is withdrawal of the person from the risks of social involvement.

Then there are the pedantic speakers, addicted to bookish phrases and big words. They do not go to the store to "buy a few things." They go to "purchase several articles." They do not "talk with friends." They "converse with acquaintances." Can this style of speaking control anxiety? Yes, if the person feels that certain kinds of intellectual achievements confer status or acceptance. This need for intellectual status to get a sense of personal worth is particularly evident when the "bookish" language is studded with words that are incorrectly used or pronounced. Here we may infer a lack of either training or capacity to sustain the erudite level of speech consistently. For other people, this style of speaking serves as a kind of restraint on impulsive reactions. They keep their distance from others and refrain from emotional involvement by using a formal, intellectual speech even when informality and colloquialisms would be more appropriate. Then, too, formality can be hostile, a rebuke to those who are acting "immature."

Narcissistic speakers insert feeling and preference reactions throughout their talk. Almost any topic offers them a chance to express their own appetites and aversions; and these feeling reactions are conveyed by means of superlatives and extreme figures of speech. Thus we may hear, "I had the most glorious time," with the "glo" heavily stressed. Or, "I was simply devastated when I realized what a frightful mistake it was." Dramatic speech of this kind suggests that the speaker needs to hold the center of attention and also that the value of external events depends upon how they affect him. It is one more way of controlling anxiety due to an assumed lack of acceptance by others. In this instance, however, the person demands that acceptance be shown by continuous attention.

Consistency of Personal Style. We have presented sketches of deferential, withdrawn, pedantic, and self-centered ways of talking. Can we say that these qualities of the stream of speech will consistently reflect the same qualities in the person being studied? At first glance, it appears that the answer is yes. Certainly it is hard to imagine that a woman using a dramatic speech style would also dress in sober, ill-fitting clothes and stay on the fringes of a party. But although she is hard to imagine, it is not impossible for her to exist. The point here is that we ought not to expect complete consistency, or what seems consistency to us, in every person.

Some of the consistency in the behavior of the individual must come from the unification of various kinds of behavior by social norms. Implicit social agreement defines what behavior shall be called deferential, intellectual, or religious. As a person comes to value and to use these characteristics, he develops a consistency in accord with the definition he was exposed to. But these definitions vary from group to group, so that different people eventually perceive different things as being deferential or as holding the center of the stage. Two people, for instance, may both try to express their superiority to others in a discussion group. The one does it by talking down all who disagree with him. The other does it by keeping an air of chill reserve.

While adolescent and adult contacts influence the definitions of social characteristics, the initial consistency depends on the way a family labels various actions. For example, consider a person who values "being religious." If his family excluded gambling from their definition of irreligious acts, this person feels no inconsistency in the fact that he both gambles and prays. But an observer who sees gambling as irreligious would regard this person as inconsistent. This example could be paralleled by illustrations of aggressive, affiliative, or masculine behavior that appear inconsistent.

Of course, other factors besides the social norms determine the consistency of personal style. Consistency is probably affected by generalization of learning, economy of effort, the limitations of individual capacity, and the rewards offered by various styles. Then, too, we should not forget that different ways of expressing ourselves may be psychologically equivalent to one other. One device for controlling anxiety may be good enough to make another unnecessary. For example, a woman who controls her status anxiety by dramatic clothing may not need to develop dramatic speech. In that case, we would not find the superficial consistency we hope to find.

The practical implications of our discussion for the clinician are evident. Realizing that consistency and unity of personal expression may be present without being obvious, he tries to be alert to them. But he knows, too, that he should not assume consistency too quickly. He must test his hunches as he investigates the specific conditions in his client's life. He will seek the consistencies that were defined by the conditions of the client's social living, not consistencies as he thinks they ought to be. Approaching the data this way, the clinician is not likely to depend on pat formulas such as "people who talk too much are showing their hostility toward others." Rather, he will recognize that this may be true for some persons; but he will wonder, too, whether overtalking may not be a misguided effort to pacify others, to avoid self-insight, to drain off tension, or even all of these at once.

ILLUSTRATIVE REPORTS

Part of the clinician's notes consists of statements about his observations. Often these notes are made part of the final report, since they are useful in supporting his conclusions. Sometimes these observations disclose the same trends that the clinician infers from his test results or from the client's story. At other times, they help him to interpret his test results more accurately. In order to show you how observations may be summarized, we have chosen some extracts from actual case reports.

A Case of Neurosis. Chalfen (3) studied a nineteen-year-old youth who complained of being depressed and lonely. Before discussing the test performance of this young man, Chalfen describes his behavior: "The patient's anxiety and tension were obvious and pervaded all areas of adaptation. His movements were jerky and overly intense; this resulted in cards being bent and lines being drawn so forcibly that pencils were broken. He perspired visibly and spoke very rapidly. On occasion he would be unable to recall simple words or to pronounce them. Task instructions were anticipated in his eagerness to avoid the distress of awaiting the unknown. Directions had to be specific in order to be meaningful to him" (3, p. 24). Notice that the last three sentences suggest that something more than anxiety is present. Actually, other findings from the study of this individual strongly suggested the possibility of brain damage. Whether or not the possibility would be confirmed by neurological examination, it is clear that his performance is easily disorganized.

Alcoholism. A fifty-five-year-old woman was hospitalized because of periodic alcoholism. Zeichner (17) reports these observations: "The patient was very talkative and generally hyperactive. She was consistently exclaiming about one thing or another in a somewhat histrionic fashion. In describing certain events, she acted them out rather than narrated them. She revealed a lack of self-confidence and made highly self-critical comments. . . . On several occasions, where she encountered difficulty with a task, she complained of physical discomfort and headache" (17, p. 52). The immaturity and self-concern indicated in this description were also reflected in her performance on psychological tests.

Schizophrenia. A twenty-six-year-old woman suffered from delusions and hallucinations. Her behavior during psychological study is reported by Wexler (14):

Initially, the patient was very shy and there was little spontaneous speech. Her voice was very low, frequently trailing off into an inaudible whisper. This was evident particularly when she had to express any kind of aggression such as the refusal to continue considering a Rorschach response. As she became somewhat more familiar with the testing situation, she displayed less tension and verbalized with greater freedom. The challenging character of the tests was reflected in such defensive remarks as "this is silly" or "you need lots of imagination to do this." . . . Occasionally her eyelids would flutter rapidly and the eyeballs would roll back suggesting that she was losing contact with the immediate situation. On the whole, the patient was pleasant, cooperative, relatively trustful, and accepted the testing procedure as a means of helping her (14, p. 18).

In this description, you should note how Wexler has told of the changes that took place during the session and how he points out the specific condition that seemed related to her inaudible speech.

An Engineering Student. Our last sample is taken from a report of the case of Earnst, who was one of a group of subjects studied for research purposes. Earnst was twenty-four, a tall, thin young man who had grown up in the rural Middle West. Although considerable information is given about him in the original report (7), our interest here is confined to the observations made by Eleanor C. Jones during informal conversations. This report differs from our previous examples in its subtlety and its more general scope. She writes:

The air of dogged patience, of tolerant resignation to an economic and emotional incubus, the overwhelming periodic fatigues, and the detached impersonality which at first appear to characterize the general behavior of Earnst are more than a little deceptive. Contrasting with these signs of an overburdened debility, one comes to discover a firmness . . . and an understated, intermittent, but accurate satire, delivered in a subtle mimicry, a few sufficient words or tones—his head resting . . . back against a chair, and just a flicker in his face, as if peace were coming at last in this belated aggression. And in spite of his desperate poverty he exhibits signs of elegance—in two rings, a striped silk muffler folded about his shoulders, the handkerchief arranged with careful negligence, and in his gray spats which, one feels, may serve a triple purpose of adornment, warmth, and a conceivable lack of socks. . . . As he sits with hunched-up shoulders, elevating himself on the toes of his sideways-twisted feet, making scrupulous, tired marks . . . one is further struck by the sudden passionate gesture of his hand to his head, a gesture which starts to be extravagantly expressive but is abruptly checked perhaps through definite control, perhaps through a compulsive regard for the arrangement of his hair. For in his use of the phrase: "I can be quite *top*, if I have to," one feels an evidence of compensation in his luxuriant, deeply wavy, always carefully washed and brushed black hair. He never wears a hat (7, p. 645).

It is worth adding that this report, based on observations in a permissive situation, does not show the aggressiveness and negativism found in Earnst's behavior at other times.

Problem 2. The following dialogue is part of an interview between a physician and a man about fifty years old:

Q: How old are you?
A: Well, I don't know.
Q: What year is this?
A: Is this 1917? I was born October 12, 1874, one Wednesday afternoon at two-thirty P.M. My father and mother kept it in a book.
Q: What year is this?
A: Is this 1917? I don't want to tell you a lie, but I think it is 1923. If that is wrong you can keep it a secret. If it is unsatisfactory for many to know, why, you are my boss. Is this rheumatism I have, Doctor? I guess it is unfavorable to me to smoke, isn't it?
Q: What month is this?
A: I don't know. I cannot write. The month of the year is nothing. All I pray to God is to get well. If God gives me back my normal mind and strength, well and good. If he sees fit to take it away, well and good. I was born October 21, 1874. What this is, I don't know. What if I say this is 1926? Or 1924? (13, p. 244).

The correct answer to the physician's question about the date was 1923. It is clear that the patient is disoriented for time, but there are additional questions to be asked about his speech.

1. Why should the patient tell the date of his birth in answer to a question about the year?

2. What could be the reason for the excessive detail in his statement about his birth?

3. How would you describe the way this patient tries to create a favorable impression on the physician?

4. What kind of disorder is suggested by this speech sample?

Problem 3. The two speech samples given below were transcribed from recordings of actual interviews. One of the interviews was with a person who was excessively meticulous, cautious, and emotionally distant from others. The other interview was with a person who suffered from a phobia, worried a good deal, and was concerned about feelings of hostility.

HAROLD: Somehow or other I have the feeling though that I could definitely forward by my efforts in this one thing, this thing of school, and show to my satisfaction through the usual methods you employ, tests and so forth, that I'm doing the work. . . . I have a feeling that a lot of these problems would, well, not disappear, but the association of similar situations in school and daily life would probably resolve themselves.

MARY [discussing her son]: He's been very, very much afraid of children ever since that. . . . Because before he wasn't like that. He made friends easily, and he was just perfectly normal, but he isn't now, he's afraid of a lot of things. All the kids out there are learning to swim this summer. There's a woman out there who teaches them, and he won't. He's scared to death to do it. And I feel awfully bad about it because he's a boy. I think boys should do these things even more than girls. But you can't hurry a thing like that either. I might just as well wait until he feels he wants to do it.

1. Which person shows the tendency to qualify and revise statements?

2. Which person is the one who is compulsive and emotionally distant from others? What is the basis for your answer?

3. Which person made the following statement? Explain your choice. "I saw *Henry the Fifth.* I saw it twice. I saw it last year when it was here, and I saw it this year. I cannot tell you why, but I think it's the greatest motion picture I've seen since the war was over. I don't know why. I've tried to analyze why—I don't know why. . . . And I don't understand why I became so excited at some of the events that occurred there."

REFERENCES

1. Allport, G. W., & Cantril, H. Judging personality from voice. *J. soc Psychol.*, 1934, **5**, 37–55.
2. Balken, E. R., & Masserman, J. H. The language of phantasy: III. The language of the phantasies of patients with conversion hysteria, anxiety state, and obsessive-compulsive neuroses. *J. Psychol.*, 1940, **10**, 75–86.
3. Chalfen, L. Organic factors in a maladjusted young male. *Case Rep. clin. Psychol.*, 1950, **1** (3 & 4), 24–29.
4. Janney, J. E. Fad and fashion among undergraduate women. *J. abnorm. soc. Psychol.*, 1941, **36**, 275–278.
5. Jourard, S. M. & Secord, P. F. Body size and body-cathexis. *J. consult. Psychol.*, 1954, **18**, 184.
6. Moore, W. E. Personality traits and voice quality deficiencies. *J. speech Disorders*, 1939, **4**, 33–36.
7. Murray, H. A. *Explorations in personality.* New York: Oxford, 1938.
8. Rokeach, M. Studies in beauty. I. Relationship between beauty in women, dominance and security. *J. soc. Psychol.*, 1943, **17**, 181–190.
9. Rotter, J. B. The nature and treatment of stuttering: a clinical approach. *J. abnorm. soc. Psychol.*, 1944, **39**, 150–179.
10. Sanford, F. H. Speech and personality: a comparative case study. *Charact. & Pers.*, 1942, **10**, 169–198.
11. Scheidemann, N. V. *The psychology of exceptional children.* New York: Houghton Mifflin, 1931.
12. Secord, P. F., & Jourard, S. M. The appraisal of body-cathexis: body cathexis and the self. *J. consult. Psychol.*, 1953, **17**, 343–347.
13. Strecker, E. A., & Ebaugh, F. G. *Practical clinical psychiatry.* (5th Ed.) New York: Blakiston Division, McGraw-Hill, 1940.
14. Wexler, M. A diagnostic and therapeutic study of a schizophrenic woman. *Case Rep. clin. Psychol.*, 1951, **2** (2), 16–27.
15. Wood, K. S. Parental maladjustment and functional articulatory defects in children. *J. speech Disorders*, 1946, **11**, 255–275.
16. Wolff, W. *The expression of personality.* New York: Harper, 1943.
17. Zeichner, A. M. Alcoholism as a defense against social isolation. *Case Rep. clin. Psychol.*, 1951, **2** (2), 51–59.

CHAPTER 6

Interviewing: The Report

In the last chapter we pointed out that some inferences about a person can be made from observations during the interview. But we were also reminded that the sample of behavior that the clinician sees is limited and may not be representative of the client's activity in daily living. If we could extend the observations to include larger segments of his life, we should have more reliable grounds for making inferences. If we could observe a client at home, at work, and at play, as he is succeeding and failing, planning and reminiscing, we could understand him better. If, in addition, we could have seen him growing, learning his social roles, acquiring his fears, attitudes, and values, we should feel more confident of our understanding. Such extended observation is rarely possible even for research programs, and it is certainly impossible for the clinician.

As a substitute for extended direct observation, we resort to reports about the client's daily living and the circumstances of his growth and learning. These reports are given by the client himself during the interview. True, reports are sometimes available from other sources: parents, school records, medical files, and the records of various social agencies. Information from these sources is likely to prove valuable even though it is sometimes meager. The time and cost required to obtain records, however, must always be weighed against their probable contribution to settling the issue at hand. In hiring a sales manager, for example, we may not wish to obtain a complete record of the applicant's marks in school, but we may be extremely interested in the way a former employer judged his performance. When people are chosen for military positions of great responsibility, extensive investigation of their reputations and behavior is undertaken. The consequences of a wrong choice for these jobs are so serious that candidates' reports must be verified. In the great majority of cases dealt with in social agencies and in educational and vocational guidance, however, the client's report is the main source of information.

To say that information given in the interview is a substitute for extensive direct observation does not mean that it is an entirely satisfactory substitute. The client's report may be deliberately falsified or unintentionally distorted. Some people can give clearer and more detailed reports than others, perhaps because of their intelligence, their verbal facility, or their training. But this unsatisfactory substitute is better than nothing, better than relying wholly upon our interpretation of the limited behavior sample available to us from observing the client. In most cases, what the client tells us about his history is probably closer to the truth than a history we could construct from our limited observations. Actually, of course, clinicians do not rely completely on the reported history or on their own conjectures. The report of the person under study is sifted and evaluated in the light of what the clinician knows about people, and all the information about the client is used as a background for interpreting specific parts of the report.

AREAS DISCUSSED IN THE INTERVIEW

What kinds of things does a clinician want to know about a client? How does he determine what information is likely to be most useful in predicting future behavior? The answer to these questions depends in part, of course, on what is to be predicted. If we are interested in whether a man will be a good auto mechanic, it is obvious that his experience and training in this work are more significant than the character of his religious training. But if we wish to know whether he will come to work regularly, we should want to know about his health, his ethical standards, and his regularity on past jobs. If we are interested in the further question of his ability to get along with his boss and fellow workers, we need to know about his attitudes toward people and his skill in interpersonal relations. Most of the predictions that interest clinicians concern broad patterns of behavior rather than specific skills or knowledge. Consequently they need information about the client's behavior in many areas of living.

However, in order to answer the questions asked at the beginning of this section, we need to inspect more closely the kind of descriptive formulation a clinician makes about the persons he studies. What he actually arrives at is a set of statements about the capacities, motives, attitudes, and traits of the person under study. All these characteristics are inferred to exist in the person at the time he is being studied. Except for capacity, these characteristics are dispositional features of the person. That is, they are dispositions or tendencies to react in one way rather than another, and they are presumed to be fairly permanent rather than temporary (1, 4). Now, theoretically, it should be possible to infer these dispositions without reference to the past. By means of tests, self-descriptions, and experiments, the existence and intensity of the various dispositions could be determined. This task has been undertaken, in fact, for a few characteristics, such as attitudes and some personality traits. But we do not have means for measuring many important dispositional variables. Moreover, even if the means were available, the results would not tell us how these dispositions affect overt behavior.

The other way to arrive at inferences about the strength of present motives, traits, and attitudes is to study the personal history of the client. Clinicians believe that if they know the kinds of situations faced by the developing person and how he reacted to them, they can infer the presence of certain dispositional variables. On the basis of theory and empirical findings, we think that certain kinds of experiences lead to certain kinds of outcomes. Knowing the treatment of the child, we assume a certain outcome, unless there is strong evidence to the contrary.

An example may clarify the kind of inference we are discussing. A man reports that his father treated him harshly in childhood and gives a few examples. The clinician assumes that the harsh treatment had the common result: hostility toward the father. But the man tells the clinician at another point in the interview that he admires his father and that there is no conflict between them. The clinician now has at least three possible inferences to choose among:

1. The report that the father was harsh is false.

2. The father was harsh and the hostility is present but unrecognized.

3. The father was harsh at one time, but his behavior has since changed enough to minimize the son's hostility.

Further discussion produces two more bits of information: The father is often sarcastic toward his son; and the son is easily irritated by his male supervisor at work. The first fact decreases the probability that 3 is true. The second fact increases the probability of 2, since the clinician is familiar with the phenomenon of displaced hostility. Both facts diminish the probability of 1. The clinician could test the assumption of repressed hostility by finding other instances of undue irritation in the presence of male authority, and by finding that the conditions for repressing hostility (i.e., anxiety) toward the father had been fulfilled.

Significant Areas of Inquiry. We may now rephrase the question that we are trying to answer: "What kinds of information will enable us to determine the important dispositional variables in this personality?" The answer to the question is that the clinician tries to obtain information about the important determinants of acquired motives, attitudes, and traits. These determinants consist of the requirements and conditions of early family living, experiences with age-mates, the nature of the school group, and special events of a traumatic or rewarding character. In addition to the information about the conditions of learning, clinicians infer what attitudes and traits have actually been learned by finding out how the client reacted to certain common problems in living. Thus, the clinician would be interested in symptoms of emotional conflict at various ages, in the job history, and in the quality of the client's social relationships.

Most published outlines for case histories include material of the sort we have just mentioned. Let us systematize the desired information a little by listing some of the areas of inquiry:

A. Family Life and Relationships. What were the dominant values and concerns of the family? How calm or agitated were the lives of the family? How did the parents feel about each other? What actions were punished? Which were rewarded? How did the parents regard and treat the client? Who visited the family? Whom did the family visit? How many children were there in the family? How did they feel about each other? How did the family change with the years? What was the financial status of the family? Were the parents gaining or losing status? What were the outstanding traits of the parents? How does the client feel about the family now?

B. Illness and Accident History. What kinds of illness did the client have? Was he frequently sick? How did the family react to his illness and to the illness of others? Was mother excessively cautious about health, always anticipating serious consequences? Were parents scornful of any physical disability? Did any illness result in lengthy separation of family and client? Were others in the family often ill? Is there a history of minor but recurrent illness appearing at certain times of the year or around times of emotional stress?

Does the client have a history of repeated accidents? What parts of the body were injured? Were there similarities in the circumstances of the accidents? What are the client's attitudes toward his accidents—does he think of them as punishments, as due to the hostility or the neglect of others, or as due to his own shortcomings? Was he a daredevil?

C. School Career. What kinds of schools did the client attend? For how long? What kinds of academic failures and successes occurred? What were the preferred and disliked areas of study? What were the parental attitudes toward school? What level of school achievement was reached by others in the family? What kinds of relationships did the client establish with his teachers? What qualities did he value in his teachers? What kinds of sports, clubs, and other extracurricular activities did he enjoy? Were there any periods of unusually poor or unusually excellent academic performance? How satisfied is the client with his education?

D. Relationships With Peers. Did the client have ample opportunity for social interaction with other children? Was he often rejected? Was he popular? What kinds of relationships does he establish—bully, hanger-on, detached observer, intellectual leader, etc.? What is his conception of a close friend? What does he value in friends? What kinds of people become his friends—intellectuals, religiously oriented, social misfits, handicapped and underprivileged, rebels, thrill-seekers, party-goers, or just people who live nearby? Have the patterns of his social relationships and values undergone any marked changes during growth?

E. Sexual Development. What were his sources of sexual information? How adequate were they? What does the client think his parents' attitudes were? What early sexual experiences did the client have? How did he feel about his sexual development at puberty? What kinds of adolescent sexual exploration occurred? Was there overconcern about masturbation, about sexual adequacy? In the case of female clients, what menstrual difficulties do they have? Was there concern over early or retarded onset of menstruation? Did they choose any particular sorts of people or circumstances in sexual relationships? Is there a history of impotence or frigidity? How satisfying are adult sexual relationships? What is the client's conception of the masculine role? Of the feminine role? Do his role conceptions seem to come completely from his parents, or have they been modified by his contacts with other people?

These five areas of inquiry will be touched in nearly every intensive interview. The questions under each heading are not intended as questions for the interviewer to ask the client; rather they are questions the interviewer should ask himself. Perhaps they can serve to enlarge the scope of your thinking about each area and stimulate further questions of your own.

The areas of inquiry that we have mentioned form only part of the information sought by the clinician. We have deliberately left the outline unfinished in order for you to create some ideas of your own in this next problem:

Problem 1. Four more general topics of interest to the interviewer are listed below. For each one of these, write eight or ten questions which the clinician should consider as he thinks about the lives of the persons he studies.

F. Vocational Interests and Occupational History.

G. Ethical and Religious Beliefs.

H. History of Emotional Conflicts and Symptoms.

I. Conception of Self.

If you were to add one more general area of inquiry in addition to the topics already listed, what would you call it and what would it include?

CONDUCTING THE INTERVIEW

The technique of interviewing is determined by the goal of the interview: to obtain as much relevant information as is possible within the allotted time. Unfortunately, the diagnostic interview has not been studied enough to give us assurance about the best methods for reaching this goal. A good deal of the research on techniques in therapeutic counseling has some bearing on this problem, however, and we shall draw upon that material for some suggestions.

In general psychological terms we can describe the task of conducting an interview as that of arousing motives to talk about significant data and decreasing motives to withhold them. The catch is that the clinician does not know what the significant data are, except in a very general way. And the client, who could give the information, probably does not see its clinical significance. One way in which specialists try to overcome these difficulties is to question the client minutely about all the areas where significant information is likely to be found. That is, they have used the "thorough search" method.

Now, while detailed questioning according to a prearranged scheme can be justified on logical grounds, it has undesirable effects on the motives to give or withhold data. For one thing, it can easily lead the client to assume that the clinician is going to ask questions about everything he wants to know. If, then, some point is not brought up by the clinician, the client is not motivated to call attention to it. It is not uncommon, therefore, for a client to mention a symptom or an interesting biographical detail only after seeing several specialists. When asked to explain why he had not discussed it earlier, he replies, "Nobody asked me any questions about it." In the second place, detailed systematic questioning may actually increase the motivation of many clients to withhold information. Such a procedure smacks a good deal of a cross-examination held for the purpose of establishing guilt. For some clients, it may arouse childhood attitudes of resistance to parental questioning; for others it conveys the impression that they are regarded as a "case." Thus, full communication is hampered.

In a few instances, the very volume of the questions may be interpreted by the client as an index of the clinician's interest in him and his thoroughness and competence. While this feeling may increase the client's cooperation, it may at the same time decrease any sense of responsibility for producing worthwhile additional information.

Decreasing "Communication Anxiety." The "thorough search" method of interviewing is based on an assumption that should be made explicit. This assumption is that clients who seek help are able and willing to give information that the clinician wants. The function of the clinician's questions, then, would be chiefly to guide the client to the relevant topics. We may compare this conception to a classroom examination: the teacher takes for granted the students' willingness to answer the examination. His task is to show them what to discuss. But is it true, after all, that clients, like students, do want to answer the questions put to them by the clinician? Of course it is true; but it is equally true that clients are, in a sense, unwilling to talk. They are unwilling because there are anxieties connected with communication of personal data. And one easy way of decreasing these anxieties is to hold back certain kinds of information.

There are many ways in which anxiety is connected with communication, but we shall mention only four that seem to be common.

1. The client may be anxious about the moral judgment of the clinician and his consequent criticism. Often the client, on the basis of his own feelings of shame and guilt, forecasts a censuring attitude on the part of the clinician and sidesteps information likely to bring on criticism.

2. The client may be anxious about placing information at the disposal of one who could use it harmfully. Giving personal information to another individual is, in a way, giving him power over you. It could be used to destroy friendships, to decrease earning power, or even to invoke the law.

3. The client may be anxious about giving information to the clinician because it will enable the interviewer to "see through" the client and discern "horrible truths" unknown to the client himself. You must remember that a good many people find their own behavior puzzling and fear the unknown forces at work in them.

4. Anxiety may be aroused by bringing up matters which the client customarily avoids thinking about, as a means of defending himself against self-hatred and self-contempt. Answers to questions touching on such areas may be evasive in order that the client can avoid further exploration.

To help you get a feel for the way that communication anxiety appears in an interview, we shall quote from a diagnostic interview reported by Dunbar (2). In this session, a forty-three-year-old woman (P) has been asked by the physician (D) to lie on an examining table. In the early part of the interview she had complained of various pains and of stiffness but denied any worries, any dreams, or any trouble sleeping.

D: You are about as stiff as a marionette, but even marionettes have joints somewhere. Couldn't you relax your arm enough so it would bend at the elbow?

P: It hurts too much.

D: How about the other arm, or one of your legs?

P: Doctor, please don't. I don't mean not to cooperate. They think I don't cooperate, but they don't understand how much it hurts me.

D: Well, then suppose you just let it rest on my hand and see if you can't make it limp. It will really help the pain if you do. . . . Nobody can relax with a clenched fist. It looks as if you wanted to hit somebody.

P: Why, doctor, I would never do anything like that! (Unclenches fist but arm remains stiff.)

At this point the doctor began to talk about puppet shows and wooden soldiers in an effort to distract her. After a short time, however, the patient stiffened again.

P: I wish you wouldn't talk about soldiers.

D: Why?

P: I don't know. I wish you wouldn't keep me lying here.

The doctor suggested that they talk about anything that the patient enjoyed. The conversation and the patient both became more relaxed, but suddenly the patient showed a good deal of anxiety and started to cry.

P: Doctor, you don't know what you are doing to me. I don't know what's coming over me. I feel awful. I feel as though something awful were going to happen. I don't know what I might do.

D: What is it?

P: Oh, I don't know, I don't know. Something terrible. I'm so frightened.

D: Nothing will happen to you. But if you'd feel better just lie down again and you can be as stiff as you like.

P: You must think I'm silly, but you see I feel safer when I'm stiff. My aggravations don't bother me so much. That's why I go to sleep stiff like that, only when I wake up in the morning sometimes I'm so stiff I can hardly get out of bed. But if I weren't stiff I couldn't even go to sleep. (Note how the patient's admission of aggravation slipped out in spite of her previous denial of worries.) [2, pp. 88 f].

In this excerpt we see that the patient's denial of trouble sleeping and of worrying was actually an attempt to avoid an area of discussion that could reveal open emotional disturbance. In the rest of the interview after this break-through, she admitted worrying about her children, hostility toward her husband and mother, and a feeling of despair that had led to a suicidal attempt. A process similar to this one occurs in many diagnostic interviews, although it is not usually so dramatic.

What can the clinician do to decrease the communication anxiety of the client? We are helped in answering this question by the work of "nondirective" or "client-centered" therapists (5, 6). If the interviewer conveys to the client a sense of his acceptance and permissiveness, he reduces the external factors that support the anxiety. That means that the interviewer must be interested without appearing to pry, be warmly responsive without being judgmental, and receptive without being demanding. Verbal reassurance does not necessarily convey this permissive quality. Saying "Now you can tell me anything," is more likely to raise the client's doubts than to allay his anxiety. The interviewer must *demonstrate* that it is safe for the client to talk. He does this by letting the client direct a good deal of the conversation, by keeping the interview calm and unhurried, and by listening sincerely without shocked or disgusted expressions.

It requires a good deal of practice to be able to deal with clients this way, but more than practice is needed. The clinician's motives and attitudes must be the sort to promote permissiveness. Here is the reason: Most of us emit vocal and gestural cues that partially reveal our feelings. You have heard voices that express impatience or a patronizing manner even when the speaker thinks he is hiding his feelings. It is a difficult task to control these cues, and if the clinician is successful he will probably seem cold and distant to a client. Consequently an interviewer who is basically a moralizer or an autocrat is likely either to reveal himself or to appear forbidding. Both outcomes fail to reduce communication anxiety. But interviewers who are actually permissive do not need to try controlling their gestural and vocal expression; they can devote their attention to the interview.

Opening the Interview. With this conception of the interviewer's task, that of building an atmosphere to make communication easy, we can inspect some specific things to do in an interview. First, how can we start the interview?

There are always a few preliminaries between the clinician and the client before the former gives the signal that the interview is starting. Usually there is a greeting, sometimes shaking hands, an indication of the location of the interview room, and an invitation to sit down. General standards of courtesy govern this interchange as they would when receiving any visitor into an office. The first few sentences, too, often consist of the same kind of conversation that you would initiate with a guest: an inquiry as to any difficulty in finding the office, a comment on the weather, regrets at having kept him waiting a few moments, helping him dispose of his wraps, etc. But there is no point in prolonging this initial phase of the conversation. The client needs a signal to know when the interview proper has begun. It is up to the clinician to furnish this signal without undue delay.

Most interviews begin by focusing the discussion on the client's interest in the professional contact—"the presenting problem" as it is sometimes called. The interviewer may say: "What was it that you wanted to see me about?" Or, "You told me over the phone that you'd been upset lately. Could you tell me more about that?" Or, "Was there something in particular that you wanted to talk over with me?" These questions serve as clear signals without delimiting the area of discussion and without sounding accusatory.

Problem 2. Inspect some other opening questions to see whether you find them satisfactory. Write a comment on each of the following signals for beginning, telling what effects they may have on clients.

    1. Could you tell me what kinds of troubles you have?

    2. How did you happen to decide you would like to talk with me?

    3. Why do you think you would like to talk to a psychologist?

    4. I was wondering whether you would like to tell me what kind of a situation you're facing?

Occasionally a client will refer to a personal-history blank that has been filled out and say, "Well, it's all down on that paper I filled out for you." Or, when a relative made the initial contact with the clinician, the client may reply to the opening question with: "I thought my wife explained that to you." In such cases, the clinician simply points out that he would like to have the story in the client's own words or in more detail. He can also choose some point mentioned by the relative or written in the personal-data blank and ask for further clarification of it.

The Presenting Problem. Once the client is launched on the problem that brought him to seek professional help, let him continue unchecked. You will want to hear how he spontaneously formulates his symptoms, how seriously he regards them, and how he relates them to his life circumstances. You will also be interested in the sequence in which the various phases of his problem are discussed. Quite commonly clients will begin by discussing a specific symptom such as inability to make decisions, inability to concentrate, shyness, or worry. As they talk about this symptom with no interruption they bring in other symptoms and often begin to discuss broad problems of human relationships.

This phase of free talk is extremely important to the clinician for several reasons. In the first place, he needs to get a clear picture of the significant problems that confront the client. If he jumps into the conversation soon after the first symptom is mentioned, he runs the risk of losing important information which comes during the broadening phase of the client's statements. Suppose that a client mentions irritability. If the clinician begins to question the client about the precise behavior he shows when irritable, about the times when it occurs, or about the people that seem to be the targets of his irritability, he tends to "freeze" the discussion to that point. Unwittingly he conveys the notion that he is quite interested in this symptom, that it is important, that a good deal of attention should be devoted to it. Now all these things may be true, but there will be time later for more discussion. During this early stage, it is better to let the client show us what *he* thinks is important and what interconnections *he* sees.

A second reason why the clinician should restrain his participation in this phase is that it gives him an excellent opportunity to convey to the client the importance of what the client is saying. Sincere listening strengthens the client's motive to talk and decreases the feeling of being a "case" to be dissected. It also establishes an atmosphere that makes transition to psychotherapy an easy matter, if that should be required.

Occasionally, of course, some clients will stick close to a few symptoms, then ask for a remedy without broadening their statements. Here the clinician may move the discussion along by asking the client to tell more about how and when he first noticed the trouble, or what he has already done to cope with it. Sometimes a productive discussion follows when the clinician asks: "These things you've told me about seem to be the things that bother you most. Are there other things that cause you trouble, even though they don't seem so big?" The main point in all these remarks is to avoid cutting off the discussion of the presenting problem too soon.

Now we are ready to look at a transcription of this phase in a diagnostic interview. A relative had made an appointment for a thirty-three-year-old woman. The following interview took place after the clinician had welcomed his patient into his office and the two were seated.

C: Your [relative] didn't go into much detail about what you wanted to talk about, so I wonder if you'd just start in at wherever you want to start in with, and tell me what kind of nervousness you have.

P: Well, it's, uh, I think if I were just to put it in, in a few words, it seems to be a, a, a complete lack of self-confidence in, and an extreme degree of self-consciousness. Now, I have always been a very self-conscious person. I mean every, just about, since I was probably fourteen years old the first I remember of it. But for a long time I've realized that I was sort of using people as crutches. I mean I, a lot of things that I felt I couldn't do myself I did all right if someone was along.

Notice that although the complaint is a common one, self-consciousness, the last sentence suggests that it is not the usual variety. The clinician here remarked, "Um-hm," and let the patient go ahead:

P: And it's just progressed to the point where I'm actually using the four walls of the house as an escape from reality. I mean I don't—I don't care to go out. I, I certainly can't go out alone. . . . It's a sort of vicious circle. I find out I can't do it, and then I'm sure the next time I can't do it.

C: Um-hm.

P: And it just gets progressively worse. I think the first that I ever noticed it when, I, I'm a nurse, and that must have been shortly after I was married, I've been married twelve years, that I first noticed it. And at that time it was a feeling of, oh, of lacking confidence in myself and, and in my work. I mean I felt it within myself, it never, there never was any criticism of my work.

And then I began, I got to the point where I began feeling so terribly sorry for people and, and, ah, taking responsibility upon myself. And you can't do that when you're a nurse. I mean you've got to feel it sort of objectively, I think, because you do meet up with so much tragedy. But the first time I noticed it was a patient that, that wasn't, I knew he wasn't going to get well. And he had a family who were very naive and kept hoping for the best. And that was sort of a horrible situation. And, and at that time I began to, oh, my hands were sort of shaky and I just, I felt then maybe it was something physical and I was tired out. And I, then it, I could always push it aside when I had that feeling. And I'd get dizzy and my heart would pound and feel I was going to faint. But I could, I still could manage to go around by myself and push this feeling away. And then, ah, my father died . . . and I felt it a good deal more after his death. And then a year after he died . . . [I went] downtown one day and got into an elevator and had this awful feeling. I mean just, I was in the back of the elevator and it was as if everybody was just pushing back against you and you can't get your breath. And that I was going to faint. And so I got out of the elevator and walked downstairs. I was way up at the top of the store. I felt I couldn't do that again, and that, since then, that's been just the last time I've attempted anything alone.

In this excerpt we find the description of the symptoms changing from a lack of self-confidence to a frank anxiety attack. Without requesting specific information, the clinician is told the duration of the condition, the patient's occupation, the length of her marriage, the fact of her father's death, and the events that led to her refusal to go places by herself. But perhaps more important than any of these items is the hint that her relationships with her family have some connection with her anxiety. Is it purely coincidence that she dates the onset of her problem at a time shortly after her marriage? Why was she so disturbed by the naïve family of a patient who was mortally ill? And is it significant that she uses the date of her father's death as a point of reference for dating the elevator episode? At this stage the interviewer does not know the answers to these questions, but he asks them of himself anyway.

Later on in the interview the clinician asked the patient what her own ideas were as to the basis for her distress. She spontaneously suggested that since she began having these feelings shortly after her marriage, she thought they could be related to her husband in some way. This statement added weight to the clinician's own hunches and sensitized him to further information about the husband.

The Middle of the Interview. The opening and the discussion of the presenting problem may take only ten to fifteen minutes. At about this time, the clinician will probably make a judgment as to how the rest of the interview time should be spent. He may feel it best to continue placing the responsibility for the direction of the interview largely on the client. The interview would then go ahead in much the same way as in the excerpt you have just read. Some of the conditions that would influence the clinician to adopt this method are:

1. Plenty of time is available for the interview, perhaps an hour and a half to two hours.

2. A further interview with the client is planned.

3. The interview will probably be the first of a series of therapeutic interviews with the clinician. In this case the diagnostic and therapeutic aspects of the interview are concurrent and not separated.

4. The client spontaneously produces a good deal of relevant information.

5. The client is somewhat fearful or resentful of psychological procedures. In this instance, a leisurely interview with little pressure from the clinician may help establish sufficient rapport for future testing or more systematic history-taking.

6. The clinician is not required to obtain systematic information about the client for records or reports to his superior.

With other clients, the clinician may decide to use the middle of the interview for a semisystematic survey of the case history. We shall describe this approach shortly, but essentially it involves directing the conversation into the major areas of inquiry listed earlier in this chapter. Clinicians are likely to use this second method when:

1. Less than an hour is available for the interview.

2. They do not anticipate a therapeutic relationship with the client.

3. No further opportunity to obtain a personal history will be available.

4. Specific, systematic information is required which is not likely to provoke anxiety in the client. This situation frequently occurs in connection with routine screening of applicants, admissions to institutions, or induction of men into military service. Ordinarily these do not require information for detailed and subtle personality evaluations.

5. The interview is being held to determine an appropriate referral for the client, that is, what kind of agency or service he needs.

6. The client seems persistently unwilling to talk unless guided by the clinician.

7. The client did not voluntarily seek out the clinician for personal help. In a number of clinical situations, clients are involuntary. They have no pressure to talk beyond what is generated by the requirements of the circumstances.

In determining how the middle interview shall proceed, then, the clinician must rely heavily upon his knowledge of the circumstances of the interview and its purposes, and upon his estimate of the productivity of each particular client. We should not think, however, that the choice between a client-guided and a clinician-guided interview is sharp and clear. Many times, the clinician brings in a question aimed at opening a new area of inquiry and then lets the client handle this discussion in his own fashion. Or, at the end of a client-guided interview, the clinician may find that certain necessary data have not been obtained; then he will ask specific questions in order to elicit this information.

If the clinician chooses to let the client guide the interview, how shall he proceed? What can he do to assist the client to communicate his pressing concerns, his conception of the important qualities of his life, his feelings about his own history? Roughly there are three main kinds of responses that he can use: signaling understanding, requests for elaboration, and reflection of feeling.

In signaling understanding, the clinician simply indicates that he is clear about what is being said. Instances of this kind are: "I see," "Um-hm," "Yes," and "I understand what you mean." He does not interrupt a client's story to make such remarks; they are useful when the client pauses or seems not to know what to say next.

Requests for elaboration may be used when the client seems to have run out of material or when he is blocked. They are questions that urge him to continue: "Can you tell me more about that?" "How do you mean?" "I'm not sure I see what happened." "How did you feel about that?"

In reflecting feeling, the clinician makes a statement that expresses his understanding of the client's feeling. It may express a feeling that the client had during some episode he is reporting. The clinician may say: "You must have been pretty mad," "You felt down in the dumps," or "Then you were sure no one cared much for you." On the other hand, the clinician may express feelings which the client seems to be having during the interview. Suppose that a client hesitates, haltingly tells about a disturbing experience, and finally becomes silent. The clinician may help him continue by saying: "It's hard to talk about that, isn't it?" Or suppose a client has been severely criticizing a member of his family, finally says that he shouldn't be talking this way, and lapses into silence. The clinician may reply: "Perhaps you wish you didn't feel this way about him." Many reflecting statements must express both sides of some ambivalent feeling that the client is struggling with: "You don't want to divorce her, but you can't stand living with her either."

Notice that all these remarks show that the clinician is listening and considering what the client is saying. They show freedom to talk without defining what is to be discussed. They are ways of telling the client: "What you say is important, and I am trying to understand you." Though they may seem simple, they depart radically from the kind of conversational interaction that the client usually has. He fights no battle to get a chance to talk, and doesn't have to listen to someone else's boring tale so that his own interesting story can be told!

Problem 3. This problem is designed to help you become sensitive to the interactions that occur in conversation. You are to listen to three or four conversations on buses, in lounges, or among your friends. These conversations need not be long—three or four minutes is enough. Choose one of the speakers for special attention and listen to his remarks with the following crude classification in mind:

Types of Conversational Reactions
1. Those meant to draw out the other person: questions, etc.
2. Those that express sympathy or pity
3. Those that are critical or that disagree with the other person
4. Those that are attempts to get sympathy
5. Those that are meant to impress the other person with the speaker's adequacy, knowledge, strength, patience, etc.
6. Those that neglect or overlook the other person: irrelevant remarks or monologue continuations of the speaker's own story

Immediately after each conversation, make notes on what you have heard and answer these questions:

1. Did the speaker spend much of his time drawing out the other person?
2. What was his most common type of conversational reaction?
3. What did the speaker do, if anything, that made it easy for the other person to talk? Was it effective?

Ending the Interview. As the time for the interview runs out, the clinician must assess the tasks remaining and allow time to finish them. He may find, for instance, that he needs special information about the client's health history or about his history of arrests and convictions. Sometimes he will decide that the client should be referred to another specialist for further diagnosis or treatment. In such cases he will allow time to discuss the referral with the client. In some clinical settings the client will need information about the next steps to be taken in the disposition of his case; or perhaps he will need to be told about further actions he himself must take. It is usually good practice, therefore, for a clinician to indicate that the interview will come to a close shortly and to introduce any special topics he feels ought to be considered. He may say, "We have only a little time left, and I wondered if we could talk for a while about . . ."—and here the clinician introduces the topic.

In addition to giving the clinician time to deal with important matters, signaling the fact that the interview will soon end has two other consequences: it diminishes a sense of abruptness—of being shoved out of the office, and it puts time pressure on the client to bring up significant matters he may have been holding back. Material produced by the client at the end of an interview often seems to be particularly valuable and revealing. This phenomenon is probably due to the fact that communication anxiety is decreasing throughout the interview and is at a low ebb in its final stages. If we add pressure to talk by way of a time warning, motives thus aroused aid communication of difficult or emotionally loaded information.

Clients often expect some definite statement from the clinician at the end of an interview. They may wish to know what he thinks of them, or what is going to happen to them next, or what the clinician is going to do with the information he has been given. Generally, the clinician ought to try to meet these expectations if he can do it in a way that is compatible with the client's welfare. For example, he may say the information the client has given will be made part of the client's file, or that it will be discussed with the specialist who referred him to the clinician. He may feel that the client needs to be reassured that the interview information will remain confidential. Often he cannot tell the client exactly what will happen next, but he can point out that the interview has provided information that will make better decisions possible. The clinician must be careful not to commit himself to a position he is not willing to defend later, nor to give the impression that he is so committing himself. Sometimes the clinician will have to say that he is sorry he cannot give a clearer answer, but that he cannot give the kind of information requested by the client.

The inexperienced clinician finds particular trouble in answering direct questions about his impression of the client. Suppose that he has conducted an interview to get a general picture of the personality of an applicant seeking a government or industrial position. Toward the close of the interview, the applicant asks the clinician to state frankly his impression of the applicant's personality. How can the clinician reply without seeming evasive or without appearing to recommend the applicant? A useful guide in such cases is to follow the principle of discussing matters that the client has talked about and to refrain from dealing with the clinician's inferences. The clinician may say, "Well, you seemed to feel that you were doing pretty well on your job and you seem to handle it without much trouble. On the other hand, you didn't feel that your family life was running along in the way you'd like. I was wondering whether that was a kind of strain on you." Here the clinician has picked out points stated by the client himself and has simply placed them together without any effort to reveal causal factors. The clinician may sense that this man is quite hostile toward his wife, but he also realizes that no useful purpose would be served by bringing up this matter. Actually, the kind of statement we have just quoted is often very satisfying to clients, may result in a fuller expression of feelings about the problem, and does not put the clinician in the position of having to defend his judgment.

When the interview time has expired, the clinician should say so. It is his responsibility to help the client make the transition out of the interview situation as well as to make the transition into it. The clinician shows the interview is over by referring to it in the past tense: "It *has been* interesting to talk with you. I hope *you* have enjoyed it, too." He may also signal closing by putting down his notes or by changing his posture. Ordinarily the clinician will rise and open the door for the client, while thanking him for coming. If the client can leave with a feeling that he has been treated with interest and consideration, the way has been prepared for further interviews, either diagnostic or therapeutic.

METHODS IN SEMIDIRECTED INTERVIEWING

Earlier in this chapter, we pointed out that some clinicians must interview clients who have not voluntarily sought help. A psychologist in the armed forces may be asked to assess men awaiting court-martial, a college counselor may routinely see students who are failing, or an industrial psychologist may interview junior executives as part of a manpower-resources survey planned by top management. In such circumstances, many interviewees are motivated to talk only by the instructions they have been given by their superiors. Moreover, they may perceive the interviewer as a threatening prober, allied with powerful figures in the organizational structure. Persons who make such estimates of the interviewer are strongly motivated to withhold information. These conditions are obviously not favorable for client-directed interview methods. To rely largely on the client for the selection and sequence of topics is to invite a good deal of carefully chosen, irrelevant material into the interview. The clinician may be able to infer the anxiety or contempt which motivates the client's evasion, but he probably learns very little more. Direction of the interview by the clinician is likely to result in more relevant information in these cases.

Some Assumptions about Interviewing the Involuntary Client. We have tried to show, in a general way, that clients who are sent to an interview are motivated differently from those who come because of personal distress. Now we shall propose some assumptions which can be useful when dealing with involuntary clients.

1. Communication is favored by the client's desire to appear cooperative. This principle implies that, although the client may be reluctant to give information, he usually cannot risk appearing too stubborn and resistant. To meet this motivational conflict, he must take a middle way:

give the minimal information requested. Thus, in these cases, an interviewer must take more responsibility for requesting the amount and kind of data to be communicated. Of course, sometimes the client loses little or nothing by being noncooperative; then the motivation to talk is extremely weak. In educational and industrial interviewing, however, the desire to appear cooperative or to satisfy one's boss helps the interviewer.

2. Reported data tend to be biased toward gaining a maximum advantage for the interviewee in the situation as he understands it. Thus, he will attempt to create a favorable impression on both the interviewer and the authorities to whom the interviewer reports. If the interviewer does not disclose his own values and preferences, the interviewee can hardly decide what kind of bias is appropriate. In this kind of interviewing, then, the questioning must be done so that the interviewer's preferences are vague, and significant questions seem innocuous. If topics do not appear to be related to the immediate reason for the interview or if the questions do not have an obviously "good" answer, biased reporting will probably decrease.

3. Reduction in bias is aided by the involuntary client's desire to appear consistent. People do not want it known that they are giving distorted accounts of their history. Intentional distortion must be introduced so that it does not conflict with other parts of the total story. In order to decrease the chances for inconsistency, the client will omit some details and enhance the significance of others. The interviewer can take advantage of the desire to appear consistent by making a thorough coverage of a number of different topics. As the amount of communicated material increases, it becomes harder for the client to bias his report without appearing inconsistent.

4. If the anxiety of the client can be decreased in the course of the interview, useful and significant information will be obtained more easily toward the close of the interview period. While the interviewer has little control over anxiety that stems from the reasons for the interview, he can reduce the anxiety that arises from the client's expectation of being treated harshly and critically. In addition, the client often becomes interested in the story of his own life as it unfolds, and he lapses from the cautious attitude he adopted at the start of the interview. The interviewer can assist this development by a friendly, considerate manner and by showing that he understands the client's feelings. He can employ the methods for signaling understanding and for reflecting feeling that were mentioned in the discussion of the client-guided interview.

We are now ready to consider some of the specific techniques that may be used in a semidirected interview.

Sequence of Topics. It is best to begin the interview with a request for information of a routine sort. Age, occupation, marital status, and similar orienting data are likely to be considered routine and nonthreatening by the client. Then the clinician may take up either the educational history or the occupational history. The client usually feels competent to report about these matters, and he does not usually think they reveal intimate facts. The recreational interests and social relationships (hobbies, clubs, friends) can be investigated next. Following this topic, the interviewer can make a fairly sharp break in the flow of conversation and proceed to the health history. During this discussion, it may be appropriate to introduce material relating to the emotional problems of the client and his sexual development. Information about the parents and the client's feelings about them may be taken up next, and this topic can naturally lead to a discussion of the client's own marriage or marital plans. In educational and industrial settings, it is appropriate to end the interview by a discussion of the client's future plans and aspirations. In other settings, the end of the interview may be devoted to consideration of the specific problem that brought about the interview. Obviously, flexibility is desirable, and the clinician should depart from this suggested sequence whenever he feels it wise. If you have had only a little interviewing experience, you may want to use the suggested sequence as a guide until you feel comfortable in the role of interviewer.

Transitional Questions. In opening a new topic, you can avoid abruptness by relating it to the topic that has just been discussed. You can also be helpful by opening with a question that is specific enough to give some guidance to the client. In making a transition from a discussion of schooling to the topic of occupation, you may say: "Did you do any part-time work while you were in school? Or work during your vacations?" On the other hand, if you want to lead into the area of social and recreational interests, you may say: "What kinds of sports and club activities did you like in school?" The topic is developed, then, by considering the chronological development of his interests up to the present.

If the topic has been health and emotional status, you may shift to talk of parents and early family life in this way: "We have been talking about your own health; can you tell me something about the health of your mother and father?" This topic can then be expanded to cover the client's attitudes toward his parents, his description of his early home life, his relations with siblings, his perception of his parents' marital relationship, and his current connections with his home.

In order to open the way for a client to discuss his own marriage, the clinician may remind him of what has been said about his own recreational interests and then ask: "What sorts of things do you and your wife like to do together?" Or he may ask for a comparison of the client's marriage with that of the client's parents: "How would you say you and your wife get along as compared with the way your own parents got along?"

QUESTIONING TECHNIQUES

There are a number of ways in which questions may be related to the context of other questions. Nearly all of these can be used at some time or other in an interview. They serve slightly different purposes, and the clinician must estimate which technique will serve his purpose best.

Narrowing. The principle in this type of questioning is to begin with a very broad question and follow with more detailed questions. It is generally a safe method to use in many situations, but is especially valuable when the clinician wants to discover the salient and spontaneous attitudes of the client. The formula for beginning is: "Tell me something about . . ." Thus the question may be: "Tell me something about how you got along with your parents when you were young." The client may answer with a general statement and then talk mostly about his relationship with his mother. The clinician may then narrow the discussion somewhat by asking: "Can you tell me more about you and your father?" This question can be followed later by: "What seemed to be the main cause of the trouble between you two?" Ordinarily the clinician will need to get more and more specific as the client's reluctance to discuss the matter increases. Narrowing gives the client a good deal of opportunity to bias his remarks in the opening phase of the topic, but he finds it harder to maintain the distortion as the questions become more detailed.

Progression. This method consists in beginning a line of questioning with a matter near to the one you wish to learn about and then following with questions that lead progressively to the specific point. It differs from narrowing in that the sequence of questions is arranged to progress from less intimate to more intimate matters rather than from broad to specific questions. Suppose that the clinician wishes to learn whether an eighteen-year-old boy has had sexual intercourse, and he believes that a direct question on this matter would meet with resistance. He arranges his questions in a progression:

"About how many dates do you have a week?"
"Where do you like to go on dates?"
"What kinds of girls do you like to go with?"
"Do many of the girls object to necking or petting?"
"Have you ever worried about getting the syph or the clap from any of them?"
"Why," or "Why not?"

In this illustration the final question is an indirect one which is ostensibly about worries. The progression prepared the way for a possibly threatening question by starting with a relatively nonthreatening series. Progression serves to introduce questions which would otherwise appear too blunt and perhaps shocking.

Embedding. This method is designed to conceal a significant question. The important question is preceded and followed by a series of questions that appear routine. The significant question is made to seem only one more detail to be explored. Here is an illustration in which the clinician was interested in the client's sexual life but did not wish to reveal this interest.

"Have you ever had trouble with your eyes or vision?"
"What about eating, appetite, or stomach trouble?"
"Anything connected with sex organs or sex activity?"
"How about trouble sleeping or getting to sleep?"
"Any skin trouble?"
"How about your legs and back?"

Here the questions are asked in such a way as to give the impression of a routine examination in which one item is about as important as any other.

Leading Questions. Sometimes the clinician realizes that a direct question will provide a clear cue as to the expected answer. He may then wish to ask questions which assume the opposite answer and see whether the client denies the assumption. For example, in interviewing supervisors in industry the clinician often wants an estimate of the interviewee's use of alcohol. A direct question on this point such as: "How much do you drink?" may lead to a biased answer if the interviewee believes that the clinician or the company opposes drinking. The clinician may ask instead: "What do you like to drink at a party?" and "About how many can you hold?" The implication here is that the clinician expects some drinking and that his main concern is tolerance for alcohol. Clearly such questions are to be cautiously used. They are safe only when there is good reason to suspect a strong bias to avoid a particular kind of answer.

Holdover Questions. Often the story told by a client raises certain questions in the interviewer's thinking, but he decides to ask them later in the interview. The clinician may feel that the question would be more appropriate in another context, that it would reveal his own interests if asked when it first arose, or that better rapport will yield a less biased answer later. Here is an example of a holdover question that changes its impact because of a new context:

Early in an interview a client reports that he got into trouble and left school in the tenth grade. He shows no inclination to talk about the nature of the trouble, so the clinician holds the question until later. During the section of the interview devoted to discussing family relationships the clinician says: "You mentioned a little while ago that you left school because you got into trouble. What did your parents say about that?"

If this question does not reveal the details of the trouble, the clinician may now inquire about it directly. The topic has been moved from the area of education into the area of home background in the hope that it will seem less threatening there.

Projective Questions. While it is common for clients to pass judgment on themselves and other people during the interview, we sometimes want to get a clearer picture of evaluative attitudes. We want to find out what standards the client applies to men as compared with women, his conceptions of authority and of support. Projective questions are designed to elicit material about these matters. Among the simplest of projective questions are those asking for descriptions of people. We may ask: "Tell me about the best boss and the worst boss you ever had. What kind of people were they?" Or we may ask a married person: "What are the qualities that your wife (or husband) has that made you want to marry her (or him)?" A variant is: "Think of your friends and pick the one that you feel is your best friend. Now, without telling me his name, tell me what it is about him that makes you admire and like him so much."

In listening to the answers to these questions, the clinician will be trying to answer some questions of his own about the client's remarks:

1. Does he give me a rich or meager description?

2. Are the traits and characteristics he picks superficial or do they show penetrating insights?

3. Does he list vague, conventional generalities (nice, good, friendly) or can he go beyond this level?

4. Are the desirable qualities of people he likes indicative of his ideals for himself?

5. To what extent does he value characteristics that reflect tendencies to moralizing or repression? For example, "My friend never says a bad word about anyone, and I've never known anyone who was so clean-minded."

6. Assuming the descriptions to be somewhat correct, what does the choice of such a person show about the needs of the client? Does he like those who permit him to dominate them, or to be dependent? Does he want approval, stimulation, entertainment, or someone to make his decisions?

Another question of this kind arouses emotional conflict in many people: "What are your strong points as a person and what are your weak points? I don't expect you to be modest in answering this." It is fascinating to see how some people avoid the first half of the question and others avoid the latter half. Even with additional reassurance that "in this situation it is perfectly all right to tell me what you believe are your assets and good points," submissive or overconventional people will protest that it is not up to them to make such remarks. Answers to this question complement those about friends and spouse, since they reveal something of insight into oneself as contrasted with insight into other people.

In *The Authoritarian Personality*, Levinson reports the use of eight projective questions which can be scored according to a scheme designed to get at authoritarian ideology. While these questions may be useful in special clinical situations, some of those which he considered promising but did not use may be of more general interest (3, p. 545). Among those he mentions are:

"What do you find most disgusting?"
"As a parent, what would you try most to instill in your child?"
"What would you protect your child against?"
"Why might a person commit suicide?"

Problem 4. A man was applying for a job in the personnel department of an industrial firm. The job required interviewing applicants and serving as a member of a committee to deal with grievances. During the interview, the prospective personnel man was asked to describe those qualities about his wife which made him prefer her to other girls he had known. After a little thought, he replied: "Well, outside of being nice and all that, I'd say it was because she was a good cook, and she wasn't high-hat, and she was a virgin." Can you make any inferences about this man's insight into others' and about his own needs?

INTERVIEWER ANXIETY

Studying information about interviewing methods may have an unfortunate effect upon you if you are a beginning interviewer. You are likely to take the information as a set of rules to be strictly followed and to measure yourself by them during the conduct of an interview. This kind of attitude is almost certain to make your interviewing more awkward and tiring than it need be. Actually, you will have to build your own interviewing style gradually. You will need to try out suggested methods critically, assimilating some and rejecting or modifying others. But the most important thing you can do in interview practice is to be aware of your anxiety and its effects. Probably the anxiety of the interviewer is responsible for more interviewing difficulty than his lack of technical know-how. While your anxiety cannot be eliminated, it may be reduced to a manageable level by understanding and recognizing it.

Causes of Interviewer Anxiety. The very fact of inexperience in a new skill causes some apprehension. A person may do a fine job of interviewing when he is talking with a friend, but he becomes tense when his conversation is called "interviewing." This normal tension is increased in students who have persisting doubts about their own ability; then the interview becomes a test of their own worth instead of a chance to get to know the client.

For other students, the client's power to withhold and distort information looms large. They become tense because they fear that the client will not cooperate. If that happens, they may have to face an unfavorable evaluation by a supervisor or instructor. Or they may have to reckon with their own stern standard of "getting everything right the first time."

Some of you will feel fairly comfortable until you reach an area of inquiry which is normally (in our society) not discussed. Then you may fear that you will offend the client and become timid and halting. If you feel this way early in an interview, it may be better to avoid that area or touch it superficially for the time being. Clients have enough trouble talking about some things without having their own difficulty magnified by a tense interviewer.

Some of you may feel a strong sense of responsibility to be immediately helpful to the client, and this may lead to overeagerness. You ought to be reminded that not everything has to be finished off in one session. If you think of your task as one of helping the client to say what he can and of making it easy for him to return if necessary, your job will be easier.

Effects of Interviewer Anxiety. While anxiety lessens the sensitivity and narrows the creative formulations of the interviewer, it also brings about some undesirable overt behavior. The common fault of overtalking is due to the interviewer's tension. He may feel that he must keep something happening every moment. Even short periods of silence will be acutely uncomfortable. Other interviewers try to control their apprehension by going out of their way to try to make the client feel at home. They may offer excessive reassurance, profuse apologies for certain questions, or repeated assurances of friendliness. Clients are more likely to be put on guard by these efforts than to be reassured by them.

Some mannerisms are traceable to tension. A constant smile may be the outward mark of a painful effort to be permissive at any cost. And the recurrent knitted brow may signal a desperate try at communicating interest and seriousness to the client. Occasionally, interviewers try to conceal their fears by assuming an air of "the expert who is penetrating mysteries." They will look sidewise at the client, lift their eyebrows as if to question, and murmur "um-hmmm" so as to leave no doubt that they have found out deep secrets.

Even worse than these mannerisms are techniques which arouse feelings of guilt or worthlessness in the client. There may be disguised belittling: under the cloak of expertness, the interviewer keeps pointing out inconsistencies in the client's story or making disparaging value judgments about the client's actions or attitudes. Or the anxious interviewer may try to discipline the client, to lecture him, and to point out the need for strict honesty and serious attention to the matter at hand. Both of these techniques permit the interviewer to cling to the fiction of his superiority and to blame the client when things go badly.

Effectively Reducing Anxiety. Experience in interviewing is the best way to reach a more comfortable feeling during an interview. But there are a few things you can do while learning. For one thing, notice where and when you become tense or anxious during interviews. Find out, if you can, what method you use to control the tension. Do you become rigid, talkative, resentful, or something else? Merely learning what you do will help you find out whether it is likely to disturb good interviewing.

Another thing you can do to decrease your tension is to recognize that actually most people have strong motives to talk about themselves. You can sharpen your awareness of this fact by listening to ordinary social conversations and hearing how people are trying to communicate their interests, attitudes, hopes, fears, and plans. Imagine yourself as unblocking barriers to this communication in the interview rather than as a cross-examiner.

You will get more help from practice interviewing than from anything else. If you have done very little interviewing before, you will find it easier if you get the assistance of a friend or another student and set up a practice interview.

Problem 5. Arrange at least one practice interview. Tell your "client" that you want some practice and explain that you are not going to analyze him or give advice. Choose any or all of these three areas for the interview: educational history, occupational history and vocational interests, and social and recreational activities. Assume that your "client" has asked for an interview to discuss his occupational plans—either to confirm or to formulate them. After the interview, both of you should answer the questions on the following brief evaluation forms.

Interview Evaluation Questions

For the client:

1. How easy was it for you to talk in this situation? Very easy _____ Moderately easy _____ Rather difficult _____

2. In which part of the interview were you most uncomfortable? First part _____ Middle _____ Toward the end _____

3. How much of the time did the interviewer seem very much interested in what you were saying? All _____ Most _____ About half _____ Less than half _____

4. Did you feel that the interviewer was pushing you to talk? Most of the time _____ Occasionally _____ Not at all _____

5. Did the interviewer seem to know what he was doing? Very well _____ Moderately well _____ Somewhat confused _____

For the interviewer:

1. How easy was it for your client to talk in this situation? Very easy _____ Moderately easy _____ Rather difficult _____

2. In which part of the interview were you most uncomfortable? First part _____ Middle _____ Toward the end _____

3. How much of the time were you interested in what the client was saying? All _____ Most _____ About half _____ Less than half _____

4. Did you feel you had to push the client to talk? Most of the time _____ Occasionally _____ Not at all _____

5. Did you feel you knew what you were doing? Very well _____ Moderately well _____ Somewhat confused _____

After these two evaluation forms are filled out independently, the interviewer and client should compare their ratings and discuss the differences in their perceptions. Further points that come to mind should be discussed to help the interviewer understand more clearly how he was functioning.

REFERENCES

1. Allport, G. W. *Personality: a psychological interpretation.* New York: Holt, 1937.
2. Dunbar, F. *Psychosomatic diagnosis.* New York: Hoeber, 1943.
3. Levinson, D. J. Projective questions in the study of personality and ideology. In T. W. Adorno and others. *The authoritarian personality.* New York: Harper, 1950.
4. Murray, H. A. *Explorations in personality.* New York: Oxford, 1938.
5. Rogers, C. R. *Client centered therapy.* New York: Houghton Mifflin, 1951.
6. Snyder, W. U. Warmth in nondirective counseling. *J. abnorm. soc. Psychol.,* 1946, **41,** 491–495.

CHAPTER 7

The Medical Assessment of the Person

By Roy M. Whitman, M.D.

Assistant Professor of Psychiatry, Northwestern University, and Chief, Neurology and Psychiatry, VA Research Hospital, Chicago, Illinois.

Up to this point, our interest has been directed toward methods for collecting data about the psychological aspects of the person. We have been concerned with the broad problem of finding out how people organize their interactions with others so as to get what they want. Before we discuss additional tools of psychological analysis, however, we shall consider some of the methods for analyzing the physical structure and function of individuals.

The biological features of the person—sense organs, viscera, bones, muscles, and so on—serve as supports for even the most complex and subtle psychological activities. Grasping a thought involves bodily activity just as surely as grasping food, although entirely different portions of the biological apparatus are mobilized in the two cases. Defects or damage of the biological apparatus will, of course, limit or modify psychological activity. This fact is obvious in cases having conspicuous defects such as blindness and deafness. Psychological clinicians would surely consider these defects when trying to make recommendations. But there are other, less manifest changes in the biological apparatus which also cripple the person and force him to change his behavior. Alterations in thyroid gland function or in brain metabolism are examples of such changes.

The detailed study of the biological aspects of the person requires special information, special sensitivity, and special equipment. For this reason, medical specialists play an important part in the study of persons. It is common practice for physicians and psychologists to work together in clinics, hospitals, and military establishments. This fact immediately raises questions about effective communication between the psychological and the medical clinician. Since their training and primary concerns are different, each may sometimes give scant consideration to the contributions of the other. Actual cooperative experience among specialists usually reduces difficulties in understanding and communication; but some preparation for this experience will help you. The purpose of this chapter is to show the kinds of contributions that medical clinicians can make to the study of persons and to tell you something of the examining procedure used by physicians.

CONTRIBUTIONS OF THE MEDICAL EXAMINATION

The medical examination typically consists of a medical history, a physical examination, and certain laboratory procedures. This kind of examination has been delegated by both time-honored convention and legal sanction to the medical profession. It is a responsibility that has been granted to the physician due to his special training. He is considered qualified to invade the bodily privacy of the individual far better than any other specialist. The physician may palpate the person's body, examine his orifices, peer through the pupils of his eyes, introduce instruments into his body, and collect samples of his fluid and solid excretions for examination.

Patients coming to a physician are willing to undergo a good deal of exposure and even embarrassment in order to receive the benefits of his expert knowledge and judgment. The contribution that the physician can make to the evaluation of the total function of the organism is therefore great; this is true of both physical and psychological aspects of the examination.

Assessment of Total Functioning. The individual may first be looked at as a holistic functioning organism. How is he responding biologically to the environment? What are his physiological resources and liabilities? More specifically, we want to know whether the elementary life-maintaining processes are functioning adequately. To survive, a person must be able to maintain internal temperature, breathe, assimilate food, excrete waste, and coordinate muscles. People differ in the adequacy with which these and similar basic processes are carried out.

Particularly concerned in the maintenance of total adaptation are the great generalized body systems: neuromuscular, respiratory, gastrointestinal, cardiovascular, genitourinary, and endocrine. Disturbances in thyroid, adrenal, or pituitary gland function, for example, can produce vast changes in the body *habitus* and in the psychological alertness of the person. Hypothyroidism produces a lethargic individual with coarse hair, rough skin, and a relative apathy to outside stimuli.

Disturbances of the central nervous system such as brain tumors may produce hyperactive individuals with distortions in their perceptual fields and in their communication with others. Toxic disorders may affect the nervous system and result in widespread signs of adaptive failure such as gross disorientation. Lead poisoning and chronic alcoholism are examples of these disorders.

Pathological involvement of the cardiovascular-respiratory system will also effect great changes, such as those resulting from anemia or high blood pressure. Fluids that bathe the body tissues may be affected by shocklike conditions, with low blood pressure; then the body tissues do not get sufficient oxygen to maintain adequate function of the organs. The brain, for example, needs a continuing supply of oxygen, and acute oxygen deprivation lasting only minutes causes the death of many brain cells.

Assessment of the Physical Results of Psychological Causes. Various psychosomatic theories have attempted to avoid the dualism of mind and body. It is still true, however, that at least a rough distinction can be made between those methods of examination that reveal the condition of the body and those that reveal the organization of patterns of behavior (5). Consequently, we can divide defects into the physical and the psychological as a useful approach in practice, even though we do not accept a metaphysical dualism.

Prolonged psychological stress may actually cause organic changes in the organism. When the person is frightened or anticipates danger, there is an increase in blood pressure, in pulse rate, in circulation time, and in clotting time of the blood. Bodily changes before examinations or sports events are common examples of this syndrome. Continued stress may sometimes result in irreversible tissue damage. For example, chronic stress may be a major contributing factor (perhaps along with unknown organic factors) to the permanent elevation of blood pressure. Eventually the individual seems to be simply utilizing an acute stress mechanism as if he had to be continuously ready to deal with disturbing situations.

Other well-known diseases in which psychological causes may be important are peptic ulcer, bronchial asthma, rheumatoid arthritis, ulcerative colitis, and neurodermatitis. Less obvious are the psychological contributions that either accelerate or impede the healing process in almost every organic illness and even in bodily wounds. Tuberculosis has often been cited in both medical and popular literature as a disease in which the so-called "will to live" is crucial. This view exemplifies the widespread recognition that the attitudes of the individual influence the outcome of the disease process.

Discovering Physical Causes of Psychological Impairment. A number of specific psychological symptoms can result from either emotional conditions or from physiological disturbance. Some of these are irritability, lethargy, feelings of weakness, headaches, and excitable restlessness. If they are due to physiological factors, treatment of the patient's emotional state or clarifying his interpersonal relations will do little to relieve them. The discovery of the physiological basis for such symptoms requires intimate knowledge of the various syndromes in which they occur and sensitivity to the subtle medical findings that may betray their origin. Physicians are obviously in a favorable position to make these discoveries during the medical examination.

Irritability is common in almost any disorder that decreases available physical energy. Thus it may be found in anemia, hypothyroidism, various chronic diseases, and in some disorders of the central nervous system. Weakness and apathy also may be traced to similar causes. Patients suffering from some continued organic disturbance will frequently complain of lethargy and lack of ambition.

Sometimes difficulty in learning, or friction in interperson relationships, may be due to undetected sensory defects. Partial deafness may prevent a child from reaching his best level of school performance; in adults, it can lead to loss and distortion of communication in social situations, leaving the afflicted person puzzled and distressed. Deafness in older people is often associated with paranoid symptoms since the deaf person cannot discover what is being said about him. Some visual defects produce headaches or vague discomfort, and these, in turn, lead to an avoidance of certain visual tasks. An aversion to reading, for example, could be due to undiscovered myopia (nearsightedness).

Some psychological symptoms can be traced to prolonged or inappropriate self-medication. Continued overuse of barbiturates ("sleeping pills") may cause defects in memory, confused thinking, and drowsiness, along with other symptoms. Even the ingestion of large amounts of aspirin may produce poor appetite, nausea, and feelings of weakness and "nervousness."

Congenital abnormalities may cause psychological difficulties, too. As an illustration, children with congenital heart disease often must restrict their activities, including social play. Thus, the defect may lead to feelings of isolation or inferiority. Recent surgical advances have made possible treatments for restoring these individuals to health, and this may lead to striking psychological improvement.

Emotional Effects of the Medical Examination. The way that a physician handles the examination is crucial as to whether it will have a beneficial or harmful influence on the patient. Often a physical examination and the discussion of it with a physician in whom the patient has confidence exerts a decided therapeutic effect. A case in point concerns both cancer and heart disease. Our culture has introduced so much fear of these disorders that almost everybody, especially in the older age groups, fears he may become a victim of these afflictions. Elimination of the physical basis for these fears along with a simple discussion of the findings is invariably reassuring.

On the other hand, the behavior of an incautious physician during an examination may be misinterpreted by some patients, and they may feel that he is holding back information that could be upsetting. The anxious individual is especially alert to facial expressions of the physician as he listens to the heart, to his comments to his nurse, and to the repetition of certain parts of the physical examination. The patient legitimately wants to know the reason for ordering additional laboratory procedures or for special examinations. There is a large group of people who suffer from "iatrogenic" heart disease. This word has been coined to describe physician-caused heart disease due to an emphasis on incidental findings concerning the heart which have no real bearing on cardiac function. Further, prescribing excessive periods of rest and restriction often leads to unfortunate attitudes of invalidism which can be eradicated only with great difficulty.

A medical examination can be more beneficial to the patient if he is told the meaning of specific findings. It is rarely enough just to name the disorder or the causative agents of a particular syndrome. Different people have different concepts of various diseases based on similar diagnoses of people they know or have read about. These concepts may be entirely erroneous or inapplicable to their own case but may cause needless anxiety. More difficult to elicit are childhood fears of certain diseases. For example, an aunt may have had a certain illness which made her a vaguely feared ogre of childhood; when the same diagnostic label is attached to the patient, he may have disturbing and unrealistic fantasies about many aspects of his personality that are not connected with the illness.

Effect of the Medical Examination on the Psychotherapist. The medical examination and its adequacy influence the confidence of the psychotherapist. One of the constant fears of any conscientious psychotherapist is that he may be treating a psychological condition that is only the superficial aspect of an underlying physical dysfunction. While he is not completely relieved of this fear by an adequate initial medical examination, he can at least proceed on the basis that a competent physician was unable to discover any underlying organic pathological defect.

A medical orientation and examination are particularly necessary when the psychotherapist is dealing with some failure of the individual's adaptation that is sufficiently severe to be called "illness." Here is a pertinent quotation from "The Resolutions on Relations of Medicine and Psychology," approved by the Board of Trustees of the American Medical Association, by the Council of the American Psychiatric Association, and by the Executive Council of the American Psychoanalytic Association:

The medical profession fully endorses the appropriate utilization of the skills of psychologists, social workers and other professional personnel in contributing roles in settings directly supervised by physicians. It further recognizes that these professions are entirely independent and autonomous when medical questions are not involved; but when members of these professions contribute to the diagnosis and treatment of illness, their professional contribution must be coordinated under medical responsibility.

Other professional groups such as psychologists, teachers, ministers, lawyers, social workers, and vocational counselors, of course use psychological understanding in carrying out their professional functions. Members of these professional groups are not thereby practicing medicine. The application of psychological methods to the treatment of illness is a medical function (8, p. 72).

If the psychiatrist, who has a medical background, is frequently concerned about overlooking a physical involvement of the person, the psychological clinician who is untrained in physical pathology should be even more wary.

Other Contributions of the Medical Examination. The initial medical examination provides a base line for future examinations when they become necessary. Then assessment of changes in the physical condition of the patient is more accurate. In other words, diagnosis is a continuing function of the person who assumes responsibility for the well-being of the client or patient. It is particularly helpful if the patient and the psychological clinician can have a relationship with a physician who is known and trusted by both of them. It is better to be known well by a physician than to be known poorly by a well-known physician.

The medical examination may also help to deny or verify hypotheses that have been arrived at on the basis of a psychological interview. There are a number of indications suggesting medical illness which may be obtained during a psychological interview. They will be mentioned later in this chapter. Also, of course, the psychologist may suspect that there is no physical basis for such complaints as headache, sleeplessness, backache, etc., and seek confirmation of his hypothesis from the physician.

THE NATURE OF THE MEDICAL EXAMINATION

The medical approach to the patient may be divided into three large sections: the medical history, the physical examination, and the laboratory examination.

The Medical History. For a variety of reasons, a physician does not usually conduct a client-guided interview. He is more likely to follow a fairly standard and systematic line of questioning. He initiates the interview by requesting complaints for which the patient has sought aid. These are usually subsumed under the category of "chief complaint" (abbreviated C.C.).

The next section is usually concerned with the "present illness" (P.I.). Here the physician elicits a history of the complaint, its duration, severity, periods of absence of the complaint, and the setting in which it began.

In the next section, "past history" (P.H.), the physician goes over the past medical background which led up to the beginning of the present illness. Obviously, this inquiry is difficult when there is no chief complaint around which the physician can orient his line of questioning. The routine physical examination and medical history may be quite unproductive when the examiner has no idea what he is looking for. This has been particularly true of military physical examinations where some abstract idea of "normality" was applied to each individual. Such criteria are helpful only where there are quantifiable measures such as blood pressure, pulse rate, and other physiological measures.

In connection with this topic, we should like to point out that when a patient is referred to a physician the referring psychologist should try to designate certain areas of doubt or weakness that he would like to have investigated. If he does not do this, but simply asks for a blanket medical clearance, both he and the physician become more concerned with achieving some sort of sanction to be free of any doubt about the patient's physical status than they are about finding particular dysfunctions.

The next section of the medical history is an inventory called "review of systems." First, a general review concerns weight changes, chills, fever, sweats, skin eruption, jaundice, tension, and allergic responses (hay fever, asthma, hives). Next, the physician begins at the top of the person to review subjective complaints.

1. The head and neck. The examiner inquires about the presence of headaches, their frequency, intensity, the location of the pain, and the presence or absence of nausea or other neurological accompaniments (e.g., light flashes). He also asks about faintness, dizziness, and periods of unconsciousness.

2. The eyes. Here the examiner is interested in whether glasses are worn, the type and extent of visual disability, pain in the eyes, photophobia (aversion to light) and disturbances in the visual field ("blind" spots or constriction of the total field).

3. The ears and nose. The patient is asked about pain, discharges, deafness, previous mastoid infections, and local infections. Obstruction of the nasal passages and intactness of the sense of smell are investigated.

4. The mouth and throat. Here the questions are about the gums, whether they are sore or bleeding; coating, soreness or swelling of the tongue; and about the teeth. The examiner also inquires about pain, hoarseness, or postnasal drip in the throat. Questions about tonsils and adenoids and their removal are usually included.

5. The chest. The lungs and heart and their functioning are of major interest. Coughs, shortness of breath, attacks of asthma, and swelling of the ankles (related to heart failure), all come in for questioning.

6. The gastrointestinal system. The investigation covers such items as: appetite, food intolerances, inability to swallow, episodes of nausea, belching, constipation and diarrhea, use of laxatives, anal itching, and rectal pain or bleeding.

7. The genitourinary system (G.U.). Is there a history of colicky pains, inability to retain urine, blood in the urine, venereal disease? For women, questions concern the menstrual cycle, miscarriages, abortions, vaginal discharges, and genital pain or itching.

8. The extremities and joints. Pain, swelling, redness, and varicosities are the usual categories about which the patient is questioned.

9. The blood system (known as the hemopoietic system) and the endocrine system can be classed together. Questions are raised about anemia, blood disorders, bleeding tendencies, menstrual irregularities, and tolerance or intolerance of heat and cold.

10. Past illnesses. The patient is asked about infectious diseases such as diphtheria, rheumatic fever, and scarlet fever and their sequelae. Previous traumatic and surgical episodes are noted. The physician is especially concerned with their influence on present adaptation, e.g., sequelae of paralyses or of head injuries.

11. The sexual history. The usual inquiries are made concerning early sexual information, onset of menses, masturbatory experience, number of marriages, health of spouse, number of children, and sexual difficulties.

The family history is next reviewed, and deaths of close relatives from such diseases as cancer, tuberculosis, diabetes, and high blood pressure come under close scrutiny. Also noted is the presence in the family history of syphilis, allergies, and some psychotic conditions.

Following this clinical history, the physician proceeds to carry out a complete physical examination with particular attention to those areas which seemed to be important in the clinical history.

The Physical Examination. The physical examination (1) utilizes four main methods: inspection, palpation, percussion, and auscultation. Inspection means looking at the person; palpation means feeling his body; percussion means tapping the body with the fingers and listening to the sounds produced; and auscultation means listening to the sounds produced within the body by physiological or pathophysiological processes.

Even though the physical examination begins after the history is taken, the alert physician is engaging in inspection throughout the history-taking procedure. He is already formulating hypotheses about the person and his illness, and these tentative formulations feed into his line of inquiry. Thus he goes into more detail as he investigates certain bodily systems and a gradually organizing line of investigation emerges.

Surgically ill patients often react quite differently to a physical examination than do emotionally disturbed patients. For the patient with an acutely painful abdomen, the inhibition of shame and embarrassment is overcome by a great need to be relieved of the pain. Psychologically ill patients, however, may be stimulated, embarrassed, or made resentful by the physical examination. The physician should, therefore, show extreme respect for their sensitivities. At the same time he should not deviate from his main purpose of conducting a thorough examination.

There is an old adage among medical practitioners that the difference between a specialist and a general practitioner is that the specialist does a rectal examination. Of course, there is sometimes justification for omitting the rectal and vaginal examinations with emotionally upset patients. Nevertheless, it seems that psychiatrists have become oversensitive about the patient's presumed reaction to the examination of these areas (12). If these examinations are carried out with restraint, dignity, and a kind, but cool, professional manner, there are few patients who will be disturbed by this sign of thoroughness on the part of the examiner.

Reactions to the physical examination have been studied by Reider (7) and reported in an interesting article. Only a few patients refused to be examined, and all of them were severely disturbed patients. He also illustrates the defensive nature of the joking that patients employ to cover up their anxiety and concern about their bodies.

The physical examination essentially follows the review of systems described in the history taking. It begins with the general characteristics of temperature, pulse rate, respiratory rate, height, and weight. Some physicians include the measurement of blood pressure as part of the general assay of the patient. They then generally progress from an examination of the gross anatomical areas of the head and neck down the body.

While we shall not go into detail about the procedures of the physical examination, we shall mention some of the observations that are usually made. The physician inspects the general conformation of the body, the amount and distribution of fat, and the characteristic posture. He notes characteristics of the skin, hair, and nails. He observes bones and joints for signs of deformity, as well as noting any structural peculiarities of eyes, ears, nose, and throat. With his fingers, he palpates the body for swollen lymphatic glands, unusual masses in the abdomen, rigidity and tenderness of abdominal areas. The chest cavity is examined by percussion and auscultation, and the heart sounds are listened to with a stethoscope.

We may profitably make a few added comments on the cardiovascular system since it is a common source of anxiety among patients. Heart murmurs as detected by the stethoscope do not necessarily indicate clinical heart disease. Failure to recognize this fact has caused a great deal of grief to many a cardiac "invalid," whose invalidism was caused by a misinterpretation of normal variations in the heart sounds.

The blood pressure is another diagnostic feature which has been grossly exaggerated. Normal blood pressure in young adults averages 120/80. (These figures refer to the height of a column of mercury in millimeters—a way of measuring pressure.) The 120 indicates the systolic pressure, which is the pressure at the moment the heart is maximally contracted. The 80 stands for the diastolic pressure, i.e., at the time the heart is relaxed. So-called low blood pressure is seemingly an advantage for it is correlated with longevity in the tables of the Metropolitan Life Insurance Company. It is rarely, if ever, the cause of dizziness, fainting spells, or tenseness, as was previously thought. High blood pressure, conversely, is often not in itself the cause of headaches, tenseness, dizziness, or weakness. It must be evaluated in the light of the total biological and psychological functioning of the organism.

The electrocardiagram should also be mentioned since it is such a commonly used test in the diagnosis of heart disease. It is the graphic recording of small electric currents which develop in the heart during each of its contractions. While it is most useful in detecting coronary artery disease, it is often used solely for reassuring the patient. In such cases, the physician unfortunately leans on a mechanical rather than interpersonal method of dealing with the patient's anxiety.

The Laboratory Examination. The third major division of the general medical examination is the laboratory examination. This may be divided into routine tests and specialized tests.

Routine tests are those that are done in the course of the initial evaluation of the patient. The first of these is the serologic test for syphilis. Syphilis is well known as a disease that may simulate any other disease. The only way to avoid overlooking it is to use the very accurate serologic tests that have been developed to detect it. It is most gratifying to have a particularly baffling diagnostic problem settled by a positive serologic finding of syphilis. This is especially true because of the effectiveness of the antibiotic substances currently used in treatment.

The most common serologic test is the Wasserman test, named after its discoverer. Other commonly used methods, relying on a slightly different principle of detection, are the Kahn and the Kline tests. Basically these tests depend on the principle that the tissues of the diseased person form substances to combat the disease. These substances are called immune bodies or antibodies. The causative disease agent is called the antigen, in this case the microorganism (*Treponema*) producing syphilis. Reactions which occur when the antibodies in the blood sample unite with the antigen or its substitute permit the laboratory technician to determine that antibodies are present.

The use of serum (hence the name serologic test) yields a result which is approximately 90 per cent accurate. In the diagnosis of neurologic and psychiatric conditions involving the central nervous system, the peripheral blood is positive (i.e., indicative of disease) in almost 90 per cent of the patients.

A sample of the patient's blood is also examined routinely for the number of red and white blood corpuscles per cubic centimeter (the "blood count"). The average number of red corpuscles is 5 million per c.c., with a somewhat lower average in women. Deviations from this figure must exceed a million to warrant attention.

The number of white cells varies between 6,000 and 10,000 per cubic milliliter. More than this usually indicates an infectious process, while a smaller figure indicates some severely debilitating or toxic process. Counting the different kinds of white cells (a "differential" count) is done routinely in some hospitals, but others do it only when the normal limits for the total white count are exceeded. The differential count is helpful in indicating the types of invaders that the white blood cells are fighting. Thus, in acute infectious diseases a certain type of white blood cell (the neutrophil) is proportionately increased, while in more chronic infections such as tuberculosis another kind of white cell (the monocyte) predominates.

Hemoglobin determinations are also routine and are indicative of the type of anemia that is present. Hemoglobin is the oxygen-carrying substance in the red blood corpuscles. The average amount of hemoglobin is about 15 grams per 100 c.c., with a lower average among women.

Urinalysis is another of the routine laboratory tests. The urine sample is examined for color, acidity, specific gravity, and the presence of albumin, sugar, and blood. The sample is also inspected microscopically. By this relatively simple procedure, diabetes, and disease of the heart, kidney, or liver may be detected.

Another procedure that has become almost routine is the chest X ray. Most medical centers and physicians now use microfilms and employ the large standard-sized plates only when there is something suspicious on the smaller, less sharp films. Although pulmonary tuberculosis, the chief reason for routine chest plates, is on the wane, the great increase in carcinoma of the lung makes the chest film a valuable adjunct to diagnosis. It is especially important since chest cancer can be operated on very successfully when detected early.

There are almost innumerable other laboratory procedures. Very often they are ordered somewhat haphazardly as a shotgun aid to an obscure diagnostic problem and are often more harmful to the patient than helpful. Specific indications from the findings of the other procedures are required before they should be requested. Certainly patients with emotional illness are the very ones in whom the physician makes a fruitless, prolonged search for the etiologic organic cause. Some of the most useful of these ancillary tests will be described under the heading of the neurological examination.

There are, however, some physical illnesses often mistaken for psychological illnesses, and laboratory procedures are helpful in their diagnosis. With symptoms referable to the gastrointestinal tract, examination of the stool specimen may reveal disease. An example is amebiasis in which infestation with small amebic parasites produces symptoms of fatigability, depression, loss of appetite, and occasional diarrheic and bloody stools. Blood in the feces is almost invariably a reason for referring the patient to a physician.

Since diseases of the endocrine glands often simulate psychogenic disorders, laboratory tests of their present status may be needed to supplement the usual medical examination. Of these, the basal metabolic rate (BMR) is the oldest and most commonly used. In hyperthyroidism the BMR is increased to a value more than 20 per cent of normal. In hypothyroidism the BMR is decreased more than 20 per cent below normal. It is important to remember that anxiety may increase the BMR by increasing the oxygen requirements of the organism. Feelings that the patient had during examination of the BMR are worth inquiring into, therefore, in order to evaluate the effect of anxiety. A newer test, apparently less affected by the momentary psychophysiology of the organism, is the use of radioactive iodine to measure thyroid function.

THE NEUROLOGICAL EXAMINATION

The neurological examination is one of the specialized examinations which supplements the general medical examination (10). It is important from our point of view because organic diseases of the nervous system may manifest themselves initially as behavior and psychological problems. A striking demonstration of this fact is given in a recent study of brain tumors (9). It was found that almost 50 per cent of such tumors first show themselves in the guise of psychological difficulties.

The neurologist as a medical specialist has lost ground to the neurosurgeon, to the internal medical specialist, and to the psychiatrist. The relationship between neurology and psychiatry has its roots in history. In the nineteenth century, the dictum was that there could be no psychological illness without underlying brain disease. This may be true, in the sense that any change in function implies a change in structure, but the structural change may often be extremely minute. It may well occur at an ultramicroscopic level or even be a transient biochemical change that cannot be demonstrated in a fixed specimen of brain tissue used for microscopic examination. The historical relationship between the two disciplines has nevertheless continued to the present; two-fifths of the examination given by the American Board of Psychiatry and Neurology deals with neurological subjects.

A trend away from the marriage of these two specialties was stimulated by the concepts of psychosomatic medicine which seemed to imply that perhaps psychiatry should be closer to internal medicine. This trend is being reversed by such findings as those of Penfield and his group showing the intimate involvement of the temporal lobes in memory (6). He did such experiments as stimulating areas of the temporal lobe under local anesthesia and evoking strikingly clear and complete memories of remote times in the patient's life. New interest has thus been evolving in the neural basis of mind. Research on the hypothalamus and deep structures of the brain showing their intimate relation to emotions has also stimulated renewed interest in structure as underlying function. The psychiatrist now operates in close contact with both neurology and internal medicine. This is in addition to his main interest in behavior disorders.

The Neurological History. Because specific impulses are carried by various neural tracts, neurological examination can often be strikingly accurate in the anatomical localization of lesions. Of course, less accuracy is possible in dealing with the higher cortical centers where function becomes less well localized. Lashley's total-brain-substance concept as the significant factor in cortical function still seems valid except for such sharply demarcated functional areas as the visual and auditory.

The neurological history does not differ greatly from the medical history already outlined. There is, however, very close and detailed questioning as to the chronological progression of the symptoms. The course of development of a symptom picture is one of the best clues to the localization of a lesion. Often the patient will attribute the onset of his symptoms to an external event such as a fall, but only rarely is the traumatic history of much importance.

Certain symptoms are worthy of mention. Headache, particularly of a fairly constant and "deep" type, is most characteristic of brain tumor. It is rarely unilateral. However, diagnosing a brain tumor by the appearance of a headache often means that the diagnosis has been made too late. The tumor usually causes headache by increasing intracranial pressure and, by the time this has taken place, the tumor is often inoperable.

The characteristic headache in migraine is usually unilateral. Here attention must be paid to accompaniments such as nausea, vomiting, peculiar visual phenomena, photophobia, and depressed feelings. These headaches are not relieved by ordinary medication such as aspirin but are relieved by special medication such as dihydroergotamine.

Another symptom which is always worthy of close scrutiny is convulsions. The history of these should be meticulously taken. Certain types of "aura" (symptoms preceding the onset of the convulsion) often provide the clue for locating the lesion which has acted as the trigger of a generalized convulsion.

A special type of convulsion that should be mentioned is the psychomotor convulsion. This kind of seizure is usually on the basis of an irritative lesion of the temporal lobe of the brain and manifests itself further by abnormal behavior with amnesia. Usually the behavior is automatic, purposeless, and occasionally destructive. It is especially important to recognize this as due to organic pathology, for drugs and surgical excision of the focus in the temporal lobe may be very useful in treatment.

A type of convulsion, which is so important as to have retained the name of the person who originally described it, is the Jacksonian convulsion. It begins as a localized convulsion, a spasm in the face, hand, or foot, and usually spreads to the entire body. The lesion is located in the contralateral motor cortex.

The Neurological Examination Proper. The most important task of the neurologist is the close observation of the patient from the moment of introduction. The patient's alertness, orientation, memory, gait, ability to stand erect must all be subject to scrutiny. The skin is carefully examined for pigmentation, changes from "normal" to dryness (often indicative of the level of a spinal cord lesion), and coarseness (a sign of endocrine disease). Examining the head for dilated veins is important. A throbbing temple artery or bony prominences are often clues to underlying growths. Stiffness of the neck is a well-known sign of nervous-system irritation. It may indicate poliomyelitis or meningitis, even though the patient is subjectively aware of only irritability or excessive tenseness.

The Cranial Nerves. Next to be examined are the areas served by the cranial nerves. These consist of the twelve nerves that bilaterally innervate the head and neck.

The first is the olfactory nerve or nerve of smell. It emerges from below the frontal lobes and may be involved in lesions of these lobes. Disease involving this nerve often results in a loss of the taste of food since much food "flavor" is actually due to odor. Simple tests such as having the patient smell cigarette tobacco in one nostril and then the other will often reveal the sensory deficiency.

The second cranial nerve is the optic nerve. Disturbances of vision are often the first symptoms of intracranial growths or irritation. The optic pathway is a long one, extending from the retina to the occipital lobes at the back of the brain. Lesions of this pathway produce different visual defects that depend upon the location of the lesion. For example, lesions impinging on the optic chiasm (the "cross-over" of the optic nerves from the two eyes) often produce hemianopsia. In this condition, the right or left half of the retina is rendered nonfunctional, and the visual field is correspondingly blocked out. Hemianopsia is usually bilateral. Other disturbances that may be mentioned by the patient are flashes of light or gaps in the visual field. Sometimes the patient is unaware of visual defects and simply reports that he often bumps into objects on the right or the left.

Swelling (edema) of the head of the optic nerve is an important neurological sign. It can be observed by looking into the eye with an ophthalmoscope. An elevation of the region where the optic nerve enters the retina will be seen. This sign, called papilledema or "choked disk," is crucial in the determination of increased intracranial pressure. The two signs of headache and choked disk, together with the symptom of vomiting, comprise the dramatic "triad" of brain tumor symptoms. Unfortunately, they are present only when the tumor is advanced.

The third, fourth, and sixth nerves (oculomotor, trochlear, and abducens) are grouped together in the examination for they supply the small muscles which move the eye about. Subjective evidence of their dysfunction is provided by the patient's report of double vision (diplopia). This symptom is almost invariably an indicator of organic involvement.

Examination of the pupils is very important. Inequality of the pupils is often a symptom of intracranial lesions such as subdural hematoma, a condition in which bleeding has taken place under the dura (the fibrous covering of the brain) and which simulates psychosis. The failure of the pupils to respond to light is often a symptom of syphilis of the central nervous system.

The fifth (trigeminal) nerve supplies the face and muscles of mastication. Tumors in the posterior part of the cranial vault often affect it. Lesions of this nerve may result in persistent pain in one side of the face. In this condition, known as trigeminal neuralgia, there are attacks of intense, shooting pain, usually on one side of the face. These attacks ordinarily last only a few minutes, and the patient may be symptom-free for long periods between them. The cause of this disorder is not known.

The seventh (facial) nerve is often the first nerve to be involved in diseases of the nervous system. Sometimes a flattening of the nasolabial fold (the crease between the wing of the nose and the corner of the mouth) on one side is the first and, for a long time, the only symptom of a brain tumor. It can often be detected when the patient smiles and shows asymmetry of the face.

The other cranial nerves are usually involved only in widespread lesions of the central nervous system.

The Brain. We shall now consider some observations related to the cerebrum or the two large convoluted hemispheres of the brain. Each hemisphere may be divided into four lobes: frontal, parietal, temporal, and occipital.

The frontal lobes were once considered a silent area, but they are now thought to be related to "higher" functions such as esthetic appreciation and the capacity for empathy. Often the first signs of disease in this region will be a deterioration of the "moral" behavior of the individual. Coarse, inappropriate behavior in social situations is often given as an example of this kind of deterioration. This area also has many connections with the hypothalamus, a structure intimately involved in emotional activity. The interruption of these connections seems to be an essential part of frontal lobotomy, a surgical procedure that sometimes helps in certain kinds of otherwise untreatable psychoses.

Destructive lesions of the frontal lobes cause varying degrees of euphoria, habit change, and loss of memory and orientation. These symptoms are most common when the dominant lobe is affected, i.e., the one on the side opposite to the handedness of the individual. It is important to diagnose lesions of this area even late in their course for large parts of the frontal lobe may be removed without disturbing the successful functioning of the individual.

The parietal lobe comprises most of the cerebral hemisphere. Its most important structure is the sensory cortex, which lies adjacent to the motor cortex at the back of the frontal lobe. A lesion of the sensory cortex produces symptoms of loss of sensation on the side of the body opposite to the site of the lesion. Many times this sensory loss is not immediately apparent to the patient. For example, a patient may burn himself repeatedly before he discovers that he feels no burning sensation.

The occipital lobe, at the back of the cerebrum, is involved in visual function. Each lobe receives impulses from the retina of the eye on the side opposite to it. Tumors in this region may result in defects of the visual field such as hemianopsia. The occipital area is often affected in children with brain tumors.

Lesions of the dominant temporal lobe often produce a peculiar feeling of "dreaminess" or a feeling of change of "self." These may be the only indication of disease in this area. One of the centers of speech is also located here, a center involved in the comprehension of auditory stimuli. Further, as recent investigations seem to show, this region may be quite significant for memory.

Detailed discussion of the cerebellum is not required here. Lesions of this small structure produce symptoms which are apparent even to relatively untrained observers. Common symptoms are unsteadiness, disturbances of gait, and disturbances of equilibrium. They obviously indicate severe disturbance of the nervous system.

The Spinal Cord. The areas served by the nerve tracts stemming from the spinal cord are examined for sensory function, motor function, and reflexes. By careful examination of these areas, a skilled neurologist can locate lesions of the spinal cord within one millimeter. This fact is of more than academic interest for it makes possible a prescription of the site of operation for the neurosurgeon. An interesting illustration is furnished by a young female patient. She was diagnosed as having a lesion of the spinal cord at the level of T-10 (the tenth thoracic segment of the spinal cord, which is divided into thirty segments). The diagnosis was possible because of close observation of a single clinical phenomenon. Whenever her umbilicus touched something cold, as happened when she did her washing at the basement laundry tub, she would involuntarily urinate. In the hospital examination, this phenomenon could be repeated by using an ice cube. Subsequent operation revealed a blood-vessel tumor at the level of T-10 in the spine.

Sensory function is examined by testing the patient's ability to sense light, touch, pain, temperature, point pressure, vibration, and point discrimination. Since these sensory functions involve different tracts in the spinal cord, location of defects indicates the location of the affected tract.

Hysterical sensory disturbances may be distinguished from those due to organic factors by the fact that the former affects all the sense modalities equally. In addition, sensory defects in hysteria usually affect the body parts that are perceived as functional units by the patient, and they have sharp boundaries. Thus we find a "stocking" or "glove" anesthesia. In genuine organic disability, the sensory loss is irregular and corresponds to the distribution of nerve pathways. An interesting question was once raised as to the kind of symptom which would be shown by a neurologist with hysteria. An actual case report of such a patient showed that he manifested the sharply demarcated glove anesthesia; apparently his intellectual functions did not participate in his emotional difficulty.

Evaluation of motor function begins with inspection. The limbs are examined to see whether they are overdeveloped (hypertrophied) or wasted (atrophied). Simple tests of strength are used, one of the commonest being to grip the examiner's hands. Not only must some standard of normal strength be kept in mind by the examiner, but he must compare one side of the body with the other, since differences in response of the two sides are more significant than absolute changes.

People are usually more aware of motor disturbances than they are of sensory loss, and they may help the examiner by telling of difficulties they have noticed. Nevertheless, psychological mechanisms of denial of disability may prevent the patient from giving a report to the examiner. Consequently the neurologist asks the patient to perform a number of simple movements in order to check intactness of motor function. Even before the formal examination begins, an experienced examiner may make a number of useful observations. For example, he may examine the patient's shoes and notice that the scuffing at the toe of one shoe is more marked than it is on the other. He infers that foot "dragging" has been going on for some time.

Because war injuries have increased the number of people with motor disabilities, it may be worth while to define some commonly used terms. The term "paraplegia" refers to paralysis of both legs. When only one extremity is paralyzed, it is called monoplegia. When one side of the body, including both the arm and the leg, is paralyzed, the condition is called hemiplegia.

Examination of the reflexes is commonly identified by the lay public as the "neurological examination," probably because there is something impressive about using a small rubber hammer to strike a tendon. One of the most commonly examined reflexes is the patellar reflex. It is elicited by striking the patellar tendon just below the kneecap to produce a kick of the foot. Not all reflexes are elicited by tapping. Some are obtained by stroking or rubbing the skin. In the case of the pupillary reflex, light is used as the stimulus.

The reflexes are used to examine the functional integrity of the spinal cord since, theoretically, it can respond at the reflex level without the participation of the higher centers. Different reflexes are available for examination from the neck down and provide valuable clues for determining which regions of the cord are intact. Again, as with motor functions, it is important to compare the findings from one side of the patient with those from the other. Very hyperactive reflexes, if equal, may indicate general bodily tension more than anything else.

NEUROLOGICAL LABORATORY TESTS

The most frequently used tests are: examination of the cerebrospinal fluid, X rays of the skull and spinal column, and recording of the electrical activity of the brain. Supplementary procedures consist of injecting air or radio-opaque substances into the spinal-fluid pathways to aid in visualization of various structures by X ray. Recently, radioactive isotopes have been injected because they seem to concentrate in tumorous areas.

The Cerebrospinal Fluid. The cerebrospinal fluid is a clear, colorless fluid which comes into contact with almost every part of the central nervous system. It can be fairly easily obtained by the puncture of the spinal canal in the low part of the back so as to draw out fluid for examination. Furthermore, at the time of the puncture, the pressure of the fluid can be measured. This pressure may indicate a disease process. For example, it may be elevated when a brain tumor is present, and normal or low in the case of tumors of the spinal cord which prevent free communication of the fluid throughout the spinal canal.

The fluid itself should be examined for color, cell count, globulin and total protein, the "gold curve," [1] and the Wasserman reaction. Abnormal findings in any of these categories indicates disease of the central nervous system. The Wasserman test for syphilis is especially important since there are a few patients who do have syphilis of the nervous system but whose disease will not be detected by the routine blood test mentioned earlier.

X-ray Examination. Plain X-ray films of the head and spinal column will occasionally reveal signs of organic pathology; but often it is necessary to inject air or radio-opaque substances such as certain dyes in order to make a diagnosis.

One reference point that can be seen in X-ray films is the pineal gland. In almost 60 per cent of adults this gland is sufficiently calcified to be visible in X-ray photographs. This gland is normally located in the midline of the skull, but it may be displaced from its normal position by some disturbance on one side of the brain. Furthermore, plain X rays can reveal changes in the bony seat of the pituitary gland or erosions of the bony container of the brain. Such findings indicate intracranial pathology.

Since 1918, air studies have been an extremely useful adjunct to the diagnosis of neurological lesions. The air is introduced into the lower spine by about the same procedure as is used in withdrawing spinal fluid. Since the air is lighter than the fluid, it floats to the skull cavity and, in various positions of the head, outlines the brain substance in quite a striking way. Many suspected neurological lesions have been detected by this method.

A small percentage of lesions not shown by air studies can be visual-

---

[1] In this test ten different dilutions of the spinal fluid are prepared. When a suspension of colloidal gold is added, various changes in color may occur. Particular patterns of color changes are associated with such diseases as central-nervous-system syphilis, multiple sclerosis, and meningitis. A negative reaction is shown by the lack of any change in color.

ized in two other ways. Injecting opaque dyes into the spinal canal (myelography) will reveal spinal cord lesions. Injections into the blood vessels (arteriography) will outline the blood supply of the brain on X-ray films.

Electroencephalography. Little more than twenty-five years have passed since the introduction of electroencephalography (EEG), but it has become an important aid to the clinician in this brief span. The technique involves the amplification and recording of the minute electrical currents produced by brain cells. It is especially useful in diagnosing epilepsy, cerebral tumors, residuals of head injury, and less common diseases such as aneurysms (small dilatations of blood vessels) and hematomas (collections of blood, usually due to trauma). Using the EEG, it is often possible to locate the site of focal lesions of the brain. This procedure was largely responsible for the discovery of a syndrome called temporal-lobe epilepsy, which is occasionally the basis for a clinical picture of psychosis or for extreme behavior deviations.

SOME SPECIFIC PROBLEMS

Physical Disease Masquerading as Emotional. A young woman presented herself at a university student health clinic with symptoms of inability to study, tiredness, difficulty in getting along with men, and a general feeling of sluggishness. Physical examination and laboratory tests revealed no abnormalities. She was treated psychotherapeutically by a psychiatric resident for some months. Although she showed gradual improvement, the feeling of fatigue never left her completely. One day the young physician suddenly had a flash of an alternative diagnosis. He got a syringe of Prostigmine from the nurse and injected it into the patient. Within a few minutes she felt better than she had in several years. He had suddenly realized that her symptoms were partially due to myasthenia gravis in which there is a blocking at the neuromuscular junction, preventing the nerve impulses from reaching the muscles. Prostigmine is a specific antidote for this condition. Psychotherapy was continued. The patient did have personality problems, but she also had a physical disorder. She continued to take Prostigmine by mouth and her tiredness disappeared completely. In psychotherapy, she worked through her interpersonal problems at a much faster rate.

This case illustrates the difficulty and complexity of the diagnostic problem. Most people do have personality disorders of some degree, but this does not make them immune to physical illness. Stewart Wolf recently reported a study in the Cornell University Medical School Clinics (12) in which it was found that 6 per cent of the psychiatric patients under treatment for psychological disturbances had also some physical disability. This figure excluded the typical psychosomatic illnesses and was based only on such organic illnesses as tuberculosis and carcinoma. Unfortunately, referring a patient for a "complete checkup" does not relieve the psychotherapist of his responsibility when physical disease is found. He has the advantage of observing and knowing the patient more thoroughly than is possible for any physician in a half-hour examination.

We need to realize that the patient soon learns to sense and use the attitudes of the person treating him. Thus, if a general practitioner is made uneasy by the patient's story of emotional difficulties, the patient may suppress such remarks, perhaps out of liking for the physician. And conversely, the patient may learn to suppress mention of his physical problems when talking to a psychologist. We should not underestimate the ability of patients to be selective and to tell us what they think we want to hear.

In a parallel fashion, we hear what we want to hear. As clinicians, differences in training and experience make us sensitive to different kinds of facts and lead us to different interpretations of the same observations. To a psychologist, the meticulous tale of a patient's last hospitalization may be uninteresting; yet the story may contain the single clue for explaining the persistence of certain difficulties despite seemingly successful psychotherapy. Much depends upon the responsibility that the psychological therapist is willing to assume. It would seem that, as an expert in human behavior, he cannot shirk the obligation to be well informed about the interrelations of organic and psychological phenomena.

One of the difficulties in arriving at appropriate treatment is that many people use the mechanism of denying physical illness. They will not go to the dentist until the pain becomes impossible to ignore. The whole system of American medicine is predicated on the assumption that the patient knows when he should consult a physician. This seems to be a vast overevaluation of the ability of the patient to judge when his own internal processes have failed to adapt. And the inability to judge is even greater in the case of psychological illness. The psychologist, therefore, must not rely solely on the patient's subjective discomfort to determine when a referral to a medical specialist is needed. Notoriously, cancer is silent until it is well along in its course; that is why there is a great deal of publicity given to the need for early examination. Similarly, many metabolic diseases do not announce themselves by pain. They manifest themselves in many subtle ways; and one of the ways is by psychological changes.

There is another mechanism which deserves attention, although it is not hard to evaluate. That is the tendency of some patients to ascribe certain disturbances to parts of their bodies that have been previously affected by another illness. Recently a patient was seen who had coronary heart disease; he referred all the pain to his back, the site of an earlier, severe injury. The back injury was like an "old friend," and pains in that location did not frighten him as much as the new symptoms produced by the heart disease.

A famous story illustrating how physical disease can masquerade as emotional concerns George Gershwin, the composer. His main complaint was persistent headache. Prior to his death, he had undergone psychiatric treatment for a long time, but the eventual cause of his death had not been detected: a brain tumor.

Emotional Disorder Masquerading as Physical. Foremost among the emotional disorders that simulate physical ailments is hysteria or psychophysiological reactions. Under this diagnosis we may find convulsions that superficially resemble those of epilepsy, restrictions of the visual field that resemble those caused by neurological lesions, and paralyses of various kinds. A dramatic psychophysiological concomitant of a hysterical reaction that is occasionally encountered is false pregnancy (pseudocyesis) in which almost all of the outward signs of pregnancy appear including absence of the menstrual period and breast changes. Obviously in all these cases, careful examination is required in order to establish the absence of organic pathology.

In World War I, the chief complaints of the soldiers centered about the cardiovascular apparatus. These symptoms were variously named "effort syndrome," "neurocirculatory asthenia," or "soldier's heart." After efforts to link the syndrome to organic disease proved fruitless, it was finally recognized as a neurotic disorder. In World War II, for unknown reasons, the majority of complaints seemed to center about the gastrointestinal system, with symptoms of diarrhea, nausea, cramps, and loss of appetite. Diligent search by medical corps physicians failed to reveal a physical basis for these complaints, but ample evidence of psychological stress was found in the personal histories and the environment of the men.

We must emphasize, however, that establishing a disorder as primarily psychological does not mean that physical changes will be missing. A hysterical paralysis can sometimes lead to atrophy and contractures of the muscles in an extremity so that genuine physical changes become the most prominent part of the illness. Peptic ulcer is probably a psychosomatic disorder, but there is a very real ulceration of the mucous lining of the stomach wall. This predisposes the ulcer patient to bleeding, with a possibly fatal outcome, and medical management should take precedence over psychological management.

Use of Drugs. The medical doctor relies rather heavily on the use of drugs in the treatment of patients. Occasionally, he may rely too heavily on their use, since drugs often prevent a real understanding of the disease process. The situation is similar to using penicillin as a kind of "shotgun therapy" for all infections. Physicians often have a tendency to prescribe sedatives to patients with emotional difficulties. Overuse of sedatives may very well mask the psychological problem and hinder psychotherapy. In some instances, of course, the converse may be true. Drugs may facilitate psychotherapy, particularly when a patient is so anxious that he deals with his problems in only an unreasoning, panicky way. A rich field for combined research is the dynamic use of drugs, i.e., finding out how the physiological action and the psychological meaning of drugs can be combined so as to be most effective.

A young pharmacist consulted a psychiatrist because of his addiction to barbiturates. He was taking Seconal tablets in the amount of ten to fifteen grains a day. The average therapeutic dose is one and a half grains a day. Psychotherapy proceeded sluggishly without great improvement, and the patient continued to take the same amount of Seconal. One day the patient brought in the following dream: He was walking along with a sack of red potatoes on his back and wanted to barter them for other goods. He went to a store but found nothing to equal the potatoes in value and decided to keep them. Once he and the therapist had discussed the fact that Seconal tablets are red, the meaning of the dream became clear. He was stating quite simply that neither the therapist nor anyone else had anything to offer him which was as good as his Seconal.

At this point, the therapist prescribed Serpasil, a new "tranquilizing" drug made from *Rauwolfia* root (an East Indian herb preparation). In one week the patient had completely given up the Seconal, which he had been taking for a year prior to coming for treatment. The therapist had offered him a drug substitute in a concrete sense when the psychological substitute was deemed inferior by him. The psychotherapy continued, of course; but the dullness of his responses due to the intoxicating effect of the sedative was eliminated. Thus, treatment could proceed at a faster pace.

The clinical psychologist, of course, cannot prescribe drugs or other medicines. In institutional settings, however, where he works as part of a team, he may consult with medical colleagues about the advisability of using drugs in specific cases. He should then be aware of both the psychological and pharmacological effects of the drug.

Dealing with Psychotic Conditions. The clinician must always be alert to the possible presence of psychotic processes (4). They are not always manifest in the clear form presented in textbook illustrations. When this is true, the clinician may commit the grave error of treating with minor methods a condition that requires more heroic measures, such as the organic and somatic therapies. He may also tamper with psychological processes which the person had safely under control, and thus touch off a major conflagration (psychosis) in order to put out a small fire (neurosis).

The traditional signs of psychosis—delusions, hallucinations, and loss of reality testing—are not present early enough to establish the diagnosis of beginning psychotic conditions such as schizophrenia. The situation is much the same as that mentioned in connection with brain tumors: by the time the symptom triad of vomiting, choked disk, and headache are present, the disease is already far advanced. To detect early psychosis, the clinician must be sensitive to minor bizarreness, seemingly small distortions of perception, and his own minimal empathy with the patient. All this requires experience that can be gained only from working with early and advanced psychotics for a considerable time. The need to develop such sensitivity is one of the best arguments in favor of the clinical psychology internship.

THE REFERRAL AND MEDICAL REPORT

Psychologists who are skillful interviewers will often elicit facts suggesting the desirability of medical studies. In many instances, all that is called for is a suggestion on the part of the psychologist that his client should consult a physician regarding certain symptoms. Thus, in vocational counseling, or in evaluating industrial personnel, the psychologist may be told about chronic gastrointestinal complaints, pains in the chest, or headaches. If the client has avoided seeking medical assistance for these symptoms, the psychologist may urge him to see his physician as part of the total planning activity. This is not a formal referral, and the psychologist does not expect a report from the physician.

In some cases, however, the psychologist has a continuing contact with his client, and medical findings may have an important bearing on his recommendations to or treatment of the client. Such situations are likely to arise in educational or vocational counseling with handicapped people, in the diagnosis of educational failure, and in psychotherapy. Here the clinician may need to make a formal referral by letter to a particular specialist, requesting specific information. Obviously, this is a matter for cooperative planning by client and clinician, and the client's permission should be obtained for the clinician to disclose some of the facts to the medical specialist. In choosing a physician, it is usually a good idea to suggest that the client discuss the matter with his regular physician and seek his advice if a medical specialist is to be chosen. If the client has no continuing relationship with a physician, the psychologist may suggest several names from which the client may choose.

If possible, the referring psychologist should write the letter of referral directly to the physician who has been selected. It should, of course, be timed so that it reaches the physician prior to the appearance of the patient in his office. The letter should include a brief statement of the psychologist's findings and the reason for the referral. The psychologist's impression of the patient should be stated or a clinical diagnosis given if it has been established. The letter should also indicate whether some particular organic condition is suspected or whether merely a general "clearance" is required. In some instances, a telephone contact may supplement or even substitute for the letter.

The medical report which will be received by the referring psychologist should, if well written, contain the chief findings elicited during the medical examination. It should emphasize "positive" findings (i.e., indications of organic disturbance) and the interpretation of these findings. If certain areas of functioning are under suspicion by the referring clinician, then the report should mention negative findings in these areas. The physician should then indicate his recommendations for further study and treatment along with his evaluation of the part that the physical functioning plays in the total adjustment of the individual.

In this communication between two disciplines, there is no substitute for face-to-face contact, even though a written report is essential. Lacking an opportunity for face-to-face contact, the two clinicians should try to have at least a telephone conversation. For the beginning clinical psychologist, medical terminology may seem quite formidable. He should not hesitate, therefore, to rely heavily upon a medical dictionary for help in understanding written medical reports (11). If questions still remain, he can at least talk more understandingly with the referring specialist after he knows the meaning of the terms used in the report.

An Illustrative Case of Referral and Report. A forty-five-year-old bachelor came to a university to take some refresher courses. He was a high-school teacher and wanted additional work in basic educational procedures. During the summer he took a room in a nearby rooming house similar to the quarters he occupied in the small city where he taught.

He came to the student health service near the end of the summer session. His chief complaints were confusion in writing term papers and in studying for his examinations. He was seen by a psychiatrist who gets many such cases as stress due to impending examinations increases. The following story was disclosed in the initial interview.

This man had always led a quite isolated life in his community and was happy only when he was teaching school. At home, he usually ate alone, and his recreation consisted chiefly of an occasional movie. During this summer session he had been particularly lonely because he felt older than the other students. In addition, he had always had difficulty making friends in new settings.

So far this was a fairly typical picture, but the psychiatrist felt there was something a bit unusual about this case. When he tried to find the reason for this feeling, he decided he was most bothered by three things: the patient's failure to remember dates exactly, his markedly dry way of talking, and the fact that he was depressed, rather than anxious as is usual, during pre-examination periods. The psychiatrist also remembered some little petechiae (small hemorrhages into the skin) that dotted the patient's forearms where he had rolled up his sleeves. These observations were sufficient to make the psychiatrist feel the need for further medical study of this patient.

He wrote out a referral to an internist (a specialist in internal medicine). He said that he had examined the patient, who seemed to have a long-standing personality disorder. He pointed out that the patient was now depressed and was somewhat withdrawn. He added that he was bothered by the slightly confused state of the individual and by the fact that his lips were so dry as to appear almost dehydrated.

The internist sent back the following report:

This forty-five-year-old man is referred for medical work-up by Dr. ——. The medical examination revealed a history of very poor nutrition for the past few years since the patient moved out of a boarding home and had begun to make his own meals. This deficient diet has become even more frugal while the patient attended summer session, for he was somewhat depressed at leaving his home town and his already finicky appetite became almost non-existent. He has actually been living on tea and toast for the past three months. Past history and family history are not significant in contributing to the present disorder; although, as the patient answers questions, one gets the impression that he has always been a finicky eater on the basis of a family where food was highly overvalued.

Review of systems reveals vague complaints in almost every body system. He complains of weight loss, poor appetite, unusually frequent colds, and makes a spontaneous observation that he has been bruising easily. He has diffuse headaches, increasing difficulty concentrating and remembering dates. His tongue is red and swollen and his mouth is rather dry. He indicates a poor appetite and occasionally has diarrhea. His muscles feel painful. He has small petechiae around the hair follicles of his arms and legs.

Blood pressure was 145/85; the pulse was 85 and regular. Physical findings merely confirmed the subjective complaints of the patient in the "review of systems." In the neurological examination there were findings of vague sensory loss in the upper and lower extremities.

Laboratory examination showed a hemoglobin of 10 grams, a red count of 3.5 million, and a moderate increase in white count (12,000) with a preponderance of monocytes on the differential smear. Urinalysis revealed a trace of albumin and was otherwise negative, as was the Wasserman. Bleeding time was increased and clotting time was decreased. A blood level of vitamin C was ordered and was almost absent in the blood.

Diagnosis: Scurvy [vitamin C deficiency]; multiple vitamin deficiency; depressive reaction; acute brain syndrome (3).

Recommendations: 1. Brief hospitalization; 2. massive doses of vitamin C and multivitamins; 3. high nutritional diet with especial attention to fruit juices; 4. further psychotherapy.

Implications of This Patient's Illness. This patient had what is now an uncommon disease, scurvy. He also had other vitamin deficiencies which can lead to difficulty in psychological functioning. He recovered very rapidly in the hospital, continued to see the internist on frequent outpatient visits during the rest of his stay at summer school, and was referred for psychotherapy once again. A psychiatrist was found for him near his home city.

It is important to recognize that this chain of events was started by psychological illness, led to a physiological illness which in turn accentuated the psychological illness, and finally led to hospitalization. Now that he has recovered from the nutritional disorder, he will need prolonged psychotherapy in order to change his isolating and food-denial mechanisms which were responsible for his inadequate diet. This is an example of truly comprehensive treatment, in which both organic and psychological factors are considered.

It is not hard to see the importance of sensitivity to the cues which enable the psychological clinician to make a referral. As we saw in the medical report of this case, almost all the findings were available from history taking and inspection of the patient. We shall discuss further both the psychological and the physiological cues that help a psychologist sense the need for prompt referral.

Psychological Cues. We have already mentioned some of the cues that aid the psychological clinician: persistent complaints of headache, unexplained fatigue, peculiar sensory defects, and periods of loss of contact with the environment. We want to point out here that medical studies are also needed when there are obvious disturbances in memory and other so-called "higher mental processes." A condition in point is the "chronic brain syndrome" or "organic syndrome" (3). It results from relatively permanent and diffuse impairment of cerebral tissue. The clinician will find an impairment of orientation, memory, apperception, judgment, and other intellectual functions. Shallow and labile emotional responsiveness usually accompanies the other symptoms.

In the "acute brain syndrome," the symptoms of disorientation and confusion are especially marked. The best-known example of this pattern is acute alcoholic intoxication. Another name often used for this acute syndrome is delirium. This term is usually employed for confused states caused by an infection with fever. It almost always has a good prognosis when treated by conservative measures.

It is important to remember that the particular form of behavior disorder exhibited by a patient with the organic brain syndrome depends upon his previous history, on the way he deals with internal threat, and on the particular kind of internal threat against which he is trying to defend himself. Thus, whether the patient becomes more or less aggressive, more or less withdrawn, grandiose or self-punishing, and so on, is not completely determined solely by the nature of the cerebral impairment.

A wide variety of substances can cause this condition, whether it is chronic or acute. Pituitary disorders, hypoglycemia, head trauma, drug sensitivity or intoxication can all cause the syndrome. It may manifest itself initially or solely as a deliroid state.

Evidence of psychotic conditions also should be a reason for referral. Psychosis should be treated strictly within medical channels for a number of reasons. It has many legal implications (2), and, of course, psychotics must often be hospitalized. In addition, the physiological disturbances that accompany psychosis need medical attention, and there is the danger of suicide or homicide, the danger of disrupting adequate defenses, and the need for drug or shock therapies (4).

Physiological Cues. To close this discussion, we may review some of the major cues of a physiological nature that indicate the need for referral to a physician. The first of these is fever. Its presence is almost never due to emotional difficulties alone. It is one of the chief danger signals that something is organically wrong and should not be disregarded. A case of persistent coma was diagnosed on one occasion by a professor of psychiatry who was idly flipping through a pile of charts while listening to a case presentation. He noted the spikes in the temperature chart. They occurred regularly every forty-eight hours. The psychiatrist immediately diagnosed cerebral malaria as the cause of the coma. Administration of quinine relieved the coma in a startling way.

Pain is another important cue to be noted. Persistent pain almost anywhere in the body is a cause for careful evaluation and medical referral.

When a patient reports the presence of blood where it should not be, a medical referral should be made. This sign of disturbance is usually reported as blood in secretions (vomitus, sputum) and in excretions (urine, stools). Since the blood does not always appear as red, the clinician should be alert to reports of dark-colored or brown tinges in the secretions and excretions, which the patient may not recognize as blood. In the stools it often appears black or tarry due to chemical changes occurring in the gastrointestinal tract.

Unusual masses or swelling in the body tissues may indicate a tumor or other serious disease process. Obviously they call for medical study.

Marked disabilities such as loss of function, weakening of function, gait disturbances, convulsions, aberrant involuntary movements (tics, tremors), inability to identify objects or to find the right words should be noted. They strongly suggest the possibility that the nervous system is damaged.

It would not be profitable to list all the other symptoms and signs which should alert the psychological diagnostician or therapist to the possibility of physical disease. They comprise the whole gamut of medical diagnosis. But after all, it is most often not the conscious knowledge of the disease which is so important; we need a cultivated sensitivity to the exquisite interrelationship of the organic and the psychological aspects of the person.

REFERENCES

1. Adams, F. D. *Physical diagnosis.* (13th Ed.) Baltimore: Williams & Wilkins, 1942.
2. Davidson, H. A. *Forensic psychiatry.* New York: Ronald, 1952.
3. *Diagnostic and statistical manual of mental disorders.* Washington: Mental Hospital Service, American Psychiatric Ass., 1952.
4. Lipton, M. A. The recognition and management of psychiatric emergencies. *Med. clin. of North America,* 1954, 38, 143–166.
5. Menninger, K. A. *A manual for psychiatric case study.* New York: Grune & Stratton, 1952.
6. Penfield, W. Memory mechanisms. *Arch. Neurol. Psychiat.,* 1952, 67, 178–191.
7. Reider, N. The reaction of psychiatric patients to physical and neurological examinations. *Bull. Menninger Clin.,* 1939, 3, 73–81.
8. Resolution on relations of medicine and psychology. *J. Amer. Med. Ass.,* 1954, 156, 72.
9. Soniat, T. L. L. Psychiatric symptoms associated with intracranial neoplasms. *Amer. J. Psychiat.,* 1951, 108, 19–22.
10. Spurling, R. G. *Practical neurological diagnosis.* (5th Ed.) Springfield: Charles C Thomas, 1953.
11. Taylor, N. B., & Taylor, A. E. *Stedman's medical dictionary.* (13th Ed.) Baltimore: Williams & Wilkins, 1953.
12. Wolf, S. The medical and psychological value of a thorough physical examination. Address presented at North Shore Health Resort, Chicago, Ill. Nov. 3, 1954.

CHAPTER 8

The Rorschach Method

What clients say about themselves is likely to be full of important omissions and distortions. In part, they intentionally suppress and emphasize in order to create a favorable impression. In part, repressive activity prevents even sincerely motivated clients from telling us about their motives. Although interviewing permits shrewd guesses about motives and attitudes that the client will not or cannot reveal, clinicians would like additional data.

Since the discovery that dreams are more likely to reveal repressed material than waking associations, it has seemed possible that imaginative activity in general could be used to reach beyond awareness. Freedom from a task with a logical solution, absence of conventional constraints, and an attitude of playful creation: these permit the unwanted, shame-provoking impulses to exert some force, even though they may still be disguised. This possibility is the basis of projective methods.

Of course, when the client and clinician know one another well, as in psychotherapy, repression is weakened along with intentional controls; then interview material is rich enough to permit confident inferences. In most diagnostic contacts, however, time does not permit building a relationship between client and clinician that will enable repressed material to emerge. Consequently, imaginative activity, or something similar, must be resorted to if we are to get "deep" material. We must set a task for the person in which he reveals himself to the clinician without realizing what he is doing.

PROJECTIVE TECHNIQUES

The Nature of Projective Techniques. Projective methods place new requirements on the client and introduce novelty into the client-clinician relationship. At one time it was supposed that these methods were, like psychometric tests, relatively independent of the social setting in which they were administered. They were considered primarily as ways of permitting a great deal of projection to take place. Projection is attribut-

191

ing our own unacceptable motives and characteristics to someone or something else. More broadly, it is perceiving the world in accordance with our own motives and beliefs instead of perceiving it "realistically." Now, while projection, in one or the other of these meanings, does take place in projective tests, many other important processes also occur. Persons taking such tests evaluate their own activity, are interested or bored, feel friendly or hostile toward the examiner, are calm or tense, and so on.

Actually, these methods are tasks requiring creative, playful imagination, and they mobilize a variety of personal resources. The tasks are rather simple and innocent-looking: telling a story, drawing pictures, making up sentences, or finding shapes in ink blots. The client does not simply project himself into reality; he creates a reality by imposing his capacities, interests, motives, fears, and preferences on amorphous materials. This playful invention occurs in the presence of another person who, the client knows, is somehow taking his actions seriously.

The interesting thing about these projective tasks is that there are no social norms—at least so far as the client knows—as to what is correct or allowable. The client cannot tell whether what he does is socially acceptable nor even whether it is acceptable to himself. Consequently, the anxiety that is needed to start and maintain repressive activity is not selectively aroused. If, for example, the client represses awareness of hostile impulses, he can do this successfully only if he knows in some dim way when he feels hostile. But in a playful activity nothing is quite serious, and he cannot really identify the unacceptable parts of himself. He does not know what elements of his performance will be evaluated by the clinician. He is not sure of the difference between a "good" and "bad" product or between an "abnormal" and "normal" approach. While he may guess that he is revealing something, he cannot say just what it is nor how he is revealing it.

In this novel situation, where the meaning of his actions is unclear, the client often becomes tense and apprehensive because he knows he is being studied. Then the stage has been set for the clinician to see how this anxiety is being managed. This is an extremely significant opportunity, because it is quite likely that the client's typical anxiety-reduction techniques will be displayed in full view of the clinician. Then the clinician can match his inferences from the client's reported history against observations of the client in a stressful situation with unclear social rules. Some people become cautious, some become servile and pleading, others become resentful, and still others suffer an impairment in their output of ideas. Usually the anxiety about the task decreases, just as in the interview, while the client becomes involved in the creative effort. Then we can observe increasing flexibility and enjoyment in the latter parts of the task.

Most projective tests include stimuli planned to arouse thoughts or feelings about common problem areas of living: sex, aggression, dependence, status, and the body. Clients are affected differently by these stimuli, and their efforts to deal with the tensions that are aroused will modify or hamper their output. By noting the kind of stimuli that cause the most trouble, the clinician can make inferences about the kinds of problems that distress the client.

In summary, projective methods enrich the interaction between client and clinician by setting a task that yields a novel kind of data. The client is asked to make a creative effort, using material that tends to touch off feelings related to personal difficulties. Since the basis for assessment is not known, repression is partly by-passed. Thus the clinician can learn more about the covert side of the client's life and about his techniques for dealing with anxiety and with social ambiguity.

Studying Projective Methods. The products emerging from the projective task are as diverse as the people who produce them. Then, too, the richness of behavior that is available to the clinician varies greatly from client to client. These complex and variable data must be systematically ordered if we are to use them. Significant information must be preserved, and unimportant facts must be neglected. How this is to be done is the nub of any projective method; and all sorts of hypotheses and hunches have been proposed to guide the sorting of data into meaningful categories. "Scoring" a projective test means applying some classification system to the client's product and to the clinician's observations. These scoring systems are complicated; they depend considerably on subjective judgment, and require much time to master.

Of course, you cannot learn to work with projective methods by studying these methods alone. Proficiency rests on familiarity with behavior pathology, personality theory, and the empirical principles of projective interpretation. Only with this kind of background can you interpret the systematically arranged data. Even then, you need a good deal of experience with the particular method you are using. A projective test is pretty much like an old automobile: only the regular driver knows how to make it go.

Giving you a complete account of any projective method is impossible in this book. It takes a whole book to describe adequately the Rorschach method alone. What we shall try to do is to give you a foundation for future study and for reading research reports. We shall try to convey the "feel" of these methods and to expose some of their weaknesses. Perhaps we can help you understand how clinicians think about projective data. More important, you may be able to develop your sensitivity and hypothesis-making skill a little more; for the study of projective methods can illuminate what is happening during interviews. It can also help you speculate insightfully about other creative activities such as hobbies, writing poetry, the selection of interior decorations, and so forth.

We shall discuss the Rorschach method first because it is so widely used and because it reveals so much about projective methods in general. If you can arrange to see a set of the standard Rorschach cards or slides, this chapter will make better sense to you. Black-and-gray reproductions of the cards will not carry the emotional impact of the originals nor disclose their associational possibilities.

THE RORSCHACH METHOD [1]

Presenting the Task. The examiner tells the client that he is going to be shown some ink blots. He is asked to tell what they might be or what they look like. After the examiner reminds him to tell everything he sees, he is given the first card. Any questions are met with the reply that he is just to tell whatever the blots look like to him, and that there are no "right" or "wrong" answers.

Examiners usually do not say anything about the purpose of the test. The fact that the examiner confidently expects the client to cooperate is enough to get the test started. If the client is hesitant, the examiner may say that this is part of the ordinary routine and that most people find it interesting. With more resistant cases, the examiner tries to get the client to speak fully about his objections and reassures him about the simple and routine nature of the test. Some clients think that the test is for "crazy people" and need to be told that it is a common method used by psychologists. When a client demands to know exactly how the examiner will use the results or how the test works, he can be promised a chance to discuss these matters after the test. With extremely stubborn clients, it is better to postpone the test and begin an interview centering about the client's attitudes toward the whole clinical situation.

The Blots. The ten cards are each 7 by 9½ inches in size. The printed blots are copies of originals that were made by folding paper to press drops of ink into random symmetrical shapes around a prominent center axis. Cards I, IV, V, VI, and VII are black and gray only. Cards II and III combine red and black. The last three cards, VIII, IX, and X are combinations of pastel colors. They are given to the client one at a time, in the sequence from I to X, and in a standard position. The client is free to turn them any way he likes.

The various combinations of blot colors and shapes produce different emotional responses. Some unpublished data from a study of the emo-

---

[1] For the historical background of the Rorschach, see the first chapter of the manual by Klopfer and Kelley (12). You will also enjoy reading Rorschach's own account of his work (18).

tional labels applied to Rorschach cards (23) reveal these differences. Subjects were shown the cards and were asked to tell which of five labels suited each card best: fear, anger, happiness, sadness, or none of these. Results indicate that the first card is most often called "fear." The next two cards, however, are more likely to be called "happiness" by normal men, although not by anxious men. The fourth card most commonly appears to represent "anger" or "fear" for normals, but anxious men use "fear" as a label for this card almost as often as for the first one in the series. No label has clear predominance for Card V. Card VI is the most emotionally confusing in the series, for it was most frequently responded to with the choice "none of these." The remaining four cards are most often called "happiness." In fact, for the final multi-colored card, X, nearly two-thirds of the normal men used this label. While we do not know the specific determiners of these emotional reactions, it is safe to say that the sequence of cards provides a shifting emotional experience. Obviously this experience will not be identical for all people.

The vertical symmetry of the blots around a center line has produced a number of areas resembling the vulva and the penis. These areas are likely to elicit sexual associations and, therefore, will often provoke anxiety. Red areas that resemble blood or fire are disturbing to many clients because of their connotation of aggression.

Recording the Responses. The favored position for the examiner is to be seated to the left and a little behind the client, although some examiners prefer a seat opposite the client. The favored position permits the examiner to see what section of the blot the client points to and allows him to take notes unobtrusively. The cards are stacked face down near the examiner. As he hands each card to the client, he notes the time elapsing before the first association is announced. He also records the total time spent in giving associations to each card. If only one response is given to the first card before the client returns it, he is asked to try to see something else. This encouragement is not strong, however, and is usually discontinued after the second card.

The examiner tries to record everything that the client says, including his comments during tests. Often something must be left out, but every effort is made to get a verbatim account of at least the associations reported by the client. Shorthand is an asset to a Rorschach examiner, but many clinicians have developed their own symbols for common remarks and associations.

During this first phase of the examination, the association period, the examiner says very little. He answers questions about procedure by telling the client to go ahead with the task in any way he wishes. He would note, however, whether the client asked permission for nearly everything he did or whether he seemed free to turn the cards and give associations of many kinds. Some mildly inhibited people need reassurance at first but become more spontaneous after seeing several cards. Others ask anxiously whether they are "doing all right" throughout the whole examination.

The Inquiry. After the client has seen all ten cards, the examiner returns to Card I and, from his notes, inquires about the basis for the various associations. The point of this questioning is to find out where each percept was seen and what features of the blot were used as a basis for the association. Was the client reacting only to the shape or form of the blot; or was he reacting to the color, shading, or textural quality of the blot? If a human figure was seen, did the client think of it as moving, or at least alive; or was the figure regarded as a puppet, statue, or silhouette? Actually, the clinician does not ask these questions outright, for he does not want to suggest that any particular basis—form, color, etc.—is more desirable than another.

The questioning should help the client elaborate on his response without guiding him in any particular direction. The inquiry must be "nondirective" and yet full enough to permit you to make certain important scoring decisions. You need to employ all the interviewing skill you can command, along with a good deal of persistence, if you are to conduct an adequate inquiry. Furthermore you will have to know what you are looking for; and that means you must be familiar with the possible scores that may be assigned. If, after further training, you use the Rorschach method, you may as well assume that at least the first half-dozen records you take will be unsatisfactory because of an inadequate or awkward inquiry.

After the Testing. Some clients are curious about the Rorschach test and ask the examiner to explain how it works or to tell what he found out by using it. Since scoring and interpretation take time, the examiner is rarely in a position to make any definite statements at the end of the test. If he simply explains this matter, the client may feel that the examiner is being evasive and that he did poorly on the test. On the other hand, it is quite undesirable for the examiner to say anything about the client's personality immediately after the test. Even if his statements were correct, the client could become so anxious or angrily defensive that further clinical studies would be hampered. Yet both client and clinician would feel more comfortable if some kind of explanation could be made. How can this be done without unduly disturbing the client?

One way of dealing with this dilemma is to discuss the associational content. The clinician says something like this: "One thing about this test is that it takes imagination to do it. I noticed that you saw quite a few different things, so I take it that it was not hard for you to use your imagination. Do you think that's true?" The client will probably have some things to say about his imagination, and these remarks can lead to a short conversation about the matters he brings up. Nothing more about the test needs to be said. If the clinician is pressed further, he can bring up specific content: "Many times the kinds of interests that people have lead them to see particular things in the blots. I notice that you saw several flowers (or maps, etc.). Have you been interested in gardening (or geography)?" Here again, the client will explain something about his interests, and nothing more will need to be said about the test proper. Of course, the examiner would not use anatomy, fire, sex, or other pathological content as his point of departure. Relatively safe associations are emblems, architecture, furniture, tools, and other commonplace objects.

With more sophisticated and educated clients, it is possible to go further, if that should be required. The clinician may make use of innocuous interpretations of the location scores: "Well, of course, we are interested in the way you look at situations as well as in what you see. For example, I noticed that you often used the entire blot to see something. Is that characteristic of you? I mean do you usually like to try to get the whole picture of every problem that you face?"

Such explanations not only help the client accept psychological procedures, but they often elicit useful information about the client's self-evaluation and insight. Obviously the clinician must try to fit his remarks to the kind of person he is testing. Most people merely need some assurance that they "did all right" on the test, but curious, anxious, or very intelligent clients will want to discuss it. The principle to use in these discussions is this: pick some obvious part of the performance, link it with a superficial aspect of the client's life, and then get his opinion of this linkage. This principle can be followed with other projective methods and even with the more structured psychometric tests. In answer to a question about an intelligence test, for example, the clinician points out that the client had some difficulty with arithmetic (or seemed to do it quite well); then he may ask him how he liked this subject in school.

Serious interpretations of test results sometimes need to be given to clients, but the time, circumstances, and context must be carefully chosen so that the client can utilize the information constructively. Interpretations of projective tests are often very threatening to clients and are more likely to be harmful than helpful.

Problem 1. Make several ink blots for yourself. Lightly crease a center line in a sheet of typewriter paper. Put a few drops of ink in or near the crease, and then press the folded halves together on a flat surface. Make one blot with black ink only, and make the other with both black and red ink. (You may have to make several until you get one that is esthetically satisfying.) After the ink dries, flatten the paper by bending the crease in the opposite direction.

Now ask a friend to tell you what he sees in the two blots. After you have recorded the things he sees, conduct an inquiry. Without directly asking, try to find out:

1. Whether a percept was based on form (shape) alone
2. Whether color or texture had anything to do with what he saw
3. Whether any human or human-like figures were seen as moving or alive

A good question to begin the inquiry is: "Will you show me where the _____ is?" After locating it, you may then ask "What was it about this blot that reminded you of a _____ ?" Don't use the words "form," "shape," "color," or "movement" in asking about what was seen unless your subject mentions them first.

Questions: 1. What are the main difficulties you found in conducting an inquiry?

2. If you or your subject became impatient during the inquiry, how did you try to handle this feeling?

A SAMPLE RECORD

Before going into the formal aspects of Rorschach scoring, let us look at an unscored record and speculate about it. Since we are interested in the client's psychological processes rather than in the mechanics of scoring, we omit the inquiry. In reading the record, note that the examiner's comments and observations are placed in brackets. Time is recorded in minutes (′) and seconds (″).

Card I. [40″.] It looks like a wolf. [*Pause. What else?*] Just simply looks like a wolf. [Can you see anything else there at all? *Client studies the card, looks at the back of it, and puts it down.* Total time, 3′ 15″.]

Card II. [*Looks briefly at back of card, then points to lower red area of blot.*] Hmm. [*Two minutes elapse as he studies blot.*] It looks like he's got a —what's the idea? [Just tell me what it looks like. *Client points to projection in upper center.*] That probably is—it's a, what is it? This is a, a . . . [*points to lower red*] that's a . . . [What does it look like to you?] I don't know what the dickens it is. [*Examiner encourages him.*] It's two. . . . [Total time, 8′.]

Card III. [*Puts card down after looking at it for a half-minute.* Can you see anything there?] Yes, a fellow can see something but. . . . [Just tell me what you see. *Client laughs.*] I don't know. [End of trial.]

Card IV. [*Client looks at back of card and puts it down after 40″.* Maybe the next one will be easier.]

Card V. [*3″.*] Oh, a bat. [*Pause.* Anything else?] No, that's all.
Card VI. [*18″.*] A coonskin. [*Puts card down.*]
Card VII. [*Puts card down after 30″. Examiner urges him to look again.*]
Two women.
Card VIII. [*7″.*] Two rats.
Card IX. [*30″.*] A couple rats.
Card X. [*18″.*] Couple of rats.

In examining this record, it is convenient to start with the client's creative product: the associations. We are struck at once with the fact that he does so little with the material he is given. Seven definite percepts are named; six of these are animals. There is no detailed description of any of them. They are simply named. In Card II, we see the beginning of another association, but there is a breakdown in the communicative process: "It looks like he's got a—what's the idea?" Obviously some kind of figure was seen, probably human, but confusion sets in before it can be described.

At this point, we need comparative data. How many percepts are commonly reported during the whole task? Is it usual to see so many animals? Fortunately, we have some normative information on these points. People are usually able to give two or three associations per card, on the average, making a total of twenty to thirty for the whole task. Among college students we often find from thirty to fifty responses in a record. While people commonly see animals, we ordinarily expect a record to contain only from 30 to 50 per cent of them. With this background we can more confidently describe this client's thought processes as meager and impoverished, that is, lacking in elaboration.

Several further observations can be made about this client's creative effort. The last three responses are the same: "rats." Although shapes that could be called rats can be found in these three stimulus cards, it is unusual to have a single response repeated in this way. The client behaves as if he had found a way to satisfy the examiner without expending much effort.

What can we say about the client's motivation as he works? Does he try hard, give up easily, or is he flighty? Actually, he sticks at the task for a surprisingly long time with only a little encouragement. He spent eight minutes on Card II, for example, although nothing definite was produced. After this point, however, the encouragement slackened, and the time spent on each card decreased. Probably the motivation of the client depended a good deal on the stimulation of the examiner. Fatigue may also be responsible for the lowered effort.

The client's language conveys the distinct impression of extreme effort which gets nowhere. With encouragement, the client tries hard but becomes confused. How does he react emotionally to this frustration and to the repeated requests of the examiner? We find little sign of emotional activity. There is embarrassed laughter on Card III, and on Card II a sign of annoyance: "I don't know what the dickens it is." But nowhere is there a request to stop the task; nor is there self-criticism, irritation at the examiner, or ridicule of the cards or the test. Apparently hostility is not easily aroused in this person. He could be described as emotionally passive in this situation.

There is one bit of behavior that should be noticed, although we cannot be clear about its meaning. Spontaneously, he inspects the backs of Cards I, II, and IV. At the very least, this is self-initiated searching activity, but it is unusual. It is reminiscent of the action of a child confronted with a novel object, an attempt at orientation toward something strange. But it occurs three times during the test.

So far nothing has been said about this client's age, sex, or background. Before we describe it, you should look at the record again to see if it contains any hints as to whether we are dealing with a child or an adult. What is your guess?

Actually the person who produced this record was a seventy-year-old man. Although largely self-educated, he had been a respected teacher and a public speaker, well known in his community. Obviously his history indicates better-than-average intelligence. Why, then, this meager record? By this time you are probably speculating about various senile disorders and their effects. The Rorschach findings and the patient's age certainly fit a hypothesis that brain damage exists. This patient had a history of increasingly severe attacks of apoplexy ("strokes") for a period of six years prior to the time this record was taken. At the time he was studied he was suffering from a severe aphasia, some loss of time sense, impairment of recent memory, and he appeared generally inert and passive. There were no indications of hallucinatory or delusional trends.

The Rorschach record in this case served no functional purpose in the disposition or treatment of the patient. The diagnosis and the treatment were sufficiently clear from interview and medical examination data. And this is often the case in other kinds of disorders. The bizarre associations of some schizophrenics, for example, appear as readily in conversation as they do in the Rorschach test. But in less extreme cases, the test permits a patient to display peculiarities of thought and emotion that are not apparent in routine or conventional situations.

FORMAL SCORING OF RORSCHACH RECORDS

The record we have just studied was interpreted in very much the way interview material would be interpreted. In order to see the special contribution of the Rorschach method, however, we must go beyond this approach and study the perceptual activity of the patient. We want to find out how and where each association is connected with the ink-blot stimulus; and then we want to be able to describe the "perceptual style" of the client. It is at this point that the formal scoring symbols are useful. They are abstractions that refer to the perceptual processes regardless of the particular content that is produced. In Table 3 you will find a list of the main scoring symbols and a brief explanation of their significance.

In order to find the value of R (total number of responses), the record must be broken into separate responses, that is, single associations, such as "bat," "men dancing" or "a fairyland cave." Comments, questions, and conversational remarks are not counted as responses.

Table 3. The Chief Rorschach Scoring Categories

Symbol	Basis for scoring	Approximate frequency in normal adult records	Approximate meaning
R	Total number of associations	20–30	Intellectual productivity
W	Use of whole blot	20–30% of R	Ability to integrate; sometimes "drive"
D	Obvious details	60–70% of R	"Common sense"; ability to use obvious facts
Dd	Unusual details	0–10% of R	Concern for detail or the unusual; meticulousness
F	Use of form only	30–50% of R	Ability to deal with objects in an objective, formal, logical way
F+	Accurate, realistic use of form	70–90% of F	Realistic intellectual control; "ego-strength"
F—	Inaccurate form perception	1–3	Distorted, unrealistic perception
M	Humans in movement	2–4	Fantasy; ability to inhibit action by thought; creativity
FC	Form used, with color as a secondary influence	4–5	Socialized, controlled emotional responsiveness
CF	Color used, with form as a secondary influence	1 or 2	Partially controlled, vivid emotionality; temper
C	Use of color only	None	Uncontrolled emotion; rage
Y	Use of shading only (occurs in combination with form also; similar to color scoring)	None	Diffuse, depressive anxiety

After breaking the record into responses, each one must be scored. First, the examiner must find the area used by the client for each response. Using specially prepared tables (2, 10) he assigns a location score: W (whole blot), D (obvious detail), Dd (small detail). He then assigns a determinant score, depending on the client's use of form, movement, color, shading, etc. This completes the formal scoring of the response, and the examiner turns to the actual content of the association.

Since there are many possible kinds of associations, scoring content is largely a matter of fitting the associations into some kind of classification scheme. Nearly all examiners use the following classes: animal (A), animal detail (Ad), human (H), human detail (Hd), anatomy (An), art or art-related objects (Art), blood (Bl), explosions and fire (Fi). In addition, special categories are invented to suit the content of some records: clothing, flowers, tools, maps, etc. The range of content produced tells something of the client's associational richness, thus indirectly revealing breadth of interests and educational background. Special preoccupations may be disclosed by a massing of responses in one content category, such as clothing, religion, or death. It is not always safe to interpret these as specific interests, however, since they may represent coping with anxiety in a way that is specific to this test. A large number of anatomy responses, for example, does not necessarily point to hypochondria. They may reflect concern with sexual adjustment or a generally anxious attitude. Vague maps and geographical forms do not usually indicate an interest in geography; they are more likely to show evasiveness, an effort to get through the test without exposing one's thoughts. Usually only one content designation is given to each response, but in some instances it is important to use two categories. The response "the Virgin Mary," for instance, would be classed as both H and Religious. "Ovaries" would be both An and Sex.

Lists of extremely common responses have been prepared so that a scoring of P (popular) is possible. Beck (2) lists twenty of these and suggests that seven to nine of them will appear in average records. Low P scores indicate an inability to accept conventional ideas or to recognize the clichés common to the community. High P scores in records of average length indicate overconformity or excessive reliance on popular, stereotyped notions. Some examiners use the score of O (original) for associations that are uncommon and creative. Others do not use this score because of the extremely subjective standards for deciding when such a score is warranted.

To show the abstract nature of the formal scores, we shall compare two responses to Card I. They are given identical formal scores, but they actually differ in important nonscorable ways.

A. "That looks like a bat."

B. "Well I'm not very good at this kind of thing. Perhaps it could be a bat or maybe a kind of butterfly. Not much of anything, really, because it's so irregular around the edges. But if I have to say something, I guess it would be a bat." Both of these responses use the whole blot, both are based on accurate form perception alone, both include a whole animal, and both are popular. The scoring is: W F+   A P.

The injection of personal feelings and self-evaluation into the second response surely suggests vacillation and self-doubt. Note also the oblique reference to coercion in: "If I have to say something." Perhaps this client projects his own standards into the external world as coercive force. Clearly, interpretation must not stop with the formal scores alone. Careful study of the actual associations yields worthwhile insights. Remember this point when you read research studies that use only the formal scores for statistical analysis.

Problem 2. The Rorschach does not really by-pass all defenses. Whenever a response can be related to social conventions, the client can control it unless he is severely damaged, as in the case of psychosis. In the Rorschach, social conventions can most easily affect the content, particularly sex responses. Experience shows that normal people do not report all of their sexual associations; their records often contain a few sex-related responses, however, such as "breast," "brassière," or "male sex organ." Two or three of these in a record of average length probably shows awareness of sexual impulses without fear of social censure for admitting them. With this background, answer the following questions.

Among what clinical types or kinds of people would each of these ways of dealing with the sexual associations in the Rorschach probably occur?

1. No sexual responses. Client has some difficulty in getting associations for areas that are often seen as sexual, e.g., the top-center details on Cards II and VI.

2. Seven or eight sex-related responses in a total of thirty associations.

3. Three or four responses which consist of names of sex organs given in crude or slang terms. Average record.

4. A third of the responses in a record are frankly sexual responses described in vulgar or obscene terms.

INTERPRETING THE SCORING SUMMARY

To show how the formal scores are interpreted we shall use the scoring summary of a record given by Tom C., a thirty-year-old single man. The arrangement of the summary is standard among Rorschach workers. The location scores are given in the first column, determinants in the second, and content in the third.

Rorschach Summary for Tom C.

W	8	23%	F	27	78%	A	9		
D	16	58%	F+	27	100%	Ad	5	A%	41
Dd	10	29%	M	5		H	3	P	4
			CF	1		Hd	10		
R	34		FY	1		(H)	1		
						Botany	3		
						Fire	1		
						Clothing	2		
						Object	1		

To start the interpretation, we look first at the number of responses (R). Thirty-four responses is greater than average. Intelligence and associational productivity seem unimpaired. Of course, we need to know more about the quality of the 34 responses in order to be sure. The location scores show an excess of small details (Dd) and a deficiency of obvious details (D). Overconcern with detail is indicated. The productivity represented by 34 R is less impressive now, and the indication of superior intelligence is weakened. What kinds of people are concerned with the unusual and the minute? We think of scientists, accountants, overanxious people who are alert to small signs of favor or rejection, obsessive-compulsive neurotics, and some schizophrenics.

The determinants are marked by a very frequent use of form (F%) and only a single color response. This man must deal with his environment in an intellectual, formal way. The absence of form-color responses (FC) suggests a lack of capacity for socialized feeling, but the one CF shows that emotional activity is not completely lacking. The color-form response (CF) may mean that it is expressed only occasionally and in a vivid, socially awkward way. All this makes us wonder whether Tom can achieve satisfying interpersonal relationships. We think of him now as a somewhat cold or withdrawn person, lacking in emotional flexibility. The hypothesis of obsessive-compulsive neurosis is fitting so far. But psychosis is not ruled out.

All his associations have forms similar to the forms of the blot areas: F+% is 100. The chances that Tom is psychotic are decreased. But several further questions arise. For one thing, it is easier to accumulate F+ by using very small areas of the blot (Dd) than it is by picking W or D areas. Is Tom maintaining realistic perception by limiting himself to details? It seems so. In the second place, we do not expect completely accurate perception even in normal people. The average person will show F— occasionally. We may infer that Tom is overvigilant and too careful in avoiding errors.

Tom gives enough movement (M) responses to indicate better-than-average intelligence. The number of M also decreases the likelihood that this is a psychotic record, provided the responses are not bizarre. Whatever restriction he has shown in emotional responsiveness, it now appears that he has a chance for some satisfaction from his own thinking and speculation. The 5 M may indicate real creative potential; but that number could also be found in suspicious folk, who constantly speculate about the motives of others. The formal scores cannot help us much in deciding how the fantasy is employed.

The remaining determinant is a form-shading combination (FY). Although it is the only one of its kind in the record, it is important because there are so few other indicators of emotional responsiveness. The hint here is that a depressive quality may appear in Tom's emotional make-up. It probably refers to sadness rather than despair. At any rate, it softens a little the cold, intellectual quality we have found so far.

For a person with the intellectual potential represented by 5 M, the content scores show a somewhat limited range of associations. Art, nature, and architecture associations are missing here, although they come easily for many people with this amount of ideational activity. Even sex and anatomy responses are absent. The range of intellectual search is narrowed. There are only three human responses and one human-like figure, scored (H). The pattern of withdrawal suggested by the lack of color responses is supported. The percentage of animal responses (A%) (based on the sum of A and Ad) is within normal limits, so that we cannot say that his thinking is stereotyped and dull. That would be suggested by an A% above 50.

Only P 4 (popular) responses are given. Surely Tom could have seen several more of these easy associations. It must be difficult for him to accept or perhaps to know the clichés of his fellows. Again we feel the distance between him and the world of people.

We can begin to construct a general picture of Tom's adjustive pattern: Self-control and correctness are important to him, and he has the intellectual equipment to achieve them without sacrificing realistic perceptions. But he does sacrifice emotional relationships, and relies instead upon his own speculation and reflections. Probably these center on minutiae. The control of anxiety is accomplished by preoccupation with details.

Turning now to the original record, we first examine the quality of the W responses. There are two bats, two butterflies, a turtle, a fan, a flower, and a burning oil well. The first six of these are easy integrations of the blots often given by adults of average intelligence. The last two represent somewhat better achievements. They are responses to Card IX, which is more difficult to see as a whole. Ability to generalize, to relate ideas to one another, is present then at about average level. More complex wholes could have been expected from a healthy person who gives 5 movement responses (M).

The Dd responses include 7 that are substantially identical: tiny faces seen as profiles on the edge of the blot. While there are people who use Dd in an imaginative and creative way, Tom is not one of them. The details he sees are repetitive and stereotyped.

Inspection of the movement responses indicates impairment in the one part of the personality that a detached person can use to preserve a sense of personal value and a relationship with others: fantasy, planning, creative thought. Tom's first two Ms appear on Card I. One is an Indian standing (a small white space is used for this), and the other is a witch riding through the air in a standing position. On Card III, Tom sees a "fellow leaning back on his forearms." This figure is later called a bear cub. The fourth M, on Card V, is someone lying asleep. This response is hardly M, and some examiners would score it F. The last one appears on Card VII: "Just a strange face there. It doesn't look much like an Indian, but that might be a feather. The two faces are noticeably looking at each other." He continues to comment and neatly removes the trace of social interaction: "You might say there's a mirror there and one is the reflection. The mirror's in between them."

These indicators of the "inner world" show no real activity; they do not suggest a thinking process that is actively coping with difficulties. Passivity, "leaning backward," and looking at oneself are the dominant trends. Healthy adults see people dancing, kissing, climbing, lifting. But Tom is inwardly at a standstill.

If we couple this passivity with the inhibition of emotional responsiveness, we can only conclude that Tom must be left with meager satisfactions in living. If we couple it with the emphasis on detail, we conclude that he must be engaged in a futile chewing-over of picayune ideas. We could go further and gather more support from the way he talks about the blots during the test, but it is time to look at Tom's background.

Tom was reared in a family dominated by a strict father, who was a Baptist minister. His mother was apparently both overprotective and moralistic. Tom worked his way through college and law school and eventually passed the bar examination. He then applied for a job in a government agency but was rejected. Following this failure he developed a number of symptoms, including weakness, stomach complaints, and headaches. After "resting" at home for several years he took a job as a librarian but was dissatisfied with it. During this period he became attached to a young woman who was married and whose husband was in military service. He felt guilty about this attachment and finally broke off the relationship. He never had sexual relations with this woman nor with any other.

Before the Rorschach was administered, Tom was interviewed by several clinicians. They described him as an obsessive-compulsive neurotic who was concerned about guilt over masturbation, small thefts, and impulses to cheat. He also worried about possible insincerity in his declaration when he was baptized as a child. His worries and obsessions preoccupied him to an extent that interfered with normal ideation and application to tasks.

The interview data and the Rorschach results are consistent with one another. Both show the rumination characteristic of the obsessive personality and the lack of satisfying interpersonal relationships. Both suggest a man of good intellectual endowment who is unable to use his capacity effectively; but knowing that Tom was graduated from law school enables us to see the impairment in the Rorschach more clearly. With the added background data the Rorschach interpretation can be extended a little.

Since Tom's condition is serious, we wonder what developments are probable. There are indications in the record that, with increasing stress, Tom could develop delusions. Consider the fact that there is enough M to indicate a great deal of associational activity and remember that the content of these Ms is passive. This combination is fertile soil for ideas that one is being imposed on and pushed around by others. The tendency to read meaning in small details could provide him with subjectively convincing evidence; while the lack of good interpersonal contact would prevent him from getting information about the real attitudes of people. All this could happen if Tom lost the awareness that his thoughts and impulses are really his—if he began to experience them as originating outside himself. This kind of break with reality has not taken place so far; perhaps it never will take place. But the Rorschach record indicates that Tom could move in that direction. Such a prediction is difficult to validate, of course, because we do not know that the additional stress needed to elicit the delusions will actually occur. If Tom becomes frankly psychotic—a paranoid schizophrenic—the interpretation would be verified, but if he does not, we could not say that the interpretation was incorrect. The Rorschach suggests the possibilities in the person; it cannot yield evidence that they will materialize.[2]

Problem 3. Sacks and Lewin (19) present a brief record and case summary to emphasize the error of using the Rorschach as the sole basis for psychological assessment. We shall reproduce the record and a por-

[2] Schmidt (21) has published the complete Rorschach record of a case of paranoid reaction. The pattern of formal scores is similar to that in Tom's record, except that there are a large number of F— responses in Schmidt's case. His patient hallucinated whispering voices and had unsystematized delusions about his wife's infidelity. You will be interested in studying the Rorschach responses of this man. Note the kind of M responses he produces.

tion of the psychiatric report. Some changes in the published scores have been made to fit them into the scheme we are using. Your problem is to study the record, construct a scoring summary, and describe the discrepancies between the record and the report. In what respects does the description of the patient fail to agree with inferences from the Rorschach? What major changes would need to be made in the Rorschach record in order to reflect the information in the psychiatric report?

RORSCHACH RECORD OF B.A.

The roman number indicates the number of the card. The numbers following the card number show the time elapsing between the presentation of the card and the first response. The inquiry is not reported, but the score for each response is given.

I. 18″	1. A crab with two fins sticking out.	W	F—	A	
II. 10″	2. The head and neck of two little dogs.	D	F+	A	P
III. 14″	3. Two men holding something. I don't know whether they hold individual things or the same article.	W	M	H	P
IV. 48″	4. Cannot make this out . . . seems to be an insect, a winged insect.	W	F—	A	
V. 6″	5. Looks like a butterfly.	W	F+	A	P
VI. 24″	6. A small butterfly; it's in different shades.	D	FY	A	
	7. Floor mat of a bear's skin.	D	FY	A	P
VII. 14″	8. Two human heads with neck and part of the body; look like children's heads.	D	F+	Hd	P
VIII. 14″	9. Two mice with tiny legs; they look like getting something to eat.	D	F+	A	P
	10. A big tree with branches and roots.	D	F+	Pl	
IX. 15″	11. Two weird nonhuman heads with big stomach. Like 1,000 years ago.	D	F+	Ad	
	12. Like flounders swimming.	D	F+	A	
X. 16″	13. Two lobsters.	D	F+	A	P
	14. Two angry looking cats' heads.	D	F+	Ad	
	15. Two sea horses.	D	F+	A	
	16. Profile of a collie dog; a peaceful-looking dog.	D	F+	A	

Excerpts From Psychiatric Report.

B.A., a twenty-nine-year-old veteran, complains about jealousy of his wife, fighting, difficulty in getting along with people and feeling watched by others. He has been married four months to a night club dancer. . . . He made excessive demands upon her, and her work aroused his anger and jealousy to the point where he became often abusive. . . . He has been infantile, impatient, impetuous, threatening and confused. While things would go well with enough reassurance, symptoms would disappear immediately. With any delay or frustration, he developed extreme intolerance and has threatened harm to his wife, her father and himself. On account of his violence, his wife has left the house and has threatened divorce (19, p. 480).

THE STATUS OF THE FORMAL SCORES

The use of separate scores implies that different psychological processes are represented by each score. Take W and D as examples. Presumably, the activity required to produce W is somehow different from that yielding D. And yet Rorschach interpreters themselves find cases where this difference does not seem to exist. In many records, the Ws do not require any more creative effort or perceptual integration than do Ds. Whole responses like "a map of some kind," or "bony structure" may reveal apathy or banality better than D responses that have been broken into parts and reintegrated. The location scores, like many of the others, are based on a mixture of logically constructed categories, approximations to actual perceptual processes, and some empirical evidence. It could very well be that a different scoring procedure would be psychologically sounder than the one currently used. For example, Beck (2) has introduced a Z score that probably reflects perceptual integrating activity more accurately than W does.

Factor Analysis of Scores. Wittenborn (25, 26) used factor analysis to explore the meaning of the separate scores. His results indicate that some of the traditional scoring distinctions may be unnecessary and even erroneous. For example, the factorial composition of FC seems to show that it is more closely related to M than it is to the other color scores. If this should turn out to be generally true, we may have to recognize that the restraint or inhibition of action implicit in both M and FC is more important than we usually suppose.

Another of Wittenborn's findings is that CF, C, and W are closely related. They have significant loadings on a factor that could be called "perceptual spontaneity." Here is a suggestion that the impulsiveness or lack of emotional restraint shown by CF may also be shown by W. With this possibility in mind, it is instructive to reexamine the record presented in Problem 3. Could it be that the lack of restraint noted in the psychiatric report appeared in the Rorschach as responses 1 and 4? Both of these are wholes with poor form quality.

Influence of Total Productivity. As the total number of responses increases, the relationship among scores in the various categories changes. The simplest illustration is afforded by the P scores. With only twenty possible popular associations, the percentage of P responses is bound to decrease as the length of the record goes beyond normal expectancy. It is hazardous, therefore, to use the percentage P in a record for interpretive purposes. Much the same thing is true of W. Apparently it becomes more and more difficult to create good syntheses of the whole blot after the first six or eight are given. Quite possibly, then, a W percentage of 30 has quite a different significance in a record of forty responses than it does in a record of twenty.

Fiske and Baughman (7) have made a detailed study of the relationship between the number of responses and the various scores. They point out that the relationship is nonlinear in some cases, linear in others. For example, FY tends to increase in a regular way with an increase in R, but the number of Dd increases very sharply in records longer than forty responses. They do not believe that the use of percentage scores adequately meets this difficulty. The whole problem is one that hampers statistical analysis in Rorschach research, because differences between group scores may be due to differences in productivity rather than to differences in the use of particular locations or determinants. Fiske and Baughman are inclined to favor using only the first three responses to each card; when fewer responses are spontaneously given, the subject should be encouraged to give at least three. While this method would lose some data, it has the very great advantage of yielding records of comparable length. Norms collected under such conditions would be more meaningful than those now in use.

Content Scores and Formal Scores. Rorschach interpretation has usually depended more on location and determinant scores than on the content of the associations. Of course, peculiar or bizarre associations are always considered in interpreting the total record, and the possibility that certain associations have symbolic meaning has been repeatedly suggested. Some investigators have presented lists of associations that are supposed to appear commonly in certain clinical groups; e.g., suspicious, paranoid individuals may see "eyes" frequently.

It is possible, however, that the content of the associations may actually be responsible for the diagnostic value of some of the formal scores. To point out one instance, consider the fact that M scores, with very few exceptions, are based on a human figure association. And remember, too, that the kind of movement (bending, fighting, standing) is ordinarily taken into account by the interpreter. Perhaps M, as now used, represents two or three different psychological processes that can be distinguished only on the basis of the associational content (1).

The same kind of speculation may apply to the color scoring. Although color is supposedly linked with emotionality in Rorschach interpretations, it seems entirely probable that the real connection is between certain kinds of associations and emotionality. The role of color is simply that it permits the appearance of significant content that would not otherwise be given. If there were no chromatic colors in the blots, it would be very difficult to elicit responses of "blood," "fire," or "inflamed tissue." Yet this kind of content is fairly frequent among emotionally disturbed people. The writer recently examined the content of the color scores in thirty-five published Rorschach protocols. The records were taken from a variety of clinical types and a few normal persons. In this small sample, some interesting trends appeared. "Blood" associations were always scored C, and they accounted for nearly half of all C scores. Anatomy was ordinarily given a CF score, although about a third of these responses were scored FC. The few fire and explosion associations that appeared were given CF scores. This relationship between certain kinds of content and the color scores could mean that any validity of the color scores is actually due to the content of such associations. Obviously, this hypothesis must be investigated further before it can be taken seriously. Evidence has already appeared, however, that casts a good deal of doubt on the presumed significance of color in the Rorschach test (13, 22).

INADEQUACIES OF THE RORSCHACH METHOD

Considered as an objective measuring instrument, the Rorschach method has severe drawbacks. We need to appraise the method critically if we are to use it appropriately. Of course, if the Rorschach is regarded mainly as a way of enriching the contact between client and clinician and of turning up data that would otherwise be missed, some of these deficiencies are not very important.

Examiner Variability. One difficulty with the Rorschach is that examiners vary in their interpretation of the same record. The Rorschach is not unique in this respect; it is characteristic of the whole clinical process. A more serious defect is that different examiners may obtain different records from the same client. One reason for this defect is that scoring is affected by the bias and training of the examiner. A response that would be scored CF by some clinicians may be called FC by others; and it is not always clear whether a response is M or simply F. Published scoring standards help to solve such problems, but difficulties are still frequent.

In addition to variability in scoring, we have evidence that the personality of the examiner affects the associational process itself (8, 15). In a carefully controlled study, Lord (15) arranged to have thirty-six college men tested by each of three examiners. Her data show that when examiners made deliberate attempts to be cold or to be accepting, the records were affected. Even more important is the fact that the examiners had different effects on the obtained records, regardless of their simulated attitudes. The coldest and most masculine of the three female examiners, for example, obtained the shortest records and the largest number of C responses. While we are not sure exactly how this influence is exerted, it probably occurs largely in the inquiry period. At any rate, we know that any given record is only one of the possible records that a client could produce.

Crudity of Measurement. The interpretation of some of the scores depends upon expected values that have a wide range. The expected value of W% among normal adults ranges between 20 and 30. Slight errors in scoring W, therefore, are not likely to have much of an effect on the examiner's interpretation. But this is not true in other cases. Scoring two responses in a fairly short record as C would make a substantial error in the interpretation, if these responses should have been scored FC or CF. Several mistakes of this kind can produce serious interpretive errors. Eysenck (6) complains of the low reliability of many of the Rorschach scores and argues for a statistical rather than an interpretive approach to the whole method. He thinks that the "intuitive approach" suffers from "the tendency of the expert to pay attention to, and base his interpretation on, minute idiosyncrasies, odd phrasings, and slight deviations from the normal which have little reliability, and consequently little validity, while giving less weight to the more reliable and valid scoring categories which are picked out by the factorial-statistical approach" (6, p. 167).

We should also note the crudeness of percentage scores in short records. With only twenty responses, a change in scoring one response will increase or decrease the percentage score by 5 per cent. For many scores, especially for those with narrow ranges, the effect is to make the error of measurement quite large. Perhaps this coarseness is offset to some extent by other factors that are taken into account during interpretation, but the correction must be quite variable among different examiners.

Lack of Clarity in Concepts. The statements made about personality on the basis of the Rorschach are usually couched in very abstract language. Too often this abstractness leads to a kind of fuzziness as to the precise nature of the motive, attitude, or capacity that is being described. Consider the concepts related to the color scores. The pure C response is related, it is said, to uninhibited emotional responsiveness, to ungovernable impulses. Sometimes it is supposed to refer to rage, but this is certainly not the only interpretation. How clear are these concepts? Are we speaking of any kind of impulse, say compulsive desire to eat or to be sexually promiscuous? How can we recognize the approximate point at which an emotion (gloom, delight, anger) should be classified as "ungovernable." We are not doubting that there is some kind of relationship between C and emotional impulsiveness, but we must insist that the hypothesis is difficult to test as long as the concepts are in their present form.

An attempt to determine the meaning of CF scores has been reported by Clark (4). He divided the group Rorschach records of 100 college students into two subgroups: those with fewer than two CF responses and those with two or more. Since these students had taken the Minnesota Multiphasic Personality Inventory, Clark could determine which items differentiated the two groups. He reports: "The higher CF score is apparently correlated with a lack of regard for social conventions and a lack of reserve or inhibition in social attitudes" (4, p. 385). These findings were cross-validated on a subsequent group of forty-one students. Despite the indiscriminate combining of records, these results are in line with Rorschach tradition. They are also a step in the direction of a clearer specification of the personality correlate of the CF score in the normal range: unwillingness to observe social conventions. By means of specially constructed attitude scales, this concept could be related to the other color scores and, even better, to configurations of scores.

Although the Rorschach is designed for a configural approach, many investigators attempt to discover the validity of single indicators, or "signs," isolated from the rest of the record. These enterprises are interesting, but their relevance to the study of the individual by the Rorschach method is not entirely clear. A good example of the confusing state of affairs is provided by some studies of anxiety indicators in Rorschach records. Williams placed subjects in an experimental stress situation by using electric shock and the threat of observation by psychologists. He found a marked relationship between the decrement on a digit-symbol test under stress and the presence of certain Rorschach signs (color and F+%). Lazarus and Carlson (14) repeated Williams' study and obtained negative results. Eichler (5) used shock as a source of stress and administered the Rorschach under stress conditions. A control group took the test without stress. He reports that only 4 of 15 indices of anxiety changed reliably in the expected direction. Berger (3) then undertook a similar study, using the stress caused by entry into a tuberculosis hospital as the independent variable. He studied both total interpretations and isolated signs of anxiety. Two judges examined the unidentified records of forty patients taken when they entered the hospital and again some six weeks later. One judge identified the "stress" record in thirty-five of the forty sets of records; the other made thirty-six correct identifications. In Berger's analysis of specific anxiety indicators he found that most of them changed as expected. Among other things, records taken under stress showed decreased R, fewer content categories, more shading responses, and more frequent rejection of the cards.

Apparently the question is not whether the Rorschach can reveal anxiety, but rather what kind of anxiety is being revealed by it. If we accept Berger's findings at face value, a further serious question must be asked: "Can we tell the difference between situational anxiety and enduring anxiety-proneness from the Rorschach record alone?" It seems to the writer that the answer is this: the Rorschach record alone cannot be used to decide between these alternatives. Only when the interpreter knows the conditions of living faced by the client will he be able to use the Rorschach material effectively.

Failure to Reveal Personal Assets. Evidence is accumulating that personality descriptions based on Rorschach records are likely to be biased in the "maladjusted" direction. In one study (9), experts rated the adjustment of 146 eighteen-year-olds who were presumably normal. These experts, using the Rorschach alone, judged that about two-thirds of the group were maladjusted. Their ratings (on a four-point scale) were compared with similar ratings made by caseworkers who had actually known the subjects over a period of years. The results showed that there was only a slight relationship between the two sets of ratings. The authors comment: "The lack of a statistically significant relationship can only lead to the conclusion that the Rorschach used blindly . . . is of little value in predicting adjustment ratings made primarily on the basis of interviews and case histories" (9, p. 17). Data reported from assessment studies of graduate students in clinical psychology (20) also indicate that ratings based on the Rorschach tend to be "derogatory."

Perhaps these findings are due to the fact that the Rorschach method has developed largely in connection with the study of abnormal persons. The chances are, however, that the method is not appropriate for determining important personal assets. An incisive statement on this matter has been made by Roe (17). Her judgment is particularly valuable because she has made extensive use of the Rorschach in studying eminent scientists. She says: "In such records as I have collected one is impressed repeatedly with the fact that the Rorschach may not give any hint of the actual life performance of the subject. It may indicate the presence of severe problems, and it must be said in justice to the Rorschach that the reality of these can usually be determined, but it very likely will give no indication of the fact that the subject has managed to cope very effectively with the problem" (17, p. 264).

An Evaluation. The Rorschach method is one of the two or three most widely used clinical tools. Despite its deficiencies and despite experimental studies critical of its assumptions, clinicians continue to prefer it to most other methods of personal assessment. Why is it so favored as a practical device?

Zubin (27) has pointed out that the Rorschach method is actually a kind of standard interview. We can go further than this and say that it is a *stress* interview. True, the stresses are not intense, but they are strong enough to influence insecure, anxious people. The result is that the clinician has a performance to observe instead of a report to evaluate. The crucial question is, to what extent is this performance characteristic of the way the person functions in general? The answer to this question is not certain at present. Probably for some people—those who are consistent or rigidly set in their ways, the Rorschach performance is representative of their general adjustive patterns. But for others, it reveals something that is true but not typical of them.

Another advantage of the Rorschach method is that it is less easily manipulated by the client than is the interview. Since he usually does not know how to act in order to satisfy the clinician and himself, his performance depends upon his preferences, aspiration level, guesses as to the clinician's expectations, fear of self-revelation—in short, upon his personal dynamics. Thus the clinician can come a little closer to seeing the operation of forces beyond the client's awareness. The Rorschach performance, then, differs greatly from methods that depend upon self-report, such as interviews and questionnaires.

The Rorschach method has another characteristic that is both a strength and a weakness: the perceptual and associational activities it requires are apparently easily disrupted by transient anxiety, marginal associations, and deliberate efforts at self-control. The ease with which Rorschach performance may be disturbed by such factors makes the test peculiarly appropriate for probing subtleties of personality. It also leads, however, to interpretations that exaggerate the importance of these subtle revelations. At present, the only real safeguard against this kind of exaggeration is to place the Rorschach findings in the context of the case history.

The Rorschach method appears to offer a good opportunity for the clinician to estimate significant trends in the client. While it hardly yields a picture of the "total personality," it can often get at personal characteristics that are of critical importance in the integration of personality. Under optimal conditions, Rorschach performance ought to be able to suggest answers to questions like these: How well organized is the client's thinking? How deviant is the content of his thought? How does he manage anxiety? How does he evaluate himself? Does he fear to reveal himself to the clinician? What does he do about sexual or hostile thoughts?

Looking at the Rorschach as a standard stress interview means that we must not stop with interpreting the formal scores. We must be sensitive to many aspects of the client's behavior during the test. Probably we must pay more attention to associational content than we have in the past, as Zubin (27) has suggested. And certainly we must be aware of his behavior style as much as we are aware of his perceptual style.

The peculiar virtue of the Rorschach, then, is that it provides data about a number of important reference points in the total pattern of adjustment. Study of these reference points turns up discrepancies. Then the interpretation of specific scores is modified to take them into account. The record is searched again with new hypotheses in hand. Now it may be found that a single response, hitherto neglected, takes on a special meaning. Finally, the broad picture emerges, the deployment of intellectual and emotional resources can be sketched, and the weaknesses of the adjustive process suggested.

The danger comes from relying exclusively on the Rorschach. It cannot give a total picture of personality, despite the claims of enthusiasts. For the person functions in a world that both helps and hinders, that contains both tolerant and intolerant people, that reacts to his actual behavior as much as it does to his potential for breakdown. Therefore you will need to look beyond the ink blots, modifying your interpretation of a life history by what you have learned from them, and changing your understanding of the Rorschach record by what you learn from studying the life history.

Does the Rorschach have enough validity to give us even the hazy outlines of a portrait? Should it be taken as seriously as we have suggested in the preceding paragraph: to modify your interpretation of what facts you know about the life of the person? The answer is yes. And this answer does not rest simply on the repeated reports of clinical usefulness in specific cases.

One of the most extensive investigations of personal assessment yet reported apparently finds the Rorschach and other projective methods to be of little value (11). But if we study the findings carefully we discover evidence that positive, though low, validities occur frequently. Morris (16) has made a detailed analysis of the relationship between certain ratings made by Rorschach examiners and ratings made by a team that had studied the subjects intensively for a week. Ten attributes were rated, including such qualities as social adjustment, appropriateness of emotional expression, intensity of inner emotional tension, motivation for scientific understanding of people, insight into others and into self. Although the examiners were apparently not all of equal skill in using the Rorschach, the validity coefficients tend to be in the low thirties. The size of these validities needs to be interpreted in the light of the subjects who were tested. The subjects in this investigation were all students who had been accepted into graduate training programs in clinical psychology. This kind of group is obviously more homogeneous in many ways than the population at large. The mere fact that they had completed college training indicates their high level of intelligence and academic drive. Let us remember, too, that the group would not include students who had been discouraged from further work because of their poor social or emotional adjustment. We may reasonably suppose that the Rorschach examiners in this study were called upon to make finer discriminations than would ordinarily be the case. On this supposition, the fact that positive validity coefficients were the rule gives us the necessary support for believing that in other situations better results could appear.

The Rorschach is not very satisfactory, but it does a kind of job which our traditional psychometric tests do not do. And clinicians feel that in their work it is a job that ought to be done. Research will undoubtedly sharpen the Rorschach method, at least by showing the places where it is weakest and should have little weight in the clinician's judgment. On the other hand, research studies will not aid in improving the Rorschach if they analyze records without taking account of patterns or configurations of scores.

EFFECTS OF THE RORSCHACH ON THE CLINICIAN

We have already pointed out that the clinician may be influenced toward "derogatory" judgments of clients by studying their Rorschach records. But there are other possible effects that the Rorschach method may have on the clinician that could be beneficial.

Problem-setting. For one thing, the Rorschach sets a stimulating problem for the clinician. After the scoring is finished, he is faced with the necessity for interpretation. Unless he gives a "cookbook" interpretation, i.e., one in which he simply lists textbook statements about the meaning of each score, he must do some creative thinking. He is challenged to develop a unified conception of the client. Hypotheses suggested by the Rorschach will spur him to search his case notes again and to reanalyze other test data. The effect of the Rorschach record, then, is to induce the clinician to pay more attention to the case he is studying. There is an enrichment of contact between him and the case materials. This stimulation of the clinician contrasts with the lack of involvement resulting from a psychometric test; in the latter case, the score is translated into a measurement or a prediction and the clinician has no further problem. Involvement must come, in such instances, from interview or case-history data.

Modification of Set. The Rorschach can serve the clinician usefully in another way, by breaking sets that he has formed on the basis of other data. After interviewing, he may have formed some conclusions about the causes of a client's difficulty or his outstanding traits. The introduction of the Rorschach record may now force him to reconsider decisions already made and to increase the flexibility of his thinking about the client. One psychologist tells of administering a Rorschach to a colleague of his, a physician. The record was somewhat surprising to the psychologist, because it indicated a person who was incapable of much emotional contact with others and who was much involved in his own thoughts and fantasies. The psychologist was surprised, because he had noticed that the physician was always eager to join an informal group or to enter into conversation. He appeared to be quite outgoing. From then on, the psychologist paid more attention to the social interactions of his colleague. Then he discovered that his previous impression, while not entirely wrong, was incomplete on account of his own insensitivity. The physician did welcome a chance to talk with others and would frequently be found in informal groups; that much was true. What the psychologist had overlooked was that his conversation was largely a monologue! Occasionally he paused to allow another person to speak, but his flow of speech and thought was not greatly influenced by the interaction.

Problem 4. Opinions differ as to the amount of information about a client that the Rorschach examiner should have before he makes his final interpretive report. Here are four possible arrangements that could be made in a clinic. Read them and answer the questions below.

1. Given the age, sex, and educational level of the client, the examiner administers the Rorschach. He is then permitted to see the case history before making his final report. This report will be presented at the case conference and included in the client's file.

2. After reading the history, the examiner administers the Rorschach. He then prepares his final report.

3. Given the age, sex, and educational level of the client, the examiner administers the test and prepares his final report. He does not know anything about the case history until he attends the case conference.

4. The Rorschach is administered and scored by one examiner, but the final report is prepared by another clinician who has never seen the client. This interpreter is given the age, sex, and educational level of the client along with the scored record, including notes on the inquiry. Neither examiner has access to the case history until the case conference.

Assume that all these arrangements are equally practicable and that the recommendations for treatment and disposition will be decided at the case conference.

1. Discuss the advantages and disadvantages of each arrangement.
2. Which arrangement should be adopted as standard practice? Why?

REFERENCES

1. Barrell, R. P. Subcategories of Rorschach human movement responses: a classification system and some experimental results. *J. consult. Psychol.*, 1953, **17**, 254–260.
2. Beck, S. J. *Rorschach's Test. Vol. I. Basic processes.* New York: Grune & Stratton, 1944.
3. Berger, D. The Rorschach as a measure of real-life stress. *J. consult. Psychol.*, 1953, **17**, 355–358.
4. Clark, J. H. Some MMPI correlates of color responses in the group Rorschach. *J. consult. Psychol.*, 1948, **12**, 384–386.
5. Eichler, R. M. Experimental stress and alleged Rorschach indices of anxiety. *J. abnorm. soc. Psychol.*, 1951, 46, 344–355.
6. Eysenck, H. J. *The scientific study of personality.* New York: Macmillan, 1952.
7. Fiske, D. W., & Baughman, E. E. Relationships between Rorschach scoring categories and the total number of responses. *J. abnorm. soc. Psychol.*, 1953, **48**, 25–32.
8. Gibby, R. G., Miller, D. R., & Walker, E. L. The examiner's influence on the Rorschach protocol. *J. consult. Psychol.*, 1953, **17**, 425–428.
9. Grant, M. Q., Ives, V., & Ranzoni, J. H. Reliability and validity of judges' ratings of adjustment on the Rorschach. *Psychol. Monogr.*, 1952, **66** (No. 2), 1–20.
10. Hertz, M. R. *Frequency tables to be used in scoring responses to the Rorschach Ink Blot Test.* Cleveland: Western Reserve Univer., 1946.
11. Kelley, E. L., & Fiske, D. W. *The prediction of performance in clinical psychology.* Ann Arbor: Univer. of Michigan, 1951.
12. Klopfer, B., & Kelley, D. M. *The Rorschach technique,* Yonkers, N. Y.: World, 1942.
13. Lazarus, R. S. The influence of color on the protocol of the Rorschach Test. *J. abnorm. soc. Psychol.*, 1949, **44**, 506–516.
14. Lazarus, R. S., & Carlson, V. R. A repetition of Meyer Williams' study of intellectual control under stress and associated Rorschach factors. *J. consult. Psychol.*, 1953, **17**, 247–253.
15. Lord, E. Experimentally induced variation in Rorschach performance. *Psychol. Monogr.*, 1950, **64** (No. 10), 1–34.
16. Morris, W. W. Rorschach estimates of personality attributes in the Michigan assessment project. *Psychol. Monogr.*, 1952, **66** (No. 6), 1–27.
17. Roe, A. Two Rorschach scoring techniques: the inspection technique and the basic Rorschach. *J. abnorm. soc. Psychol.*, 1952, **47**, 263–264.
18. Rorschach, H. *Psychodiagnostics.* Berne: Hans Huber, 1942.
19. Sacks, J. M., & Lewin, H. S. Limitations of the Rorschach as sole diagnostic instrument. *J. consult. Psychol.*, 1950, **14**, 479–481.
20. Samuels, H. The validity of personality-trait ratings based on projective techniques. *Psychol. Monogr.*, 1952, **66** (No. 5), 1–21.
21. Schmidt, H. O. The Rorschach test in a case of paranoid reaction. *J. consult. Psychol.*, 1949, **13**, 134–143.
22. Wallen, R. The nature of color shock. *J. abnorm. soc. Psychol.*, 1948, **43**, 346–356.

23. Wallen, R. Emotional labels and projective test theory. *J. proj. Tech.*, 1954, 18, 240–247.

24. Williams, M. An experimental study of intellectual control under stress and associated Rorschach factors. *J. consult. Psychol.*, 1947, 11, 21–29.

25. Wittenborn, J. R. A factor analysis of Rorschach scoring categories. *J. consult. Psychol.*, 1950, 14, 261–267.

26. Wittenborn, J. R. Level of mental health as a factor in the implications of Rorschach scores. *J. consult. Psychol.*, 1950, 14, 469–472.

27. Zubin, J. Failures of the Rorschach technique. *J. proj. Tech.*, 1954, 18, 303–315.

CHAPTER 9

The Thematic Apperception Test

In 1820, Thomas Brown wrote: "To the cheerful, almost every object which they perceive is cheerful as themselves. In the very darkness of the storm, the cloud which hides the sunshine from their eye, does not hide it from their heart; while, to the sullen, no sky is bright, and no scene is fair" (4, p. 127). After relating mood to perception, he discusses the more enduring dispositions of the person:

. . . emotions of a stronger and lasting kind must influence the trains of thought still more;—the meditations of every day rendering stronger the habitual connexions of such thoughts as accord with the peculiar frame of mind. . . . We see, in every thing, what we feel in ourselves; and the thought[s] which external things seem to suggest, are thus, in part at least, suggested by the permanent emotion within (4, p. 127).

These propositions express the central assumptions which, in the twentieth century, are embodied in the Thematic Apperception Test. Of course, since Brown's time, unconscious motives have been added to the "permanent emotions" which he mentions.

Brown also hints at the stumbling block that trips the twentieth-century psychologist in his efforts to interpret the thoughts and perceptions of his client. ". . . in part at least," we are told, the character of perception is determined by motives, attitudes, emotions. But what part? What rules shall we follow to find the points where the inner world of the person guides thought and those where external social and physical reality have shaped its course? The value of the Thematic Apperception Test (TAT) as an instrument for revealing personality depends on our ability to answer these questions. Let us look at the nature of this projective method.[1]

ADMINISTERING THE TAT

The materials for the TAT are twenty black-and-white pictures. The pictures vary somewhat in size, although they are printed on cardboard

[1] Historical background for the TAT will be found in the first chapter of Tomkins' book (27).

with standard dimensions of 9½ by 11¼ inches. A few of the pictures are rendered with photographic clarity, but most of them have been drawn without fine detail and with soft lines, like charcoal sketches. We shall describe the pictures later. Most of them can be used with either sex, but a few are used exclusively for males or for females.

Administering the Test. After making the client comfortable, he is given these instructions:

I am going to give you a test of imagination. I'll show you some pictures and I want you to make up a story about each one. Try to make up a good dramatic story. Tell what led up to what you see in the picture, what is happening now, and what the outcome will be. Tell what the characters are thinking and feeling. Just tell me the story as you think of it, but be sure to tell what is happening, what led up to it, what the characters think and feel, and what the outcome will be. Do you have any questions?

These instructions are adapted from those given by Murray (19) in the manual for the test. Examiners make changes to suit the particular client they are testing, but the instructions always include a request for prior events, present situation, thoughts and feelings, and outcome. Ordinarily, if clients omit any of these four elements in giving a story, they are reminded of the omission and encouraged to tell the part they left out. Subjects are expected to spend about five minutes on each story and to give a story of around 300 words in length (19). Children's stories run about half as long. Examiners encourage reticent or unproductive subjects to tell longer stories, but, of course, they avoid demands which would destroy rapport. If stories become excessively long and rambling, the examiner may suggest that they be shorter.

The seating arrangement of the examiner and client is frequently the same one used in administering the Rorschach. Many examiners, however, prefer to face the client as he tells the stories. This position permits the examiner to notice the client's facial expression and establishes an easy conversational atmosphere.

The entire series of pictures is not usually presented at one sitting. Giving stories for ten pictures requires about an hour, and both the client and the examiner are likely to be fatigued by the end of that time. Murray (19) suggests that at least a day should elapse between the first and second sessions, but this rule is not invariably followed. For the second session, the client is often asked to make up still more dramatic and exciting stories than he did in the first session. The length of time required to administer the whole picture series makes the TAT inconvenient to use in most clinical settings. Therefore clinicians commonly select eight to twelve of the pictures and administer them all at one session.

Writing down the client's stories is a hard job. Ideally, every word should be taken down, but examiners frequently cannot write fast enough. It is permissible to ask the client to go more slowly or to repeat something he has said. Even then some words will be missed. Many psychologists, therefore, are using tape and wire recorders to get an accurate record of the stories. The recordings may be transcribed at leisure, and they have the additional merit of allowing the examiner to hear the client's tone of voice when the story is being analyzed.

The Inquiry. While the examiner is usually silent and does not interfere with stories, he should inquire about unclear or confusing stories. Ordinarily, this inquiry follows the end of each story. It must be a subtle, nonsuggestive probing. When important objects in the picture have been omitted from the story or mislabeled, questioning about them should probably be deferred until the end of the session. Then there is less chance of making the client aware of his distortions. Some examiners interview the client after the test is finished. They then encourage the client to tell about his stories, their sources, which ones he liked best, and what he thinks about his plots and characters.

SOME SAMPLE STORIES

To get an idea of the kinds of stories clients give, we shall compare three different stories for Card 1. This picture shows a boy gazing at a violin on the table in front of him. He is supporting his head on his hands as if resting. The first story was given by a single woman in her middle thirties. She is an intelligent person without any evident neurotic symptoms.

Well, it's a desire to study music but a lack of lessons—a forlorn feeling of "I wish I knew how, but I have nothing to work with," a sort of despair feeling. The outcome of this will be that if he ever has the money or the time he will devote it to the study of the violin. I guess that is about all. I'm not very good at storytelling. That is one thing I don't do, is dramatize things. I have one girl friend at work who does that kind of thing all the time.

The second story was given by an epileptic man in his late twenties. He showed a number of neurotic symptoms including temper outbursts and sexual difficulties.

This boy is sitting there dreamy-eyed. He doesn't like to play the fiddle but he's forced to play it because his mother wants him to learn it. He'll go ahead and play it, because he's forced to. But he won't want to. That's about all. He must not be interested in music because he lets it lay under the violin. He's got a smirk on his face, like "I'm gonna show you."

The third story was told by a single woman of thirty. She has had psychotherapy. Her chief complaints were: inability to stand up for herself, feelings of inadequacy, and a tendency to withdraw from social situations.

He's been practicing and—he's dreaming of what he might do with it another time—what he might go on to be as a violinist. He looks like a prodigy, I mean he doesn't look like a regular little American boy on account of the haircut. Then, too, he might have a little bit of a foreign, of a foreign, something like Yehudi [*laughs*]—not Yehudi, but what's his name, the violinist? [Examiner: Yehudi Menuhin?] It looks as though it might be he. I think that's about as much as I get out of that one. [What will the outcome be?] Well, it looks as though he might, he might succeed inasmuch as he seems so very much interested in it. The only thing would be, does he have the talent? Which is, of course, exactly what I wonder about me. Well, it seems to me that a little boy who would, who would sit down and dream about, about being a violinist after having practiced, instead of being, wanting to go out and play baseball. If he's got the talent, he's certainly got the appreciation and the willingness to study, he might succeed. Seems as though music would always mean a great deal to him.

As you study these stories, notice that, in addition to the actual story, two of the clients make comments about their own relationship to the task. The first woman excuses herself in a rather defensive way for the story she gives. Nobody has criticized it; she does that herself. Indirectly, the criticism is aimed at the examiner for requiring such a stupid task. In the third story, the client spontaneously recognizes that her own feeling of inadequacy influences her conception of the outcome. The boy will fail, she thinks, not from lack of interest but from lack of talent. And that is how she feels about herself.

Let us look at some of the chief features of the stories. The first emphasizes the lack of means—time or money—for reaching the goal. The barrier is external to the central character. In contrast to this, the third story indicates that the barrier—lack of talent—is internal. The second story shows a boy who is coerced by his mother into practicing. The coercion cannot be defied by refusal to practice but only by a smirk.

The crucial question about these stories is how they are related to the personality of the narrators. Do they tell us how the narrators see themselves or how they see children in general? Do the actions and thoughts of the central characters show how the narrators think of themselves as children or as they are now? Do they tell us what they are or what they would like to be? The various schemes that have been proposed for interpreting the TAT are attempts to answer these questions. There is no conclusive evidence that one set of assumptions is more appropriate than another, but certain similarities among the schemes can be found.

We shall discuss the problem of interpretation in more detail later. Let us now turn to one of the first steps of interpretation that is found in nearly all schemes.

ABSTRACTING THE STORY

Reading only a few records will convince you that some assumptions about the meaning of TAT stories are of little value. One of these is that the stories duplicate in slightly disguised fashion the actual experiences of the narrator. The number of killings, suicides, and jail breaks found in the recordings of normal people is enough to show the falsity of any such view. After all, the instructions invite people to indulge their imagination and to dramatize. Small wonder, then, that they choose the kind of events dramatized in the news and the movies.

Another assumption that should not be made is that the events in the stories are events which narrators wish for. If a man tells a story about a wife who is unfaithful, we are not justified in assuming that he *wishes* his own wife were unfaithful. Nor can we properly assume that he *fears* his wife has been or will be unfaithful. Interpreting stories on any such concrete basis will lead to ridiculous results. Nevertheless, the story is there and it must be related in some fashion to the man who told it. How shall we proceed?

Nearly every TAT analyst begins by abstracting events and persons from the stories. That is, they regard the concrete events as examples or illustrations of more general categories. A murder, abstractly regarded, is an example of a personal attack. Still more abstractly, it is a manifestation of hostility. On the most abstract level, it is a form of behavior. At this last level, we have drained out all the characteristics of murder except that it is a human action. The same abstracting process can be applied to the people in the stories. Thus a young married woman belongs to the class of "married women" (neglecting her age), to the more general class of "women" (neglecting her marital status), and to the still more general class of "persons," if we neglect her sex. For any story, then, it is possible to construct a number of abstract versions. To illustrate, we use a story told by a married man in his early twenties:

This is a doctor. He's a rather sinister figure. He's been called in because—he's somewhat of a fraud—called in by the boy's parents who are unversed people. The boy is seriously ill. The doctor will treat the symptoms only. The boy will think he is better. The parents will be relieved. The doctor will collect his exorbitant fees and depart. The boy, no doubt, will die later, say of cancer.

In constructing abstract versions of this story we may begin with the doctor. He may exemplify "male experts," "experts," and finally "people." The boy may exemplify "young people," "dependent people," and finally "people." The death belongs to the class of "getting worse," and this in turn belongs to the class of "failure to receive benefit." By neglecting the parents mentioned in the story, we get a low-level abstract version like this:

A doctor treats a sick boy superficially, and the boy later dies.

By substituting extremely abstract categories for the persons and the actions, we arrive at this version:

1. A person helps another person, but the second does not benefit.

A story at an intermediate level of abstractness could read this way:

2. An expert treating a person makes him worse.

Now, these versions all depend upon leaving out the term "fraud" that was used in the original story, and they neglect the statement that the parents are "unversed people." If we consider these elements in constructing an abstract version, our story would appear rather different:

3. Ignorant people employ an expert who is a fraud to treat a relative. The relative dies.

Version 1 is a statement of the impossibility of help from other people. Version 2 is a criticism of experts. But version 3 may reflect the narrator's realization of the plight of ignorant people. Which version should we choose to represent the meaning of the original story? There is a rough guide for choosing, but before we present it, let us point out that there is no necessary incompatability among these versions. Is it not possible that, for this young man, there is truth in all of them? It is. And therefore we would be wise not to throw away any of our versions but to hold them all as possibilities. We need other stories before we can choose among them.

The choice of an appropriate abstract version of a story depends on finding another story that yields about the same set of relationships. As we construct abstract versions for this new story, one will usually be found which is the same as, or quite similar to, one version of the first story. Then we choose the lowest level of abstraction that will include both stories. Among the stories given by the young man who told the "fraudulent doctor" tale there is another that is similar. In this story, a father is giving advice to his son. The advice is actually designed to gain something for the father. Although the son modifies the advice, he will still make the wrong decision and be harmed by it. We may construct the following version:

An older man gives help to a younger man in such a way as to hurt him.

At once we see that it is possible to construct a version of the "fraudulent doctor" story that coincides with this one. The fact that two stories can be unified in this way indicates that this belief is probably of special significance to the storyteller.

Abstracting is a first step in TAT interpretation. It enables us to generate a number of versions of the same story that are simple enough to be dealt with easily and at the same time preserve essential meanings. Sometimes abstracting must be done a number of times for the same story, using different elements as components. In the story about the doctor, version 3 shows the effect of introducing the parents into the story. Actually, it is probably more appropriate to neglect the parents in this case. The narrator spends more time describing the doctor than he does the parents, and thus singles him out as a prime figure. Had the story emphasized the stupidity of the parents and minimized the physician, it would have been better to construct an abstract version that neglected the physician. Since the clinician's judgment is involved in abstracting, versions of the same story constructed by different clinicians may not always be the same. Finding similar versions of several stories should aid in removing some subjectivity, however. Another difficulty is that some stories cannot be abstracted because there is no plot: the characters are simply described or are said to be thinking. Such stories should be looked at carefully to see whether they have any common elements. Often some general statement may be made about the characters or the situations yielding these plotless stories.

ORGANIZING THE DATA

Another activity in TAT analysis is organizing the story material. A wide variety of organizing principles can be used, and they yield somewhat different data. One widely used type of analysis requires listing the characteristics of the central figures, the forces acting upon them, and the outcomes of the stories. The essentials of this kind of organization were originally stated by Murray (19), although many variants of his method have been proposed. Another method requires the application of Mill's canons of experimental inference (27) in such a way that causal factors producing outcomes are made visible. The method we shall follow here is a simple scheme proposed by Arnold (1). It organizes stories as units into categories of interpersonal relationships. While it does not yield quantitative data and is less objective than some of the other methods, it is a good one to begin with because of its simplicity.

Arnold's method requires an abstract version of each story, constructed in about the way we have already described. The simplified versions are then arranged into groups on the basis of the sex and relationship of the characters in the story. In Group I are placed all stories dealing with parent-child relationships. A subcategory is provided for stories showing child with mother and another for father-child stories. Another could be added for stories where both parents are brought into the story. Group II includes stories with heterosexual situations, with subdivisions for married and unmarried characters. Group III is devoted to stories where the characters are all of the same sex. There is a separate category for each sex. Group IV includes stories where only a single person is present. Again there is a category for males and one for females. The last group, V, is for miscellaneous stories in which humans are unimportant. Let us apply this organizing scheme to a sample record.

A SAMPLE RECORD

We shall present the stories given by Tom C., the man whose Rorschach record was analyzed in the last chapter. Before each story we shall briefly describe the picture he was viewing. The descriptions are adapted from those of Murray (19).

1. [A boy, head in hands, gazes at a violin on the table before him.]

I don't have much imagination, but. . . . Here's a child taking lessons. He's practiced quite some time. Now he's through practicing. He's tired and thinking about what he's been doing. He'll probably either practice a little more or. . . . He looks as if he's through or wants to be. He'd like to leave it. You can also see that he is studying the instrument itself: what it is made of, how it's built, and so forth. He's in deep thought about that instrument. Maybe the outcome is that he'll take it up and play some more.

2. [A young woman is holding some books. Beyond her a man and a horse are working in a plowed field. A woman leans against a tree at the right.]

This young lady has been to the library in the city. She's coming home. Bringing books to read. Thinking about what has taken place during the day and. . . . Or she could be thinking about what she might do at home. Her thoughts do look far away. The man is plowing of course. He has a beautiful white horse. He is a man of physical strength. His wife has been talking to him. She's daydreaming, thinking. The girl with the books is going into the house. The man, of course, will continue working and the woman will stay out a while. In the background is a lake, trees, hills. . . . Perhaps they might have all been discussing something. The woman is thinking. The girl will go up to the house, and the man will go to work. It looks like it's cloudy or late in the day. The girl is college age. Nice and neat to be out on a farm. The man is younger than the woman.

3 BM. [Seated on the floor leaning against a couch is a boy. His face is not visible. A pistol is on the floor near him.]

This child is crying because he didn't have his way. His feelings were hurt some way. He's been out playing. He didn't get his own way. Looks like a gun there. Maybe someone was rough with him or. . . . I don't know whether he was spanked or not, could be. He's crying hard as if his heart would break. Of course, I think he's feeling deeply about it now but will soon get up and start doing something else or go back out and play some more. . . . He's not asleep in that position. He's just come in. I can't tell what's beyond outside. No, someone may have taken advantage of him or he didn't get his way. He came running in the house in order to get away and give vent to his feelings. To tell what started his crying, I'd have to think back and see what makes little boys do that. Perhaps he and another boy were playing and, playing robber or soldier and began to scuffle. This one was gotten the best of. It looks like it might be a girl. I never thought of that. Girls don't usually play with guns. He has long hair and maybe a skirt. After his feelings are vented, he'll go out and start play. He'll start with a single fellow or maybe just with himself.

4. [A man is turned away from a young woman as if he were pulling away from her.]

This picture looks like the boy has. . . . He's thinking of something other than the girl. Maybe he has some other girl in mind. Could be he's just told her that he didn't love her any more. He may be fixing to leave her. She's inquiring what the trouble is all about. She's in love with him, but he's going to leave her. He's thinking of something else. She's looking at him wondering what he's thinking about. Could be he's had some trouble and she's trying to console him. The outcome of course he will be leaving in just a minute. She'll go back inside. I don't know what the sign represents. He looks more like a worker than a soldier. He's expressing, a look far away, some discouragement. Hers [her expression], encouragement or connected with his having told her about not loving her any more and wondering. I can't tell where they are. The door and curtain . . . not a home. Reminds me of a picture show. The man was afraid to go up in high places. The girl encourages him. He's afraid. The man is husky and the girl is very neat. Her hair is pretty. The main thing I think I see is love and the breaking away.

5. [A middle-aged woman is looking into a room through the doorway.]

A noise, the woman heard a noise. Either someone at the door or just some noise. She has come to investigate. She's wondering. She might be saying, "Who is it?" or calling someone. It is in the living room or library. She's cautiously looking in. She'll either go back, finding no one there, or go ahead and open the door. It looks like it's late, but she's still up. The lantern is burning. She has been for some reason. . . . She is opening the door, not closing it. She's not afraid. There's a sense of wonder.

6 BM. [An elderly woman stands with her back to a young man who seems to be confused or frowning.]

Well, well. Looks like the son has done something to disappoint the mother. He's worried. She's turning away. Boy! I [*shakes head*]. . . . They are in the house. He's had some bad news for her. She isn't comforting him in any way. She doesn't give him any comfort. As to what he's done, it's hard to say. He's so. . . . He's old enough to be married. At least thirty. She's about sixty. Maybe she's. . . . Well, maybe she's a very religious woman. He's had some family troubles, wants to marry again. She won't listen to him. It's contrary to her feelings. He's confused and discouraged, about his feelings. He doesn't know what to do. The outcome of course will be that he will have to go out and make some decision. Just what he'll make is hard to say. More than likely he'll go ahead and do what he wants to do. He's confused now. He wanted to talk to his mother about it. It doesn't look like. . . . Ordinarily a mother would be encouraging if he was in trouble. She would not be like this. She would face him and hold his arms, give comfort. But here he doesn't. She turns away sternly.

7 BM. [An older man with a mustache is looking down toward a younger man. The young man gazes into space with a set or sullen look.]

The men are sitting together discussing current problems. The older fellow is, has just finished saying something. He's interested in the younger man's reaction. The younger man is pondering what the older man has said before he says anything. The older one expresses a sense of satisfaction. The younger expresses, I wonder. . . . It looks like he might not agree with the older man. Of course the outcome will be that they will continue their conversation. Finally, whether they agree or not they will just converse. They could be father and son. The father talking to the son about something, giving advice. He's made some statements the son is pondering. The father looks like he's fatherly in giving advice. The son has a downcast mouth, somewhat bitter. The father has a kind expression. The son may or may not agree with the father. He looks like he's independent as yet. He's not discussing it with the father. He's listening but doing his own independent thinking.

8 BM. [A boy, in coat and tie, gazes straight out of the picture. A kind of montage background shows a surgical operation. A gun is partly visible at the left of the picture.]

Here's youth. A few years before the war he was just a freshman in high school. He looks young. About fifteen years of age. All dressed up thinking only of things happening in civilized life. War is a thing far away. He's from a nice home, neat and ambitious. Before you know it, he has reached the age of service. Then he is wounded. They are cutting out a bullet. Two doctors work on him in the operation. There is a gun lying by the bed. He's developed into a husky youth from that small fellow. This place might be, hmm, it's a rigged-up place, not permanent. The doctor is old. There might be a doctor that old in the service but it detracts. . . . The young fellow has, it could be . . . the outcome is that this boy . . . he. . . . Oh, yes . . . I can see intense suffering on the face of the person being operated on. The importance is in the eyes of the doctor. The young fellow is dreaming of the future when he will get in the war or when he might become a famous doctor. Well, times as they are now [*laughs*]. Well, he might [*laughs*] . . . let's make him a doctor.

9 BM. [Four men are relaxing on the grass. One rests his head against another's back. They appear to be in work clothes.]

Oh, these are Negroes, aren't they? It's dinner time. They've put in a hard day in the field. Now they're taking it easy, resting. Two of them are resting. One looks like he's in charge, sitting up. He's more awake than the rest. It certainly looks like they're resting from their work. They'll snooze awhile longer. They've had their lunch. They'll go back to work. They're in a grain field. They all feel satisfied.

10. [Close-up view of a woman leaning her head against a man's shoulder.]

That looks to me like a mother and son. The mother is experiencing great feeling, love for her son. He's returning it with a kiss on the forehead. Looks like he's a soldier. He's neither arriving nor leaving. It's just an occasion where he has feeling for his mother. She has her hand on his chest. Both have their eyes closed and a deep expression of love. They'll carry on a conversation and then go about their respective ways. Or it could be an older man, husband and wife. But it's the same thing anyway, love between them.

11. Second session. [A murky picture of a road along a cliff, vague figures in the distance, and a dragon's head and neck on the left.]

A man is in a dangerous crevice or canyon, and he is with some group of animals. And he is going up now, fixing to cross a bridge, encouraging others to cross the bridge. He's pushing them. It's a place of danger. They've just passed over a narrow place. Behind is a monster likely to attack them any minute. It's dark in the distance. He's working hard to encourage them to go over. Perhaps he'll somehow manage to go on to where he wants to go. The animals sense great danger. The man also realizes, but he knows they must push on. And that's what he's helping them to do. After they cross the bridge, they'll be able to go ahead and they'll feel freer. At the present time they are in trouble.

12 M. [A young man lies on a couch with closed eyes. An older man stands beside the couch, leaning forward slightly and stretching one hand out.]

Looks like a case of a man having hypnotized a boy. The boy has perhaps just about passed out under the spell. The man will proceed to ask the boy questions. If it stays as hypnotism it can't be very exciting. He will just ask him some questions. Maybe I can ask some exciting questions. The man first asks about his age . . . I don't know much about that. Let's switch over.

The boy is reclining on a couch. A man slips in and sees the boy there. The boy is of a wealthy family. The man is fixing to grab him in the mouth so he won't be able to holler. He's acting now slowly and carefully not to disturb him before he silences him. Then he will tie him up and proceed to go over the rest of the house. It's nighttime. After taking care of the boy, he will burglarize the house.

13 MF. [On a low bed, a woman lies with breasts exposed. A man stands beside the bed but turned away from it, his forearm covering his eyes.]

Oh, my! My! This is a murder. The husband comes in and finds his wife has been attacked and murdered. She's lying there as the person left her. The husband is showing great sorrow as he looks at the body and turns away. The man is suffering from shock and grief. He will report it to the police and they will come out and make an investigation, gather the evidence, and search for the person who committed the crime. A very young couple in moderate circumstances.

14. [In silhouette, a man stands gazing out a window.]

Here's a picture of a young man at the window. It's late in the day or nighttime. He's taking it easy looking out and thinking of things. Perhaps he's thinking of his best girl, and what he might do on the coming weekend. Of course, his mind will wander to athletics or the day when he'll be drafted into the service. He's looking at the moon, stars, clouds, anything in the yard, anything that might pass by. A picture of relaxation, thought, and meditation. He may be thinking of his family, his work, or his plans.

15. [A stylized picture of a gaunt man standing in a graveyard.]

A graveyard and the old fellow is grief-stricken. He's mourning over the grave of someone. The man may be considered as death. He looks dark, thin, and lifeless. Instead of his hands pointing up to heaven, they are pointing down—another sign he might be death. He's a sad creature. It's a dark gruesome picture, and everything in the picture is—there's nothing cheerful at all.

16. [Blank card. Here the subject is instructed to imagine a picture, then to tell a story about it.]

This is a picture of a beautiful farmhouse with a barn, one that can be utilized, a fine barn. An old colonial house way out in the country. There are cows, chickens, ducks, and turkeys, a beautiful orchard. It's spring and everything is in bloom. Trees are bursting forth. The house is surrounded by farm land on the left and pasture and wooded land on the right. There is a group of hills a half-mile beyond. Out of the house come two couples. One of them is visiting the other. They go for a walk over the pasture land that has wild flowers on it. At a certain spot there's a clear-water stream fed by springs. They roam around out there and then return. ["What I was dreaming there was what I'd most enjoy," Tom said at the end of this story.]

17 BM. [A naked, muscular man clings to a rope.]

This man is a prisoner. He somehow managed to get a rope and he's escaping over the walls, cautiously coming down the wall, letting himself down. As he goes down he surveys the country so he'll know what way he wants to leave. He's barefooted. Maybe he has trunks on, but other than that has no clothes. My imagination must have gotten away from me to make him a prisoner with no clothes. Perhaps he's looking for someone who will furnish him clothes. That's it—someone is helping him. He'll get away but not for long. They'll get their hands on him and catch him before he gets too far.

18 BM. [Three hands clutch a man, who is looking to one side.]

A murder has been committed here. It reminds me a little of a picture show. Is that all right? The man has been murdered and has been carried to an auto for the purpose of disposal. There are two people working on him. We can't see them. They have their arms around him. They will put him in the back seat of an auto and dispose of the body in a field, lake, or railroad, so it will be hard to find. The man apparently has been slugged to death. There's no evidence of blood; it could be he's been shot. Probably was beaten to death on the head. He's a member of the gang who squealed and they are trying to get rid of him.

19. [A snow-covered cabin and cloudy sky rendered in unconventional shapes. The picture is ambiguous as to content but eerie in mood.]

[*Laughs.*] This is a picture of winter. There's been a big snow, and there's snow on the ground and on top of the house. The people inside are comfortable and warm but—no, let's not have them comfortable and warm. There's no smoke coming out. They are having a hard time. They are cold. Work is hard to get; food is scarce. The spirit of winter is in the background, hovering over as they suffer. And the lack of necessities and the sheer fear of what's ahead in the coming winter months. The spirit of winter and the thoughts they have.

20. [A half-illumined figure of a person stands near the post of a lighted street lamp. The rest is dark, except for some light spots in the upper left.]

This is the middle of the night, while people are off the street. We can make this two or three things. A man is on the street for no good reason, looking for what he might get into. We'll just make him an officer. He doesn't have the cap, so it's hard. It's a cold night. He has something around his neck, a hat on, his hands in his pockets. He's on his beat. He looks to the left. He is looking to see if everything is all right. Then he'll go ahead and cover the beat. Across the street is a square and some trees. It's a cold night.

Problem 1. Before trying to interpret the stories in a TAT, it is wise to examine the record for the way in which the subject undertakes his task. That is, we look for formal or stylistic features of the subject's behavior as a storyteller. Inspect Tom's record for the answers to the following questions.

1. Analysis of Tom's Rorschach responses revealed obsessional trends in his behavior. Is there anything in the way he tells his TAT stories

that is consistent with this conclusion? Cite the evidence for or against your answer.

2. Tom's stories are shorter than the 300-word average found by Murray. What is the possible significance of this fact in Tom's record?

3. A good part of Tom's stories consists of description or enumeration of objects in the pictures. This tendency is not so marked in an average run of stories. What hypothesis could account for this aspect of Tom's behavior?

INTERPRETING THE SAMPLE RECORD

To apply Arnold's method of organizing the TAT stories, we first arrange them under the five category headings. Table 4 shows where Tom's stories fit. Then we make slightly abstract versions of the stories. Under the category of parent-child situations, Tom gives four stories.

Table 4. Classification of Tom's TAT Stories

I. Parent-child situations
    Mother: 6, 10
    Father: 7
    Both: 2
II. Heterosexual situations
    Married: 13, 19
    Unmarried: 4, 16
III. Same-sex situations
    Males: 8, 9, 12, 18
IV. Single situations
    Males: 1, 3, 11, 14, 15, 17, 20
    Females: 5

Here are the simplified versions:

2. A girl comes home from the library, enters the house after a discussion with parent.

6. A mother refuses to comfort a troubled son who wishes to marry again.

7. A son listens to father's advice but thinks independently.

10. Mother and son experience a deep feeling of mutual love.

What kind of relationships are pictured here? It is obvious that the emotional involvement between son and mother is greater than between son and father or between daughter and parents. The mother-son relationship is thus marked with special significance. The two stories about mothers are quite different, however. In the first, a son does not receive aid and comfort. In the second, the love is mutual. Tentatively, we may say that Tom has an inconsistency in his conception of the mother-son relation. If we reread stories 6 and 10 with this in mind, we discover some enlightening details. In story 10, the mutual love takes place in a psychological vacuum. Tom not only failed to give us the events leading up to this scene; he carefully stated that the son was neither arriving nor leaving. He has, in a sense, erected barriers between this episode of deep feeling and all the rest of life. At the end of this episode, he remarks that it could be husband and wife, and says, "But it's the same thing anyway, love between them." Thus he reveals a conception that parental love is the same as married love.[2]

What kind of man is most likely to have this conception of love? We are reminded at once of the classical Oedipus situation as described by Freud. Possibly Tom's feelings about his mother and himself fit into this pattern. If this is the case, we should expect to find at least two other conceptions present in the stories. One would be that the father (or figures representing the father) would be conceived of as punitive and forbidding. The other conception would be that sexual activity is wrong because it resembles or is related to incest.

The parent-child stories give us only one clue as to the father-son relationship. In picture 7 the father is not seen as punitive but, on the contrary, as helpful. Nevertheless, the son is not accepting this help. The evidence here is weak but not contradictory to the hypothesis that Tom conceives of his father as an adversary. Story 12, however, is of great interest in this connection. Here we see an older man gag and tie a younger one so that he may rob the house. The conception is that of the power and aggressiveness of the older man and the helplessness of the younger. This story, then, provides more positive evidence in favor of the Oedipus hypothesis. But what about Tom's sexual conceptions?

Heterosexual Relationships in the Record. Three stories clearly fall under the heading of heterosexual situations: 4, 13, and 16. Perhaps story 19 could be classed here, although the sex of the people is not mentioned. They can be simplified thus:

4. A man leaves a girl who loves him.

13. A man finds his wife murdered. Overcome with grief, he will call the police.

16. Two couples roam a beautiful farm in spring.

19. People in winter suffer.

No frankly sexual relationship appears in any of the stories. This, in itself, has some significance since several of the twenty pictures often stimulate some sexual material. Picture 13 shows the exposed breasts of a woman,

[2] Interpreting TAT material as showing conceptions of the narrator is often done, although it is seldom made the central principle of an interpretive system. Hall (8) has developed this principle most fully in his study of dreams. While the interpretation of the TAT differs in many respects from the interpretation of dreams, the notion seems fruitful that both creations reveal the subject's conception of himself, of others, and of the causal factors in human relationships. In addition, it is one of the most parsimonious assumptions that can be made about the meaning of fantasy material. As Hall points out (8, p. 14) these conceptions are not to be construed as necessarily revealing objective reality.

and the situation is usually interpreted by narrators as having sexual overtones at least. According to Tom's story the woman is murdered. No reason is given for the attack, and Tom does not even state that the murderer will be caught. It hardly seems correct to say that the story reveals Tom's conception of marriage; more probably it reflects a conception of the dangers of sex.

This interpretation is strengthened by the story for card 4: A man leaves a loving woman. Now it happens that a detail of this picture shows a semiclothed woman in the background. Here again is a suggestion of sexual interest, and here again the story is one of a relationship that is broken off. The two stories, 4 and 13, can be connected by the following abstract version:

Male-female relationships with sexual implications will not last and will end in grief for the man.

The story for the blank card, 16, seems to be an exception to this attitude. Here the heterosexual situation is a happy one. But we should note that the human beings in this story are almost incidental; most of the storyteller's time and emotional intensity are spent on the environment. Tom does not tell us whether the couples are married or unmarried. And possible sexual implications in the story are guarded against by having four people roam the fields instead of two! The story, moreover, is deliberate wish fulfillment on the conscious level, as Tom indicates by his comment at the end.

One further point should be indicated before we leave our exploration of the Oedipus hypothesis. The story for Card 6 showed a mother failing to comfort her son. This maternal attitude is surprising to Tom, and he comments that ordinarily a mother would help her son. What are the conditions, then, that Tom conceives could bring about this rejection? The answer is clear: the desire to marry another woman. But there is a bright spot in this story, for Tom conceives of the possibility that the boy can make his own decision and will go ahead and do as he wishes. Even mother's disapproval can be borne.

Same-sex Relationships. Tom tells four stories that contain only male characters:

8. A boy grows up, is wounded in military service, and is operated on by two doctors.
9. Negroes who have been working are resting after lunch.
12. A man grabs a wealthy boy, ties him up, and robs the house.
18. A gang member who squealed is beaten to death.

Only one of these stories (Card 9) has a peaceful mood, and that deals with members of a minority group. As in story 10, Tom gives no outcome: the satisfied, restful feeling is essentially walled off from activity.

There is a static quality about both stories. All this sounds very much as if Tom conceives of enjoyment largely in a passive sense. It reminds us of the passive trends detected in his Rorschach record. We see other manifestations of passivity in the remaining stories in this group. In 8 and 12, Tom shows us a conception of youth as impotent against older men, and in 18 the squealer is murdered.

If Tom conceives of male authority figures as powerful and potentially harmful, we may wonder how he acquired this conception and what effects it could have on him. The most plausible answer to the first of these questions is that he acquired this conception from his relationship with his own father. This answer is not supplied by the TAT material, of course. It stems from theoretical notions about the source of deep and pervasive attitudes toward authority. In this instance, we know that the case history supports our conjecture: Tom's father was described as a strict and dominating Baptist minister.

What effects could this conception of authority have on Tom? Again we must go beyond the TAT for an answer. One effect would probably be to produce a good bit of hostility toward authority. At the same time, Tom would have to repress hostile urges, since open avowal of them would be punished. Perhaps we have here the clue to the passive trends that are so marked in Tom's personality. Inactivity and lack of initiative are safe, even though they may not be otherwise rewarding.

Single Situations. We shall not list the abstract versions of the remaining stories. You should try your own hand at this task. If you do, you will find that most of them are not even stories as defined by the TAT instructions. They are characterized by inactivity, by thinking, and by dreaming. One story, however, deserves special comment because it is an exception to the general tone. In story 17, a prisoner is attempting to escape. Despite the fact that someone is helping him, he will eventually be caught. On one level of abstraction, this story reveals Tom's conception of the inevitability of punishment: "A wrongdoer cannot escape punishment." In the light of Tom's religious training, there can be little doubt that he is deeply convinced of this belief. But the story tells us something else.

If we abstract it differently, this story becomes "A man who tries to find freedom will fail even with help." The futility of striving for independence that Tom reveals here is echoed in some of his other stories. Reexamine the end of story 4 in which a man leaves a girl. Tom talks of discouragement and of a picture show where a man feared to go up in high places. Look again at story 6. The son is going against his mother's wishes. Tom speculates that the outcome will be an independent decision, but the price is confusion and the loss of maternal support. In story 7 the son is said to be doing his own independent thinking, but there is no outcome in action. The son refrains from even discussing his thoughts with his father. The consistency among these stories is possible because we are dealing with abstract versions which transcend the specific circumstances of each story. This is the kind of unity we try to seek out in TAT interpretation.

Context Determines Interpretation. It would be a serious mistake to assume that similar stories given by different clients have similar meanings. The significance of a story depends on the context formed by the other stories. In stressing the futility that was expressed by Tom in story 17, we are not suggesting that every story of an escaping prisoner who is caught indicates the same thing. Support for that interpretation had to be found in the discouragement and confusion revealed in other stories of independent striving. Then, too, the presence of so much inactivity in the stories makes this interpretation more plausible. If this same story were given in a record filled with stories of successful independent action, we should interpret it quite differently. We must use the same principle of configural interpretation that is required in dealing with the Rorschach.

The necessity for viewing a single sample of behavior within a context or framework does not arise only in interpreting projective tests. It is one of the distinctive features of the clinical method, and it is required just as much in understanding behavior in life situations as it is in interpreting imaginal productions. What does it signify when a boy fails in school? Does it mean he was stupid? Uninterested? Ill? Or does it mean that he was rebelling against adult authority in one of the few ways left to him? We cannot know without a knowledge of his achievement pattern, his family, his health, of the norms of his friendship group, and so on. And what shall we say of a foreman who plays yes man to his factory manager? Nothing, until we know the context of his actions. He may be abiding by the social norms in his factory; or he may be clinging to a technique he used to influence his father years ago.

Problem 2. As you study a TAT record, generalizations emerge, and a certain feeling-tone or atmosphere seems to characterize the whole record. Against this background a story, hitherto casually treated, sometimes stands out as exceptional. In Tom's record, story 11 is a good example of such an exception. Read this story again, bearing in mind the interpretation of the record we have developed. What is there about this story that makes it exceptional? Discuss the possible significance of this story in the light of the rest of the record.

Some Final Remarks about Tom's Record. We have pointed out the main trends in this set of TAT stories: concern for relationship with mother figures, fear and helplessness before male authority, inability to accept heterosexual impulses, lack of faith in the outcome of independent action, and a general emphasis on fantasy (meditation and thought) rather than on action. Several other characteristics of this record should be noted, not so much for improving the interpretation as for the sake of suggesting approaches that are useful in all TAT interpretations.

How can we describe the general nature of the human relationships in this record? In most of the stories people are not very deeply involved with one another; the words "transient" and "superficial" come to mind as descriptive terms. The prototype of this conception occurs in the second story. Only one relationship term is used in describing the three figures in the picture, "wife." In the main, they are simply a young woman, a woman, and a man. Only the use of the word "home" suggests that this story may be classified as family situation, but even then it is not clear that these three belong to the same home. Another fact that points toward weak human relationships is the large number of stories concerned with only one character. There are eight of these, twice as many as there are in any other category. It would have been easy enough to introduce at least one other character into some of these stories, but Tom does not do it.

Another interesting feature of this record is the presence of alternative stories or the beginnings of alternative stories. In 2, after telling one story, Tom remembers a movie in which the girl encourages a fearful man. In 8, another "end-story" is given. This time the boy dreams of becoming a famous doctor instead of being wounded, as in the first story. The story for Card 12 begins with a common theme: hypnosis. But it is quickly altered on the very doubtful grounds that it won't be exciting enough. In 19, Tom first characterizes the people in the house as comfortable and warm and then describes them as suffering from cold and want of food. In the very last story, 20, a man is on the street "for no good reason, looking for what he might get into." Abruptly, Tom changes him into an officer who is covering his beat.

In thinking about these shifts, notice that the alternate versions in 2 and 8 consist of "undoing," that is, the end-stories essentially negate the kind of relationships or outcomes originally stated. The changes in the last three stories, however, occur early in the story. They constitute defenses by interrupting anxiety-producing lines of thought. In the hypnosis story, it seems that Tom must avoid the possible revelations that could be made by the young man. In the twentieth story, he avoids talking about antisocial behavior by changing the central figure into a policeman; reaction formation occurs in full view. Story 19 provides no clue as to the reason for the shift.

The record contains four references to military service. They are in stories 4, 8, 10, and 14. Actually Tom was in military service at the time these stories were told. He had been drafted but had not been sent overseas. These references probably reflect his surroundings and perhaps his concern about combat (story 8).

THE NARRATOR AND THE CENTRAL CHARACTER

The chief assumption we have used in interpreting Tom's record can be stated this way: the stories tell us the beliefs or the conceptions of the narrator about people, their motives, their difficulties, and their successes. In order to formulate these beliefs, we seek for similarities among the stories and use the stories as concrete instances of more general beliefs. Thus we have referred to "male authority" rather than to the client's own father, or to "love relationships" rather than to the client's own wife or sweetheart. Beliefs about causal relationships appear when the stories are rephrased in "if-then" language. For instance, several of Tom's stories can read: "If a man and woman are in love, grief will follow."

In order to relate these conceptions to the personality of the narrator, we have to ask further questions:

1. What are the characteristics of a person who believes these things?
2. What motives and attitudes will he have?

These questions will have to be answered on the basis of our ideas about the dynamics of personality. The TAT stories themselves will not hold the complete answers. Thus on the basis of Tom's belief about love and grief, we may infer that he himself would be fearful of a love relationship. Then, if our theory of personality dynamics includes the principle that both social and organic pressures push men to seek love relationships, we would think that Tom had conflicting motives in this regard.

This interpretive approach, then, involves two steps:

1. The discovery of the belief patterns of the narrator
2. The use of these to make inferences about his motivational, emotional, and attitudinal structure

Another kind of assumption is possible and has been widely used. This assumption is that the central figures (or heroes) in the stories reveal the characteristics of the narrator.

Attributes of the Hero Assumed to Be Attributes of the Narrator. One of the clearest statements of this assumption has been made by Murray in the TAT manual published in 1943:

. . . two tentative assumptions are made, to be corrected later if necessary. The first is that the attributes of the heroes (needs, emotional states and sentiments) represent tendencies in the subject's personality. These tendencies belong to his past or to his anticipated future, and hence stand presumably for potential forces which are temporarily dormant; or they are active in the present (19, p. 14).

Murray then points out that this representation is generally symbolic, not literal. The attributes may be personality forces that the narrator is not entirely conscious of, or they may be feelings that the narrator is currently experiencing. They may reflect what the subject has wanted to do or has felt in the past, or they may indicate something he would like to do in the future. With all these possibilities, it is no easy matter to disentangle those forces which are active from those which are dormant, nor to discover which tendencies are known and which are unknown to the narrator. In practice, interpreters who use this kind of assumption tally all the needs shown by the heroes; then they interpret these data in the light of the total pattern of the stories.

Some interpreters are more cautious in using the assumption that the needs and emotions of the central characters reflect needs and emotions of the narrator. For example, Vorhaus (28) regards moods ascribed to the central characters as "consistent with the subject's own feelings." On the other hand, she suggests that most of the attributes ascribed to the central figures will show what characteristics are used by the narrator in his self-evaluations and also whether he is favorable or unfavorable in his evaluation of himself (28, p. 8). Apparently, she does not think that unconscious needs will be directly expressed by the central figures.

Determining the Hero. As a general rule, the hero of a TAT story is the person who is most like the narrator. Similarities in age and sex are the most common indicators. In addition, we can look for similarities in occupation, interests, or in values and goals. The hero of a story usually is the one about whom the story centers, and he is the one who plays a leading role. Commonly, the central character is chosen from the persons depicted on the TAT card. There are times, of course, when the sex of the narrator is not the same as the sex of the hero. An example of this discrepancy occurs in the second story told by Tom. Here, we must assume that the studious, daydreaming girl is the central figure, and that her attributes probably represent Tom's own attributes. On the other hand, it is quite doubtful that the female character in the fifth story can be taken to represent Tom. In this meager story, there is no reason to assume that the age, sex, status, or goals of the central figure are sufficiently similar to Tom's to permit an equating of the two.

Investigations show that several readers can agree fairly well on which figure in the story is the hero. A study by Mayman and Kutner (16), for instance, found that two relatively untrained raters agreed in 89 per cent of ninety-one stories. But this does not demonstrate that the central figure is always the one that reveals the narrator's personality. In fact, Murray (19) thinks that there may be primary and secondary heroes or even a number of figures through which the narrator reveals his attributes. If these possibilities occur with any substantial frequency, the various studies showing agreement among raters concerning the hero may actually be unimportant so far as interpretation is concerned.

Piotrowski's Assumption. Piotrowski (21) has proposed a substantial modification in the interpretation of the hero's attributes. He suggests that every figure in the stories represents some aspect of the narrator's personality. The impulses that are most acceptable to the narrator would appear in the central figure or hero. Less acceptable impulses would be found in story characters having the same sex as the narrator but differing in age. The least acceptable impulses would be revealed by characters differing in both age and sex from the narrator. Thus, a hierarchy of impulse acceptance can be established for the narrator.

One interesting consequence of this approach is the possibility of detecting conflict and poor integration of motives by analyzing the differences in motives shown by figures in the same story. Piotrowski suggests that when the several characters in a story show marked differences in motives or when their motives are quite incompatible, we should expect to find tension, impulse fear, and poor integration in the narrator. Examples might be stories where sexual activity is desired by one character and rejected by another, or where one values success and another devalues it.

These various assumptions about the attributes of the hero and the attributes of the narrator have been reviewed by Lindzey (15). In the light of the available evidence, he can find no clear demonstration that one set of assumptions is more useful than another. Of course, there is a scarcity of investigations designed to test these specific points.

HOW ARE CHARACTERISTICS OF THE NARRATOR SHOWN?

Some investigators have used the TAT or similar techniques as a research instrument rather than as a clinical device. Out of their studies we can glean some ideas about the kind of interpretive assumptions that may be useful, although their investigations were not always directed to this end.

Effect of Mood on Picture Descriptions. Leuba and Lucas (13) used hypnosis to induce three moods in each of three subjects. The induced moods were: happy, critical, and anxious. The subjects were asked to describe each of six pictures (not the standard TAT cards) during each of these moods. The results indicated differences in the number of mood-related statements made under the three conditions. Fortunately, Leuba and Lucas report the actual descriptions given by the subjects, so that it is possible to tell how these moods were reflected. A study of the data shows that moods were more likely to be revealed by the subject's reaction to the picture than by statements attributing the moods to the characters in the picture. This finding is clearest in the case of the critical moods. In this condition, the subjects expressed their own criticism of the pictures rather than describing the characters as mean or critical. During the anxious-mood condition, one subject typically invented some kind of catastrophe that could happen to the pictured characters. But another subject, more commonly, mentioned his own feelings of anxiousness.

The fact that the moods were hypnotically induced is reason to be cautious in generalizing these results. Then, too, we cannot be sure that the experimenters would have found the same data had they asked for stories instead of descriptions. But there is a suggestion here that should not be overlooked: different subjects may not use the same avenue of expression in revealing their moods. Perhaps some narrators express their current mood directly as their own; others may impute their moods to their characters.

Effects of Aggressive Feelings on TAT Stories. Several investigators have attempted to make subjects angry and to note the effects of this emotion on TAT stories. Bellak (3), for example, criticized subjects after they had told five stories and kept up the criticism for the remaining five stories. He found that simply counting the number of nouns and verbs connoting aggression was enough to show differences between the control stories and those told during anger. Lindzey (14) subjected college men to physical discomfort and then to a social situation in which they failed. This treatment increased the frequency of incidents in which the story heroes acted aggressively. Discussing these results in another paper, Lindzey (15) indicates that there was also an increase in the number of aggressive acts shown by figures other than the hero.

These two studies seem to show that it is not necessary to assume an identification figure in order to determine current feelings of aggression in the narrator. They also demonstrate that temporary or transient states of the person affect the stories he tells. Whether chronically aggressive people would reveal their aggression by aggressive language or by a greater frequency of aggressive actions in the story cannot be decided on the basis of these studies.

Pittluck (22) has directly approached the problem of the kinds of stories chronically aggressive people tell. She obtained ratings of the aggressive behavior shown by seventy-two nonpsychotic, male neuropsychiatric patients. These ratings were compared with various aspects of the TAT stories told by the patients. There was not a clear-cut relationship between amount of aggressive behavior and the frequency of stories with an aggressive quality. She did find, however, that aggressive men were more likely to use defense mechanisms to modify the aggressive actions occurring in the stories than did nonaggressive men. The aggressive narrator tended to disapprove of the aggressive acts of a story character, to excuse them as accidents or as deserved punishment, or to begin telling of an aggressive act and fail to complete it.

The curious inference that follows from Pittluck's data is that openly aggressive people apparently feel more guilty for aggressive fantasies than do those who are less openly aggressive. We would ordinarily think that the inhibitory anxiety attached to fantasied acts would be less than that attached to overt acts. Whether her findings would hold in the case of other socially disapproved impulses is hard to say. Perhaps the stories told by the aggressive men simply reflect the practice they have had in giving excuses and defensive interpretations of their own aggressive behavior.

Inferring Repressed Motives from the TAT. In actual clinical practice, it is probably hazardous to make inferences about repression on the basis of the TAT alone. Tomkins (27, pp. 77–82) has proposed an elaborate way of estimating the strength of repressed wishes from TAT stories, but it rests on a series of assumptions that are not entirely acceptable. The chief difficulty in relying solely upon the TAT, however, arises from the nature of repressive activity itself.

If a motive is to be called repressed, at least two conditions must be fulfilled: 1. The client must be unaware of the motive. That is, he must deny that he feels a certain want or thinks of certain goals. 2. On the other hand, he must show some behavior that indicates the actual existence of such a motive. Now it should be clear that there is no way of discovering whether the client is aware of his wants except by asking him to talk about himself, his wishes, and his feelings. The evidence for condition 1 can be obtained only from sentences in which the client is referring to or describing himself. In the TAT, however, clients are *not* engaged in the task of describing themselves; they are actually talking about the characters shown in the pictures. Consequently the stories, as stories, provide no basis for deciding whether the client would admit or deny any of the characteristics he attributes to the hero or other story figures. Of course, incidental comments referring to the narrator himself could show something about his awareness of his motives.

The evidence for condition 2 above may very well be derived from the TAT. Dominant concerns may be revealed by the frequency with which certain emotions, motives, or goals are mentioned in the stories; or perhaps by a few stories where very intense motives are introduced quite arbitrarily. We could properly infer the *existence* of a motivational trend under these conditions; but its *repression* can only be demonstrated by the direct statements of the client about himself.

An example may help clarify our point. Let us see how repression may be inferred without using the TAT. A woman tells a clinician that she is disturbed by the fact that she reads so many newspaper stories about crime, accidents, and cruelty. She says that she would like to get her thoughts away from such topics but cannot do it. These remarks lead the clinician to infer that she is concerned with hostility, perhaps has hostile impulses herself. The fact that she feels compelled, against her expressed wish, to read items dealing with death and cruelty suggests the possibility that her hostile impulses are repressed. But the crucial evidence of repression comes when she tells the clinician that she rarely feels anger even when she is mistreated, that she feels nothing but affection for her family and friends, and that she never has thoughts of wanting to hurt somebody. Here, talking about herself, she reveals no awareness of hostile feeling in circumstances where it usually arises.

How can we explain her continued reading of news stories centering around hostility? Simply that the hostility seems external to her. It is projected, shown by other people, and, so far as she knows, has no bearing on her own attributes. And, in a similar way, the client telling TAT stories believes he is talking about others. The way is open for both repressed and nonrepressed motives to be revealed. To distinguish between the two kinds, however, we must also find out how the client describes himself when he knows he is doing it.

Of course, not all repressed motives will be revealed by the TAT. Undoubtedly, some people have repressed an impulse so strongly that it is literally unthinkable, even in fictitious stories. Then a complete absence of a motive that normally appears in the stories would suggest repression; but we should have to seek outside the TAT for evidence that the motive exists.

Effects of Experimentally Aroused Needs on TAT Stories. McClelland and his associates have explored the effect of experimentally aroused needs on TAT productions. In one experiment (2), stories told by hungry subjects were compared with those told by nonhungry control subjects. In another experiment (18), achievement needs were aroused by causing subjects to fail in some laboratory tasks. A number of different scores were developed and applied to the TAT stories. Three of these various measures increased under conditions of both food and achievement deprivation:

1. Frequency of story plots dealing with deprivation of the goal of the need being measured
2. Frequency with which characters in the stories are described as wanting or desiring the goals related to the need being measured
3. Frequency of mention of successful activities or methods for reaching the goal (18, p. 252)

Perhaps the first measure listed above increased because of the technique used by McClelland to arouse or intensify needs. It does not seem, at present, that deprivation plots will be found in instances where the need is aroused in some other way. Neither can we be sure that these measures, obviously useful for detecting currently active needs, would reflect long-term needs, or "need dispositions" (17). They are in line with clinical usage, however, and to some extent support Murray's suggestions about measurement of needs by the TAT. One obvious limitation of these findings is that they may not apply to needs that are socially unacceptable, and these are, of course, the very needs that clinicians want to measure.

One attempt to study the expression of unacceptable needs has been reported by Clark (5). He intensified the sexual need in college men by showing them pictures of female nudes. In another experiment, need arousal was produced by using an attractive female experimenter. Under these conditions, the aroused subjects did not include sexual references in their stories as often as the presumably nonaroused control subjects. This finding indicates that increased need intensity is not always accompanied by increased frequency of reference to need-related topics. It appears that the social acceptability of the need in question is of critical importance. If the presence of a need arouses anxiety, then there may very well be a decrease in the indicators of that need in the TAT stories.

Clark (5) tried to decrease inhibitory anxiety in one of his groups. He administered the nude pictures and the TAT cards at a fraternity beer party. Presumably the social situation and the alcohol decreased some of the anxiety about sexual references in the stories. The results were consistent with this expectation. Here, the experimental group showed more sexual imagery in their stories than did the control group. For this comparison, Clark properly tested his control group in a beer-party setting, but the nude pictures were not shown to them.

One further finding from Clark's studies should be mentioned since it seems to parallel Pittluck's results on aggression. Clark found that any group that was high on sexual imagery score was also high on a score that measured guilt about sex. We may tentatively conclude, then, that unacceptable impulses may have one of two effects on the stories: either there will be a decrease in need-related imagery in the stories or the imagery will increase but with more indications of guilt or defensiveness.

Types of Stories Associated with Personality Traits. From a study conducted by Hartman (11) we can get some idea of the kinds of persons that tell various types of stories. Hartman designed his study so that thirty-five adolescent boys were studied by a psychologist who then rated each one of them on forty-two graphic rating scales covering as many different personality traits. The psychologist used social-history materials, several psychometric tests, and an interview lasting at least two hours, as a basis for his ratings. Later the TAT was administered. Among others things, the TAT stories were analyzed according to an elaborate outline which included scoring the formal characteristics, the themes, and the feeling-tone of the stories. Biserial correlations were computed between the frequency with which each category appeared in the records and each of the personality ratings. From several of Hartman's tables (11, pp. 14–16) it is possible to extract some fairly consistent patterns.

Emphasis on achievement, i.e., on themes of striving to gain recognition or social approval, is positively related to ratings of extroversion, popularity, happy temperament, of preference for active recreation, of compliance with adults, of close attachment to father, and to a few other ratings. This relationship between a cluster of socially valuable characteristics and stories of achievement is one of the strongest and most clear-cut in the entire study.

On the other hand, an emphasis on themes showing the characters failing to satisfy their needs or to reach their goals is related to ratings of poor emotional adjustment and of emotional deprivation. The remaining variables that correlate significantly with this kind of story indicate that intellectual brightness and retarded sexual development may contribute to such stories also. These findings suggest that the narrators constructed their stories in such a way as to reveal their conceptions of the social world around them. Further support for this view is found in another set of correlations. Boys who give stories where the environment is described as benign tend to be rated as extroverted, well adjusted, emotionally stable, and realistic.

Some of the other relationships are not so easily explained. For example, emphasis on anxiety, uncertainty, and worry did not correlate reliably with degree of rated anxiety. Subjects who told stories with a good deal of anxiety in them tended to be lacking in energy, passive, neat, and dependent. The meaning of this relationship is not clear, although several plausible speculations could explain it. At least it warns us against a direct translation of story characteristics into personal characteristics of the narrator.

Sadistic emphasis in the stories is related to a cluster of traits that include conventional standards, weak appearance, anxiety, preference for sedentary recreation, close attachment to mother, and many nervous symptoms. There is a strong temptation to speculate that emphasis on violent incidents or on cruelty signifies a hostility that is repressed by a process of reaction-formation. Another way of looking at this result is to assume that these anxious, conventional boys are depicting the world as they see it—a world that has resulted in emotional stultification for them.

This brief review may be summarized by saying that there is evidence that moods, transient needs, and more enduring traits affect the TAT stories. At the same time, we lack a reliable guide for deciding, from the stories alone, which qualities are temporary and which are enduring. We need to know something of the current stresses on the narrator in order to make this distinction. It is also clear that we are not in a position to defend some single principle as a basis for interpretation. To say simply that the narrator projects his own needs into the stories is to say little that is helpful. Even to assume that the stories show the narrator's conceptions of his social world leaves many specific interpretive questions unanswered.

Problem 3. An intelligent, single woman in her late twenties volunteered to take a series of psychological tests to help a friend who needed some practice. In two sessions she gave stories to the entire set of TAT cards. At the end of the second session, the student presented card 17 BM and obtained this final story:

This man had been going along just like any other young man until he wandered into the woods the same day, and he fell into this pit. It wasn't just a plain pit used for catching animals. This was the plan of some fanatics to capture a human being and to observe him through a series of experiments that they had invented. When he first fell down, it was a blank empty cavern with cement walls on all sides. He just sat there for days, staring at the blank walls. Occasionally food was dropped to him by a long rope. He saw no one. After several days of this emptiness, he noticed animals coming out of the walls. They were like lizards, horrible, slithering back and forth. He thought they'd drive him crazy, until that day they dropped his food and forgot to take the rope away. He jumped immediately for this means of escape. He didn't think he could get very far, but he tried. He grabbed the rope and crawled up, expecting any minute to find one of his secret torturers discovering him. But they didn't. Maybe somehow they were caught. He climbed up into the world of reality and thought of his sojourn into the depths of the earth as just a memory. [What had become of his tormentors?] He doesn't know— never found out anything about them. They just disappeared. [What does he think about them?] He doesn't know. [Who do you think they were?] They were fanatics, sort of like Communists or Fascists, or a group of scientists that were trying an experiment on human behavior. [What do you think of their motives?] They were brilliant men, but somehow they had gone off the beam. They wanted to find out about human nature, but yet they thought nothing of the subject they were using. [Does it appear to you that he's without clothes?] Yes, I noticed that. After this captivity down there, they practically rotted away or were eaten away by lizards.

1. Assuming that this story indicates some transient state on the part of the narrator, what do you think this state is?

2. Assuming that the story could indicate some enduring character-istics of the narrator, what do you think it shows?

3. Assuming that the picture itself was disturbing to this woman, how could this account for any features of the story? (The picture is that of a naked, muscular man clinging to a rope.)

AN EVALUATION OF THE TAT

In trying to evaluate the TAT, we must remember that we are judg-ing the interpretive assumptions and scoring method. Since there are so many different assumptions in current use, we can hardly judge the value of *the* TAT. Then, too, the results will vary even among inter-preters using the same scoring system. Research data on the TAT must be studied with these points 'n mind. A study showing that the TAT lacks validity may be showing that either a particular scoring method or a particular interpreter lacks validity.

Many of the weaknesses of the Rorschach method are present in the TAT even at its best. The concepts used in writing interpretive reports are often hazy and ill-defined. The measurement of underlying variables, whatever they may be, is relatively crude. Subjectivity plays a large part in interpretation. In addition to these inadequacies, normative data have not yet accumulated for the TAT in satisfactory amounts. Despite these barriers, clinicians continue to feel that TAT data are useful. And there is some evidence to support their feeling.

Validity. In one part of Hartman's study of adolescent boys (11), he determined the agreement between ratings of specific traits made by a TAT interpreter and those made by a psychiatrist who studied the sub-jects without using the TAT. The median correlation between the inter-preter's ratings and the psychiatrist's ratings was only .17, although about a third of the correlations were in the low .30s. The TAT inter-preter worked "blindly"; that is, he knew only the age of each subject and the general nature of the group being studied. Another rater had interviewed and tested the subjects and had social histories available. His ratings showed a median correlation with the psychiatrist's ratings of .44.

A somewhat better result was obtained in the Michigan Assessment Study according to Samuels (23). Median correlations between inter-preter and pooled ratings of judges after intensive study are of the order of .30. Of course, this study used an entirely different set of varia-bles for rating than did the Hartman study. Six TAT interpreters were used in the Michigan study, and Samuels found substantial variation in the validity of their individual ratings.

Several studies by Harrison (9, 10) indicate that he was able to achieve better than chance accuracy in matching TAT interpretations with case histories. In one part of the investigation, thirty of thirty-nine cases were correctly placed as to major diagnostic category.

In a different kind of study, Murray and Stein (20) used five TAT cards as a basis for rating the leadership ability of ROTC men. They obtained a rank-order correlation of .65 between the ranking based on the TAT material and the ranking made by superiors of the men.

At present, it appears that we can expect validity coefficients to cluster around .30, depending on the kinds of traits or qualities used and on the adequacy of the interpreters. But it should be noted that most of the studies have used fairly small samples, and that cross-validation studies are conspicuously missing.

Attempts to validate the TAT bring to the fore some painful complexities in the validity problem, complexities that are connected with nearly all projective methods. If we want to predict overt behavior from the TAT, we can choose some fairly clear-cut, but narrow, criterion such as number of arrests, amount of sexual activity, or presence of psychosomatic ailments. We then attempt to find out those features of a record that will enable us to predict the criterion. But it is often said that the TAT is not designed to do this kind of job, and that may be perfectly true. It is further said that the proper function of the TAT is to reveal needs, attitudes, and similar covert variables. If we wish to demonstrate this kind of validity (construct validity) we face two problems. First we must show that the interpreter can, in fact, estimate the covert variables with some degree of accuracy. Ordinarily, this demonstration consists of showing a positive correlation between an interpreter's ratings and the ratings by judges who base their ratings on interviews and observations of behavior. Assuming that this validity can be shown, we are faced with the second problem: how are these covert variables related to the broad areas of action that we must finally estimate?

Let us take a specific illustration of this last problem. Suppose we show, by means of rating validation, that certain features of TAT stories really measure unconscious hostility toward women. And suppose that a young man stands high on this variable. What can we say about him that makes a difference? Is it safe for his fiancée to marry him? Should he be allowed to supervise women workers? In other words, how valid are the predictions of overt behavior from covert variables? This last question is crucial, for covert variables that tell nothing about overt behavior are useless to the clinician.

This matter of the relationship between inferred variables and observed behavior is, of course, part of the problem of personality and of motivational psychology. It is not forced upon us solely by projective methods; it arises whenever we make inferences about the underlying variables of personality in order to predict a person's probable courses of action. The usefulness of projective tests, then, is intimately related to the general progress of psychology. The situation is summarized this way by Korner:

Since, in predicting behavior from projective techniques, we have to rely on psychological inference, it is the function of general psychological research, rather than that of endless pragmatic studies with projective techniques proper, to establish predictive criteria. In other words, if we wish to know what kind of a person would make a good engineer, a good pilot or a good psychoanalyst, let us first establish clinically and theoretically what kinds of needs, what patterns of impulse-control are helpful and which are a hindrance in a given field. After these clinical criteria are validly established, projective techniques will be very helpful, and will constitute a short cut in the selection of candidates (12, p. 627).

Pessimistic Bias. Like the Rorschach, the TAT seems to lead interpreters to take a dim view of the client's adjustment. Soskin (25) was able to show this by means of an ingenious research method. After intensive interviews with a subject whom he names "Linda," he constructed a twenty-four-item multiple-choice test covering her attitudes and specific events in her life. The choices offered for each item varied in the degree of adjustment or maladjustment they suggested. Novices studying TAT interpretation were initially given the test with only background data available: age, sex, educational achievement, marital status, etc. Then they were permitted to study Linda's TAT stories and answer the test again. The results showed that these judges considered her more maladjusted after seeing the TAT results than they did before. And the degree of maladjustment they attributed to her was greater than the maladjustment indicated by the correct answers. Experienced clinicians, too, showed the same tendency after examining Linda's TAT record.

This tendency is probably not due simply to increased familiarity with the subject. In another study Soskin (24) constructed a similar test for "David." Judges answered the test, then observed David in nine role-playing situations. Retests after the observation period did not reveal shifts toward judgments of poor adjustment. Clinicians who based their answers on the Rorschach test did show such shifts, however.

At present, we cannot certainly say that the TAT cannot reveal personal assets. Perhaps it can, and perhaps clinicians fail to see them because they are oriented toward the discovery of pathological trends. But present interpretive methods neglect personal assets and stress liabilities.

The Need for Normative Data. Responses to the TAT cards depend to some extent on the pictures that are used. For this reason, we need information on the common ways in which people react to them. Without such data, we cannot really say whether a narrator is telling many or few success stories, aggressive incidents, and so on. Several studies to establish normative data have been carried out by Eron (6, 7). He considered the emotional tone of the stories, their outcomes, the themes told, and several other characteristics. Some of his data from male groups (6) force a revision in our notions about reasonable inferences from the stories. To illustrate, about two-thirds of the stories told by normal subjects were rated on the "sad" side of the emotional tone scale. Consequently, a record with a majority of sad stories may not indicate any peculiar deviation on the part of the narrator.

Some experts claim that misidentification of the sex of the figures in the pictures is an indicator of marked pathology. Eron did not, however, find significant differences among normal and pathological groups in this respect. Confusion of the sex of the male figure on card 3 BM has been especially mentioned as an indication of feminine personality trends in males. Over half of the 150 male subjects studied by Eron showed this confusion, but of seven known homosexuals in the group, not one misidentified the sex of the figure. In the face of this evidence, it seems unwise to rely on confusion about the sex of the figures as an indicator of feminine trends. Eron also failed to find evidence that other kinds of perceptual distortions were characteristic of his pathological cases.

Eron's data show that certain kinds of themes are quite common. The five most common themes in Eron's female group (7) are the same as those found in his male group (6). These themes are: pressure from parents, aggression arising from an impersonal environmental source, aspiration, curiosity, and succorance from parents. Presumably these themes are common because of the nature of the stimulus cards and the nature of culture in the United States. Their presence in a record would not lead us to any unique interpretation. On the other hand, absence of these themes should probably alert us to the possibility of special, unique attitudes in the narrator.

Much more normative data is needed than we now have. It would be helpful to know the incidence of certain kinds of themes, moods, outcomes, and perceptual distortions in groups representing different socioeconomic levels. And normative data on special groups such as homosexuals, schizophrenics who later recovered, or head-injury cases would illuminate the nature of the TAT as well as aid diagnosis.

The Clinical Use of the TAT. The TAT seems to yield more hints about interpersonal relationships than the Rorschach does. Also it is more likely to indicate something about the client's conception of himself. Frequently, the clinician can get some idea of the kinds of values that the client habitually applies to the social environment, i.e., whether he is concerned with morals, conventional success, intellectual understanding, or interpersonal feelings. For these reasons, the TAT is a useful supplement to the Rorschach.

The TAT can also be used as part of an interview. Several cards are selected, and stories obtained according to the standard instructions. These stories may be used as a basis for further discussion of biographical data. Under these conditions there is no need for scoring nor for extensive interpretation. The interviewer may simply point out some interesting feature of the stories and ask the client for his own comments.

The TAT may also be used in this way during psychotherapy or counseling. Client and clinician may actually engage in a cooperative interpretive effort, focusing on whatever aspect of the client's life is relevant at the time. Tomkins (27, pp. 270–286) points out that TAT stories can aid in recovering repressed memories, in estimating the client's current attitude toward therapy, and in promoting catharsis (talking about emotional material without holding back the emotions). He warns, however, that the TAT may arouse great anxiety in acutely disturbed clients and thus lead to depression or anxiety attacks.

An interesting use of the TAT as a therapeutic device has been reported by Sutter, Kell, and McGuire (26). They obtained self-ratings from thirty graduate students on twenty different personality characteristics. Next, each subject told stories to ten TAT cards, speaking into a sound recorder. Three judges listened to the sound recordings and rated the subjects on the twenty scales. Two weeks after the stories were told, the subjects listened to playbacks of their TAT stories. Then they rated themselves again. The data indicated that the second ratings were more nearly like the ratings of the three judges than the initial ratings had been. This shift in ratings was not found in a control group that was not exposed to the "audio-mirror." The investigators think that this method can be used to bring repressed memories to awareness.

The TAT as a Stimulus to the Clinician. As with the Rorschach, the TAT provides data to challenge and interest the clinician. The task of interpreting the stories involves him more deeply with the person he is studying. It stimulates him to form explicit hypotheses about the motives and attitudes that underlie behavior. But in view of the difficulties and uncertainties connected with the test, these hypotheses must be checked against other data. They are not conclusions but beginnings.

The final caution to the interpreter is to remember that he is a person, too, and is not beyond the influence of the very forces he finds in his clients' stories. "TAT stories offer boundless opportunities for the projection of one's own complexes or one's pet theories, and the amateur psychoanalyst who is disrespectful of solid facts is only too apt to make a fool of himself if, in interpreting the TAT, he gives free rein to his imagination" (19, p. 6).

REFERENCES

1. Arnold, M. B. A demonstration analysis of the TAT in a clinical setting. *J. abnorm. soc. Psychol.*, 1949, 44, 97–111.
2. Atkinson, J. W., & McClelland, D. C. The projective expression of needs: II. The effect of different intensities of the hunger drive on thematic apperception. *J. exp. Psychol.*, 1948, 38, 643–658.
3. Bellak, L. The concept of projection: an experimental investigation and study of the concept. *Psychiat.*, 1944, 7, 353–370.
4. Brown, T. The secondary laws of learning. In W. Dennis (Ed.), *Readings in the history of psychology*. New York: Appleton-Century-Crofts, 1948. Pp. 125–128.
5. Clark, R. A. The projective measurement of experimentally induced levels of sexual motivation. *J. exp. Psychol.*, 1952, 44, 391–399.
6. Eron, L. D. A normative study of the Thematic Apperception Test. *Psychol. Monogr.*, 1950, 64 (No. 9), 1–48.
7. Eron, L. D. Responses of women to the Thematic Apperception Test. *J. consult. Psychol.*, 1953, 17, 269–282.
8. Hall, C. *The meaning of dreams*. New York: Harper, 1953.
9. Harrison, R. Studies in the use and validity of the Thematic Apperception Test with mentally disordered patients. II. A quantitative validity study. *Charact. & Pers.*, 1940, 9, 122–133.
10. Harrison, R. Studies in the use and validity of the Thematic Apperception Test. III. Validation by the method of "blind analysis." *Charact. & Pers.*, 1940, 9, 134–138.
11. Hartman, A. A. An experimental examination of the thematic apperception technique in clinical diagnosis. *Psychol. Monogr.*, 1949, 63 (No. 8), 1–47.
12. Korner, A. Theoretical considerations concerning the scope and limitations of projective techniques. *J. abnorm. soc. Psychol.*, 1950, 45, 619–627.
13. Leuba, C., & Lucas, C. The effects of attitudes on the descriptions of pictures. *J. exp. Psychol.*, 1945, 35, 517–524.
14. Lindzey, G. An experimental examination of the scapegoat theory of prejudice. *J. abnorm. soc. Psychol.*, 1950, 45, 296–309.
15. Lindzey G. Thematic Apperception Test: interpretive assumptions and related empirical evidence. *Psychol. Bull.*, 1952, 49, 1–25.
16. Mayman, M., & Kutner, B. Reliability in analyzing TAT stories. *J. abnorm. soc. Psychol.*, 1947, 42, 365–368.
17. McArthur, C. The effects of need achievement on the content of TAT stories: a re-examination. *J. abnorm. soc. Psychol.*, 1953, 48, 532–536.
18. McClelland, D. C., Clark, R. A., Roby, T. B., & Atkinson, J. W. The projective expression of needs: IV. The effect of need for achievement on thematic apperception. *J. exp. Psychol.*, 1949, 39, 242–255.
19. Murray, H. A. *Thematic Apperception Test Manual*. Cambridge: Harvard Univer. Press, 1943.
20. Murray, H. A., & Stein, M. Note on the selection of combat officers. *Psychosom. Med.*, 1943, 5, 386–391.
21. Piotrowski, Z. A new evaluation of the Thematic Apperception Test. *Psychoanal. Rev.*, 1950, 37, 101–127.

22. Pittluck, P. *The relation between aggressive fantasy and overt behavior.* Unpub. Ph.D. thesis, Yale Univer., 1950.
23. Samuels, H. The validity of personality-trait ratings based on projective techniques. *Psychol. Monogr.*, 1952, **66** (No. 5), 1–21.
24. Soskin, W. F. Influence of information on bias in social perception. *J. Pers.*, 1953, **22**, 118–127.
25. Soskin, W. F. Bias in postdiction from projective tests. *J. abnorm. soc. Psychol.*, 1954, **49**, 69–74.
26. Sutter, E. L., Kell, B. L., & McGuire, C. Some audio-mirror effects of TAT stories upon self-awareness. *Amer. Psychol.*, 1953, **8**, 444.
27. Tomkins, S. S. *The Thematic Apperception Test.* New York: Grune & Stratton, 1947.
28. Vorhaus, P. G. *TAT summary record blank: Manual of directions.* Yonkers, N. Y.: World, 1952.

CHAPTER 10

A Variety of Supplementary Methods

Clinicians do not always undertake complete personality studies. Often they are asked to assess persons for special purposes that require only limited information. They may be called on, for example, to choose persons with great or little tolerance for stress. In such cases it helps to have a projective method that is brief yet "hits the high spots." This chapter describes a variety of these methods.

Several of the techniques mentioned in this chapter are well suited to clinical use in business and industrial settings. In this kind of work, the clinician must evaluate executive and supervisory personnel in a limited time, and he may prefer to spend most of his time interviewing. To supplement the interview, one of the briefer projective devices may be used. The sentence completion test, for example, can be administered by an assistant and interpreted at the clinician's leisure. Conclusions arrived at in the interview may be confirmed or modified by the added data.

In military work, techniques are needed which are applicable to large-scale screening of recruits. One method that has been tried in military screening is the Group Rorschach. There is also the need for short, individually administered methods in military clinical work. Often the pressure on a psychiatric unit is very great, and clinicians want added data without spending much additional time. Drawing analysis is potentially useful in such a situation. Its value is heightened by the fact that the military clinician encounters a large number of men with verbal handicaps which make methods like the TAT or the sentence completion test inappropriate.

Most of the methods in this chapter can be adapted for group administration. And, with the exception of the Group Rorschach, they do not require a highly trained professional person to administer them. The important requirement is that the administrator should know how to do testing in large groups.

The methods described in this chapter are not on an equal footing so far as general acceptance and demonstrated validity are concerned. As with the TAT and the Rorschach, the clinical skill of the interpreter and his familiarity with the test are crucial for using these supplementary methods well. The fact that they are administered easily does not mean that they can be interpreted easily. But they are ways of obtaining data that will stimulate the clinician to frame hypotheses about his clients and to reexamine hypotheses he has formed on the basis of other information.

None of these methods can be described as well-developed probing devices, although they appear to be worthy of further investigation and refinement. Perhaps you will be able to think of some research that could be done to improve them, or you may get notions for new methods. Many knotty problems arise in developing soundly based projective techniques, and ingenious research methods must be devised to solve them. If you are interested in clinical problems but do not care for actual clinical work, you may find satisfaction in this kind of research.

THE SENTENCE COMPLETION METHOD

In a sentence completion test, the stimuli are sentence fragments, called "stems," arranged to allow space for writing the completion of the sentence. Persons taking the test are expected to finish sentences with words that express their own feelings or thoughts. Here are some sample stems:

"At night I feel . . ."
"Secretly I . . ."
"When he failed . . ."

There is no single standard list of stems. Investigators have felt free to borrow and to invent them to suit their own purposes. The number of stems used is ordinarily from forty to a hundred. Instructions usually request subjects to work rapidly and complete the sentences with the first thought that comes to mind. Obviously, however, the subject has ample opportunity to withhold or to modify his responses.

The content of the stems is naturally decisive in determining the meaning and interpretation of the responses. Therefore, stems are chosen to fit the clinician's purpose and the setting in which the test is to be used. A test blank for industrial use will contain more stems dealing with the boss, with conditions of work, pay, and ambition than one for use in a public mental-hygiene clinic. School psychologists will want more items about teachers, grades, and classroom activities. In nearly all forms of the test, however, there will be some items related to family, reactions to authority, friends, important wishes, fears, moods, and attitudes toward the opposite sex. Items dealing with the same topic are usually scattered randomly throughout the list.

Stems may be phrased in the first person ("I fear . . ."), third person ("He fears . . ."), or proper-name forms ("Mary fears . . ."). Some lists use all these forms, while others rely exclusively on first- or third-person phrasings. Sacks (6) compared first- and third-person versions of the same stems to find out which form is more useful. His results led him to conclude that the first-person form yields more accurate estimates of emotional disturbance. Hanfmann and Getzels (3) found that adolescent girls admitted responding to stems using proper names as if they were thinking about themselves or a girl they knew. This finding may not hold for sophisticated adults, however. It may be worth while to use a few third-person or proper-name stems in a list simply in order to disguise the test better or to prevent the subject from making routinely favorable or evasive completions.

We have pointed out that subjects can control their responses to the test without difficulty. Thus, we would rarely expect to find completions that obviously violated common expectations about "good" or "right" feelings. Suppose that applicants for a foreman's job are faced with the stem "People who work for me . . ." Few of them are likely to reveal their preference for strong-arm supervisory methods by saying: ". . . soon learn I'm boss." The clinician would have to search for this kind of attitude by studying the applicant's completions relating to obedience, to respect for authority, to attitudes toward parents, and to punishment.

In many instances, of course, subjects do not know the interpretation that a psychologist will place upon their completions and must either tell what they consciously feel or what they believe will create a favorable impression. Thus, a man may carefully refrain from making any response that would reveal hostile feelings, because he does not realize that psychologists can accept such feelings as part of an adequately functioning person. His wariness indicates his concern, and perhaps his difficulty, in connection with these feelings. Or a man may give responses showing that he idealizes his mother and mistrusts women in general. He is not aware of revealing anything important about himself; such remarks are acceptable in most social groups. The clinician, however, would see here a hint of a hampering emotional dependence and an inadequate conception of the masculine role. He would search for other evidence to confirm or deny this hypothesis.

The degree to which psychological defenses are by-passed by the sentence completion test, then, depends upon the inferential activity of the clinician. And, in this respect, it is much like the interview. We must be careful, however, not to overwork interpretations about deep personality trends. For instance, flippant or humorous remarks on a sentence completion test could lead to speculation about the evasive hostility that is being displayed toward the test. Actually, such remarks do not seem to indicate emotional disturbance (5). Unless they pervade the whole record, they probably indicate a normal interest in concealing information about oneself.

Numerical Scoring. Rotter and his associates (5) have developed a numerical scoring system for their version of the sentence completion test. The system is based on the principle that responses conveying conflict or "negative feeling-tone" indicate emotional disturbance. The scoring manual (5) provides standards for rating each response on a scale running from extremely positive feeling-tone to extremely negative feeling-tone. For the stem "My father . . ." a response such as ". . . isn't close to me" would receive the most extreme negative rating. On the other hand, a very positive rating would be given to the response ". . . is a wonderful man." Total scores based on the summation of individual item ratings have shown correlations of the order of .60 with clinician's estimates of maladjustment. Moreover, in one study cited by Rotter (4), these scores seemed able to reflect improvement due to psychotherapy. The scores, then, are promising as indicators of general emotional disturbance.

If this scoring method is to be used for detecting persistent emotional disturbance, it should not be sensitive to transient emotional upset. Batman (1) has investigated this point and gives some evidence that the Rotter scoring method meets this requirement. He administered the test to college students after they had been frustrated by forced failure in an intellectual task. Scores for these frustrated students did not differ reliably from the scores of a control group that had completed the task successfully.

The value of Rotter's work goes beyond merely providing a way for detecting emotionally upset people. A number of simpler methods do a fairly good job in this respect. More important is the possibility that the principle of scoring feeling-tone is sound enough to be applied to separate areas of the blank, such as family, self-evaluation, and so on. If this idea should be correct, the way would be open for using subscores to aid in sketching a picture of the motivational and attitudinal characteristics of the person. Since most blanks have only a few items in each topical area, the reliabilities of the conflict scores in each area would probably be low. Yet at least the beginning of an integrated interpretation would be possible.

Numerical scoring schemes at present cannot reveal the kinds of subtle interpretations that can be extracted from a study of the content of the responses. For example, to the stem "Money . . ." we may find the completion ". . . is essential to happiness." If this response occurs in a record that expresses an interest and concern for human relationships, status, and personal enjoyment, we could interpret it as a realistic attitude toward money. On the other hand, if the rest of the record shows exclusive concern with "getting ahead," we should regard this response as further evidence of a driving competitiveness.

Qualitative Interpretation. One way to begin analyzing sentence completions is to group together all stems referring to a common topic and study their completions (7). The interpreter notes the feeling-tone of the various responses, their length, style of expression, inconsistencies, and peculiarities. He also looks for erasures, repetitions, and misreading of the stems. He notes his hunches and inferences. As he proceeds from one group of stems to the next, he accumulates a context for his interpretation. Eventually, he reexamines the first sentences he worked with in the light of the total record.

A further step is to inspect the completions for common words or ideas, disregarding the stems. Groups of similar completions are formed, and the stems are studied. Sometimes the sheer number of items that have similar completions will be significant.

Hanfmann and Getzels (3) have suggested an interesting aid to interpretation: after the test is finished, the examiner asks the subject to tell which items were completed in a way that is true for himself. The number and kind of items indicated will reveal something of the subject's insight into himself. Items that the subject says do not refer to himself may indicate motives that are repressed or, at least, unacceptable to himself. Evidence supporting the usefulness of this suggestion has been found in a study of the sentence completions of authoritarian and nonauthoritarian college men (2). This kind of inquiry, called the "self-reference technique," can be carried out with groups by simply asking them to place a check mark next to the items that refer to their own feelings or lives.

To illustrate the interpretation of sentence completions we shall give some responses from two men. They were studied to determine their suitability for positions in several business firms. The tests were administered by psychological consultants as part of the psychological evaluation requested by the firms concerned. The two applicants, Al and Bill, are both married, and they have both had at least ten years of business experience.

In presenting the responses, we organize the sentences into groups based on the content of the stems. The order used here is not the order in which the stems actually appeared on the sentence completion blank.

My mother:
AL: . . . is the nicest person on earth.
BILL: . . . is my ideal in most respects and devoted to me as I am to her.

My father:
AL: . . . is a good fellow.

BILL: . . . was an admirable, lovable, honest, and righteous friend.

Brothers and sisters:
AL: . . . I have many
BILL: . . . are wonderful companions, standing by each other whatever happens.

Our family:
AL: . . . is not very close.
BILL: . . . functions as a unit, where all participate in decisions based on the fact we love each other.

Obviously, Bill is more wordy than Al. But Bill's choice of somewhat pedantic words shows that he is less spontaneous in expressing his feelings than Al. Both have favorable attitudes toward their parents, although Al seems to overidealize his mother. Al makes a neutral remark about his siblings, while Bill's attitude is consistent with his attitudes toward his parents. It should be noted that Al's completion "I have many" is awkward and does not really form a complete sentence with the stem. Perhaps the stem aroused an emotional response that temporarily interfered with his intellectual activity. Tentatively, we may say that Bill feels more affectional support from his family than does Al. The latter, on the other hand, is more spontaneous in expressing feeling.

Other people usually:
AL: . . . like me.
BILL: . . . like me, respect me, and work well with and for me.

People think of me as:
AL: . . . a good fellow.
BILL: . . . a leader with my feet on the ground—one who is substantial and sincere.

If people only knew:
AL: . . . my ability.
BILL: . . . how to build relationships, the world would be a happier place.

People are slow to:
AL: . . . to realize my ability.
BILL: . . . judge unfairly.

In this group of completions, we see that Al is concerned about his ability. His last two responses are considerably more self-centered than Bill's. Human relationships are stressed by Bill, although with a somewhat moralizing tone. He seems to have a broader base than Al for self-acceptance, if we assume that their views about what other people think reveal what they themselves find important. Again Al fails to build a complete sentence; he repeats the "to" in the last stem quoted above. He understands the instructions. We know that from his other completions. Haste and impulsiveness could be responsible for his carelessness.

I wish I:
AL: . . . had a million bucks.
BILL: . . . could right the ills of the world.

If I had my way:
AL: . . . I would be a success.
BILL: . . . we'd all believe in and live by certain basic principles.

I will do anything to:
AL: . . . to be on top.
BILL: . . . serve God and my fellow men.

My greatest ambition:
AL: . . . is to be in good health and financial security.
BILL: . . . is to succeed.

Al's self-centeredness becomes even clearer here. And his concern with a rather narrow concept of success is equally clear. His completion of the last stem is one more evidence of carelessness in his grammatical construction. Bill, on the other hand, sounds concerned about humanity and principles. If it were not for his completion to the last stem, we might imagine that he is unable to accept his own needs as legitimate. At the same time, such a need for service to others opens the possibility that he may be too self-critical and overconscientious. Furthermore, his completion to "If I had my way" contains a hint of domination.

Grouping the sentences according to completions reinforces some of these conclusions. For this purpose, the entire hundred completions in the test taken by these men were studied. Al gives a total of six completions using the words "success" or "successful," while Bill gives only two. Al completes four stems with phrases using the word "fun." Bill uses this term only once—in connection with work. Bill uses some form of the word "plan" in five completions; Al does not mention planning or plans in any item.

The pictures of the two men that are taking shape can be summarized this way: Al is a self-centered person, who is somewhat immature, but who expresses his feelings spontaneously and openly. He is overconcerned with success, and is prone to be careless and impulsive. Bill has a broader conception of success, is consciously humanitarian and interested in principle. He does not show a great deal of personal warmth toward others, however, since he exerts a good deal of rational control over his feelings. His emphasis on planning indicates at least mild obsessional trends. His "righteousness" could alienate some of his associates and may lead at times to efforts to control others by moralizing. At the same time, he is probably dependable and conscientious.

The value of these sketches must be determined by comparing them with other information about these men. As Symonds (8) points out, the sentence completion test is not a safe guide for prediction. But, he thinks, it can illuminate overt behavior by suggesting causal factors, by revealing inconsistencies in the interview and by showing personality trends that, while presently inhibited, may break through under stress.

Problem 1. We shall present more items from the tests of Al and Bill. Study these in the light of those already analyzed and answer the questions that follow.

I get down in the dumps when:
AL: . . . if I am sick.
BILL: . . . someone very dear to me lies at death's door.

I suffer most from:
AL: . . . the atomic bomb.
BILL: . . . the failures of others.

Nothing is so frustrating as:
AL: . . . a traffic jam.
BILL: . . . being apparently unable to come up with the right answer on the spur of the moment.

I failed:
AL: . . . to cross the street.
BILL: . . . to get an order because I temporarily lost sight of the prospect's interests.

What gets me into trouble is:
AL: . . . robbing banks.
BILL: . . . sometimes expecting other people to reach or go into action as quickly as I do.

1. Which man's father was a minister?
2. Which man is currently earning the most money?
3. Which man told an interviewer that "no woman is superior to a man?"
4. Which man was pampered by a mother and three sisters during childhood?
5. What interpretation do you place on the last three completions listed above for Al?

PROJECTIVE INTERPRETATION OF PERSONAL DATA

In Chapter 4 we saw how background data could serve to orient the clinician to the social roles and status of clients. It is possible, however, to extract more information from such data by taking account of the client's expressed preferences and manner of response to the various items. This possibility was first explored by Worthington (13, 14).

To use a personal-history blank for projective interpretation, we need more than the simple form shown in Chapter 4. In addition to the questions used in that form, we ask about school progress, courses liked and disliked in school, extracurricular activities, details of occupational history, and additional details about marriage, family, and health. It is not necessary to ask questions about religious preferences or sexual attitudes. Clients are asked to fill out the blank using a pencil so that erasures can be noted.

Interpretation of a personal-history form by Worthington's method is rather complex, but we can indicate roughly how it is done. On the basis of psychoanalytic theory and empirical observation, Worthington assigns scores to both content and style of answer. These scores are presumably indicative of various defense mechanisms (withdrawal, repression, compulsiveness, and so on); type of character structure (passive, narcissistic, oral-sadistic); and specific emotional characteristics. After the scoring has been finished, a personality interpretation is arrived at by considering the scores in relation to one another, somewhat after the fashion of Rorschach interpretation.

Examples of a few of the kinds of items scored will show what the interpreter considers. Indicators of a high activity level with feelings of confidence and elation include: using dashes to indicate punctuation, using dashes after words, majoring in business administration in college, engaging in selling as an occupation, and expressing dislike for detailed work in a job. On the other hand, meticulousness and social reserve are indicated by such things as: using small dashes where items do not apply, writing out addresses, improving a letter by retracing it, or giving month, day, and year in dating jobs held over ten years ago. Certain kinds of erasures are taken to indicate anxiety. One interesting feature of the scoring method is that a particular indicator may be scored for more than one characteristic, i.e., it is taken to reveal more than one kind of personality trend (13).

Obviously, normative data are required in order to discover whether a given score is high or low. This in turn means that a standard blank must be used, for the size of the scores will vary with the number of items on the blank. For example, if each erasure contributes to the score for anxiety, long blanks requiring a great deal of writing would have larger average anxiety scores than short ones. Worthington has developed a standard form for a personal history along with record forms for scoring.

Some published evidence suggests that this way of scoring a personal history form may be useful. Le Shan (9) studied accident-prone persons by this method and found personality patterns that were in line with theoretical expectations. His study suffers, however, from a lack of control groups to serve as a basis for comparison. More positive evidence is provided by Spencer and Worthington (11) in their study of salesmen.

Their data indicated that the method could help to predict sales success.

In an unpublished study, Nevis (10) applied the Worthington method to data from a hundred captains in the U.S. Air Force. These men had been studied intensively by projective methods and by situational tests such as group discussion and observation under varying degrees of social pressure. As a result of this study, ratings on thirty variables were available for each man. Since the thirty rating variables were not the same as the scoring variables used in the Worthington method, Nevis developed patterns of Worthington scores which should theoretically predict the rating variables. These patterns were then correlated with the ratings. His results show that the estimates based on the Worthington scores had generally low but positive correlations with the criterion ratings. Over-all military effectiveness, level of drive (perseverance and directed energy), and executive leadership ability were among the variables best estimated from the personal-history blank. On the other hand, fair-mindedness, likability, and physical health and stamina were poorly estimated. While these data cannot demonstrate the correctness of single scores in the Worthington scoring scheme, they indicate at least as much validity for score patterns as has been reported for the TAT or Rorschach.

The practical advantages of interpreting a personal history form are great. It can easily be administered to groups, and it can be used in business settings where the TAT or Rorschach would be inappropriate. Furthermore, it probably evokes less defensiveness in clients because it does not appear to be a "test." For these reasons, the Worthington technique may prove to be of unique value in the study of persons.

Another type of blank has been used in somewhat the same way by Wertheimer and McKinney (12). Their case-history form was developed for use with college students and includes many items dealing with attitudes and feelings in addition to the standard background data. When they compared the responses of 200 unselected students with those of 200 neurotic students, they found that, in general, the latter more often expressed feelings of misery, uncertainty, and fear. More novel is the finding that neurotics used the space on the blank oddly. They were more likely to write between the lines and on the back of the page in answering the items. The extent to which these findings can be generalized to non-college adults is not known.

Problem 2. On personal data blanks there is usually a request for the client's hobbies or spare-time activities. These activities are interesting to think about because they ordinarily represent the client's free choice and show something about his motives. Consider the hobbies or spare-time activities in the list below. What kinds of people could be interested in them? For each item, make some plausible inferences about the personality or about the needs of adult males who would choose it as a major spare-time enjoyment.

1. Outdoor camping
2. Reading the *National Geographic*
3. Practicing magic tricks, putting on magic shows for clubs
4. Raising orchids
5. Stamp collecting
6. Being scoutmaster of a Boy Scout troop
7. Building model railroads
8. Reading psychology, especially Freud's books

MODIFICATIONS OF THE RORSCHACH METHOD

Scoring by Adding "Signs." Many times clinicians want to use the Rorschach method for making a diagnosis rather than for constructing a personality sketch. They want to say that a given patient is psychotic, or homosexual, or suicidal. Such statements may be extremely important in deciding whether the patient should be hospitalized, be given electro-convulsive therapy, be closely guarded, and so on. Since the complete study of the usual Rorschach record is quite complex and time-consuming, clinicians have searched for ways of simplifying the analysis of the record when making a diagnostic decision. One way of doing this is to make a list of "signs" or indicators of behavior disorder and count the number of signs in the patient's record.

The usual method for compiling a list of signs that characterize a particular disorder is similar to the item-analysis methods applied to psychometric tests. Suppose, for example, we wish to find a list of signs that indicate neurosis. We would choose a sample of known neurotics and a sample of normal persons and administer the standard Rorschach test. Then we would systematically compare the formal and content scores of the two groups. Whenever we found that the two groups differed with respect to a given scoring category, we would include that score in our list of signs that indicate neurosis. Of course, we would retain only scores that differentiated between the two groups in a statistically reliable way.

The outcome of such an investigation would be a list of eight or ten characteristics indicative of neurosis. The list of signs might include such things as: more CF than FC, fewer than two M responses, F% greater than 50 per cent, fewer than two FC responses, and a total number of responses that is below twenty. Armed with such a list, we could inspect the record of a patient and count the number of neurotic signs it contained. The total number of signs can be considered as a kind of "neuroticism score," that is, a high score would mean that the patient is probably neurotic.

A number of research studies have been directed toward discovering signs that are associated with neurosis, brain damage, schizophrenia, homosexuality, and other specific kinds of disorder. These investigations have turned up interesting and illuminating data, but the actual application of the schemes for scoring by adding signs has not worked very well in everyday clinical practice. There are several reasons for the failure of these scoring methods.

In the first place, many of the lists of signs have not been adequately cross-validated (see Chapter 2). Many of the statistically reliable differences between the normal and abnormal groups studied in one investigation will not be found when the study is repeated.

Another reason why we cannot place much confidence in lists of signs arises from the nature of present diagnostic categories. The various types of neurosis are separated from one another largely on the basis of symptoms. This basis for classification probably covers up marked differences in the dynamics of these disorders. For example, even though two patients may be classified as hypochondriacs, their attitudinal and motivational patterns may be quite different. In one, the symptoms serve to control unacceptable sexual impulses; while in the other, they serve to control and manipulate members of the patient's family. In some ways, then, patients who belong to a single diagnostic group may be quite unlike one another. This statement is probably just as true of psychotic diagnoses as it is of neurotic diagnoses. If the Rorschach really goes beyond the surface of the personality, it may not be an appropriate tool for classifying people into the categories currently in use.

A further reason for doubting the value of adding signs is that such a practice violates the principle of configural interpretation. This principle is one of the unique contributions of projective methods to clinical work. We have seen in earlier chapters that the meaning of a client's response depends upon the rest of the responses he gives to the test. Simply tallying indicators of a disorder does not reveal indicators of resources appearing elsewhere in the record.

Lists of signs may be helpful as rough guides in interpreting individual records. They may call the attention of the interpreter to significant features of the Rorschach protocol, but they should be evaluated in the light of the entire record. If the sign approach is used as a substitute for skilled interpretation, we cannot expect a great deal from it.

The Inspection Technique. Munroe (18) has proposed an "inspection technique" that seems to be an improvement over the simple summation of signs. Essentially, it is a method for summarizing the outstanding features of a Rorschach record. First, the record is scored in the usual way. Then entries are made on a check list covering twenty-eight different items. Deviations from the optimum scoring levels for W, D, FC,

CF, M, and other scores are weighed in accordance with the degree of deviation. For example, a record with 50 per cent W responses would receive a single "plus" on the check list. One with more than 75 per cent W would be entered as a double "plus" in the W category. A record with less than 15 per cent W would be given a "minus" entry. Other scores would be entered in the proper places on the check list. The end result is a condensed summary of the record using symbols that show significant departures from presumably normal functioning.

When the check list has been completely filled out, the signs of deviation can be added to give a total adjustment score. High scores would indicate marked deviations from the optimal adjustment range. These scores would not, of course, show the nature of the maladjustment; they would, however, enable an examiner to locate quickly those records that deserved more complete analysis. Munroe points out that the total score should not be used alone for predicting the adjustment of an individual. On the other hand, it is useful for screening purposes and for research studies in which groups are to be compared. Using the check list gives some guarantee of a standard approach to the interpretation of a number of records.

One reason why the Munroe inspection method is an advance over the simple addition of diagnostic signs is that, to some extent, it preserves configural interpretation. This is accomplished by making some of the entries on the check list depend on the joint presence of several factors. For example, a marked deficiency in W is recorded if there is only one W in the record and it is a popular association. And the same deficiency score is used if there are two Ws that are quite vague or of poor form. In other words, a deficit in the *quantity* of W is not recorded without considering the *quality* of the W. This use of contingent scores deserves more thorough exploration in research studies. It is not enough to show that two groups differ in the amount of M, for example. Rather we are interested in the difference in Ms that are of "good quality" and also optimally related to the rest of the record. In practice, this would mean giving a score for one particular sign only when it occurred along with several other signs.

Group Administration. Another modification of the Rorschach has been to administer it to groups by projecting the blots on a screen. Harrower and Steiner (16) have described a way of doing this. The slides are shown in a partially darkened room, and the subjects write their responses on special blanks. Subjects see each slide for three minutes. After all the slides have been shown, instructions are given for indicating the location and determinants of the associations. The slides are shown again so that the subjects can write down where they saw each percept and explain how form, color, movement, or shading influenced them. After the blanks have been collected, the examiner can then score each record in the customary way and proceed with the interpretation.

This modification raises some serious questions. For one thing, we want to know whether the use of slides changes the norms for location and determinant scores. Can we be sure that subjects will find about the same proportion of whole responses or movement responses in slides as they do in the standard cards? Then there is the question as to the effect of limiting the time for giving responses. Surely, the records of some persons will be very much shorter when the group method is used than they would have been had the test been administered individually. But will this curtailment alter the interpretation enough to make a real difference?

Perhaps the most serious question of all concerns the effect of conducting the inquiry in the group setting. In our earlier discussion of the Rorschach, we pointed out that the way the inquiry was conducted could influence the scores. If experienced examiners have difficulty in deciding whether a given response is FC or CF, surely naïve subjects, who know nothing of the issues involved, will often fail to give sufficient information for scoring. To some clinicians, the group inquiry seems to compound the unreliability of an already dubious scoring method.

Harrower believes that skillful administration can overcome the objections that may be raised against group administration. She says: "Essentially the same material, then, is available to the examiner as the result of the Group Method of presentation as is available to him through the individual method if he has conducted his group procedure successfully" (15, p. 148). And she affirms her faith in the method: ". . . while many investigators have embarked on this new method with some feelings of misgiving and even skepticism, they have found that in this respect the Rorschach is foolproof" (15, p. 147).

On the other hand, Hertz (17), writing about a year after Harrower's evaluation, is sharply critical. In a thorough review of the present status of the Rorschach, she says: ". . . to date no group method has been reliably established as valid, scoring norms for such factors as normal details, popular responses, form quality, and the like have not been determined. . . . It has not even been systematically established that the same principles of interpretation upon which we proceed with the individual record operate with the group record" (17, p. 325).

Probably the safest course is to regard the group Rorschach as a new test that strongly resembles the individual Rorschach. It may be useful for crude screening purposes and, perhaps, even for some specific selection problems. But we cannot assume that the values of the standard Rorschach will automatically be carried over to responses given to the slides.

DRAWING ANALYSIS

Asking a client to make a drawing presents a different kind of creative problem for him than is posed by either the Rorschach or the TAT. In drawing, verbal skills count for little; thus the task does not penalize persons who are taciturn or linguistically undeveloped. On the other hand, the drawing task is mildly stressful for people who depend heavily on words. For the examiner, the use of a drawing task offers a chance to see a sample of muscular coordination and to hear the client's comments on his own productions. At the very least, then, the clinician can get an idea of the generality of attitudes of self-depreciation, hostility toward the examiner, or tendencies to offer excuses and rationalizations. But it is possible that drawings can reveal more.

It has been known for a long time that drawings could be used to estimate the intelligence of children (28). More recently, Berdie (24) has shown that the Goodenough scoring method for children could be used with adults for purposes of screening men with defective intelligence. His data indicate that scores based on the drawing of a man are at least as valid as single subtests of the Wechsler Mental Ability Scale when used with adults of less-than-average intelligence. In the course of using the Goodenough method, examiners occasionally noticed that seriously maladjusted children made drawings which were peculiar or even bizarre. Naturally enough, some clinicians began to wonder whether emotional and motivational features of personality could be inferred from drawings.

Drawing a Person. One of the most ambitious attempts to use drawing analysis for the diagnosis of personality has been reported by Machover (30). To use her method, the client is given a sheet of paper 8½ by 11 inches and a medium-soft lead pencil with an eraser. The instructions are simply to draw a person. After the first figure is finished, the client is requested to draw another figure on another sheet of paper, but his second figure is to represent a person opposite in sex to the one initially drawn. An inquiry as to the age, occupation, and personal characteristics of the figures completes the administration of the test.

Machover (30) makes a number of suggestions for interpreting the drawings and presents analyses and case data for seven subjects. No satisfactory data are given to validate the presumed meanings of the various drawing characteristics, but the method is reported to be useful in the hands of skilled clinicians. Interpretation depends heavily on psychoanalytic theory and some plausible, but inadequately established, empirical findings. We can show something about the interpretive principles by reporting some of Machover's suggestions. As in other projective methods, the proposed meaning of individual items must be modified by the interpreter in the light of the total drawing.

One feature to notice is the content of the drawings. The interpreter looks for parts that are missing or that have been elaborated. Special treatment of a body part may indicate conflict relating to that part or to the functions it stands for. Thus, at the crotch of a figure, there may be an erasure, a break or reinforcement of the line, or heavy shading. The clinician would then infer anxiety or conflict about sexual matters. Other information about the client would help the clinician decide whether this was normal or pathological anxiety. Sometimes omission of a part, such as the mouth or hands, indicates problems centering around oral needs or aggressive impulses. In one record, Machover (30, p. 131) interprets omission of the hands as an indicator of guilt over stealing.

The amount and kind of clothing is also noted. Most people vaguely draw a few articles such as shirt, trousers, and dresses. A few, however, spend a great deal of time dressing their figures, thus revealing immaturity, egocentricity, and perhaps some sexual maladjustment. These drawings are apparently more common among socially oriented persons, while lack of clothing and emphasis on muscles is more likely to be found in the drawings of introverted people who turn to their own fantasies for satisfaction. Emphasizing buttons by shading, heavy lines, or odd placement is supposedly characteristic of immature, dependent people. The necktie is thought to symbolize the male sex organ; therefore a large or elaborate tie may reveal overcompensation for sexual inadequacy. Other sexual symbols in line with psychoanalytic tradition are pipes, cigarettes, and canes.

Differences in the way the client draws the male and female figures are also considered significant. A masculine woman may make the male figure smaller than the female or may give it a childish appearance. When males draw female figures that are powerful and maternal, they may be showing their dependence on and fear of a dominating mother. Males who draw the female figure first are thought to have at least mild homosexual tendencies.

In drawing analysis, the examiner must also note the style of execution of the drawing. Does the client use heavy thick lines, perhaps indicating vigorous and uncontrolled emotionality, or does he make dim, faint marks, as if he feared to commit himself to the task? Is he concerned about minute details in an obsessive way? Or does he content himself with stick figures, thus evading the task while seeming to comply with the instructions? Is the drawing task carried out painfully? Or does the client use it as an opportunity for enjoyable self-expression?

Obviously, drawing a human figure provides considerable material for the clinician to think about. Obviously, too, as a personality test it is well disguised and therefore suitable for disclosing attitudes and concerns that are not directly reportable. But the relationship between drawing and personality is sufficiently unclear at present to make us cautious about accepting current interpretive propositions. They must be tested and validated further before analysis of human-figure drawings can be more than an interesting clinical puzzle.

Some Studies of Drawing Analysis. Systematic investigations of human-figure drawings are scattered and conflicting in their findings. As with other projective methods, the reports of clinicians are more enthusiastic than are warranted by the findings of controlled studies. This difference is not due merely to the subjective bias of clinicians; it stems in part from limitations in the methods of scientific investigation. Controlled studies must quantify data in order to determine the statistical reliability of their findings. In order to accomplish this, they often resort to comparing several diagnostic groups on each of a number of scorable items. In a study of drawings, for example, products of anxious and nonanxious subjects may be compared with respect to shading, number of erasures, size of figures, and intensity of line. Such item-by-item comparisons violate the injunction to interpret the configuration or pattern of diagnostic indicators. At the same time, however, studies using this design may turn up useful indicators which were not derived from theory.

An example of this last point can be found in a study by Royal (31). He compared veterans having diagnoses of anxiety neurosis or anxiety state with a nonanxious veteran group. Many of the drawing characteristics studied did not differentiate between the two groups, but eight indicators survived which, used together, do differentiate anxious from nonanxious males. Royal had modified the Machover technique by having both figures drawn on the same page, and one of the discriminating items was that anxious men drew figures separated by a distance greater than two inches. Anxious men also drew figures with absence of heavy lines, many erasures, one figure higher on the page than the other, one figure markedly greater in length than the other, and coincidence of lines for body and for clothes. Some of these items are mentioned by Machover, but some are new.

Another study in which single items were used as a basis for scoring was concerned with predicting nonimprovement in psychotherapy. Fiedler and Siegel (26) chose twenty-two items from the Goodenough scale and used them to score the drawings of patients who had improved and patients who had not improved in psychotherapy. All their items concerned only the face of the figure drawing. Total scores based on these items reliably differentiated between the two groups. Scores were not related to intelligence, so that we cannot attribute the predictive power of the drawings to that factor. If the measure used in this study continues to differentiate improved and unimproved patients in further studies, we shall have a useful technique for diagnosis. Also, as Fiedler and Siegel suggest, the findings may be evidence that the faces of human-figure drawings reflect the social attitudes of the client.

Albee and Hamlin (20) obtained a good agreement between estimates of adjustment made from drawings and rankings of adjustment based on complete case-history material. In their study, judges had a chance to use the over-all approach to the drawings instead of relying on separate items alone. Possibly the results in this study are partly a function of the wide range of levels of adjustment covered by the ten cases that were rated. This interpretation is supported by the fact that in a further study (21), Albee and Hamlin found that clinicians using drawings could differentiate between normals and patients, but they could not reliably differentiate between anxiety cases and schizophrenics.

In an effort to use drawings for the screening of student pilots, Anastasi and Foley (22) found some items that differentiated between fifty well-adjusted cadets and fifty poorly adjusted cadets who had failed in their training. These items did not continue to differentiate when subjected to cross-validation, however. We are forcibly reminded again that cross-validation procedures are essential, particularly with this type of material.

Whitmyre (32) has reported an attempt to estimate over-all adjustment from drawings, but his findings do not support the promising results of Albee and Hamlin. He asked trained clinicians to use drawings as a basis for rating the over-all adjustment of twenty-five psychiatric patients and twenty-five normal men. All subjects were veterans of World War II. The correlation between the criterion (status as patient or normal) and rated adjustment from drawings was positive but not statistically reliable. More striking is his finding that ratings of adjustment show high and significant correlations with the rated artistic excellence of the drawings. The ratings of artistic excellence were made both by artists and by psychologists; both sets of ratings were positively correlated with rated adjustment. This finding casts serious doubt on claims that drawings can reveal the client's general adjustment, and it casts doubt on the supposed independence of clinical drawing analysis from esthetic considerations.

Failures of specific drawing indicators to stand up under critical examination have also been reported. Fisher and Fisher (27) were unable to verify Machover's suggested indicators for paranoid schizophrenia. They utilized an item-by-item approach to this problem, and they also permitted clinicians to use a global impressionistic approach. Either way, their results provide scant support for the view that the drawings of paranoid schizophrenics are distinctive. In another study of specific indicators,

Barker, Mathis, and Powers (23) compared the drawings of fifty homosexual soldiers with those of thirty-five normal controls. Features such as large eyes and lashes, full lips, and emphasis on the hips of the figures did not differentiate the two groups. One outcome was in line with current drawing interpretation, however: homosexual men more often drew female figures that were distorted.

One study of drawings focused attention on the clinician instead of on the client. Although the number of clinicians used was inadequate, the findings are so pointed as to be worth reporting. Hammer and Piotrowski (29) asked six clinicians trained in drawing analysis to rate the amount of aggression shown in the drawings of children.[1] A list of signs of aggression was furnished so that the clinicians would have a common guide. After the ratings were completed, it was possible to compute an index for each clinician representing his tendency to make aggressive ratings. Each clinician was also rated by his supervisor as to the degree of hostility he displayed in interpersonal relationships. An extremely high degree of agreement was found between the clinician's own hostility and his tendency to assign aggressive ratings to drawings. There is an obvious lesson here for clinicians.

Problem 3. The pair of drawings shown in Figures 6 and 7 were spontaneously produced and brought to a clinician by a woman at the time of her third therapeutic interview. She was an intelligent woman of twenty-six with several years of college work. She was self-effacing and overly eager to please others. She had been divorced and was living with her parents. For the last few years her social contacts had been sharply restricted. Try to answer the following questions about the drawings:

1. Look at the drawings as a whole. What feelings do you get as you look at them?

2. Describe the outstanding characteristic of each drawing.

3. What evidence can you find to indicate that the client is: a) Hostile toward people? b) Disturbed about sexual matters? c) Attached to her parents?

4. What could be the significance of the way the hands are drawn in the male figure?

MIRROR-TRACING

Another method for exposing the client's motor coordination patterns is the mirror-tracing test. It has been traditionally used in psychological

---

[1] The drawings used in this study were those of a house, a tree, and a person. This method, called the H-T-P Test, was developed by Buck (25). While its value is not yet established, it has the advantage of providing a wider sample of drawing behavior than the simple drawing of a person.

laboratories for the study of bilateral transfer of training. Essentially, the test consists of tracing a geometrical pattern with a pencil while viewing the pattern in a mirror. The mirror is placed at a right angle to the median plane of the subject, on the far side of the pattern. A shield prevents the

Figure 6. Drawing of a man.

subject from seeing the movements of his hand directly but permits a view of the mirror. This arrangement produces a conflict between established habits of visual-motor coordination and the novel visual-motor relationships required by mirror vision.

The motor conflict creates a miniature stress situation that is often quite frustrating. The frustration is heightened, of course, if the client is intent upon creating a good impression. This situation allows an examiner to observe the client's emotional reactions and his comments about his

Figure 7. Drawing of a woman.

performance. But whatever the client says, the problem remains. Words will not push a pencil around the pattern to be traced!

Ordinarily, the tracing pattern is a six-pointed star having a continuous path about a quarter of an inch wide. The client is first asked to trace the path using direct vision. He is instructed to stay within the pathway and to work as rapidly as possible. The shield is then placed over his hand

and a clean blank pattern is inserted. One or more trials with mirror vision are requested. The time required to complete a tracing of the entire path is recorded in seconds. Peters (35) used the total time for four mirror-vision trials as the score. He counted a trial a failure when the subject tried to quit after the examiner had urged him three times, or when less than half the star was traversed in ten minutes.

Several investigators agree that unstable people use more time in this task than do normals. Louttit (34) found that psychiatric patients and prisoners spent more time than a control group of naval personnel. Peters (35) found similar results, and he also found that, among psychotics, delusional cases failed more often than nondelusional cases. Brower and Weider (33) report that the mirror-tracing test has demonstrated its value in studies of over 4,000 cases, although they do not present their data. Peters and Jones (36) used mirror-tracing as part of a battery to evaluate improvement in schizophrenic patients receiving group therapy. Although their control and experimental groups were small (eleven and ten cases respectively), they found smaller time scores and fewer failures on the posttherapy test. The control group showed no such improvement.

A number of qualitative observations can be made in connection with the test, and these are probably as useful as the time scores. Peters (35) believes that behavior during the test may reveal tendencies to give up under difficulty, poor emotional control, degree of self-criticism, meticulousness, and tendencies to rationalize. He reports that the majority of his subjects dropped their pretentions and affectations after the test, presumably because they had already disclosed so much weakness. Some of the subjects in Peters' investigation were quite upset. Weeping, dizziness, and hypomanic episodes occurred, primarily among the psychotic cases.

Mirror-tracing is obviously a supplementary procedure. Its most appropriate use is as a stress test when that seems needed in a total study. When given by a skilled examiner, the reactions of the client may yield information not easily obtained in an interview. The time scores and actual tracings are objective data, easily filed for future research.

PERSONAL DOCUMENTS AND OTHER WRITTEN MATERIAL

Clinicians can often obtain written materials from their clients and may find them as revealing as projective tests. Sometimes they get personal documents such as letters, diaries, or poetry. Sometimes they request a specific kind of writing. For example, the client may be asked to write an autobiography, or a description of the personalities of his parents. Since the writing can usually be done by the client alone, the clinician's time is not used for "administering" this technique. On the other hand, a good deal of time may be required to read and interpret the written material.

The ease with which large amounts of written material may be collected from high-school or college classes makes such data useful in clinical research. Hall (40), for example, has applied this method to the collection of series of dreams from college students. Other kinds of information may be extracted from themes on life ambitions, on the ideal woman, on what to do with $100,000, and so on. Students may be asked to keep a diary for several weeks in which they note episodes of anger, or fear, or moodiness. These methods could be applied to individual diagnostic work in certain settings, although that is rarely done. In some clinics, for example, a fairly lengthy waiting period must elapse between the first contact and the first appointment. Perhaps case studies could be facilitated by asking clients on the waiting list to provide written material, such as autobiographies, to the clinic.

Personal documents such as letters or diaries from various periods in the life of the client will sometimes show significant changes in values, concerns, or in interpersonal problems, and these may aid the clinician's assessment of the client's present condition. Occasionally, a single document will show clear pathology. An example is this advertisement, written as a school assignment by a nineteen-year-old girl:

> GOODYEAR TIRE—Oh! That Nasty Tire.
> > These are gorgeous tires,
> > They walk, sing, sleep and dance.
> > These tires are so valuable,
> > That we named them the
> > > GOODMAN TIRE
> > GOOD, SOUND TIRES.
> > They're a Humbug, those tires
> > TRY ONE TIRE ON YOUR AUTO
> > They're marvelous, you would enjoy a long trip and
> > Come home and congratulate
> > These are AIR PROVE TIRES.
> > I can't do any more than sell you a tire
> > So I am much pleased.
> > Give 'em air once in a while
> > But don't fuss too much.
> > > So long   Callagain.
> THESE TIRES GIVE ME A PAIN A RIPE PAIN IN THE NECK B. (41, p. 512)

The curious twists of thought shown in this sample were present in the girl's other written work, too. It will be no surprise to learn that she was given a diagnosis of early schizophrenia after psychiatric study.

Spontaneous written productions are also useful in psychotherapy. Short stories, poems, letters to the therapist, and essays may reveal ideas that are not brought into the therapy discussions. Sometimes patients deliberately choose to bring a problem to the therapist's attention by giving him something they have written. At other times, patients will show their increasing trust in the therapist by letting him read a literary effort they have shown to no one else.

Interpretation of Written Material. There is no set of clearly formulated principles for the interpretation of assigned or spontaneous writing. Stories and other fantasy productions may be approached in much the same way as the TAT. But this frame of reference may not be appropriate for letters and diaries. Probably the first thing we must do in considering a personal document is to ask how it came to be written. This question immediately raises speculations about the motives for writing it and about the interpersonal relationship of the author with the intended reader. What kind of impression did the writer hope to make? What would he probably not want to say? These questions help us form the context within which we would make a more detailed analysis.

A general principle used in interpreting most written material is that the frequency of a topic, of a description, or of a stated condition is a rough indicator of the intensity of the personal motives centering around that topic. This principle was used by White in his analysis of Richard Wright's autobiography, *Black Boy* (45). White shows that the most frequent descriptive category used in connection with the parents was "dangerous." Rarely are they described as "loving" or "affectionate." Furthermore, Southern whites are most commonly described as dangerous. Surely, the inference that Wright sees his social environment as essentially hostile is justified. If this is true, the clinician would want to know how this hostility affected the author. Again tabulation suggests an answer: aggression is one of the most commonly mentioned goals or "values" in the book. Of course, sheer frequency of mention is not the only way of communicating the importance of a motive or attitude. Sometimes a single dramatic and terrifying episode should count heavily as an indicator of concern or disturbance.

Another guide to use in interpreting written materials is to look for common associations between ideas or topics. Thus, in a number of stories we may find that a writer mentions a certain kind of female character in connection with violence. It may happen that no causal relationship is expressed between these two notions. Perhaps it is only that the woman is the one who first learns of the violence, or that she is a witness. The frequency with which the association occurs will suggest that some special relationship between these ideas must exist for the writer. Baldwin (37) has applied this kind of analysis to a series of letters.

More generally, we search written material to discover what the author sees as valuable, significant, frightening, helpful, repugnant, and so on. This is done more easily when the writing is intended to express the writer's own feelings than when it is fantasy material. Thus, a man writes to a friend: "It has been wonderful to meet Mr. Foreman. He is such a man of principle." We may infer in this case that ethical values are important to the writer, perhaps more important than personal warmth or status. But if this writer had created a story in which one of the characters expressed admiration for a man of principle, we could not draw this inference. We should have to consider, in this latter case, what attitude the writer held toward the character who expressed this view. If the character were portrayed in a generally unsympathetic way, we should infer that the author did not regard this standard of judgment as important or legitimate.

One of the most rewarding kinds of information to be obtained from autobiographies and personality sketches is the psychological insight of the writer. Tomkins (43) has pointed out that in TAT stories the narrator cannot attribute more awareness of motives to his characters than he himself possesses. And he cannot attribute complex patterns of motivation to his characters if he does not have insight into these patterns. There is every reason to think that the same thing would be true in interpreting written material. It seems safe to assume also that unexpected and deviant accounts of psychological dynamics probably represent significant and distorted notions that the writer has about his own life.

Interpreting written materials also includes noting the style or expressive techniques of the writer. We may characterize writing as flat, factual, emotionally dramatic, didactic, hostile, or "full of sound and fury, signifying nothing," according to the way it makes us feel. Probably style of writing is not related to personality in any simple fashion, however. An "inhibited" style may not necessarily mean an inhibited person. Like clothing, gesture, and speech, written expression results from a complex of determinants: ability, training, sensitivity, and immediate purpose. The style of writing, therefore, reveals one more facet of personality; it does not necessarily reveal the most central or enduring qualities.

Scoring Written Material. Several methods of analyzing written material so as to yield numerical scores have been proposed (38, 39, 45). These methods depend upon counting the frequency of certain kinds of words or ideas. For example, Dollard and Mowrer (39) have proposed a "discomfort-relief quotient" (DRQ). The written sample is first divided into thought units according to instructions. Then the number of discomfort units is found by counting all expressions of pain, discomfort, want, tension, or drive. Relief units are found by counting all expressions of pleasure, reward, relaxation, or drive reduction. Neutral or mixed expressions are not counted. The DRQ is simply the ratio of discomfort units to the total of discomfort and relief units. Presumably this index measures the tension or over-all dissatisfaction of the writer, but some research raises doubt about whether this tension measure indicates poor adjustment (42).

These methods were developed primarily for following the changes in social casework and therapeutic contacts. Little effort has been made to apply them to autobiographies, letters, and diaries, but it is possible that they may be usefully employed with these materials. Here again are some interesting research possibilities.

Problem 4. In this problem you will have a chance to see how you react to written material and to try a simple experiment in matching two kinds of written productions. First, we shall present the replies of three female students of different ages to the following request: "Write several paragraphs telling what things in life are most important to you, that is, what you are going to try to get out of life." These replies will be labeled A, B, and C.

Then we shall give you the replies of these same people to one part of the Similes Test (44). For this test, subjects are asked to make up as many similes as they can for a number of adjectives: pathetic, meek, dangerous, exciting, and so on. They are given two minutes to write as many similes as they can for each adjective. We present their responses to the word "delightful." The responses of the three subjects will be numbered, but they will not be listed in the order in which their paragraphs are presented.

Your task will be to match the sets of similes with the proper paragraphs. Indicate your matching by placing the letter of the paragraph with number of the simile set that was given by the same person. Then write a paragraph describing your basis for matching.

A. My immediate interest is to finish and finish *well* my work for a Bachelor's Degree. That is my principle concern right now. Not only will this be beneficial to me extrinsically (more money) but I honestly want to be a more educated person, i.e., I want to learn—I like it!

Eventually (I might add it had better be soon) I want to marry and have a family. But I absolutely refuse to marry just to escape the scourge of "old maid." I have to be really in love. Funny ("they" said it was true) but the older I get the more it takes in a man to even make him a likely candidate.

B. Most important things in life are family, interesting work, worthwhile work and friends to enjoy. A family is important, gives one others to be with, others to think of, feeling of belonging and sharing fun and troubles. Worthwhile work, why put forth the effort if it has no value or satisfaction, or others are not to gain.

Hope to live a life that is helpful and find pleasure in doing it, work with little children gives it, also worries.

C. Life in general is very interesting to me. Every day that I live I find there are so many things to learn about and become interested in. In my work the fields are so varied and so wide that I find I can't learn fast enough all the things which interest me. Getting a degree has given me a still wider and greater degree of intellectual curiosity. The most important thing in life, however, is to live right and just in the sight of God. Of course, that covers a lot of territory. Secondly, I'm very interested in my family—Mother and Father. And my work is a very important part of life also. I want to put all I can into my work and I want to get the greatest amount of happiness life can offer by serving others in my capacity.

Responses to "As delightful as . . ."

1. A summer day, ocean blue, pleasant surprise, singing birds.

2. Chocolate ice-cream sundae with whipped cream & nuts, fresh clean white linen dress, new fluid-drive Chrysler convertible, fried chicken, seeing a very sick baby up and well again, meeting an old friend, buying a present for mother.

3. A summer breeze, a rose, as a day in June, a happy child, a walk in the woods. [Note: Crude norms for this group indicate that about four similes is average for the word "delightful," and that about one of these will refer to a human being.]

REFERENCES

Sentence Completion Test

1. Batman, R. H. The sensitivity of a projective test to transient frustration. Unpublished master's thesis, Western Reserve Univer., 1953.
2. Dorris, R. J., Levinson, D. J., & Hanfmann, E. Authoritarian personality studied by a new variation of the sentence completion technique. *J. abnorm. soc. Psychol.*, 1954, **49**, 99–108.
3. Hanfmann, E., & Getzels, J. W. Studies of the sentence completion test. *J. proj. Tech.*, 1953, **17**, 280–294.
4. Rotter, J. B. Word association and sentence completion methods. In H. H. Anderson & G. L. Anderson (Eds.), *An introduction to projective techniques.* New York: Prentice-Hall, 1951. Pp. 279–311.
5. Rotter, J. B., Rafferty, J. E., & Schachtitz, E. Validation of the Rotter Incomplete Sentences Blank for college screening. *J. consult. Psychol.*, 1949, **13**, 348–356.
6. Sacks, J. M. The relative effect upon projective responses of stimuli referring to the subject and of stimuli referring to other persons. *J. consult. Psychol.*, 1949, **13**, 12–20.
7. Sacks, J. M., & Levy, S. The sentence completion test. In L. E. Abt & L. Bellak (Eds.), *Projective psychology.* New York: Knopf, 1950. Pp. 357–402.
8. Symonds, P. M. The sentence completion test as a projective technique. *J. abnorm. soc. Psychol.*, 1947, **42**, 320–329.

Personal Data Blanks

9. Le Shan, L. L. Dynamics in accident-prone behavior. *Psychiat.*, 1952, **15**, 73–80.
10. Nevis, E. C. The effectiveness of the Worthington personal history technique in assessing air force officers for command and staff leadership. Unpublished Ph.D. thesis, Western Reserve Univer., 1954.
11. Spencer, G. J., & Worthington, R. W. Validity of a projective technique in predicting sales effectiveness. *Personnel Psychol.*, 1952, **5**, 125–144.
12. Wertheimer, R., & McKinney, F. A case history blank as a projective technique. *J. consult. Psychol.*, 1952, **16**, 49–60.
13. Worthington, R. W. *The Worthington System: a scoring manual.* Mimeo. Copyright, 1948.
14. Worthington, R. E. Use of the personal history form as a clinical instrument. Unpublished Ph.D. thesis, Univer. Chicago, 1951.

Rorschach Modifications

15. Harrower, M. R. Group techniques for the Rorschach Test. In L. E. Abt & L. Bellak (Eds.), *Projective psychology.* New York: Knopf, 1950. Pp. 146–184.
16. Harrower, M. R., & Steiner, M. E. *Large scale Rorschach techniques.* Springfield, Ill.: Charles C Thomas, 1945.
17. Hertz, M. R. Current problems in Rorschach theory and technique. *J. proj. Tech.*, 1951, **15**, 307–338.
18. Munroe, R. L. The inspection technique for the Rorschach protocol. In L. E. Abt & L. Bellak (Eds.), *Projective psychology.* New York: Knopf, 1950. Pp. 91–145.
19. Munroe, R. L. The inspection technique: a method of rapid evaluation of the Rorschach protocol. *Rorschach Res. Exch.*, 1944, **8**, 46–70.

Figure Drawing

20. Albee, G. W., & Hamlin, R. An investigation of the reliability and validity of judgments inferred from drawings. *J. clin. Psychol.*, 1949, **5**, 389–392.
21. Albee, G. W., & Hamlin, R. Judgment of adjustment from drawings: the application of rating scale methods. *J. clin. Psychol.*, 1950, **6**, 363–365.
22. Anastasi, A., & Foley, J. P., Jr. Psychiatric selection of flying personnel. V. The Human-Figure Drawing Test as an objective psychiatric screening aid for student pilots. USAF, Sch. Aviat. Med., *Proj. Rep.*, 1952, No. 21-37-002, Rep. No. 5.
23. Barker, A. J., Mathis, J. K., & Powers, C. A. Drawing characteristics of male homosexuals. *J. clin. Psychol.*, 1953, **9**, 185–188.
24. Berdie, R. F. Measurement of adult intelligence by drawings. *J. clin. Psychol.*, 1945, **1**, 288–295.
25. Buck, J. N. The H-T-P Test. *J. clin. Psychol.*, 1948, **4**, 151–159.
26. Fiedler, F. E., & Siegel, S. M. The free drawing test as a predictor of non-improvement in psychotherapy. *J. clin. Psychol.*, 1949, **5**, 386–389.
27. Fisher, S., & Fisher, R. Test of certain assumptions regarding figure drawing analysis. *J. abnorm. soc. Psychol.*, 1950, **45**, 727–732.
28. Goodenough, F. L. *Measurement of intelligence by drawings.* Yonkers, N. Y.: World, 1926.

29. Hammer, E. F., & Piotrowski, Z. A. Hostility as a factor in the clinician's personality as it affects his interpretation of projective drawings. *J. proj. Tech.*, 1953, **17**, 210–216.
30. Machover, K. *Personality projection in the drawing of the human figure.* Springfield, Ill.: Charles C Thomas, 1949.
31. Royal, R. E. Drawing characteristics of neurotic patients using a drawing-of-a-man-and-a-woman technique. *J. clin. Psychol.*, 1949, **5**, 392–395.
32. Whitmyre, J. W. The significance of artistic excellence in the judgment of adjustment inferred from human figure drawings. *J. consult. Psychol.*, 1953, **17**, 421–424.

Mirror Drawing

33. Brower, D., & Weider, A. Projective techniques in business and industry. In L. E. Abt & L. Bellak (Eds.), *Projective psychology.* New York: Knopf, 1950. Pp. 437–461.
34. Louttit, C. M. The mirror tracing test as a diagnostic aid for emotional instability. *Psychol. Rec.*, 1943, **5**, 279–286.
35. Peters, H. N. The mirror-tracing test as a measure of social maladaptation. *J. abnorm. soc. Psychol.*, 1946, **41**, 437–448.
36. Peters, H. N., & Jones, F. D. Evaluation of group psychotherapy by means of performance tests. *J. consult. Psychol.*, 1951, **15**, 363–367.

Written Material

37. Baldwin, A. L. Personal structure analysis: a statistical method for investigating the single personality. *J. abnorm. soc. Psychol.*, 1942, **37**, 163–183.
38. Bugental, J. F. T. A method for assessing self and not-self attitudes during the therapeutic series. *J. consult. Psychol.*, 1952, **16**, 435–439.
39. Dollard, J., & Mowrer, O. H. A method of measuring tension in written documents. *J. abnorm. soc. Psychol.*, 1947, **42**, 3–32.
40. Hall, C. S. Diagnosing personality by the analysis of dreams. *J. abnorm. soc. Psychol.*, 1947, **42**, 68–79.
41. Howard, F. E., & Patry, F. L. *Mental Health.* New York: Harper, 1935.
42. Meadow, A., Greenblatt, M., Levine, J., & Solomon, H. D. The discomfort-relief quotient as a measure of tension and adjustment. *J. abnorm. soc. Psychol.*, 1952, **47**, 658–661.
43. Tomkins, S. S. *The Thematic Apperception Test.* New York: Grune & Stratton, 1947.
44. Wheeler, D. R. Imaginal productivity tests. In H. A. Murray (Ed.), *Explorations in personality.* New York: Oxford, 1938. Pp. 545–550.
45. White, R. K. Black Boy: a value analysis. *J. abnorm. soc. Psychol.*, 1947, **42**, 440–461.

CHAPTER 11

The Clinical Use of Psychometric Tests

We shall use the phrase "psychometric tests" to mean the traditional question-and-answer psychological tests. The most familiar examples are tests of intelligence and of achievement in school subjects. In addition, the name applies to a host of special-ability or aptitude tests, interest and attitude tests, and questionnaires or inventories for assessing emotional qualities or social behavior. Many of these tests are paper-and-pencil tests in which the items are verbal. Some, such as musical-aptitude tests and measures of manual dexterity, use nonverbal stimulus material. Most of these tests are capable of group administration, and many of them can be given by relatively untrained examiners. These advantages have led to widespread use of psychometric tests in educational, industrial, and military situations, in which partial assessments of large numbers of people must be made at fairly low cost. Except for intelligence tests, however, clinical psychologists have not been inclined to rely on psychometric devices. We shall discuss some of the reasons for this, but we also want to suggest that they may be more useful to clinicians than they sometimes believe.

In this chapter, we shall discuss the use of a battery of tests as part of the study of a person. We shall not describe in detail the specific tests used for illustration. The understanding of particular tests is part of the clinician's general knowledge and can be acquired in courses devoted to psychometric testing. If you need background to understand the tests mentioned in this chapter, you can get help from the Mental Measurements Yearbook (10, 11). They contain descriptions and critical reviews of every important test available.

In the same way, we shall assume that you have at least a speaking acquaintance with derived scores such as percentiles and standard scores. Background for understanding these and related statistical ideas can be found in Cronbach's chapter on interpreting test scores (14). More extensive treatment is given in the text by Goodenough (18).

Psychometric tests are often called "structured" in contrast to the unstructured projective methods. This means that the stimulus material is familiar to the subjects, and that the instructions present definite tasks of solving problems, of making choices, of giving an answer, or of demonstrating a skill. Thus, in a clerical aptitude test, the subject compares pairs of numbers and marks them "same" or "different." Psychometric tests are structured in another way also: the subject does a task which can be evaluated by norms that are roughly familiar to him. In the case of ability and achievement tests, the notion of a "right" and "wrong" answer is familiar to most subjects in United States culture. There is no "right" way to respond to the ink blots or to the TAT pictures, however, and the subject has no way of knowing how "well" he is doing.

The usual content of a psychometric test is a list of items. They can be objectively scored and readily subjected to statistical treatment. Projective test data, on the other hand, must usually be broken into items, for they come in "chunks" that are larger than item size. Objective scoring is important, too. For one thing, it reduces scoring time. It also reduces the influence of personal bias and other kinds of error at the data-gathering level. Some psychologists seem to think that objective scoring removes the need for clinical interpretation altogether. This is not the case. Objective tests simply postpone the clinician's interpretive activity until the scoring is finished.

Another distinguishing feature of psychometric tests is that they must be interpreted on the basis of scores rather than by analyzing the psychological processes used in answering. The scores are usually arrived at by adding all the items answered in a specified way and by using this total to find the subject's position relative to a normative group. Thus we may arrive at percentiles, standard scores, age-level, or grade-level scores, depending on the purpose of the test. The development of numerical scores has been an outstanding achievement of psychology; they open the way to refinements and discoveries that make modern tests far superior to the tests of a half century ago. On the other hand, the value of scores for research should not blind us to the fact that they are, for the study of a person, far removed from the richness and concreteness of acts and feelings. Scores are symbols of useful but high-level abstractions.

Unlike projective methods, psychometric tests do not set creative tasks for the subject. Although intelligence tests sometimes set problems, they are solvable by methods that have been taught in school. Actually psychometric tests appear to require a reproductive or reporting activity. This is obviously the case in ability and achievement tests. In testing interests and social adjustment the subject is usually asked to report his preferences or customary behavior. Tests of motor proficiency or sensory acuity do not call for creativity but for a demonstration of skill.

THE ISOLATION OF TRAITS

Psychometric tests and projective methods stem from different conceptions about the nature of personality. The psychometric conception in pure form is that personality is composed of ingredients (abilities, traits) that can be studied separately and that exist in "amounts." Thus, we can speak of a person as "having" so much intelligence, literary information, prejudice, manual dexterity, and emotional stability. The projective conception, on the other hand, would regard personality as a gestalt or organized totality. Such a conception would insist that abilities and traits can be understood only in relation to other salient features of the person. It would require that whatever aspects of behavior are singled out for study as abilities should be related to the motivational pushes and adjustive efforts of the individual.

We can illustrate the difference between these two points of view by elaborating upon an example given by Allport (1, p. 331). He describes a professor who is very neat and orderly about his own possessions but is quite disorderly in his handling of the departmental library. Presumably, if a "neatness test" were devised, this man would score somewhere near the average. Does this score really tell us how neat the professor is? Perhaps, in the sense that it shows we cannot expect extreme neatness nor extreme disorder from him. But the score covers up the fact that neatness is incidental, even irrelevant, in describing this person. Allport points out that actually the professor is a self-centered egotist whose orderliness expresses his high regard for himself and his low opinion of others.

It would not help, either, to build another test, this time for "self-love," and administer it to the professor; for the addition of more isolated information could hardly reveal the dynamic relationships that make his neatness understandable and, in fact, more predictable than by using a test.

It is this separation of traits from the whole personality that has made clinicians turn away from psychometric tests. To many of them it seems that by the time human behavior has been squeezed into a percentile it is too abstract to be of much value. And yet abstracting is surely a legitimate activity. In fact, it is essential to science that we deal in abstractions, that we neglect some phenomena for the sake of labeling and identifying others. The risk comes only from taking our abstractions too seriously, from failure to remember that the "reality" of these isolated traits is no greater than the "reality" of some other convenient constructs.

Incidentally, clinicians and global personality theorists may be wrong in assuming that no traits can be assessed in isolation from the rest of the personality. Quite possibly, a few characteristics can be assessed this way but others cannot. In fact, it is probable that the nature of public-school instruction, the competitive character of our society, and the tremendous reliance of Western culture on verbal abstractions has actually made possible the isolation of a few aspects of behavior. To illustrate: laboratory attempts to measure the auditory acuity of primitive peoples would fail, because such individuals could see no significance in pure tones presented outside the context of hunting or dancing. But with training and the development of social norms that make "experimental" situations part of real living, they could exercise this sensory function apart from the complex matrix of their daily activity. So too with intelligence, knowledge, or special abilities. They are always intermixed with wanting, feeling, imagining, and with remembering in specific situations; but people in Western culture have become adept at responding to requests that they act now intelligent, now dextrous, now musical, now literate, and so on. If this view has any truth, the isolated traits of the psychometrician are not entirely artifacts but are parts of our social reality.

The isolation of traits may lead us into another trap besides the failure to see that real characteristics seldom exist alone. That trap is the belief that the trait we study is solely the property of the individual. We may come to think that we are measuring some "organized neuromuscular predisposition" that exists independently of the environment. According to present conceptions of the relationship of the individual to social groups, the consistency and predictability of the individual's behavior are due largely to continuing external pressures. To the extent that a person is supported and encouraged by a group, he will standardize much of his behavior around the norms of that group. Thus, an alcoholic can change his behavior considerably by affiliating with Alcoholics Anonymous. Let this social support be removed and the behavior of the alcoholic will change.

The intelligence which we so neatly measure and call a property of the individual may turn out to be almost as much a function of our culture as the alcoholic's sobriety is a function of his A.A. membership. If we seriously changed important values (for example, if we stressed the esthetics of action, thought, and learning instead of efficiency) our tests of intelligence would appear ridiculous. All this does not deny the usefulness of such tests in our present culture.

THE PROBLEM OF MEASUREMENT

Another conception on which psychometric tests are based is the idea that traits are present in varying degrees in different individuals and that they can be measured. In fact, the phrase "mental measurement" is often applied to the whole enterprise of psychometric testing. This idea of measuring the "amount" of some individual characteristic needs careful examination if the clinician is to use psychometric devices appropriately.

It is generally agreed that, if tests are measuring a trait, they do not measure it directly but only by inference. Even in the case of an achievement test, we do not measure all the knowledge in chemistry or English that a person has; rather, we assume that the sample of information we obtain is a fair indicator of the total stock of information he has. Now, if we are going to measure by inference, we must know how the obtained score is related to the inferred trait. For example, does a zero score on a test mean zero amount of the trait? This assumption has been thoroughly debated, and no one now seriously defends the view that a zero score shows the complete absence of the trait. Nor can we say that a perfect score means the maximum of the trait. Furthermore, we cannot say that equal gains in score represent equal gains in the trait. Surely a method with these limitations should not be called measurement.[1] And there are still other, serious difficulties.

In some instances, we cannot even be sure that higher scores actually mean greater amounts of the measured trait. The discovery of over-compensation and reaction-formation makes the assumption of a one-to-one relationship between trait and score untenable in some cases. Certain personality inventories, for example, purport to measure feelings of inferiority. Low scores mean that few questions were answered in the way self-confident people answer them. High scores mean that many questions were answered in a self-confident way. Are people with very high scores supremely self-confident, then? It does not seem very likely. More probably, they are covering up their real feelings behind a defensive bravado. In this case, both high and low scores mean lack of self-confidence; the difference in scoring level would be due to the degree of awareness that accompanied this lack. High-scoring people may be fooling themselves into believing they are confident.

Probably the situation just described does not often occur in the case of ability, aptitude, and achievement tests. We do not think that people can show more ability, or proficiency, or knowledge than they actually have. Sometimes, of course, special coaching and previous experience with tests may raise scores beyond the level that would have been attained without them. More commonly, the scores on such tests may be lowered by the conditions of testing. For instance, some persons are

[1] Problems of the zero point and the unit of measurement are discussed by Goodenough (18) and Peak (26). A sophisticated discussion of measurement that distinguishes between nominal, ordinal, interval, and ratio scales has been prepared by Coombs (13). Important criticisms of tests as measures can be found in a monograph by Thomas (30).

emotionally aroused by tests that have a time limit. They may become so disturbed by the pressure for speed that they perform below the expected level. When this happens, the test score cannot be used to estimate the level of ability or achievement, except to say that we have a minimum estimate.

It is usually taken for granted that a test measures the same underlying trait at all points on the scoring scale. In fact, this is a necessary assumption if we are to believe we are measuring at all. We should hardly know what to do with a tape measure that measured length up to a certain point and then began to measure temperature. Yet this kind of thing apparently happens with some tests. Consider, as an illustration, a test of manual dexterity that involves fairly complicated directions for turning and placing blocks of various colors. Low scores on such a test can result either from poor manual dexterity or from inability to grasp and remember the instructions. After a certain point on the scoring scale, differences among test scores will be due almost entirely to differences in dexterity. Something like this can happen on tests of interest and emotional stability, too. Since many of these tests were designed for college students, they require a high level of reading comprehension. When the tests are given to persons below this level of comprehension, deviant scores may reflect reading difficulties rather than lack of interest or emotional instability.

Even with tests that are more carefully constructed and used than those just mentioned, there may be doubt as to whether the same trait is being measured at all points on the scoring continuum. It frequently happens in sensory measurements that quantitative increases in stimulation finally produce qualitative shifts. For example, increasing the frequency of sound vibrations results in higher-pitched tones up to a point. After that, nothing is heard. Or, increases in the temperature of an object held against the skin produces increased feelings of warmth, but finally a critical temperature is reached and painful burning occurs. It is entirely probable that this kind of effect, this change of quality at extremes of the scale, happens in some kinds of psychometric measurement. Consider an interest test that includes a scale for measuring interest in social-service occupations. Is a low score on this scale simply an indicator of very low interest? Or could it represent a genuine aversion to helping people in face-to-face situations? There is a real difference between these two interpretations of the score, particularly if we are trying to relate interests to other aspects of the person.

We can summarize our discussion by saying that, so far as the clinician is concerned, it is not very useful to think of psychometric tests as measuring devices that reveal the amounts of various ingredients in the make-up of a person. They do permit the grouping of people with respect to certain qualities of behavior, and, in this sense, they provide the clinician with reference points to use in constructing an integrated description of the person. Test scores are facts, but they do not stand alone. They require understanding and interpretation just as much as facts about a person's dress, speech, or behavior in the interview.

THE PROBLEM OF VALIDITY

Construct Validity. It has been clear for a long time that the name of a test does not tell us much about the meaning that should be attached to scores on that test. Nor does the fact that a test contains questions or problems that appear to test dominance or mechanical ability guarantee that it does test these qualities. Consequently, there has been an increasing demand for proof that tests measure what they purport to measure. This is the way that test validity is sometimes defined. A test is said to be valid to the extent that it measures the trait that it claims to be measuring. This concept of validity has been termed "construct validity" (32).

Construct validity is not easy to establish for two reasons: the exact nature of the trait to be measured is often not agreed upon; and no criterion can be found which is a sufficiently pure measure of the trait to serve as a validating criterion. Establishment of the fact that a test actually measures a trait must depend upon the convergence of a number of lines of evidence. We must have a theory that tells us that a particular trait will be related to some performances but not to others. Then we can proceed to examine a number of performances to see whether the test correlates with them in the expected way.

Presumably this is how we know that intelligence tests really measure intelligence. But despite a tremendous amount of experimental, statistical, and theoretical work, it must be admitted that the construct "intelligence" is far from clear. Cattell says:

". . . a survey of current literature reveals every possible variety of divergence as to the objectives of intelligence testing. Intelligence is abstract thinking; it is concrete thinking; it is verbal skill; it is manipulative ability; it is innate; it is a set of acquired skills; it occurs equally in all activities; it cannot be measured by sampling; it is one thing; it is a host of things; it is a few distinct, clear-cut aptitudes" (12, pp. 162 f).

And what Cattell says of intelligence testing is even more true of the traits that are presumably measured by other psychometric tests.

Why then, in the light of this confusion about constructs, have intelligence tests been so useful? The answer to this is straightforward: they have consistently shown positive correlations with socially significant criteria. From this point of view, it does not really matter much what an intelligence test is measuring. The question that interests the clinician is "what does it predict?"

Predictive Validity. What is to be gained from giving any test? Basically we gain economy of time, effort, and expense. Tests enable us to make estimates of some performance without having the subject actually engage in that performance. Our estimates may not be very good, but they provide additional data that enable decisions to be made. We know, for instance, that the Ohio State University Psychological Test correlates in the neighborhood of .50 with grades earned in certain colleges. The test requires about two hours to complete; college requires four years to finish. Now for some people, the time and expense of going to college to find out whether they will succeed is of no moment. Most students, however, would prefer to know that the odds are not against them before they commit themselves. And college faculties want a similar assurance before admitting their students. The value of the test comes from the fact that a relationship has been demonstrated between it and future academic success, over a long period.

Sometimes we want to make predictions that do not refer to the future. We may be interested in how others perceive a person. Do they regard him as friendly, as a good employee, as a leader, and so on? In these cases, there must be a demonstrated relationship between test scores and ratings. Sometimes we want to know how experts would rate a person after extensive study. For example, we may want to know what diagnosis psychiatrists would give a person; then we need proof that a test predicts psychiatric diagnosis. Tests, then, are short-cut substitutes for extensive studies.

In all these instances, we are dealing with the relationship between two samples of the individual's performance or the social impressions he makes. The validity coefficient expresses the degree to which one sample can be accurately estimated from the other. If a test (the small behavior sample) can enable us to improve our estimate of some criterion (the large sample) that is significant for the person or for society, it is valid for that criterion. Tests, then, cannot be properly described as simply valid or invalid. They are valid to differing degrees for various criteria. Thus, an interest test may validly predict whether an individual's expressed preferences for activities are like those of art students; but it may not be able to predict the grades he will make in art classes (9).

This emphasis on predictive validity requires a rejection of certain common clinical practices in dealing with test scores, as Anastasi (2) has forcefully pointed out. She notes that clinicians are prone to argue that the test scores of certain people are too low or too high because of some extenuating condition. For example, they may say that lack of environmental stimulation, or frequent illness, or a language handicap results in an IQ that is too low. But is this really true? In order for the IQ to be considered too low, we must know that the criterion scores (school grades) in such cases are consistently higher than those predicted on the basis of the known correlation between test and criterion. Anastasi argues that this discrepancy will not occur. For, she says, the handicapping factors that determined the IQ will also influence behavior in the criterion situation.

Of course, measures may be taken to remedy the conditions that interfere with school performance. The child may be given special tutoring. In that case schoolwork would probably improve; but so would the IQ, tested after the handicap had been overcome! Taking scores as predictors instead of measures, we have no basis for calling them too low or too high unless we know that transient events during testing affected the score. Obviously, illness or fatigue during testing lowers the test score without lowering the criterion performance. The meaning of such disturbances, however, is not that they interfered with the measurement of a trait, but that they prevented the examiner from getting an adequate sample of the individual's test behavior.

The difference between thinking of tests as predictors and thinking of them as measures of an underlying trait that exists in a fixed amount is so important that we shall add another example. Suppose that a student is being studied in order to determine whether or not he should go to college. A group test of academic ability is administered, and the student scores below the critical level required. Further study reveals that the student reads very poorly. The clinician decides that the test was "unfair" to the student and did not really show his ability. He administers an oral test, say the Wechsler-Bellevue, and discovers that the student does substantially better on it, when the scores are properly compared. Should he now recommend that the student ought to enter college? The answer to this question depends on the validity coefficients of the two tests when the criterion is college success. If the group test has a higher validity coefficient in this situation, the clinician should base his estimate of probable success on the group-test score. This estimate does not end the clinician's work, however. Knowing that a reading difficulty is present, he would suggest that special training in reading is needed. After the training is finished, a retest may show that the student has a better chance of doing good college work.

One further point should be noted in connection with predictive validity. The criterion used to establish predictive validity does not usually sample all of the activities in the life situation we are trying to anticipate. There is more to college than earning grades, and to say that a student will pass does not mean that he will be socially effective or personally happy. Similarly, in selecting men for advancement in a business organization, our tests may show that they can probably do what is expected; but they may not show that they will develop emotional tensions in their work. The clinician tries to go beyond the sampled aspects of the criterion in making his predictions.

Psychometric test scores, then, represent factual data that are not essentially different from other kinds of observations. Although they are more refined, objective, and permit more accurate comparisons of individuals than many observations, they require understanding. They set problems for the clinician rather than simply give him answers. Anastasi remarks:

Quite apart from the question of validity, the examiner should, of course, make every effort to understand why the individual performs as he does on a test. The fullest possible knowledge of the individual's pre- and postnatal environment, structural deficiencies, and any other relevant conditions in his reactional biography is desirable for the most effective use of test data. But to explain *why* an individual scores poorly on a test does not "explain away" the score (2, p. 70).

Content Validity. In the case of achievement tests for school subjects, validation is not ordinarily carried out by using an external criterion or by attempting to validate a construct. In using achievement tests we are primarily interested in finding out whether a subject has reached a given level of proficiency or information. We are interested in the behavior itself rather than in the predictive power it may have. Therefore we want to know whether the achievement test is actually a satisfactory sample of the person's knowledge in a particular subject.

To determine whether a test has content validity, we need to know what kind of achievement is to be tested. Presumably, for any school subject, there are thousands of facts or relationships that are potentially knowable. The test, however, gets at only a few of these facts. The question that we ask, therefore, is: Do the items in the test represent an adequate sample of the items that constitute this kind of achievement? Ideally, the test builder would answer by defining a universe of items and then showing that he had drawn a sample of representative items from this universe. For example, in building a vocabulary test, the universe could be all words in a particular dictionary, and a sampling method would be chosen so as to draw an unbiased sample of these words (32, p. 20). This way of getting content validity cannot be applied in many other cases, however. In testing achievement in mathematics, biology, or the social sciences, we may have to rely on the judgment of experts as to whether there has been an adequate sampling of the universe of items.

In using achievement tests, we need to distinguish between knowledge and proficiency in using that knowledge. It would be simple to construct a test of knowledge about automobile driving. It would include items about the use of the clutch, brake, and starter, as well as items about traffic rules, hand signals, and safe driving practices. A high score on such a test, however, would not guarantee actual skill in driving. It takes more than knowledge to keep from cracking up a car!

Test Intercorrelations. Test builders sometimes short-cut the validation problem by showing that the new test predicts scores on a familiar one. This procedure may be useful if the new test is shorter and more economical than the familiar one. It is not entirely satisfactory as a substitute for direct validation against an external criterion. If a well-known test predicts an external criterion, the fact that the new test shows a high correlation with the familiar one yields only presumptive evidence that the new test will predict that same criterion. A far better method is to offer new data to establish the predictive validity of the new test.

The fact that tests do show substantial intercorrelations provides a useful tool for the clinician. Knowing that several intelligence tests should yield similar scores for the same person makes it possible to find discrepancies due to motivation, to speed pressure, to conditions of testing, and the like. Then, too, since we usually expect positive correlations among intelligence, achievement, and reading tests, discrepancies in scores made in these kinds of tests point to special problems. When achievement scores are significantly lower than would be predicted from ability scores, we may look for such things as poor schooling, antipathy toward school, or interference of competing interests.

In order to be sure that test scores deviate from expectations, fairly large deviations must exist. For example, suppose that an academic-ability test has a correlation of .50 with an achievement test in English grammar and punctuation for a particular school. A student scores at the 84th percentile on the ability test. What is his probable score on the English test? Using the regression equation, we can compute his probable percentile in English achievement as 69. But it is possible to estimate the probabilities that he will score higher or lower than this. By applying the appropriate formulas, we can show that there is a probability of about .68 that his English score will lie between the 34th and the 91st percentiles. Put another way, we should not think of his English score as deviating from our expectations unless it is outside the range of scores from the 34th to the 91st percentiles.[2] If the correlation between

---

[2] The values in the illustration were computed by using standard scores in the regression equation. Once the estimated standard score on the criterion was found, the coefficient of alienation was used to find the limits within which the criterion score would probably fall. The customary limits of plus and minus one standard error were used. Percentile scores were found after the computations were complete. The formulas are given in many statistics texts, but one of the clearest discussions is by Bingham (7, pp. 260–263).

test and criterion were substantially greater, the probable limits of the expected criterion score would be much narrower. The point is, that under the usual conditions of test usage, we should not attach much significance to small deviations from predicted scores. A person who scores ten percentiles higher or lower than expected is not really deviant enough to warrant special consideration, unless his expected scores are either quite high or quite low. It is a waste of time to spin hypotheses explaining differences that may not really exist.

Problem 1. Suppose that you are a clinician engaged in consulting with business and industrial firms. Your chief task is the assessment of supervisors and minor executives, so as to locate those who are potentially promotable. A new paper-and-pencil test purporting to measure ascendance and submission in social situations is published. It is easily scored and requires only twenty minutes to administer. You want to consider using it in your work.

1. What kind of information on test validity would you like to have?

2. Suppose that the only validity information supplied is that test scores showed a correlation of .60 with instructors' ratings of social ascendance for 150 students in five college classes. Could you justify using the test in your work? On what grounds?

THE PROBLEM OF NORMS

One of the very great advantages of using psychometric tests is that they provide data on the distribution of scores made by various groups of people. These normative data give the clinician a much broader basis for interpreting scores than he gets from his own experience. They permit him to see how well his client has responded to the test as compared with various defined groups. It is important, then, that normative data be reported in such a way that the clinician knows what kind of comparisons he is making.

The essential statistics that should be reported for the score distributions of norm groups are means and standard deviations. It is useful to show also the complete distribution for each separate group. The test manual should give percentile or standard score equivalents based on each norm group. But these statistical data mean little if the character of the norm group is not adequately reported.

There are a number of facts that should be reported in describing norm groups: the age distribution, education, sex composition, locale of residence, and year in which they were tested. The method by which the normative sample was drawn is also useful information. This last requirement is very important when the norms are supposed to be representative of the general population. It is well known by now that general population norms usually are somewhat biased because the sample contains too many professional people and too few unskilled or agricultural workers. Fortunately, general population norms are not really needed for a good deal of clinical work.

Norms are more likely to be stable if they are based on large samples; e.g., at least 200 or 300 people. With samples of this size, we can be fairly confident that means and standard deviations will not be reflecting random fluctuations due to chance factors in sampling. On the other hand, a large sample is not valuable if it is a biased sample. Increasing sample sizes does not automatically make them adequately representative of the population from which they are supposedly drawn.

As social conditions change, norms may easily become outmoded. For example, the norms for a group intelligence test based on a sample of college students in 1925 are not very useful today. In 1925, fewer students attended college and they were more likely to be highly selected with respect to academic aptitude than is the case at present. Thus, the mean test score of a present-day sample of students is likely to be somewhat lower than the mean of the earlier group. Another case of the effect of social change on norms has been noted in connection with the interest patterns of psychologists. An interest test constructed in the 1920s (the Strong Vocational Interest Blank) used a scoring key for "psychologist" that was similar to the key used for physician. At that time, psychologists were mainly oriented toward semiphysiological experimentation in laboratories. Today, more psychologists are interested in personality, social psychology, and the applications of psychology. Consequently test builders have had to develop new keys and new norms.

You must pay particular attention to the norm groups whenever you give a battery of tests to one person. Even though the scores for all the tests are given in comparable units (percentiles), individual profiles are greatly affected by the nature of the norm groups used. Since the tests in the battery have been standardized on different norm groups, we cannot assume that a given percentile means the same on one test as it does on another. Suppose we are using only two tests, one for academic ability and one for English grammar. A client scores at the 60th percentile on both tests. This result tempts the clinician to describe the client as "slightly above average" on both tests. But he discovers that the norm group for the ability test consists of college freshmen in a large state university, whereas the norms for the grammar test are based on sophomores in private colleges. The latter group undoubtedly stands higher in ability and achievement than the former. Consequently, the clinician must correct the grammar score to put it on the same basis as the ability score. The best guess would be that the client stands somewhat better in grammar than he does in ability. Although the correction is guessed, it is probably safer to make it than to assume the two scores are equal.

When testing adults beyond the age of thirty, the absence of appropriate norm groups raises a serious problem. Many tests give normative data for only high-school or college students, and we have no way of knowing how mature adults perform on them. Usually, clinicians use norms for the highest school grade completed by the adult client. This practice makes no allowance for the deterioration of reading skills and information level that takes place after formal schooling ends. Again, subjective corrections are called for, and they must take account of how occupational and leisure-time activities may have influenced test scores.

Problem 2. Suppose a test for "neuroticism" has been standardized and validated on a large number of students in several Middle Western universities. The external criterion predicted by the test is psychiatric diagnosis. Critical scores indicating that neurosis is probably present have been established on the college sample.

1. Would you be justified in using the norms and critical scores on students in an agency where the clientele consisted largely of people from thirty to fifty years of age? Explain.

2. Would you be justified in using published norms in working with senior high-school students in the Middle West? Explain.

Because information on normative groups is often badly reported or is out of date, many agencies prepare local norms. By keeping adequate records, it is possible to prepare, for an entire battery of tests, norms that are based on the same sample. Test profiles are more meaningful if such a common base is used. Local norms may also be compared with published norms in order to reveal special characteristics of the agency's clientele.

INTERPRETING A TEST BATTERY

Two Aspects of Interpretation. The clinician looks at scores on a battery of tests from two points of view. First, he is interested in what the scores mean in terms of the client's future. He wants to say that a client probably will succeed in college, in sales work, in the ministry, and so on. These forecasts obviously depend upon the predictive validity coefficients of the tests. When these validities are known to be substantial, clinicians cannot safely disregard the test scores in making predictions. No matter what extenuating circumstances are present, the test with the best validity for a given criterion can probably predict better than the clinician. Of course, these predictive validities are often not available. For example, a client wants some estimate of his probable success as a director of television programs. No investigations of the predictive power of tests for this job have been reported. Consequently, the only thing the clinician can do is to make a cautious forecast on the basis of the similarity of this job to others that have already been studied. Probably he would use an academic-ability test and a vocational-interest test as a minimum battery.

The second way that a clinician looks at test scores is to regard them as outcomes of living. From this point of view, his job is to understand what influences determined the client's behavior in the test situation. This task is the same kind of task that the clinician has when he tries to understand why a person is a hypochondriac or why he has delusions of grandeur. Test behavior, like any other behavior, is the outcome of the person's previous experience, his physiological equipment, his motives, his favored adjustive techniques, and his perception of the immediate testing situation. And, in so far as he can, the clinician wants to relate these factors to the observed test behavior.

What is gained by this second kind of interpretive activity? Probably the most important result is the discovery of correctable defects or liabilities. Moreover, the clinician may be able to suggest the most appropriate kind of remedial work. Let us take a fictitious example. A young man in college shows better than average college aptitude and a high level of achievement in various subject-matter tests. His score on a mathematics achievement test is conspicuously low, however. This poor performance would be of no consequence were it not for the fact that the client wants to enter an occupation requiring more than mediocre skill in mathematics. Suppose that the clinician, trying to understand the score in relation to the life history, finds that the young man probably hates mathematics because his father, whom he also hates, placed a high value on skill in this subject. The objection to mathematics is basically an objection to pleasing or resembling his father. Consequently, the son has been poorly motivated in mathematics courses and has failed to learn. If this hypothesis is correct, there is little point in telling the client that he must take more courses in mathematics if he is to enter his chosen occupation. The problem is rather to help the young man shift his attitude so that he can stop defeating his own efforts to get what he wants.

A Sample Case Study. We can show something about test interpretation by presenting an actual case. The data we give were collected in a vocational-counseling agency that routinely used an extensive test battery. Not all the tests given to this client were really necessary, but they provide good material for illustration. The tests included in this battery sampled academic aptitude, scholastic achievement, special aptitudes, interests, and emotional adjustment.

Mary D. was a thirty-seven-year-old woman who had completed ten grades in school. She told the counselor in a preliminary interview that she thought she would like to take some college courses as a part-time student. She wanted to know whether she could do this successfully. (A nearby college admitted adult students to courses on a noncredit basis even though they had not finished high school.) She also wanted to know what kind of work she was best suited for, since she had to earn a living. The counselor interviewed her to get information about her background, and planned a testing program for her. We shall first consider the results of the psychometric tests.

Academic Ability. Mary was first given the Otis Self-Administering Test of Mental Ability, Higher Examination. There is a time limit of thirty minutes for this test. The items are heterogeneous as to content and include arithmetic, analogies, definitions of words, interpreting proverbs, following directions, syllogistic reasoning, and a few others. Mary's score on this test yielded an IQ of 91. When compared with the norms for college students furnished with the test, she scored at the 4th percentile. This score certainly does not indicate that Mary would be able to do work at the college level.

Several characteristics of the Otis test, however, make it desirable to verify the inference that she would probably fail in college courses. For one thing, the Otis norm group of college students is outmoded and probably averages higher on the test than a present-day group. Perhaps Mary's score seems low because she is being compared with a group that does not represent the kind of competition she would actually meet in college. Then, too, she may have reacted adversely to the time pressure imposed by this test. We expect a person of thirty-seven to be somewhat slower than a person who is younger and also accustomed to taking tests in school. The counselor asked the psychometrician to administer two other tests.

One of these tests was the Ohio State University Psychological Examination, Form 22. This test is untimed, but it can usually be finished in two hours or less. Its norms for college freshmen are based on a large number of entering students in Ohio colleges. Validity coefficients, using a criterion of freshman grades, have been relatively high, and at least one coefficient of .68 has been reported (10, p. 244). The test is heavily loaded with vocabulary, verbal analogy, and reading comprehension items. Mary's percentile on this test was 38, based on college freshman norms. While this result allows us to predict a somewhat better outcome for her, it is low enough to indicate that college-level work will be quite difficult for her.

In order to get an estimate of Mary's academic ability in a face-to-face situation, she was given the Wechsler-Bellevue Intelligence Test.

This is an individual test with normative data based on adults. Thus it offered a chance to assess Mary's academic ability relative to her own age group. The verbal part of the test has subtests of information, arithmetic, similarities, comprehension, digit span, and vocabulary. The performance part of the test requires identifying missing parts of pictures, arranging sets of pictures to make a story, reproducing block designs, putting together simple jigsaw puzzles, and learning a nonverbal code. The Wechsler-Bellevue is rarely used to predict college success, but it correlates quite well with other individual tests of intelligence and with teachers' estimates of the intelligence of high-school students. Mary earned an IQ of 108, which gives her a percentile rank of 69 relative to a norm group in their late thirties. This group is presumably representative of the general population at that age.

The three tests permit the inference that Mary probably cannot do adequate college work. But the Wechsler-Bellevue indicates that Mary's success at academic tasks would be slightly above the average for her age. To the extent that this kind of learning is required by a job, Mary would probably turn in a performance at least as good as the average person.

Scholastic Achievement. Mary was given two sections of the Progressive Achievement Test, Advanced Battery. One was a reading test and the other a language test intended for high-school students. Her scores on these tests were compared with norms for the tenth grade, the highest grade she had completed. On the vocabulary part of the reading test she scored at the 70th percentile. This is a high score considering the fact that she had been out of school for more than twenty years. She probably would not have scored much higher than this when she was in the tenth grade. On the reading-comprehensions section of the reading test she scored at the 60th percentile. Although this score is lower than the vocabulary score, the difference is not great enough to be of any practical significance.[3] If the comprehension score were markedly lower than the vocabulary score, we might suspect that speed pressure or lack of practice in reading was responsible for the discrepancy. If the client's history showed little reading in the last eight or ten years, we could account for the low comprehension score. But then we would try to explain why the vocabulary score was higher.

The language test is composed of items requiring knowledge of Eng-

---

[3] The difference between these two percentiles amounts to about one quarter of the standard deviation of the distribution of scores. But at another point on the distribution, a difference of 10 percentiles would be a very substantial difference. For example, the difference between the 80th and 90th percentiles is about a half of the standard deviation. This curious inequality of seemingly equal differences between percentiles may easily lead to erroneous interpretation of profiles reported in percentiles. Standard scores, or their derivatives, do not have this disadvantage.

lish grammar, punctuation, and spelling. Mary's score on this part of the achievement test was only at the 20th percentile. Probably this low level of achievement was due in part to a lack of concern with the formal aspects of grammar since leaving school. She has not been in work that called for skill in written English. Besides, she is not prepared for such work now without further training.

No more achievement tests were given to Mary. Had she been interested in training requiring mathematics, chemistry, or physics, the counselor would have suggested a test in one of these subjects. When such tests are given, one point must be kept in mind: school courses do not always cover the same material tested in achievement tests. A particular school may have a chemistry course, for example, that does not attempt to cover material that is called for in a chemistry-achievement test. Sometimes this is because of the special educational goals of the school. Sometimes it is because of the fact that the test and the course were built at different times.

Suppose that we had tested Mary's knowledge of chemistry with a recently published test. The test is presumably based on current views about the appropriate content of a high school chemistry course. These views may differ from those held some twenty years ago, when Mary was in school. Consequently, a low score could be due to a poor sampling of what Mary was taught rather than her lack of mastery or inability to remember. A similar conclusion would hold if we used a test built twenty years ago to measure the achievement of a recent high school graduate.

Aptitude Tests. Four tests of special aptitudes were given to Mary. The counselor hoped that the results would suggest some employment possibilities. Two of these tests were designed to predict success in mechanical or in engineering occupations. One test was the Bennett Test of Mechanical Comprehension. The items in this instrument are pictorially presented problems requiring a knowledge of mechanical principles for their solution. Although a special form of the test is available for women, Mary was given one of the men's forms. Her score placed her at the 77th percentile as compared with a norm group of employees in mechanical work.

The interpretation of this score is difficult because we do not know exactly what the Bennett Mechanical Comprehension Test predicts. Some evidence indicates that it can predict success in operating machine tools, but in at least one study it was less useful than an intelligence test in making such predictions (3). Scores on the test are also related to success in courses dealing with applications of physics and engineering principles. Perhaps we can only say of Mary that she could probably do mechanical work adequately.

The other mechanical ability test given to Mary was the Revised Minnesota Paper Form Board Test. This test requires the subject to visualize how a set of geometrical forms could be assembled to make a larger form. Since the parts are shown as diagrams, they cannot be actually manipulated. The subject must arrange the parts on a symbolic level, probably by using visual imagery. The test apparently predicts success in courses in descriptive geometry, mechanical drawing, and some of the skilled trades, but the reported validity coefficients are rarely above .45.

Mary's score on the Paper Form Board placed her at the 45th percentile relative to a norm group of adult women. We must conclude that she would be able to do mechanical work, but would not be judged as very good or very poor. Had Mary made extremely high or extremely low scores on these two mechanical tests, the counselor would want to investigate her background to find out about the part mechanical activities played in her personality. For example, it could be that close association and admiration for a mechanically talented father along with a rejection of female domestic activities could lead to high mechanical-test scores.

The Minnesota Clerical Test was administered to Mary to throw some light on her suitability for office clerical work. The test has two parts: one requires the subject to compare pairs of names and to judge whether they are the same or different; the other requires the same kind of judgment about pairs of long numbers. It is a speed test and can be administered in about fifteen minutes. Using supervisors' ratings as criteria, validity coefficients of around .40 have been reported between test scores and rated success in office work. Mary's score on both name and number checking placed her at the 10th percentile of the norm group of women clerical workers. This low score strongly indicates that she would not do well in such work as filing, operating office machines, and routine bookkeeping. But there is more to be said about her performance on this test.

The items in the Minnesota Clerical Test require a painstaking approach to detect small differences in material that is essentially repetitive and meaningless. In some ways, the test demands a performance that is like the activity involved in picking out small details in the Rorschach blots. Now there are some people who can do this kind of thing well but do not like it. There are others who find security and perhaps even some pleasure in discovering demonstrable errors in material that is not personally relevant. Although both kinds of people could make fairly high scores on this test, they would probably differ on a test of interest in clerical work. The former would show weak interest in clerical occupations; the latter would show strong interest.

What could lie behind low scores? Immediately we think of impulsiveness and aversion to careful inspection. People who dislike a detailed task and want to finish it quickly could pile up errors. But some would object mainly to the meaningless content or repetitive nature of the items. We do not mean that these various motives would be aroused for the first time during the administration of the test. Rather, the test would actually be one more instance of a kind of task they had often found distasteful in the past. Their aversion would hinder both the acquisition of the name and number checking skill prior to the test and the application of painstaking effort during the test.

At this point, we cannot say what conditions affected Mary's score. We should consider the possibility, however, that she may be impetuous and poorly motivated to pay attention to details.

Because Mary had expressed a possible interest in artistic activities, the counselor asked her to take the Meier Art Judgment Test. In this test, the subject is shown a series of black-and-white pictures in pairs. One member of each pair reproduces an original painting or drawing, and the other is a distorted version with alterations in composition or design. The subject indicates which version he thinks is better artistically. A choice is counted correct if it agrees with the one selected by a group of art experts who aided in constructing the scoring key. Essentially, then, the test score shows how closely the subject agrees with art experts. Factors such as color, style of execution, and originality of conception play no part in determining the judgments. It is not very clear just what criteria this test will predict. Usually art students make higher scores than nonart students, and high-school students do better than grade-school students. But there is little evidence that future employment or training in art fields will probably turn out well for those with high scores.

Mary's percentile score of 19, based on adult norms, indicates that she knows little about good composition in the fine arts; at least, it indicates that she doesn't agree with the experts. Whether she can draw or not, we do not know. Meier's Test is not intended to reveal that kind of talent.

Had Mary's score been high or had her expressed interest in an art occupation been strong, the counselor could have administered a test of drawing ability, such as the Horn Art Aptitude Inventory. But a more economical method would be to find out the role art had played in Mary's life. Did she take art courses in high school? How well did she do in these courses? Is drawing an avocational interest for her? If so, in what media does she work? What kinds of paintings does she like? Does she visit museums? How enthusiastically does she talk about art? These and similar questions would be important in any instance where art interest is expressed strongly. And a comparable exploration is called for whenever a client expresses an interest in some specialized work, such as music, dramatics, or writing.

Mary's history showed no avocational activity of an artistic kind nor much concern with appreciation of art. Since she was thirty-seven, further training in art would be dismissed as irrelevant to her employment plans. That would not preclude the discussion of training in an art-related craft such as weaving, metalwork, or hatmaking.

Interest Test. Mary was given the Kuder Preference Record (Vocational) to survey her interests systematically. This requires the expression of preferences for various types of activity. Each item presents three different activities to be ranked in order of preference. This is a "forced choice" technique which prevents a subject from earning high scores on all nine of the subtests.[4] Choosing the answers referring to one interest area automatically excludes some answers referring to other areas.

Kuder scores have moderate validities with respect to a number of different criteria. One review of research on the Kuder Record (29) indicates that the interest scores differentiate among students preparing for different occupations, as well as among people actually engaged in different occupations. A few investigators have shown that some of the Kuder scores show low positive correlations with success in related college courses. Barnette (4) found that Kuder scores differentiate between engineers who are successfully following their vocational plans and those who are unsuccessful in following their plans. A similar differentiation was found between successful and unsuccessful accountants, but this was not true of salesmen. Barnette's study strongly suggests that Kuder scores predict satisfaction in certain vocations. Levine and Wallen (25) have shown a positive relationship between Kuder scores of adolescents and the type of occupation entered seven to nine years after the test was taken. However, their data on the artistic, musical, and social-service scales are not adequate enough to lead to any conclusions about those fields.

Mary's percentiles on the nine scales are based on the norms for adult women. They are as follows:

Mechanical	52
Computational	13
Scientific	55
Persuasive	12
Artistic	84

---

[4] At the time Mary filled out the Kuder Record, keys for only nine scales were available. Newer versions of the Record have an additional scale for measuring interests in outdoor activities.

Literary	67
Musical	92
Social Service	30
Clerical	4

The most striking finding is her low interest in clerical-computational work. It would probably be safe to say that she has an aversion to this kind of occupation. This result adds weight to our earlier speculation that Mary objects to exacting, painstaking effort.

Mary's highest scores were on the three scales sometimes called the "culture triad." They include art, music, and literary interests. The interpretation of scores in this area cannot be made without reference to the case history, for these interests function differently in the lives of different people. We must digress, therefore, to consider the psychological meaning of interests and to introduce some additional information about Mary.

Interests are essentially motivational phenomena. A vocational-interest inventory describes the person's wants in terms of occupations or occupational types that presumably satisfy his distinctive pattern of motives (8). But a given kind of occupational activity may satisfy more than one motive, and different people perceive an occupation as a satisfier of different wants. Thus, in the case of the culture triad, the activities may be seen as conferring intellectual status. Knowledge of art, literature, and music is commonly identified as a mark of membership in the "cultured," upper middle class. These fields are also seen as "creative," offering a chance for "expressing oneself." Or they may appeal to people who find face-to-face relationships difficult and trying. (Shy adolescents discover that the high-school band provides social life without much personal involvement.) Sometimes these activities are regarded as routes to fame and fortune on the stage. Again, the chief motive may be an intrinsic interest in the content itself, due to special training or long familiarity.

Now Mary's history shows no evidence of home or school training that would lead her to know and value art, music, and literature. She came from a lower middle-class background and has worked mainly as a waitress. During World War II, she engaged in semiskilled factory work. These facts suggest that status aspirations may lie behind her scores on the culture triad.

Mary said that her favorite recreations were attending concerts, photography, movies, and reading philosophy and psychology. None of these is a genuinely social activity. The interest in philosophy and psychology sounds a bit strange in the context of her education, academic ability, and home background. Is this another evidence of status hunger, or are we dealing with more deeply rooted needs related to her personal difficulties? People who are emotionally detached often seek help from books instead of from other people. Then too, those who are cut off from others often become concerned about cosmic problems. The extreme of this is seen in bizarre schizophrenic delusions; but the poorly socialized and detached person also has a stranger thought-life than is commonly suspected. Perhaps Mary's statement that she had been studying philosophy and psychology for ten years shows deep concern about her life and the existence of a fantasy world, developed without the corrective influence of social interchange. Support for this speculation comes from a remark she made about being particularly interested in the people of Tibet and Africa. This interest has the full flavor of escape into exotic, far-off lands.

Her high scores, then, suggest status aspirations and some possible need for isolation and detachment. What about her low score on the persuasive scale? High scores on this scale are made by men in occupations requiring face-to-face contacts, such as salesmen, and by men who have dominant positions, such as supervisors and executives. Low scores are common among mathematics teachers, chemical engineers, toolmakers, and farmers. These occupations require little social dominance. In terms of personality, the persuasive scale appears to reflect an interest in face-to-face power relationships, with low scores indicating submissiveness and social isolation. A similar statement holds for women's occupations.

Mary's persuasive score thus fits with one guess about the meaning of her high scores on the culture triad: she is not emotionally close to people.[5] And in addition, she may be submissive, perhaps unable to take her own part in competitive situations.

Problem 3. Among women, members of the following occupational groups make high and low scores on the social service scale:

High scores	Low scores
Religious workers	Retail buyers
Social workers	Tearoom managers
Trained nurses	Librarians
Home demonstration agents	Teachers of commercial subjects

1. Describe the difference between these two sets of occupations with respect to the kind of human relationships they require.

[5] Further evidence of the schizoid quality of Mary's personal adjustment was provided by her extremely high scores on the Religious and Theoretical scales of the Allport-Vernon Study of Values. Extreme elevation of these two scores always suggests that the clinician should probe for preoccupation with abstractions and cosmic speculations along with inadequate social contacts. Of course, data from the life history are needed to find out whether these tendencies have been integrated into the person's life in a satisfying way, or whether they are destroying his happiness and effectiveness.

2. Which set of occupations would be more appealing to women with strong needs for achievement? For nurturance? For openly dominating others?

3. How would you interpret Mary's social-service score in the light of her other interest scores and the background information you have?

Personality Testing. Since Mary had told the counselor that she had been divorced twice, he thought it would be worth while to administer a test to reveal possible emotional maladjustment. His choice was the Minnesota Multiphasic Personality Inventory (MMPI). This test includes nine diagnostic scales and four validity scales. The latter are intended to expose records that cannot be interpreted because of evasive answers, intentional deception, or failure to carry out directions. Keys for other special-purpose scales such as social introversion, dominance, and prejudice, have also been developed.

The items in the MMPI are statements describing symptoms, preferences, actions, beliefs, and events that may have occurred in the personal life of the client. Examples are: "I like children," "I am a special agent of God," and "At times I think I am no good at all." People taking the test are asked to classify each item as true or false as applied to themselves. A category titled "cannot say" may be used when the respondent cannot decide the truth or falsity of a statement.

The score on each scale shows the degree to which the client's answers are similar to those given by a group of patients with a common psychiatric diagnosis. For example, the key for the hypochondriasis scale was developed by finding those items that differentiated between hypochondriacs and normals. A high score on this scale would indicate that the client answered the items in very much the way hypochondriacs do. Thus, each scale is basically an attempt to predict the diagnosis that the client would receive from psychiatric study.

One difficulty that arises immediately is that diagnostic groups cannot be neatly separated from each other on the basis of the kind of items used in the MMPI. Hypochondriacal behavior can be observed in cases of depression and schizophrenia, for example. And depression may occur as a secondary feature in almost any other diagnostic category. This complication forces the clinician to examine the whole profile of scores in order to say something meaningful about the client. A case in point is the fact that neurotics frequently make high scores on three scales no matter what specific diagnosis they may have. These scales have even been termed "the neurotic triad." They are the hypochondria, depression, and hysteria scales. Other common patterns have also been discovered. A good idea of the relationship between types of MMPI profiles and case-history material can be obtained from reading *An Atlas for the Clinical Use of the MMPI*, by Hathaway and Meehl (20).

A number of studies show that the MMPI scales are related to more than psychiatric diagnosis. Some evidence is available to show that psychotherapy and electrical-shock therapy result in lower scores (17, 27, 28). Thus, the MMPI may be able to reveal the *degree* of emotional disturbance as well as its nature. There is also a possibility that the MMPI may be able to predict how the normal client will be perceived by others. Hovey (22) has shown that, among student nurses, scores on some of the scales were related to supervisors' judgments of certain personality characteristics. High scores on the hypochondriasis scale indicated a lack of alertness, and high scores on the depression scale showed shyness, a low degree of initiative, and poor social poise. These findings seem to fit the kind of personality traits we would expect in the clinical groups used to build the scales, but other findings do not. It is not clear, for example, why Hovey should find that those nurses who made high scores on the schizophrenic scale should be described as active participants in group discussion. At any rate, there is a possible relationship between these scales, originally built to detect pathology, and normal personality characteristics.

Scores for the MMPI are not given in percentiles but in T-scores. These T-scores are standard scores transmuted so that the mean score for every scale is 50 and the standard deviation is 10. Scores above 70 (i.e., about the 98th percentile) are considered high enough to raise doubt as to the adequacy of the client's adjustment. Obviously, however, one high score is not very strong evidence. In fact, it is common to find college students with several scores above 70 who appear to be functioning adequately. On the other hand some profiles seem to be unusually low on most of the scales, with only one score near 70. Then it is wise to investigate further, for it can happen that a sophisticated subject may give "normal" answers, not be detected by the validity scales, and still be maladjusted.

Here is Mary's pattern of scores on the MMPI:

Scale	T-score
Hypochondriasis (Hs)	44
Depression (D)	40
Hysteria (Hy)	50
Psychopathic deviate (Pd)	55
Masculinity (Mf)	63
Paranoia (Pa)	38
Psychasthenia (Pt)	37
Schizophrenia (Sc)	49
Hypomania (Ma)	40

The validity scores were all well within the normal range, so that we have no reason to think the record has been distorted by faking or by a desire to create a good impression. On the other hand, these scores are low enough to make us suspect that Mary somehow suppressed "maladjusted answers." Assuming this is the case for the moment, what is most noticeable about these scores? The T-score of 63 on the masculinity-femininity scale indicates that Mary gave more masculine answers than 90 per cent of the female norm group. This score is made more significant by the fact that it occurs in a context of low scores. One minor bit of additional evidence for its significance is the score of 55 on the psychopathic deviate scale. Scores on this scale often rise along with the masculinity-femininity score; and it is the second-highest score in this record.

What meaning could this masculinity score have? The authors of the manual for the MMPI are careful to point out that the Mf scale should be taken to indicate masculinity or femininity of *interests*. In fact, they call it an interest scale. They also point out that, while feminine scores among men may show homosexual tendencies, masculine scores among women may not indicate homosexuality. Nevertheless, in this instance, the counselor should ask himself what these masculine interests signify in Mary's personality. The fact that she was divorced twice suggests, at the very least, difficulty in her relationships with men. But this history in itself points simply to a sexual problem. We cannot say that it is a homosexual problem. The data from the MMPI, however, suggest that possibility.

It is possible that Mary's low scores on the MMPI were due in part to her spare-time reading. She did not describe in detail her reading in psychology, but she mentioned that she had read a number of books by Freud. Her sophistication about symptoms could lead her to avoid admitting, even to herself, the truth of many of the items in the test.

INTEGRATING BACKGROUND DATA WITH TEST RESULTS

So far, we have examined Mary's test results without much reference to her history. In general, the interpretation of a battery should start this way. Then, the test scores serve as independent sources of hypotheses, and their interpretation is not contaminated by biases stemming from a knowledge of the case history. But the final interpretation must take the client's history into account. Ideally, one person should interpret the test battery and another should interpret the life history. The final report should be the joint product of these two interpreters; then, conclusions arrived at independently could be found and accepted with more confidence than the conclusions of a single interpreter. This procedure is too expensive, however, to be commonly used.

Mary's History. When Mary was a child, her parents were divorced and she was sent to live in an orphanage for several years. Following this, she was taken to live with her grandmother. She described this woman as a domineering person who strictly enforced orthodox Protestant moral and religious beliefs. She left school in the tenth grade, when she was about seventeen years old.

At eighteen she married, and after about a year and a half of marriage she had a child. This marriage lasted only four years. It was not clear to the interviewer why this marriage broke up. Mary's daughter had been living with the divorced husband for some time. In her early thirties, Mary married a second time, but this marriage lasted only two months, because her second husband was an alcoholic.

Although she worked as a waitress for a number of years, she found this work distasteful, because she didn't like dealing with the public. She had also worked as a riveter and as a plasterer. These jobs were held during the war years. Although they are unusual jobs for a woman, such work was often done by women during the war. She expressed no liking for these jobs and regarded them merely as sources of income. She had not worked for the last year. She had been able to stop working because of a small income in the form of alimony from her second husband.

Her social life had been meager. She belonged to no organizations at the time of testing. She had belonged to a Protestant church many years ago but was not affiliated with it any longer. She stated that she had no close friends and that she didn't have dates with men. According to her, she had become increasingly shy during the last three or four years.

She said that her health had been good. She admitted that she drank heavily some years ago but denied drinking at the time her history was taken. When she was asked what kind of work she would like, she mentioned color photography. She also said that she would like to fit colored glass into church windows, because she liked working with her hands and working with color.

An Interpretation of the Data. Test results show that Mary could perform slightly better than the average person in jobs requiring verbal intelligence. Her work history, however, suggests that she has not quite achieved this level. Special training to give her some "salable skills" would improve her earning power, but her motivation for added training is probably weak.

Her interest in college may be due largely to an intellectual status need. Her distaste for her past jobs may reflect, in part, lack of status satisfaction offered by them.

She shows no evidence of special abilities or talents either in her history or in her tests. Job choice, then, must be guided by her emotional and motivational requirements. Her low persuasive score, indicating social submissiveness, suggests that sales and managerial work will be unsatisfying. The moderately low social-service score seems to eliminate face-to-face service occupations.

Mary's recreational interests and Kuder scores indicate tendencies to withdraw into a preoccupation with her own emotional problems. Her interest in the job of fitting colored glass into church windows suggests an unrealistic assessment of job opportunities. It may stem from a desire for atonement, because two divorces and a period of heavy drinking must have produced considerable guilt and self-devaluation. Also, her early years were marked by strict religious instruction.

The fact that her second marriage lasted only two months indicates that her choice of a husband must have been based on a distorted perception of what she wanted and what her husband was. Such distortions are not simply mistakes; they betray the force of repressed needs. The masculinity shown by the MMPI is probably related to her difficulties with men; but whether it represents homosexual trends or a more recently acquired masculine protest cannot be decided from the data. She is not as well integrated as the low MMPI scores seem to show. Emotional withdrawal and autistic fantasies are efforts to compensate for her personality disturbance. More data are needed to determine the severity of this disturbance and its probable dynamics.

Further Data about Mary. Because the counselor inferred that Mary was a disturbed person, he asked that she be given a Rorschach Test. Unfortunately, the Rorschach examiner was not a skilled clinician, so that a thorough interpretation of the record could not be obtained. Several findings were clear, however. Mary gave far more than the average number of responses, and the record was similar in many ways to schizophrenic records. These findings offer some confirmation of the emotional detachment and autistic thinking shown by other data. They do not mean that Mary is a schizophrenic.

In the course of her final interview, Mary talked a great deal about her strong sexual drives. She said that her first sexual experience at seventeen was due to a desire to hurt her mother, whom she described as promiscuous. For the first time she openly admitted an intense hatred for her mother. When her mother died a few years ago, Mary developed strong feelings of guilt which persisted. In addition, she said that her religious beliefs conflict with her sexual impulses and produce additional guilt feelings. Six months ago, she claimed, she stopped having any sexual relations. She did not spontaneously admit any homosexuality, and the counselor did not probe this area.

The counselor suggested that Mary should seek psychiatric help. This suggestion surprised Mary. She said that she was able to analyze herself and that she had developed "the ability to bring anything up out of my subconscious." These remarks only confirmed the counselor's impression that Mary was a deeply disturbed person. Further confirmation came when, two days later, Mary returned to ask the counselor to serve as therapist. She told the counselor that she had been so upset by the final interview that she got drunk on the evening after the final session. Since the counselor was not a therapist, Mary's request was refused; but she was told where she could find professional help.

Problem 4. Although successful psychotherapy would probably change Mary's interpersonal relationships enough to modify job recommendations for her, we should be prepared to suggest some occupation that she could follow now. In the light of what you know about Mary's ability and her personality, what suggestions would you make about further schooling and about the kind of job that would meet her needs at present?

MAKING HYPOTHESES ABOUT TEST DATA

In Chapter 3 we pointed out that inconsistencies and deviations from group norms set problems for the clinician. They require him to make hypotheses which show how unexpected findings can be explained. However, these hypotheses have implications beyond the specific discrepancy to be explained, and these implications can be tested to see whether the hypotheses are plausible. Clinicians draw their hypotheses from personality theory and from empirical generalizations that seem useful.

Interpreting psychometric data requires the same kind of activity. We are required to look for discrepancies and then to guess what they mean. The test data themselves do not contain the answers; they must come from the clinician's own background. But he must realize that the behavior behind the test scores is the product of a person and not some disembodied ability or interest. That is, test scores are somehow influenced by the residuals of training, by the physical equipment, by the emotions, and by the motivational pattern of the person. It is not easy to work from the separate scores of a test battery back to a unified description of a person, but if a history is available, it can be approximated.

We have tried to show by example how this kind of interpretation is carried out. Now we shall summarize by listing some questions that the interpreter of psychometric batteries can ask himself.

1. Are ability predictions, education, and occupational status related in the expected way?

2. If tests indicate special abilities or talents, does the history confirm

them by showing either how they were acquired or how they are being used?

3. Are interest test patterns consistent with the broader motivational and adjustive trends in the client?

4. Does the client's perception of his abilities and interests roughly agree with the test data?

5. If personality disturbances are indicated by the test results, are they also found in the history?

If the answer to any of these questions is in the negative, then the clinician must set to work to find out why. First, he must look to superficial reasons for discrepancies: low test validity, failure to follow directions, illness or low motivation during testing, or inaccurate scoring of the test. Once these are ruled out he may proceed to ask whether the results could have been caused by deliberate faking, by lack of specific opportunities in school or home, by the impact of a regional culture pattern, and so on. Finally, he will inspect his data from the standpoint of personality dynamics: masculine protest, oedipal attachments, conflicts with authority figures, repressed hostility, and so on.

A particularly instructive example of the relationship between test data and life adjustment is the case of Philip Bronson, reported as part of the Dartmouth investigations of visual factors in college performance (5). Philip scored at only the 5th percentile on the scholastic-aptitude test given him at the time of his entrance to Dartmouth. On a reading-comprehension test, he scored at only the 6th percentile. These scores were not in error, yet he managed to graduate from the college in four years. He even earned part of his own expenses. Now the question here is this: What kind of personality pattern does it require to unite such surprising discrepancies? The answer, given in fascinating detail in the original report, is that Philip became a compulsive person with no social life. He turned into a kind of intellectual machine devoted solely to getting through his courses. He was chronically fearful of making a mistake and expended great effort in mastering trivial details. He found it difficult to adapt to new situations. While he repressed many of his feelings, he was sometimes frightened by a dim awareness of his impulses. Tendencies to be hostile, to indulge himself, or to depend on others seemed potentially destructive of his ability to complete the task he had set for himself. But Philip was regarded as dependable and conscientious by the faculty. And his orientation toward people was basically humane and democratic (5, pp. 185–201).

In conclusion, we can say that psychometric tests yield useful data about a person; but these data must be integrated with other information if we are to understand their full significance. Since they are objective, psychometric tests decrease the chances of wild speculation. They place limits on the hypotheses that can be reasonably accepted. Since they depend on the client's activity rather than on his report of his life history, these tests eliminate some of the bias caused by the client's desire to make a favorable impression. Since the test scores depend on norms derived from groups far larger than the groups usually seen by a single clinician, they permit more accurate comparisons of the client's performance than would otherwise be possible.

One other point should be mentioned. In our discussion of projective methods, we suggested that they often lead the clinician to an unnecessarily pessimistic view of his client. They do not seem fitted to reveal the client's personal assets. Psychometric tests, on the other hand, can show strengths that could be missed in an assessment by projective methods. High achievement in school subjects, good reading ability, and special talents or interests can be valuable resources; and psychometric tests bring them sharply to the clinician's attention. When they are interpreted with proper consideration for other kinds of data, these tests may offset some of the unfortunate bias imposed by an emphasis on pathological trends. Psychometric test results must be counted as important facts in the study of persons. But they do not tell the whole story.

PSYCHOMETRIC TESTS IN SCREENING

The clinician in military service faces the special problem of detecting men who are psychologically unfit for service. Among the large numbers of recruits who are to be trained, a small proportion will be unfit because of inadequate ability to learn or because of behavior disorders. If each recruit were carefully studied by a clinician, most of these unsuitable deviants could be located. This is impossible, however, because of the time and expense involved. Administering an individual intelligence test such as the Wechsler-Bellevue would require about an hour of the clinician's time for each man. And a rapid assessment of emotional disturbance by interviewing would take at least an additional half hour. If we assume a relatively small number of recruit arrivals, say a hundred a day, it would take at least fifteen clinicians to make even such limited studies, disregarding the time needed to write reports. In a military installation during wartime, recruit arrivals may easily reach five or ten times this figure. Even if the expense were warranted, it is doubtful whether there would be sufficient clinical manpower available to staff all the training centers.

One way of solving this problem is to use rapid screening tests (24). These tests must be short, be easily administered, and be easily scored. If possible, they should be group tests. Every recruit takes the screening test, and those who make deviant scores are selected for intensive individual study. If the test correlates even as low as .20 or .30 with final judgment of suitability for service, it can be useful. The group of men selected for intensive study will probably contain a higher proportion of deviants than is found in the total recruit group. The clinician, then, invests his effort where it counts most. Of course, the screening test will miss some of the deviant men; that is the price that must be paid for the efficient use of clinicians.

Types of Screening Devices. One interesting proposal for screening individuals with defective intelligence has been made by Hildreth (21). He lists a series of items to be used in a rapid screening interview. The items have been chosen so that passing any one of them indicates that the respondent probably has a mental age of at least eleven years. This mental-age value is used because it corresponds to an IQ of about 70 for adults. A recruit who fails several of these items should be given an individual intelligence test. A sample item is this: The recruit is shown a card bearing the following numbers:

$$1 \quad 2 \quad 4 \quad 8 \quad 16 \quad \underline{\hspace{1cm}}$$

and is asked, "What is the next number?" He passes the item if he correctly gives the answer and can explain that each number is double that of the preceding number. Of course, in actual practice the clinician would not need to ask every recruit one of these "single-item tests." Men who have completed at least eight school grades are almost certain to pass the minimum requirements.

A more elaborate screening test for individual administration has been developed by Hunt and his coworkers (23). Two subtests from the Wechsler-Bellevue Scale—comprehension and similarities—are used along with a fifteen-word vocabulary test. This test has proved to be effective in detecting mentally defective individuals. Although it is a very short test, the fact that it must be individually administered means that it is not entirely suitable for administration to the total group to be screened. It could be most effectively used by administering it to all recruits who had completed fewer than six school grades.

Since illiteracy is a severe handicap in military service, the psychologist must be prepared to detect it. Recruits are usually required to be able to read at least as well as the average child in the fourth grade before they are considered literate. By simply using passages from standard reading tests, a psychologist can administer a short literacy test that is adequate for screening. The passages should include both fourth- and fifth-grade material. After a little practice, a psychologist can tell in less than a minute whether a recruit should be selected for further study.

Another kind of problem in military screening is the detection of men with disabling psychopathology. Many kinds of deviants must be detected. They include not only neurotics and psychotics, but also psychopathic deviates (the so-called "constitutional psychopaths"), homosexuals, enuretics, and queer people that do not fit standard diagnostic categories. Since the mere presence of a personality disturbance does not, in itself, disqualify a man for service, each case must be individually evaluated. The purpose of a screening test is to select as many deviants as possible for individual study, and to eliminate as many normal men as possible from further consideration.

There is good evidence that a number of paper-and-pencil tests of "adjustment" are useful in this kind of screening (15). The Cornell Selectee Index is one example of a brief questionnaire that works fairly well in a military setting. The questions are direct and undisguised. They ask for information about previous commitment to a mental hospital, about the history of convulsions, and about psychosomatic ailments. This kind of instrument appears to work better in military settings than in civilian settings. In part this is because the recruit group as a whole is less sophisticated about these tests than are the college students who have usually provided validation data. Then too, there are undoubtedly pressures for truthful answers in the military setting that are missing from civilian situations.

A few studies indicate that psychometric screening devices can be constructed which are less transparent than the usual neurotic inventory and are less time-consuming to administer and score. Asking recruits to check all the foods they dislike from a twenty-item list has proved to be surprisingly effective as a screening method (19, 31). High food-aversion scores are found in a number of different disorders. A twenty-two-item check list of recreational interests, compiled by Berdie (6) can also be used as a disguised test for detecting men with psychiatric disabilities. Both of these instruments can be administered in about three minutes and are suitable for either group or individual oral administration.

Setting a Cutting Score. An important practical problem in using a screening test is the location of a cutting score. This score determines which recruits shall be selected for individual study. Recruits scoring below the cutting score are considered probably suitable for service. Those who make scores equal to or greater than the cutting score will be called in for clinical study. Since most screening tests yield continuous distributions, the location of the best cutting score is partly an arbitrary matter. We shall propose a way of looking at this problem, however, that clarifies the practical issues that must be considered.

In the first place, we must realize that validity coefficients do not help solve this problem. They are required when we are deciding which of several screening tests to use. Several simple methods have been proposed for rating the relative efficiency of a number of screening tests (16, 24), but after the best test has been selected we must still choose a cutting score.

In the second place, the choice of a cutting score depends on the actual operating conditions in a given military establishment. The number of available clinicians must be considered in relation to the number of recruit arrivals and to the efficiency of the screening test. If more clinicians become available, the cutting score may be lowered. If more recruits arrive, but the number of clinicians is constant, the cutting score may be raised. There is no way of finding a cutting score which is best for all conditions.

The method we shall use involves finding out how many working days will be required for studying the men selected by the screening test. Since the number of clinical working days varies as we change the cutting score, we can weigh this information against the number of deviant men that are left undetected. We can explain more clearly by using the data shown in Table 5. These are hypothetical but typical data. They could be obtained by giving the screening test to a large group and then carefully locating every deviant man in the group by clinical study of the entire group. (In practice, data of this kind can be derived from a study of a group of known deviants and of a group of normals, but a correction must be made to keep the proportion of deviants about the same as it is in the total recruit population.)

The basic data in Table 5 are two cumulative frequency distributions: one for deviants and one for normals. The entries are read this way: five deviant men made a score of 7 on the screening test; twenty-five made scores of 6 or higher; and seventy-five made scores of 5 or higher. The entries opposite the lowest score show the total number of men in each group. They indicate that there are 100 deviants (about 9 per cent of the total) in the entire group of 1,100.

Table 5. Cumulative frequency distributions for normals and deviants on a hypothetical screening test

Score	Deviants	Normals	Work load	Working days
7	5	0	5	1
6	25	0	25	3
5	75	50	125	16
4	95	250	345	43
3	100	750	850	106
2	100	950	1,050	
1	100	1,000	1,100	

Inspection of these two cumulative frequency distributions will show that, in general, the deviant men made higher scores than the normal men. The point biserial correlation between test score and classification as deviant or normal is .31 for these data. This value may be slightly conservative but it is not far from the usual validity coefficients under these conditions.

The column headed "work load" shows the total number of men selected for clinical study by using each score as a cutting score. With a cutting score of 5, for example, 125 men would be chosen for individual study. If a cutting score of 4 were used, 345 men would be selected.

The column headed "working days" shows the number of days a single clinician would have to work in order to finish each work load. It is based on the optimistic assumption that a clinician could adequately study about eight men in a working day. The figures in this column may also be interpreted as showing the number of clinicians needed to finish each work load in a single day.

The table shows that it takes only three clinician-days to handle the work load generated by a cutting score of 6. If a cutting score of 5 is chosen, about five times as many working days are required, but the lower cutting score enables us to locate only three times as many deviants as the higher one. This outcome is common in screening work. It is very much more expensive to detect the last few deviants than it is to detect the first few. Consequently, we must ask: How much damage will be done by allowing any given proportion of deviants to go undetected?

The answer to this question cannot usually be precisely determined, but we can see that some kinds of military assignments impose more stringent standards than others. Extremely stable and competent personnel are required to operate aircraft and submarines, for example. A severe neurotic or psychotic episode suffered by one man may seriously impair group morale or endanger the lives of the crew. For assignments like these, screening tests may be useless, since every person engaged in this kind of work should be studied individually anyway. On the other hand, more deviants may be tolerated in limited-duty assignments where combat stress is missing and the damage done by a severely disturbed person is apt to be less serious. In addition to the risk that deviant men may impair the effectiveness of combat units, we must consider the time and money cost for their treatment, hospitalization, and eventual pension, if they break down in military service. These costs are often great enough to justify the clinical study of many suitable men in order to locate a very small number of unsuitable men.

Of course, not all the deviants missed by a screening test will remain forever undetected. In actual practice, the stress of military training alone will disturb some men so much that they will be referred to psychiatric units for study. If noncommissioned officers are taught some elementary facts about behavior disorders and mental defects, they can help greatly in the detection of unfit men. Thus, the training period itself serves a screening function.

REFERENCES

1. Allport, G. W. *Personality*. New York: Holt, 1937.
2. Anastasi, A. The concept of validity in the interpretation of test scores. *Educ. psychol. Measmt*, 1950, **10**, 67–78.
3. Anderson, R. G. Test scores and efficiency ratings of machinists. *J. appl. Psychol.*, 1947, **31**, 377–388.
4. Barnette, W. L., Jr. Occupational aptitude patterns of selected groups of counseled veterans. *Psychol. Monogr.*, 1951, **65** (No. 5), 1–49.
5. Bender, I. E., Imus, H. A., Rothney, J. W. M., Kemple, C., & England, M. R. *Motivation and visual factors*. Hanover, N.H.: Dartmouth College Publications, 1942.
6. Berdie, R. F. Range of interests and psychopathology. *J. clin. Psychol.*, 1946, **2**, 161–166.
7. Bingham, W. V. *Aptitudes and aptitude testing*. New York: Harper, 1937.
8. Bordin, E. S. A theory of vocational interests as dynamic phenomena. *Educ. psychol. Measmt*, 1943, **3**, 49–66.
9. Borg, W. R. The interests of art students. *Educ. psychol. Measmt*, 1950, **10**, 100–106.
10. Buros, O. K. *The third mental measurements yearbook*. New Brunswick, N.J.: Rutgers Univer. Press, 1949.
11. Buros, O. K. *The fourth mental measurements yearbook*. Highland Park, N.J.: Gryphon Press, 1953.
12. Cattell, R. B. The measurement of adult intelligence. *Psychol. Bull.*, 1943, **40**, 153–193.
13. Coombs, C. H. Theory and methods of social measurement. In L. Festinger & D. Katz (Eds.), *Research methods in the behavioral sciences*. New York: Dryden, 1953.
14. Cronbach, L. J. *Essentials of psychological testing*. New York: Harper, 1949.
15. Ellis, A. & Conrad, H. S. The validity of personality inventories in military practice. *Psychol. Bull.*, 1948, **45**, 385–426.
16. Eysenck, H. J. A comparative study of four screening tests for neurotics. *Psychol. Bull.*, 1945, **42**, 659–662.
17. Gallagher, J. J. MMPI changes concomitant with client-centered therapy. *J. consult. Psychol.*, 1953, **17**, 334–338.
18. Goodenough, F. L. *Mental testing*. New York: Rinehart, 1949.
19. Gough, H. G. An additional study of food aversions. *J. abnorm. soc. Psychol.*, 1946, **41**, 86–88.
20. Hathaway, S. R. & Meehl, P. E. *An atlas for the clinical use of the MMPI*. Minneapolis: Univer. Minn. Press, 1951.
21. Hildreth, H. M. Single item tests for psychometric screening. *J. appl. Psychol.*, 1945, **29**, 262–267.
22. Hovey, H. B. MMPI profiles and personality characteristics. *J. consult. Psychol.*, 1953, **17**, 142–146.

23. Hunt, W. A. & French, E. G. The CVS abbreviated individual intelligence scale. *J. consult. Psychol.*, 1952, **16**, 181–186.
24. Hunt, W. A., Wittson, C. L., & Harris, H. I. The screen test in military selection. *Psychol. Rev.*, 1944, **51**, 37–46.
25. Levine, P. R., & Wallen, R. Adolescent vocational interests and later occupation. *J. appl. Psychol.*, 1954, **38**, 428–431.
26. Peak, H. Problems of objective observation. In L. Festinger & D. Katz (Eds.), *Research methods in the behavioral sciences*. New York: Dryden, 1953.
27. Schofield, W. Changes in responses to the Minnesota Multiphasic Inventory following certain therapies. *Psychol. Monogr.*, 1950, **64** (No. 5), 1–33.
28. Schofield, W. A further study of the effects of therapies on MMPI responses. *J. abnorm. soc. Psychol.*, 1953, **48**, 67–77.
29. Super, D. E. The Kuder Preference Record in vocational diagnosis. *J. consult Psychol.*, 1947, **11**, 184–193.
30. Thomas, L. G. Mental tests as instruments of science. *Psychol. Monogr.*, 1942, **54** (No. 3), 1–87.
31. Wallen, R. Food aversions in behavior disorders. *J. consult. Psychol.*, 1948, **12**, 310–312.
32. Technical recommendations for psychological tests and diagnostic techniques. *Psychol. Bull.*, 1954, **51** (No. 2, Part 2), 1–38.

CHAPTER 12

Individual Psychotherapy: Initial Steps and Aim

In all the work of a clinical psychologist, nothing is as absorbing and as exciting as psychotherapy. Here, the study of the person becomes more continuous, more detailed, and more intimate than in any other context. But the clinician's fascination for psychotherapy is not due simply to the opportunity it offers for understanding his client. He is drawn to it because it is a creative activity that gives him a lively sense of being needed and helpful. In therapeutic work, his knowledge, skill, and sensitivity are utterly challenged and he feels that they really make a difference in human living.

At the same time, psychotherapy is full of unanswered questions, ambiguity, and discouragement. Despite ingenious theories and practices, we have no clear evidence that any one method of therapy is superior to all the others. We do not even have adequate criteria for evaluating the results of psychotherapy. One survey of the outcomes of psychotherapy questions whether any kind of therapy does much good: "The figures," Eysenck says, "fail to support the hypothesis that psychotherapy facilitates recovery from neurotic disorder" (8, p. 323). No wonder that one psychologist is reported to have said: "Psychotherapy is an undefined technique applied to unspecified problems with unpredictable outcome. For this technique we recommend rigorous training" (12, p. 93).

These somber remarks remind us to be modest about therapeutic work, but they ought not discourage that work. Eysenck's statistical evaluation of psychotherapy is not the definitive statement about the present state of affairs, as Rosenzweig (16) has shown. Superficial comparisons of the incidence of recoveries under different methods of treatment overlook too many crucial variables. For one thing, different agencies attract different types of patients. We know, too, that therapists do not agree in deciding how much a patient has improved. And we know that many changes in the lives of treated patients cannot be detected by present methods of measurement. We must also admit that we are not sure which variables in the complex of activities we call "therapeutic technique" are really responsible for improvement when it does take place (18). It is possible, although unlikely, that the prolonged and friendly interest of the therapist is more significant than anything else in therapy. Or it could be that reduction of anxiety is of critical importance. Research will eventually help us decide what is happening in psychotherapy. Already tape and film recordings have enriched our understanding of therapist-patient interaction. The "client-centered" therapists have employed these records for vigorously investigating their own methods (15). The fact is, however, that we know precious little about a "science" of helping people change. Psychological therapy is still an art.

In the meantime, people are asking for help. The clinician, as practitioner, can hardly refuse them on the grounds that all the data are not yet in. After all, he has some resources. A half century or so of therapeutic experience gives him some guidance, and the psychology of learning and motivation tells him something about how people change. Clinicians, aware of the complexities of personality, are more likely to be successful in the art of therapy than are self-styled counselors who rely on half-baked formulas from physiology or religion. The psychological clinician, then, has a responsibility in the area of treatment, even though he is dissatisfied with the amount of factual information he has.

This chapter and the next deal with intensive individual psychotherapy as it is used with neurotic persons. Therapy with children and with psychotics poses special problems which are better taken up after studying therapy with neurotics. Group psychotherapy, too, will be better understood after an acquaintance with individual therapy. These topics are properly placed in advanced courses and will not be discussed in this book.

SOME COMMON PROBLEMS AMONG PATIENTS

People who seek psychological help complain about many different troubles. Some emphasize bodily aches, some tell of excessive fear, anger, or sadness, and some are disturbed about conflicts with wives, children, or relatives. Often, elementary biological functions are impaired: sleeping, eating, and sexual activity are commonly affected. On the other hand, some people report only a sense of vague dissatisfaction with their work, with their level of achievement, or with their human relationships.

The wide variety of specific complaints conceals certain common problems shared by poorly adjusted or neurotic people. When we hear them talk at length about their lives, we discover important similarities among them. Although these similar features are not present in every case, they occur so often that a psychological therapist is continually alert to their possible existence. Here are some of them:

Failure in Human Relationships. Patients report that they have not been able to get sufficient satisfaction out of their relationships with others. This lack is most noticeable, of course, in those relationships that are intimate and continuous: with parents, spouse, children, and close friends. Often the dissatisfaction is described in terms of lack of affection, lack of warmth, of closeness, or ability to enjoy the other person. Sometimes patients will say that compliments, praise, and affection that are given to them have not seemed genuine; at least, that they do not feel loved and wanted. People give different reasons for this lack of affectional satisfaction. Some think that it is because of their own shortcomings; some believe that other persons are at fault. But even in the latter case, it is worth noting that the dissatisfied patient has done little to find other, more satisfying relationships. Thus, a wife who complains of a lack of closeness with her husband may not have established close relationships with friends or relatives that are available.

The inability to get affection from others is often accompanied by a sense of inability to give affection. Patients tell us that they are not responsive or demonstrative, and they regret this deficiency. Sometimes it is not a question of giving affection, but rather an inability to live up to other people's presumed expectations of strength, consistency, or virtue. Then the patient has the feeling that he is disappointing to others and so is failing in his human relationships.

Self-devaluation. Another common characteristic of patients seeking therapy is a feeling of being "bad" or "worthless." They do not like themselves. Achievements and actions that could be considered praiseworthy are overlooked or ascribed to luck, to the incompetence of others, or to special talents which seem unimportant to the patient. At the same time, failures (or what seem to be failures) are stressed and magnified. The therapist gets the impression that the patient somehow needs to take a dim view of himself and selects evidence to support his stand.

In some instances, self-devaluation is not immediately evident, because it is covered by excessive self-praise. Boasting occasionally occurs, but more often the therapist will hear favorable self-judgments delivered in a tone of defiance or of pleading. Therapists soon hear, however, this compensatory self-praise replaced by self-condemnation.

Puzzlement. In one way or another, patients express disturbance over their inability to explain their actions and feelings to themselves. They do not know why they do some of the things they do. They are unable to account for feelings of sadness, of fear, or of irritation. They can't understand why they have the thoughts they have. All these things are related to a sense of helplessness; patients feel that their behavior is forced, not chosen, and that they are at the mercy of uncontrollable impulses. Sometimes these impulses are ascribed to other people, but even then the patient is puzzled, for he cannot understand why others should behave the way they do.

Inability to Reject Alternatives. Many patients report a number of episodes showing that they have difficulty in fully committing themselves to a course of action. Sometimes this is described as difficulty in concentrating on a task that presumably interests them; they are bothered by intrusive thoughts about other things. They may speak of indecision, or of decisions made but continually doubted and reexamined. They may put off decisions about even such small matters as buying clothing or accepting an invitation.

The inability to reject alternatives appears in other activities besides intellectual decision making. Sometimes it is shown by an inability to enjoy the concrete situation faced by the individual at a given moment because of intrusive desires to be doing something else. Conversely, the person may be unable to reject a situation as unsatisfactory; he cannot leave it or try to change it, nor can he withdraw into his own thoughts. For some people the difficulty is mainly in the field of interpersonal relations. They cannot say no to requests from others even when saying yes interferes with important plans of their own. Again, patients complain of ambivalent attitudes, such as liking someone on one day and disliking him the next.

Unhappiness. The common troubles of maladjusted people so far mentioned contribute, naturally enough, to misery and unhappiness. Patients are often so emotionally wrought-up that they feel they "can't stand it any more," or are "on the edge of insanity." Usually, the unhappiness seems connected with some specific problem such as marriage or career, and the patient is not likely to see that it is related to many other areas of his life. Often the unhappiness is ascribed to symptoms such as obsessional thoughts, neurotic fatigue, sexual impotence, or a phobia. While such symptoms do make life more difficult and miserable, these are certainly not the basic cause of the unhappiness.

HOW PATIENTS REPORT PROBLEMS

Patients do not report these difficulties all at once. The psychologist will hear them inserted into a number of interviews and related to a variety of circumstances. In order to show how patients talk about these matters, we shall present excerpts from transcripts of recorded interviews. The first of these is taken from the initial interview with a thirty-year-old single man. Early in the interview, he had said that his main trouble was in concentrating. After fifteen or twenty minutes, the conversation took the following turn:

P (patient): And when I get to the—to a certain page, I try to think back, what has occurred? I have a very poor memory. It's intolerable.

T (therapist): At the time that you're reading this you have the feeling that you're concentrating a great deal on it, but later on when you come to, uh, to try and recall it, you can't.

P: Um-hm. [*Pause.*]

T: So you feel that it's your memory that's slipping.

P: I have a feeling that it, my, my memory is—along with other things—is affected too.

T: What do you mean by other things?

P: Well, I mean not only I can't remember things, but I am confused about them. I, uh, uh, actually I don't know what attitude to adopt toward life. That, that, that's the point. I, I have no use for, as I told you, I don't have much use for people. I, I withdraw from my family. I, uh, have, uh, can't stand gossip. And most of the conversations that I hear in the society in which I find myself, I don't enter into them. I'm the type of individual that most people call, tag as, a character, queer. I find it very difficult to, to make compromises with what you *have* to do and what I *want* to do. That I think is, uh, uh, my basic problem.

This passage tells of failure with people and of puzzlement and confusion. In the third interview, two weeks later, we find a self-devaluating statement:

P: It's true I'm not sure of myself, or my abilities. And I have a, well, I believe that I must reach a, reach a, my attainments academically because I feel that is the only way that I, will be successful or have an opportunity for success.

A few minutes later he reverts to the theme of his relationships with people:

P: I like to do things for people, and do things for people and their betterment, but not when I have to be in continuous contact with them all the time.

T: You like to think about people, but you don't like people.

P: Um-hm. I like humanity, but I don't like humans.

T: That's it.

P: Um-hm. I wrote that in a theme, and I'll have to rewrite the theme and say what I mean by that statement. I like humanity, I, I, I've a love for humanity but I dislike human beings, and I, I, I don't like to be with people.

Three weeks after this interview, his feelings about personal contact with people again come out. This time, during the sixth interview, he reports some misery that he has not discussed before:

T: What is this feeling you have about just people? I mean dealing with them as, as individuals, not in abstract ideas of humanity but as actual individuals. There's something that you don't like and you described it as torture. What, what kind of a thing is that, anyway?

P: I don't know.

T: What sort of feelings do you have?

P: I get kinda sick inside, I guess that's the thing. I get tense, build up a tension, I suppose, inside of me, and the only release I have is to take myself away from them. A large group of people. I get restless and nervous.

Our next excerpts are taken from interviews with a twenty-two-year-old married man. His initial complaint was that he became aggressive and insulting when he drank. He had been in trouble several times because of fighting while drunk, and he hoped that psychological treatment could prevent further difficulties. During the second interview, he shows how self-devaluation affects his relationship with others while he is drinking:

P: A lot of times I've been with people that I know very well and that I have reason to believe are fond of me and that's a, when I get so far, why, I just feel cut off from all that. I just have a feeling that: you're silly, you're making a fool of yourself coming to those conclusions, and this is obvious, this proves how everybody feels or something. And then I walk out.

T: It proves that they really, that underneath they really don't like you.

P: That's what I feel at the time.

T: Yeh. [*Thirty-second pause.*]

P: Sometimes I go out with people and after I've had a few drinks I accuse them of different things. All sorts of things that I know are untrue.

In this same interview, he shows how important affection is to him. He tells of his fear that his wife may leave him if he continues drinking and says:

P: She's, she's the one thing that continually holds me to any career that I might eventually try and to my education and to most of the decent things in life, to the better side of the tracks, something like that, whatever you want to call it. Otherwise it's highly probable that I'd drift back to sea for a couple of years and wander around the country and end up not much of anything.

T: Then what you really feel is that she's just about the only thing that stands between you and a kind of complete dissolution.

P: That's right. I guess if she left me, why, I would complete my self-destruction in a hurry.

These last comments not only show the young man's need for his wife, but they also reveal a complete lack of faith in his own resources. He feels helpless to pursue education or career without her guidance. More than that, he feels aimless; without her, he thinks, he would only destroy himself.

In the fifth interview, the problem of affection is again discussed, and, for the first time, it is connected with his aggression:

P: I hate a lot of people, and I love very few. I'm afraid of being hurt. It's always a lot easier to hate people than it is to love them.

T: Depends on who you are. Some people, it's easier for them to hate.
P: It's safer. If you hate somebody and they hurt you, it's what you expect.

With this description of the means for keeping safe, it is hardly surprising that his wife, important as she is to him, should be a target for hatred, too. In the sixth interview, this possibility is injected into the conversation with a jolt:

P: I've been fishing, got a suntan. Nose got sunburned, rather.
T: Where have you been fishing?
P: Oh, the lake. Oh, it's awful. We're with the rest of the mob, you know, casting out there. People three feet on the right of you and two feet on the left, or something like that. It's awful. Where I come from, if you came down there and saw somebody half a mile away you'd move down. Somebody's crowding you. You don't do things like that, it's impolite and it's rude. Jesus! You know it's, why do I hate my wife?

A few minutes later, in the same interview, he recognizes the ambivalence in his feelings about his wife:

P: Well, I am mixed up about it. Now I don't know whether I hate her personally or whether I hate her for what she stands for. But I've always missed her very much when I was away from her the slightest bit. I've been very much in love with her.

Motivational Force of These Problems. The statements you have just read suggest some of the reasons why people seek psychotherapy. The unhappiness and dissatisfaction reported by these two patients reveal powerful motives for starting psychological treatment. But they are also important in keeping the patients in treatment once they have started. As they explore their lives and their feelings, they see more clearly how pervasive their unhappiness is and how much there is to understand.

Psychotherapy is a kind of relearning process, and, as in all learning, the learner must be motivated to keep at the task. Psychotherapy takes time and painful effort if it is to be successful; therefore it requires a high degree of motivation to see it through. The initial reason for undertaking therapy may be strong enough to keep patients coming back for a time; but when they find out how many problems they have, valuable supplementary motivation is added.

Some people begin psychotherapy because of pressure from others. A man, faced with the threat of a divorce, may come to the therapist in order to satisfy his wife and discourage her from legal action. Or a young woman may request treatment because of parental urging. Such pressure does not supply sufficient motivation for protracted psychotherapy; in fact, it may sometimes lead to resistive and uncooperative attitudes toward the therapist. In these cases, it is important for the therapist to indicate that he is interested in those matters that are seen as problems by the patient himself. Only by helping the patient experience his own dissatisfactions will sufficient motivation for therapy be generated. The therapist tries to elicit remarks about the patient's own feeling of unhappiness and thus establish a better basis for therapy.

DIAGNOSIS AND THERAPY

The mere fact that a patient *wants* psychological treatment is no reason for believing that it is what he *needs*. In Chapter 7 we pointed out that patients cannot be trusted to diagnose themselves. That warning is worth emphasizing again. The psychotherapist has a background of knowledge and experience that the patient lacks, and an important part of the therapist's work is to decide whether psychological treatment will be helpful and whether it alone will be sufficient. If other forms of therapy seem desirable, the therapist has an ethical responsibility to suggest consultation with another specialist.

The kinds of diagnostic decisions that must be made when the patient arrives for treatment can be put in the form of three questions:

1. Is this patient likely to need institutional treatment?

2. Is this patient in need of treatment other than individual psychotherapy?

3. What level of psychotherapy is likely to be most useful?

We shall consider each of these questions briefly.

Institutionalization. The problem here is to determine the severity and probable course of the disorder. If the patient is psychotic, it is likely that hospitalization will permit more effective treatment. For one thing, it removes him from the stresses imposed by a hostile or competitive social environment. In a mental hospital, less is expected of the psychotic patient than in his normal setting, and there are fewer people who are frightened or resentful of his actions. Living in a hospital regime also safeguards the patient from committing acts that are criminal or seriously detrimental to the welfare of those around him. In one sense, the psychotic person does not really *want* to commit offenses that will later make him remorseful; but he needs help in avoiding such actions. Protection against suicide is another value of hospitalization.

In a hospital a patient has an opportunity to receive intensive study and treatment of a kind that is not available elsewhere. The medical studies made at the time of admission can be followed up by observation, by psychological tests, and by trials of various drugs to test their therapeutic value. The ingestion of toxic substances such as bromides, alcohol, and the barbiturates can also be regulated or prevented. And, of course, the more radical therapies, such as brain surgery and insulin comas (17, pp. 125–133), must be given under the conditions provided by a hospital.

It is better, of course, if the patient willingly agrees to enter the hospital. Sometimes this can be accomplished by pointing out his poor physical condition and the need for improving it before other help can be given. Some patients react favorably to the idea that a period in the hospital will give them a chance to get away from many irritating demands and actions of their families. But there are a number of patients who are so resistant to the idea of entering a mental hospital that they must finally be forced to go. Since commitment to a public mental hospital deprives patients of many citizenship rights, it is understandably surrounded with legal restrictions. Court action and the testimony of a physician are usually required. This means that psychologists must work cooperatively with medical personnel in these cases. Restriction to a private hospital, though less complicated, also must be carried out by physicians.

Alternatives to Individual Psychotherapy. Once the therapist has decided that the patient is not likely to require hospitalization, he must determine whether or not other therapies are likely to be preferable to psychotherapy. Sometimes, of course, it is a matter of deciding whether other therapies should be utilized along with psychotherapy.

The first decision is whether or not the patient needs medical treatment. Some aspects of this problem were discussed in Chapter 7. Here we should point out that the therapist often asks patients about their last physical examination and requests them to visit their own physicians for another checkup. Even then, however, the therapist must be alert to such disorders as petit mal, epilepsy, migraine, or endocrine dysfunction.

In some instances, where an emotional problem is clearly present, medical treatment may be preferable to psychotherapy, at least for a time. Thus, depressed patients often benefit from electrocoma treatments and become more accessible to psychotherapy. Or acute panic states may need heavy sedation and rest immediately.

Even though medical treatment is not required, that does not mean that the patient should receive intensive psychotherapy. In a few instances, the psychologist may conclude that the patient chiefly needs information, and he will suggest some reading (bibliotherapy). Books on marriage, child-rearing, or mental hygiene may be recommended. Such reading will not greatly change the patient, but it may serve to reassure him and even bring about some desirable attitude changes. Again, legal or financial questions may be pressing and may need to be dealt with prior to psychotherapy. The clinician may ask the patient to consult specialists in these matters. Some patients profit from information about social or recreational activities in the community.

These superficial methods of dealing with problems can be helpful. Sometimes there are reasons for delaying individual psychotherapy, even though we may sense the deeper sources of a patient's problem. A patient's job may make it difficult for him to visit a therapist regularly; or he may live far from centers where professional help is available. His current problems may seem to be temporary and not likely to warrant the time and expense of intensive psychological treatment. Occasionally, a patient is not motivated to undertake intensive treatment until he has tried to settle his problems by some of these superficial methods.

Of course, a therapist who suggests measures of this kind will not propose them as roads to final solutions. Rather he will say that they are worth trying; if they fail, more intensive treatment should be started. The point is that the therapist should not neglect simple, common-sense approaches to some patients merely because he feels that most patients need deep psychotherapy.

LEVELS OF PSYCHOTHERAPY

Psychologists can do a number of things to help people, and these measures may be crudely classified according to the amount of effort devoted to changing basic personality characteristics. Some kinds of help, although not aimed at bringing about personality change, are often quite useful. Remedial training in reading or vocational counseling are examples. On the other hand, some people cannot benefit from such help until their emotional problems have been solved. Let us look at the kinds of psychological treatment that focus directly on emotional difficulties.

Counseling. The shortest and least intensive treatment may be called "simple counseling." Usually it is limited to six or eight interview sessions and centers on the particular stress situation that brought the client to the psychologist. The counselor encourages the client to talk fully about his problem and to express his feelings about it—a process sometimes called "ventilation." The counselor does not encourage the client to explore the relationship between the two of them, and he is not concerned about promoting insight into the client's repressed motives and feelings. He hopes that the client can reach a decision or accept his situation more comfortably in the friendly, undemanding atmosphere of the counseling interview. Most counselors give little advice, since the client has usually heard it before and has been unable to act upon it.

Simple counseling can be helpful when people, previously happy and productive, face a temporary difficulty. They may meet with loss of a job, with failure in professional school, with the death of a child or spouse, or with an unexpected marital conflict. If the client has been able to cope well with his previous problems and if he is free from obvious neurotic symptoms, simple counseling may help him through a trying time.

This brief description of simple counseling does not show its intricacy.

It is not easy to help a failing student reach a decision to give up school, nor is it easy to lessen the discouragement of a man who has been fired from a job. Moreover, the counselor needs considerable diagnostic skill if he is to pick out those people who can profit from only a few interviews. Sometimes his aim will be to help a client realize that he needs intensive psychotherapy. This is a valuable service but is not easy to accomplish.

Supportive Therapy. A somewhat more intensive treatment is "supportive therapy." Here the therapist assumes the role of continuing guide and counselor. He encourages free expression of feelings and does not expect that the therapy sessions will be devoted to one or two main problems. He may comment on the possible reasons why the patient acts as he does, and ask questions to make the patient reexamine the effect of his actions. The therapist attempts to be a kindly representative of social reality, reminding the patient of his unrealistic attitudes without scolding him, and revealing his resources without requiring perfection. He provides a periodic retreat for the patient to examine his own life and reorient himself.

In supportive therapy, the therapist accepts limited goals. He does not try to explore deeply repressed parts of the personality. He hopes to keep the patient's life situation from becoming worse, and to stabilize his earning capacity and his social relationships. He knows that certain kinds of crises will probably recur, and he makes no claim to be helping the patient achieve his maximum effectiveness and satisfaction. He does believe that by occasional interviews over a long period his patient will be able to function better than he would without support.

Supportive therapy will be chosen when the therapist believes that exploration of the patient's repressions will provoke anxiety that the patient cannot tolerate, or when more intensive therapy would disrupt his life too much. Sometimes he makes this judgment because of the attitudes and power of the people who have the most intimate contact with the patient, and who may be so rigid and unyielding that they would withdraw their emotional support of the patient if he changed in a significant way. Sometimes the patient is physically handicapped to such an extent that he is genuinely dependent upon others; then supportive therapy may help him adjust to circumstances he cannot alter. Occasionally, the therapist may choose supportive therapy because he feels that the patient could not withstand the shock of self-understanding. Consider, for example, a shy and socially withdrawn young man. As the therapist listens to him ventilate his feelings, he discovers some fantastic, almost bizarre, thought processes that resemble those of psychotics. He also infers that the patient is repressing homosexual impulses. In the face of these findings, he may fear that intensive psychotherapy would bring about an open psychosis. Consequently, he devotes his efforts to helping the patient improve his social skills, to building his confidence by sympathetic understanding, and to explaining the attitudes of the patient's associates and community.

One of the risks in supportive therapy is that the patient may develop an excessive dependence on the therapist. It is undesirable to encourage patients to come to the therapist with every new problem they face or to judge themselves largely by what the therapist thinks of them. Yet supportive therapy may have these effects unless the therapist helps the patient see the value of independent action and gradually withdraws his support. It may very well be, however, that some people need a kindly supervision for years and that a forced independence would have unfortunate consequences. If a therapist chooses a supportive role, he must recognize the risk of overdependence and be prepared to accept the responsibility it imposes.

Insight Therapy. Under this heading we class all those forms of intensive individual therapy that aim at significant and lasting changes in personality. Instead of being concerned about the immediate and specific problems in the patient's life, the therapist is concerned about those forces that make it difficult or impossible for the patient to deal with problems by himself. The therapist deals with attitudes, with motives, and with feelings that pervade many situations, and helps the patient to recognize and change them. An important part of this intensive treatment consists of analyzing the relationship that the patient establishes with the therapist, using insights gained from this experience to clarify other important relationships in the patient's life. Because the next chapter will describe this kind of intensive therapy in more detail, we shall not discuss it further now. Instead we shall list some of the signs indicating that such treatment may be useful.

In general, the various types of neurosis are improved by psychotherapy. It is useful also in psychosomatic disorders such as asthma, gastric ulcers, and some forms of high blood pressure, in which emotional distress aggravates the physical disorder. In addition, a number of people have few specific neurotic symptoms but feel handicapped by being excessively submissive, too dominant and overbearing, or by being cold and distant toward people; intensive psychotherapy may help them. Sometimes patients want help because of an emotional crisis brought on by a sudden gain or loss of occupational status, by marital conflict, or by the death of a member of the family. After a few interviews, the therapist may see that the emotional crisis is only one resultant of a personality pattern that is responsible for many other puzzling difficulties; as the patient comes to realize this fact, too, he may desire further psychotherapy.

There are a few signs that roughly indicate whether or not a patient will be a good therapeutic risk. One study suggests that intelligence is correlated with patients' continuation in therapy (1). Quite probably, direct-interview therapy will not turn out well for people who are below average in intelligence. In such cases, supportive guidance and changes in environmental pressures are more likely to help.

Another study that suggests some indicators of a favorable outcome in psychotherapy has been reported by Barron (2). He used items from the Minnesota Multiphasic Personality Inventory to build a scale for predicting improvement in psychotherapy. The scale was cross-validated and showed correlations of about .45 with rated improvement in psychotherapy. Inspection of the items in his scale suggests that patients who improve are likely to have the following characteristics prior to beginning treatment:

1. They report that they are generally in good health.

2. They seem relatively free from seclusiveness and obsessional brooding.

3. They appear to reject fundamentalist religious beliefs (e.g., in miracles) although they go to church.

4. They are able to admit their impulses to go counter to some of the trivial dictates of conventional morality.

5. They have not had "strange" or hallucinatory experiences.

6. They feel able to cope with the ordinary problems of living. Apparently, Barron's scale is measuring something like "ego-strength" or "capacity for personality integration."

Some other factors contributing to a favorable prognosis for psychotherapy have been suggested by Rogers on the basis of clinical experience (14). It seems that patients who are quite dependent upon their families and are subject to a high degree of control by them are not likely to benefit as much from therapy as those who are more independent. This independence is probably related to another factor: the patient's ability to initiate environmental changes. If therapy helps the patient arrive at some important decisions about his life, it is reasonable to suppose that his improvement is partially dependent upon his ability to act upon these decisions. If, for example, the patient's circumstances hinder him from changing residence or occupation, therapy cannot produce maximum benefits for him. This factor, along with physiological decline and insecurity about giving up old ways, will contribute to an unfavorable prognosis in some people over fifty-five or sixty years old.

We do not mean to imply that therapists should refuse help to people who do not fit the pattern of favorable prognostic indicators. There are too many other variables that may influence outcomes so that we cannot be sure that a given patient will or will not improve. We do not really know much, for example, about the possible influence of the therapist's personality and method. Perhaps patients who do not improve with one therapist would do better with another. Then too, we know little about the effects of various kinds of environmental support on therapeutic success. It may be that finances or family attitudes toward therapy play a critical role in the improvement of some patients. We may guess that an optimal environmental situation would be one which frustrates the patient sufficiently to motivate him to do the work of therapy without placing almost insurmountable obstacles in his path. In many instances, intensive psychotherapy is worth a try, but we must remember that other measures may be needed too.[1]

THE EFFECT OF DIAGNOSTIC PROCEDURES ON THERAPY

Traditionally, the diagnosis of a patient's difficulties takes place before any program of treatment begins. Commonly this diagnostic work includes a detailed case history, a physical examination, and psychological testing. In clinics where the patients usually have problems that are clearly psychological, the physical examination may be omitted (as in marital-counseling agencies). In hospitals, on the other hand, a physical examination is a routine necessity. It will be supplemented by direct observation of the patient's behavior for a short period. In private practice, however, the therapist may use only the scantiest of formal diagnostic procedures.

Although the custom of carrying out diagnostic procedures before beginning treatment is widely approved, it may not always be necessary or even desirable. Let us first consider the necessity for diagnostic procedures.

Diagnosis and Choice of Treatment. Any diagnostic method ought to be judged in terms of its consequences. Will the findings significantly alter the method of treatment? In the case of deciding whether physical or psychological treatment is preferable, the answer to this question is clearly yes. But after the physical factors have been evaluated, are elaborate diagnostic methods needed in order to determine whether psychotherapy should be started? The answer to this question is often no. In most instances, psychological tests and a detailed case history cannot really tell us whether the patient is a good therapeutic risk. The indicators of a favorable prognosis that we have discussed are only rough guides, but they can usually be discovered without tests or systematic questioning. Actually, an unstructured, permissive interview will reveal a great deal about the patient's ability and motivation to use psychotherapy, and

[1] A recent study gives evidence that different socioeconomic classes have different attitudes toward psychotherapy (13). Patients coming from the unskilled and semi-skilled occupations and having poor educational backgrounds do not understand what the psychotherapist is trying to do. They are prone to regard the therapist as an authority who should tell them what to do. Perhaps supportive therapy is more effective for these patients than the uncovering, insight therapy.

it has the additional advantage of starting to build the therapeutic relationship.

One of the few studies of the consequences of detailed diagnosis has been reported by Dailey (4). He was interested in the effect of clinical diagnostic reports on the clinician's choice of treatment. In the hospital where the study was conducted, Dailey found that there were thirty-two decisions possible as to treatments for patients. He gave clinicians a list of these decisions and asked them to indicate the treatments they would recommend for the average or typical patient admitted to the hospital. The next step was to let the clinicians read diagnostic case reports on nine actual patients. The clinicians were then asked to indicate their choice of treatment for each of these patients. Dailey found that, for the average patient, certain treatments were very commonly recommended; occupational therapy and group therapy are examples. The effect of reading actual case reports was to change only about a fourth of the recommendations that would have been made if these nine patients had been treated as "average." This finding suggests that, even in a hospital setting, case data have little influence on choice of treatment. Of course, we do not know how important the few altered decisions were. Even though there were not many, they could be crucial for the patient's well-being.

Closely related to choice of treatment is the matter of forecasting risks that may arise in the course of treatment. As an illustration, we may take the possibility of suicide. Therapists would like to estimate the probability that a given patient will make a suicidal attempt. If such an attempt is predicted, relatives should be warned of the possibility, and perhaps the patient should be admitted to a hospital. The trouble is that detailed studies do not help us much in making this kind of prediction. We know that the danger of suicide is greater if the patient is depressed, if there have been previous suicidal episodes, or if a long period of discouragement has led to frequent suicidal thoughts. But elaborate case studies are not required to discover this kind of information; it can be elicited in therapeutic interviews. Perhaps projective tests can assist in making these predictions, but evidence of their value in this respect is still weak.

Diagnosis and the Conduct of Psychotherapy. Some therapists want extensive preliminary psychological studies because they feel that the psychological data will help determine the strategy of psychotherapy. That is, even though they have decided to offer psychological treatment, they believe that the tests will influence the technique they use. Whether this is true or not is open to question.

In the first place, it does not seem that knowing the diagnostic label of the patient aids psychotherapy. Patterson (11) has pointed out that our traditional diagnostic categories are not really based on differences in the underlying causes of different neuroses and that there are no specific therapies for specific kinds of neurotic disorders. We may expect to find certain distinctive difficulties in the treatment of, say, obsessives, but that fact probably does not change our therapeutic approach.

In the second place, even if knowledge of the psychodynamics of the patient alters what we do in therapy, we may doubt whether preliminary testing affords the most accurate and useful knowledge. The events taking place in the therapy sessions are better guides for the therapist's activity than an abstract account of the patient's personality given by tests and case history. Some therapeutic methods do not even conceive of the therapist as "planning the strategy and tactics" of therapy. For example, client-centered therapists see their task as one of communicating understanding and acceptance to the patient. They would use the same approach no matter what psychological study revealed about the patient.

Possible Effects of Preliminary Psychological Diagnostic Procedures. When patients come to a clinic, they are not likely to see the point of the various preliminary steps. They want help, and hope that they will get it quickly. The intake interview, the psychological tests, and the initial therapeutic session are not sharply different for them, and they may be baffled when they find themselves referred to several different specialists within a few days or weeks. As they meet each new clinician, they must be asking: "Is this the one who will help me?" Even when the various diagnostic steps are carried out by the same person, the patient tries to utilize whatever he can from them, hoping that the clinician has at last found something that will help.

These preliminary steps may create or foster a misconception about psychotherapy. The misconception is that "the doctor will find out about you and then tell you what to do." Because many therapists believe that the patient's willingness to assume responsibility for his own psychological growth is a crucial matter, they do not like to strengthen the belief that they are taking responsibility for the patient's decisions. Rogers remarks about the reaction of the patient to an initial history-taking: ". . . he expects to receive the solutions to his problems. Any effort to get him to take the responsibility for his own situation, to try to find the type of adjustment which is realistic and within his own powers, must necessarily be interpreted by him as a deliberate refusal on the part of the counselor to tell him the answers" (14, pp. 81 f). When the patient feels this way, the counselor may seem to be a threatening figure, capable of manipulating the patient by using secret information. Thus, therapy becomes more difficult.

Some patients, of course, may be reassured by the competence and interest demonstrated by painstaking diagnostic studies. The tests may be proof that the therapist will leave nothing undone to help them. The chances are, however, that this kind of reassurance can be given equally well by considerate listening.

One of the chief values of detailed psychological diagnosis may lie in its effect upon the therapist's anxiety. If he believes he understands a case before starting treatment, he may feel more comfortable than if he faces the patient in utter ignorance of him. Then, his own confidence may aid effective therapy, even though he never paid any attention to the diagnostic formulation. For the beginning therapist, case data may be helpful in this way. With experience, however, therapists will find that they can usually learn most of what they need to know during the course of therapeutic interviews.

Diagnosis during Therapy. If we want to keep diagnostic activity from interfering with the therapeutic relationship, we need to look at the whole problem in a new way. In the first place, we should realize that diagnosis is going on throughout therapy. The therapist is always acquiring information about the meaning and severity of the patient's symptoms, and he is in a good position to notice tendencies and changes in the patient's behavior. The fact that he is engaged in therapy does not diminish his sensitivity to underlying motives. Actually, he is likely to be more aware of them.

Secondly, if special tests are needed they can be administered any time during the therapeutic process. After the patient has established a relationship with the therapist, he is less likely to regard testing as relieving him of the responsibility for his own decisions. Furthermore, the therapist can choose diagnostic procedures that will answer questions relevant to the therapy. Instead of using a standard, routine battery for all patients, he selects tests that will clarify specific problems. Generally, of course, it is best to have someone other than the therapist carry out the testing and interpretation. This practice does not interfere with the therapeutic relationship and provides an independent check on the therapist's own interpretations.

Problem 1. In some clinics, psychologists wish to gather test data for research purposes. They need routinely to test all patients who are treated. How can this testing be carried out so as to gain the patients' cooperation and not convey the impression that the patients' part in therapy is to accept passively the advice of experts? How should the testing be explained to patients?

THE GOALS OF PSYCHOTHERAPY

At the beginning of therapy, the patient's aims are clear and straightforward: he wants to get rid of whatever distress brought him to the therapist. He may have anxiety attacks, compulsive habits, sexual impotence, fear of small rooms, insomnia, or excessive indecision. He is likely to think of therapy as a way of getting rid of these handicaps without affecting the rest of his life. Often, he expects that the therapist will give some advice or prescribe a course of action that will remove the symptom.

The therapist, however, sees the matter differently. Because of his training and experience, he believes that the patient's complaints are only signs of more pervasive trouble. The symptoms are, presumably, necessary outcomes of difficulties in the integration or reconciliation of various needs and wants. If the distressing symptoms are to be permanently destroyed, the underlying causes must be removed. Consequently, he is inclined to formulate the goal of therapy more broadly than the patient. He thinks in terms of personality change instead of symptom removal.

This difference in viewpoint could seriously interfere with therapy if it were openly expressed in the early interviews. Most patients are not ready to hear that their personalities must be reconstructed; that is a frightening prospect to some and a completely irrelevant aim to others. If the therapist holds his tongue, however, the patient will soon learn from his own explorations that his symptoms are related to attitudes and behavior that once seemed irrelevant. He will discover that a phobia, for instance, is somehow connected with a mistrust of his family. Moreover, as therapy goes on, he will find that he wants more than mere relief from his symptoms.

One patient, initially hoping to get rid of disturbing sexual thoughts, may later search for a sense of independence; another, worried about his lack of achievement, may eventually become more interested in warm relationships with others. As the patient begins to seek positive satisfactions instead of relief, he feels the need to change his life more than he had originally expected.

Therapists, however, should not lose sight of the fact that symptom removal is an important aim of psychotherapy. Sometimes a patient improves in many ways but still has the symptom that brought him to the therapist. Then the therapist may decide that his task is to help the patient learn to live comfortably with the symptom—to "accept" it. For example, a woman began psychotherapy because of a peculiar "catch" or break in her voice at certain times. After a year of treatment, the symptom was still present despite the fact that her self-confidence and her relations with others had vastly improved. At this point, the therapist took the position that, since the patient was getting so many real satisfactions, the voice break was not a serious barrier to her happiness and could be overlooked. This kind of attitude is defeatist, and such treatment probably ought not to be called therapy (3, pp. 230–232). One of the goals of psychotherapy must be the removal of symptoms due to psychological factors.

Normality as the Goal of Therapy. We have pointed out that symptom removal on any lasting basis usually requires personality changes, i.e., changes in the pattern of motives, feelings, attitudes, and behavior of the patient. We must then ask: What is the desired end-state? What kind of outcome is wanted? One way of answering this is to say that the patient should have the "normal" motives and attitudes. And these normal characteristics are implicitly defined as the "usual" ones. Such an answer is a statistical one: the goal of therapy is to help the patient become more like the modal or the average person. The objection to this answer is twofold: it takes the already existing state of public psychological adjustment as the desirable one, and it assumes that we know, or can find out, the amount of sexuality, hostility, dependency, and so on that characterizes the modal person. Actually, our complex society contains many kinds of modal people depending upon the stratum and locality studied. (Perhaps among some occupational groups the modal person has ulcers!)

Another, more subtle version of this answer is that normality can be defined in terms of the cultural norms or ideals. Therapists are to move patients toward a better approximation of what society regards as desirable. In practice, this would mean that the therapist would try to get his patients to be ambitious, monogamous, religious, patriotic, etc. That is, he would attempt to finish the socializing task started by the family and the school. The trouble is that many patients with distressing symptoms are already normal in this sense; in fact, their symptoms may be due to their anxiety about deviating from the cultural ideal. Furthermore, in a heterogeneous society like our own there is no clear and single cultural ideal, despite the contrary belief held by many patients.

Probably no therapist openly advocates the conceptions of the therapeutic goal we have just stated. But some definitely aim toward getting the patient to conform to certain religious or ethical standards. They seek, unwittingly perhaps, to preserve a marriage, to encourage continued employment, to stimulate good citizenship, whether or not these goals are announced or accepted by the patient. Doubtless a skilled therapist can guide a patient toward such goals; but there is a serious question whether such guidance will effectively reduce the patient's distress and confusion in the long run. Not only that, such guidance may alienate patients so that they discontinue treatment. If they feel unable to live up to what is expected of them, they may become more discouraged and self-devaluing.

Problem 2. One published report of a case treated by psychotherapy deals with an ethical problem in the initial interview (6, pp. 32 f). The patient was a forty-year-old woman who complained of feeling depressed.

In the first interview she told how she planned to pay for treatment by stealing money from her housekeeping funds. She didn't want to go to her husband for the treatment fees nor to tell him that she was being treated. The therapist's supervisor describes this plan as an "immoral proposal," and insists that the husband must be told of the treatment. At the end of the first session the therapist did, in fact, tell the patient that he could not continue the treatment unless she told her husband. In the light of this information answer the following questions.

1. What is your guess as to the way the patient felt about the therapist's stipulation that he would not treat her unless she told her husband?

2. Would the therapist's stipulation be more likely to strengthen the desire for treatment or to weaken it? Why?

3. What effect would the therapist's action have on the patient's willingness to share her thoughts and feelings freely with the therapist?

4. What motives probably prompted the patient to conceal her psychotherapy from her husband? Can you make any inferences about her relationship with him from her deception?

5. Is it possible that the patient would like to feel free to tell her husband about her therapy? If so, on what basis did you infer this?

6. What speculations can you make about the therapist's motives for making his stipulation?

Psychological Health as the Goal of Therapy. Sometimes the idea of healthy functioning is substituted for the concept of normality in defining the goal of therapy. This kind of thinking originated in a somewhat dubious analogy between "physical" health and "mental" health. Presumably the "mind" is capable of functioning in a certain way if it is undisturbed, just as the body will function in health. If the mind is not functioning this way, it is "ill" or "diseased." The "disease" concept is not a very useful one, however, in dealing with psychological problems (10). It seems now, in the light of studies of psychologists and cultural anthropologists, that what was called "mental" is profoundly shaped, even created, by culture patterns as transmitted through family groups. Hallucinations, a sign of mental illness in our culture, seem to be "healthy" in some other cultures.

Actually, neurosis does not seem to be an illness with a definite causative agent, with a specifiable course, and with a possible "cure." It is better described as a way of living that brings emotional misery. And this way of living depends upon attitudes, emotional responses, and assumptions that were gradually learned as a result of the patient's specific life circumstances. This description, of course, does not sharply differentiate neurotic people from nonneurotic ones. Both have acquired attitudes and motives that result in certain ways of living. The crucial difference between them is in the degree of satisfaction that they obtain from their ways of living. If you accept this viewpoint, then you will see that the goal of therapy can be to increase the neurotic's ability to find satisfactions in living, not to "cure an illness."

Increased Satisfaction as the Goal of Therapy. If we think of the goal of therapy as helping the patient find more satisfaction, we approach psychological treatment with a completely different yardstick for determining improvement. Instead of imposing an external standard on the patient, we can use his own feelings as a standard. Our criterion of adequate psychological functioning is autonomous—derived from the patient instead of from an average, a cultural ideal, or a psychological ideal. This way of looking at therapy has a number of advantages.

If the therapist sees his task as increasing the patient's ability to get satisfactions from living, he is not committed to evaluate the patient against any given ethical code or currently fashionable ideal. Thus, he has nothing to defend or justify to the patient in this respect—he represents no special interest group. This clears the ground of many potential differences between patient and therapist that could lead to unproductive arguments. It does not mean, of course, that the therapist is amoral or without conceptions of the ideal person; it simply means that he is not prepared to use his own conceptions as a standard for the patient.

Once the patient realizes that the therapist wants to help him find his own satisfactions, a powerful motive for therapy is invoked. This goal is something the patient wants and can understand. He and the therapist stand on common ground and can work together. And this feeling is valuable because the work entails much painful facing of anxiety-producing thoughts and impulses.

Another consequence of this notion of the therapeutic goal is that the responsibility for choices obviously lies with the patient. While the therapist is always willing to explore the possible consequences of a decision and the patient's feeling about it, he will not say that a given line of action should or should not be followed. The success, and therefore the satisfaction, of a course of action depends greatly upon the motivation behind it. And if the patient takes action primarily because someone else thinks it is best or most virtuous, his motivation is not very great. Any choice means giving up some satisfactions in order to obtain others. What can be sacrificed depends upon the patient's understanding of his own needs, not upon the therapist's hunch or belief concerning what is best for him. For only as the patient perceives that what he gives up would bring him less satisfaction than what he selects will he pursue his choice with zest and hopefulness. We cannot really say, therefore, that a patient should or should not forsake his job, his marriage, his aspirations, or anything else. The ingredient essential to a happy outcome must be created in the act of making the choice: a sense that "this is what I really want and will forgo the other to get it."

One of the clearest and most challenging statements of the view that the therapist must not evaluate the patient's search for satisfaction by external standards has been made by Rogers (15). He asks whether the therapist is completely willing for the patient to direct his own life:

Is he willing for him to choose goals that are social or antisocial, moral or immoral? If not, it seems doubtful that therapy will be a profound experience for the client. Even more difficult, is he willing for the client to choose regression rather than growth or maturity? to choose neuroticism rather than mental health? to choose to reject help rather than accept it? to choose death rather than life? To me it appears that only as the therapist is completely willing that any outcome, any direction, may be chosen—only then does he realize the vital strength of the capacity and potentiality of the individual for constructive action (15, p. 48).

Perhaps you wonder whether defining the goal of therapy as increasing the satisfaction of the patient could result in antisocial, selfish people? After all, a person could apparently get the most satisfaction by doing whatever he wanted without regard for others. That would be true if actions did not have social consequences. But many actions do have social consequences that affect the satisfactions of the individual. We can alienate others so that they will not cooperate in giving us what we want; or we can stimulate others to help. We must not overlook the fact that some of the satisfactions we want involve the friendliness or attentiveness of others. Such motives may vary in strength from person to person but they are part of the total set of forces that determine action. Taking account of the feelings and possible actions of others, then, is necessary in so far as they can give satisfaction: affection, help, stimulation, attention, money, jobs, and so on.

One final point needs emphasis. It is not the therapist's goal to provide satisfactions for the patient; that could be done only for the duration of the therapy. The fundamental task is to help the patient acquire the means for obtaining his own satisfactions. Then, after therapy is finished, the patient is better able to cope with the social environment around him. He is not a contented, completely satisfied person; rather, he is free of important inner obstacles that have interfered with his ability to choose and to obtain what he wants.

PSYCHOLOGICAL OBSTACLES TO OBTAINING SATISFACTION

Helping the patient learn to get what he wants more effectively is not a matter of teaching him new skills. Learning to dance, to drive a car, to converse, or to dress attractively may be desirable acquisitions for some patients; but they are not hard to come by, once the patient sees their relevance to his life and does not fear them. People can usually prescribe such things for themselves if they know what they want. Therapists are concerned about removing the obstacles that prevent patients from learning new ways of doing things or from seeing the need for new learning.

There are many ways of describing the reasons for neurotic inability to get satisfaction from living. Neurotics are said to be inflexible, to use inappropriate defense mechanisms, to be emotionally immature, to have insatiable demands, and so on. Here, we shall describe the neurotic's handicaps under three headings: insensitivity, inadequate forecasting, and anxiety-proneness. These three kinds of handicaps are interrelated and indicate the kind of work that must be done in therapy.

Neurotic Insensitivity. One of the most important characteristics of neurotic people is that they are unaware of significant motivational and emotional processes within them. They do not know some of their own desires and feelings. These unconscious processes affect the actions of the neurotic person, even though he does not know about them. Consequently, he is surprised or puzzled by some of the things he does, and feels that his actions are not under his own control. Also, as Kubie points out, behavior determined by unconscious forces is relatively unaffected by reasonable arguments or by rewards and punishments (9, p. 14). Finally, such behavior is not likely to reduce motivational tensions very well because the neurotic cannot use his knowledge to get satisfactions for wants that are unknown.

This lack of sensitivity to inner processes can be described in a number of ways. Traditional psychoanalytic terminology calls it "repression." Rogers refers to it by saying that "the organism denies to awareness significant sensory and visceral experiences, which consequently are not symbolized and organized into the gestalt of the self-structure" (15, p. 510). Dollard and Miller think of it as an inability to label drives or feelings correctly (7, Chap. XII). We should also remember another point: the repressive process itself is automatic and unknown. That is, the neurotic does not know (a) what is repressed, and (b) when repression is taking place.

The failure to discriminate, to label, or to be aware of inner bodily events is usually matched by insensitivity to some external events. These events are usually the actions of people. Thus, a person may fail to hear the sharp, aggressive tone in the voice of another just as he overlooks the same quality in his own voice. Or he may see and react to only one part of another's action and neglect the rest of it. Some people actually do not look at others well enough to note changes in facial expression; careful study shows that their visual contact with others is maintained by intermittent, rapid glances. This kind of behavior yields inadequate data so that a person's fixed opinions about other people are not given the chance to change.

One of the specific tasks of the therapist, then, is to "make the unconscious conscious," to promote awareness, or to restore the ability to label inner processes accurately. Success in this task will decrease the puzzlement of the patient, restore some sense of choice, and enable him to bring his intellectual resources into the service of his wants.

Inadequate Forecasting. To some extent, our actions depend upon the consequences we think they will have. We imagine or assume that our gifts will elicit thanks and that arriving home late for dinner will bring criticism. These assumptions are not always present as subvocal sentences or as images. Mostly they are "built into our behavior," so that we act upon them without really making them explicit. In driving, for instance, we stop at a red traffic signal without saying to ourselves that we are avoiding arrest or a serious accident. There is no reason, under ordinary circumstances, for us to examine the forecasts that are embodied in our acts; they turn out to be correct often enough that we need not question them. But when we fail to solve problems, i.e., fail to discover how to satisfy our wants, we need to reexamine the assumptions we are using. It may be that we are disappointed because we learned wrong assumptions about interpersonal relations.

During childhood, we learn that parents and other powerful adults will react in predictable ways to our actions. We gradually find out what pleases, what annoys, what pacifies, and what shocks. These discoveries serve as a basis for our forecasts about the social consequences of our behavior. As long as parents continue to react in the expected way, we can avoid trouble fairly well and still manage to extract whatever satisfactions are available. Two complications arise, however, that make many of these childhood social assumptions inadequate.

In the first place, as children grow, they develop more intellectual and physical resources. They can calculate the potential dangers and advantages in various courses of action for themselves, and increased strength and skill make a wide range of independent action possible. For example, the growing ability to establish new social relationships or the increasing opportunity to earn money make the adolescent less dependent upon parents than he was a few years earlier. Therefore the importance of basing actions upon the expected reactions of parents diminishes greatly.

Secondly, the reactions of parents are in many ways unlike those of other people. What they will praise or condemn is often a poor sample of what others will praise or condemn. Furthermore, their reaction to the child is determined in part by their responsibility for him and their view of him as a public representative of the family. But other people in the social environment react to the growing child on an entirely different basis; this is even more true when he has become an adult. Failure to realize these facts leaves the old social assumptions unaltered.

If the adult continues to forecast that the social consequences of his behavior will be about the same as those he discovered in childhood, he will make many mistakes. Instead of being loved for servility and lack of self-assertion, he is avoided as a kind of pathetic object. Instead of getting attention for irritability and temper, he gets social isolation. Instead of being praised for meticulousness and perfectionism, he is regarded as slow, rigid, and lacking in spontaneity. These changed consequences do not alter the neurotic's forecasts, however, for he does not see the connection between his action and the results he gets. The rules he goes by are unexamined for the most part, and even when examined they seem obvious and right to him. If other people do not behave in accordance with his assumptions, he thinks there is probably something wrong with them. Thus, if he believes that only great effort deserves praise, he cannot feel the sincerity of praise given to him for something he has done easily.

One effect of these automatic forecasts is that the neurotic often restricts his behavior unnecessarily. Then he has no chance to learn that the assumed painful outcomes of certain actions will not always occur. If he assumes that refusal will nearly always follow open requests for help, he will not ask openly. He deprives himself of help that would sometimes be willingly given. Or he may cling to a childhood assumption that failure to obey another always results in loss of the other person's affection. Not wanting to lose affection, he is carefully obedient. Thus he has no way of finding out that some people do not require obedience as a condition of affection. In fact, he may discover that, in some instances, his obedience does not guarantee continued affection—an outcome that increases his bewilderment.

An important task for the therapist, then, is to help the patient make his social forecasting explicit. He will also try to create a situation in which the patient can actually experience the fact that the assumed consequences of his behavior do not always occur. And finally, he hopes to develop a relationship in which the patient feels secure enough to try out new assumptions. The new forecasts will take more account of concrete circumstances and of his adult status.

Anxiety-proneness. Since the early work of Freud, it has been increasingly clear that anxiety is one of the most important features of neurosis. We do not mean that all neurotics are anxious; many are fairly calm people. But the neurotic person is continually engaged in a struggle to control or decrease anxiety. And the ways he uses to control it seriously interfere with his ability to get satisfactions for many important wants or desires.

To understand the role of anxiety in neurotic behavior, we must realize that it is not only a feeling, but it is also a drive (7, pp. 190 f). Like other physiological drives, it involves bodily changes leading to heightened, restless activity and searching for relief. Apparently, the anxiety drive can be readily conditioned to a wide variety of stimuli, including our own thoughts. Furthermore, it tends to resist extinction (19). Once an event or object has become an anxiety-arouser, it is hard to diminish its potency.

One of the most effective ways to relieve anxiety is to get away from the anxiety-producing situation (withdrawal behavior). But we can also prevent anxiety from being aroused by staying away from anxiety-producing situations (avoidance behavior). If, then, awareness of our own impulses has become a source of anxiety, we can stay comfortable by avoiding the awareness (whether it is labeling, imaging, or some other kind of discriminative response). This avoidance results in what we have called insensitivity to our own inner processes. It is repression.

The neurotic suffers from repression because he has learned to be anxious when he knows that certain motives are present. He is "bad," that is, anxious, if he feels sexy, aggressive, status-hungry, or lazy. He is bad if he wants to get his own way or to indulge himself. In order to avoid the constant self-devaluation that would occur if he knew these wants, he represses them. Not knowing what he wants, he cannot satisfy them effectively. He wins comfort in one way while losing it in many other ways.

Anxiety is also connected with what we call inadequate forecasting. Even when the neurotic person knows what he wants or what he feels, he is prevented from expressing it because he forecasts disapproval or social rejection. It is true, of course, that unfortunate consequences do occur if certain wants or feelings are expressed in words or actions in some social situations. But the neurotic is anxious about expressing them in any situation. He neglects those aspects of a social situation that would enable him to differentiate between appropriate and inappropriate expression. Thus, he often loses the chance of getting his known desires satisfied.

We can see, then, that another therapeutic task consists of reducing the patient's anxiety about awareness and about communicating his wants and feelings. As the patient becomes less anxious, he becomes more likely to find out what he wants and to take appropriate measures to get it. Since he has many wants, and they are not always compatible, he must also learn how to integrate them for maximum satisfaction. He must find out not only what he wants but how intensely he wants it.

Then he will be able to act reasonably, not irrationally. As Dewey puts it: ". . . reasonableness is in fact a quality of an effective relationship among desires rather than a thing opposed to desire. It signifies the order, perspective, proportion which is achieved . . . out of a diversity of earlier incompatible preferences" (5, p. 194).

Problem 3. The following transcript is taken from a recording of the initial interview with a thirty-five-year-old man. He had been referred to the therapist by a vocational counselor. After the patient was seated, the therapist spoke:

T: I wonder if you'd give me a little background on the problem that you and Miss —— were discussing and so forth.

P: Well, I'm not sure. I plan to change jobs. I'm with a company now that I don't think is quite right for me and there's an individual who is my superior that is most difficult not only with me, but with others, so that I feel that perhaps it would be best to change. So I went to her with the idea of taking a complete series of tests to find out where I best fitted. You see, during the, for ten years I was with the X Company, which is an excellent company, and during the war years I took the place of a veteran. And when he returned, they didn't give him his job back immediately as they did the other boys. They let us share responsibility, which was wrong, because he felt that I had usurped his job. They transferred me then to . . . doing strictly accounting work, which I'm not suited for I've found. And I developed a very bad attitude and didn't know quite what was wrong. I almost had what I felt was a nervous breakdown. And, uh, so they, they eventually, then, too, I had an overpowering ambition to be somebody or to be a manager of some sort, and I told them that. And I think they felt that my, I was reaching for something which wasn't available in their company and they discharged me, which was a great surprise to me because my work over a period of years had been most satisfactory. I'm pretty sure of that. The personnel manager said when I left that he felt that it was for my own good. In other words, that I'd be a better man for the experience. So that I went out then and sought this job with this other company, and I am an office manager now. A relatively small company. And, but I find that I have an emotional anxiety and it evidently came out in these tests. She said that I have a maladjustment, a personality maladjustment. And she says it's a sex maladjustment which was more or less a surprise to me. My relationships have been none other than with my wife in a sex act way. I've been married more or less happily for years. Two children. Own my own home. Although it isn't surprising that she told me I had a maladjustment of some sort because I, I am in a, a state of anxiety.

T: Can you describe that a little bit to me?

P: Yeah. Now, last night I went home, course it's the end of the week, and I live under more or less of a tyrant boss. He's noted for it and during the war he had a constant turnover, because people can't take it. But if, if I were strong enough mentally to know him as he is, certainly, I, I could be able to take that. But anyway I came home last night, and it's been pretty much all work. Work at the office and work at home. And, and you feel like you're on a merry-go-round, you know, quite a few people do, I mean. And, gosh, before I sat down to dinner, I went upstairs, and I broke down crying. I felt that things were too much for me. I was exhausted. You know, I don't know quite what's eating me. There's a bug eating me. I don't quite know what it is.

T: In other words, you cried because you felt all upset and a lot of strain on you, but you didn't know the exact reason for it.

P: I don't know the reason, yes. There's an overpowering, you see, I've pushed me, I think what I need is a little change. Now last night we went to the movie. We haven't done that recently. And Sunday, my folks are going to take the two children and just my wife and I are going out. I think that'll do me a world of good. I think I'll go back Monday morning, and to all appearances I'll be perfectly happy, a normal and adjusted individual [*laughs*]. But the same thing will re-occur because it has in the past. Now I've had rather a tough time. I was fired from this job. It was a great shock. I mean, it really hit me hard.

T: Yeah.

P: 'Cause I thought that was the company I was going to stay with till I died. [Portion omitted] The thing that bothers me a little bit is that I'm very meticulous, and I, I'm a little slow. And, according to the counselor I have ability and I'm not, I wondered whether I was subnormal or something. I have ability but she feels that there's an adjustment there that keeps me from doing my best. She gave me this ink-blot test, and from those she says I have a sex maladjustment. Now, here I am complaining about my work situation, I haven't said anything about sex.

T: Well, but isn't it actually true that *you* don't feel any sex maladjustment yourself?

P: Yeah, that's true. Except this, that now she's told me that, I kind of think back, you know.

T: Yeah.

P: And search my own mind as to what, uh, it is true that I, uh, I look at girls on the street, I get a great amount of interest and pleasure out of, you see a sweater girl, why I'm very much interested, that is, I mean, even when I'm with my wife, you know, take a great deal of joy in that (*laughs*). I, I have no illicit relationships at all. And I love to be with other women, I like to dance, and I like to, I suppose I'm, I, I'm oversexed to the extent that I like to dance close. But there's no going out with other girls at all. I guess maybe there's a subconscious desire maybe to do that. But I'm restricted from it because of my marriage, I don't know.

1. Does this patient have a persisting maladjustment or is his difficulty due mainly to the stress of his present situation? Support your answer.

2. What indications are there that this patient is suitable for psychotherapy?

3. Leaving aside the judgment of the vocational counselor, does this patient really seem to have a sexual problem? Explain your answer.

REFERENCES

1. Auld, F. Jr., & Eron, L. D. The use of Rorschach scores to predict whether patients will continue psychotherapy. *J. consult. Psychol.*, 1953, **17**, 104–109.
2. Barron, F. An ego-strength scale which predicts response to psycho-therapy. *J. consult. Psychol.*, 1953, **17**, 327–333.
3. Braatøy, T. *Fundamentals of psychoanalytic technique.* New York: Wiley, 1954.
4. Dailey, C. A. The practical utility of the clinical report. *J. consult Psychol.*, 1953, **17**, 297–302.
5. Dewey, J. *Human nature and conduct.* New York: Holt, 1922.
6. Dollard, J., Auld, F. Jr., & White, A. M. *Steps in psychotherapy.* New York: Macmillan, 1953.
7. Dollard, J., & Miller, N. E. *Personality and psychotherapy.* New York: McGraw-Hill, 1950.
8. Eysenck, H. J. The effects of psychotherapy: an evaluation. *J. consult. Psychol.*, 1952, **16**, 319–324.
9. Kubie, L. S. *Practical and theoretical aspects of psychoanalysis.* New York: International Universities Press, 1950.
10. Marzolf, S. S. The disease concept in psychology. *Psychol. Rev.*, 1947, **54**, 211–221.
11. Patterson, C. H. Is psychotherapy dependent upon diagnosis? *Amer. Psychol.*, 1948, **3**, 155–159.
12. Raimy, V. C. (Ed.) *Training in clinical psychology.* New York: Prentice-Hall, 1950.
13. Redlich, F. C., Hollingshead, A. B., & Bellis, E. Social class differences in attitudes toward psychiatry. *Psychosom. Med.*, 1955, **17**, 60–70.
14. Rogers, C. R. *Counseling and psychotherapy.* New York: Houghton Mifflin, 1942.
15. Rogers, C. R. *Client-centered therapy.* New York: Houghton Mifflin, 1951.
16. Rosenzweig, S. A transvaluation of psychotherapy—a reply to Hans Eysenck. *J. abnorm. soc. Psychol.*, 1954, **49**, 298–304.
17. Skottowe, I. *Clinical Psychiatry.* New York: McGraw-Hill, 1954.
18. Snyder, W. U. The present status of psychotherapeutic counseling. *Psychol. Bull.*, 1947, **44**, 297–386.
19. Solomon, R. L., & Wynne, L. C. Traumatic avoidance learning: the principles of anxiety conservation and partial irreversibility. *Psychol. Rev.*, 1954, **61**, 353–385.

CHAPTER 13

Psychotherapeutic Methods

Most people, hearing about psychotherapy for the first time, find the whole notion somewhat mysterious. "How," they want to know, "can simply talking about your problems help you?" They will admit that a frank discussion of disturbing emotions can bring temporary relief: "Getting something out of your system makes you feel better." But they correctly realize that this does not bring lasting improvement.

At a more sophisticated level, people think that psychotherapy works because the patient finds the origins of his problems. By exploring his developmental history, he can learn how he came to have the feelings and attitudes, the symptoms and fears that now distress him. At the same time, people who accept this point of view are puzzled as to how knowledge of causes can bring about changes. And it does seem unlikely, in fact, that merely knowing how we learned to fear something will substantially decrease the fear.

Psychotherapists today are not inclined to stress the importance of talk in helping people change. True, speech is necessary to communicate and to direct attention to certain psychological processes. But therapeutic sessions are more than talk. They involve the emotions of both therapist and patient, and they involve efforts by the patient to stimulate or to manipulate the therapist in his characteristic way. Here, in the realm of emotional experience and interpersonal behavior, is the opportunity for relearning to take place. Therapy is not simply a matter of giving the patient an outlet nor of getting him to understand childhood origins of difficulties; it is a matter of arranging circumstances so that he can unlearn inappropriate feelings, attitudes, and assumptions and acquire new, more satisfying ones. Therapy is, as Alexander and French (1) put it, a corrective emotional experience.

Therapists, then, have as their immediate aim the construction of a situation where the patient can have experiences that are novel and illuminating. It must permit him to become aware of his typical response and also to try out new ways of looking at himself and at his relationship to others. The prime factor in this special situation is the relation-

351

ship between therapist and patient. We shall, therefore, first discuss the therapeutic relationship and then turn to specific methods that can be used in therapy.

PSYCHOTHERAPY AS A SOCIAL RELATIONSHIP

From the standpoint of social psychology, psychotherapy is a relationship deliberately created in order to change the patient. Of course, it is not the only relationship of this kind in our society. Teacher-pupil and warden-prisoner relationships are also social arrangements for producing change. Probably psychotherapy most closely resembles the teacher-pupil relationship in tutoring. The purpose of both tutoring and therapy is not to solve a particular problem for the client but to help him acquire skills, information, and sensitivities so that he can solve problems by himself. This aim is different from those found in medicine, law, or dentistry. The consultant in these professions is usually engaged to solve specific problems *for* the client. Any understanding or sensitivity acquired by the client is only a by-product of his contact with the consultant. In therapy, however, the gain in self-understanding is primary, and when it occurs patients report that they can deal with specific problems that were not even discussed with the therapist.

In passing, we should point out that this conception of therapy differs radically from the view that it consists of "curing a mental disorder." The "curative" view is a carry-over from medicine. It also reflects the nineteenth century notion of the social role of the medical authority figure. The epitome of this conception was probably reached in the hypnotic treatment of hysteria during the latter part of the last century. In that treatment, the ignorant and sick patient turns himself over to the "expert," who manipulates and suggests until the symptoms have vanished and the "disease" is "cured."

Today, the therapist does not establish an authoritarian relationship with the patient. Even when hypnosis is used as part of therapy, it takes place in a context of mutual cooperative effort. The modern psychotherapist hopes to promote the growth of the patient by providing appropriate conditions for learning. He is an expert in the procedures that encourage the development of awareness, but he is not an expert in knowing how to manage the patient's life. He may know more than the patient; he does not know "better" than the patient.

The "curative" conception of psychotherapy is particularly inappropriate in dealing with a class of patients sometimes described as having "character disorders." They do not show clear-cut neurotic symptoms that can be fitted into the classical diagnostic categories. Rather, they suffer from traits or "styles" that handicap them, although they are not obviously abnormal. Thus, some people are unable to form love relationships, others sacrifice themselves, and others are excessively shy and timid. Psychotherapy for such people is not a matter of curing them but of aiding them to achieve optimal satisfaction.

Group Norms and Social Relationships. Social relationships are built upon a basis of shared expectations. Two people, for example teacher and student, expect certain attitudes and overt behavior from each other. The student expects the teacher to set learning tasks for him and to evaluate his learning. And the teacher expects the same things of himself. The student, on the other hand, is expected to attend to the tasks and to submit to evaluations. When both parties have a common understanding about their joint activity, the relationship is clear and communication is easy. Of course, in addition to these shared norms about the basic behavior to be expected, there are other activities that are permitted but not expected. Thus, teacher and student may become friends, but this is not commonly regarded as a necessary part of the relationship.

Our society has many of these interlocking roles, and there is widespread understanding of at least the minimum requirements to be fulfilled by the participants. We may mention parent-child, boss-worker, physician-patient, salesman-customer, policeman-citizen, and pastor-parishioner relationships as examples. All these permit different kinds of behavior, require different attitudes, and provide different possibilities for individual satisfaction. We expect to earn money as workers, to obtain police protection as citizens, and to preserve our health as patients. In other words, we utilize these different relationships to satisfy different desires.

Our way of looking at psychotherapy is to regard it as a special relationship created to provide experiences that are not otherwise readily available. Obviously, we can find therapeutic values in other relationships such as marriage and friendships. But they are not deliberately arranged to bring about personality changes. Psychotherapy, in a sense, distills the effective growth-producing qualities from these relationships and intentionally uses them to promote personal change. For example, we sometimes discover that the quiet, comfortable manner of a friend listening to us calms our emotions, and we are better able to explore the consequences of a difficult decision. This accepting attitude is an important part of psychotherapy, made possible by the therapist's training and experience.

Norms in Psychotherapy. What are the norms that distinguish the therapeutic relationship from others? How does it offer possibilities not usually found in other social connections? The answers to these questions differ somewhat for the various therapeutic approaches: orthodox psychoanalytic technique and gestalt therapy (6) open different opportunities. But there are a few norms that are applicable to most kinds of modern psychotherapy.

The most common expectation is one that applies to all consulting relationships: one person is the helper and is paid, and the other wants help. The therapist is not expecting personal help from the patient. True, the relationship has possible therapeutic value for the therapist, but that is clearly not the goal. If the therapist wants to talk about *his* problems, he should find another therapist or a friend. And therapists often do this. It is one of the arrangements that helps a therapist continue to keep the patient's goals central.

Another norm of the therapeutic relationship is that the patient is expected to have problems he cannot solve alone. We may call this "the expectation of dependency." It contrasts with the usual requirements that we be independent, mature, strong, fearless, and so on. If we really are all these things, the therapist has no time for us. Therapy is open to those who fail, or think they fail, to meet the social ideals of independence and maturity.

In therapy, it is expected that the patient will talk almost exclusively about himself, his history, his feelings. This "expectation of self-orientation" is another reversal of ordinary social standards. Few of us have ever been told to go ahead and talk about ourselves all we please. We know that it is polite and correct to let the other fellow occupy the center of the stage part of the time. Not so in psychotherapy! The patient who insists on yielding his time to the therapist may be evading therapy.

Another characteristic of therapy is that it violates the social prohibitions against discussing tabooed subjects. The norm of therapy is: "You may talk about anything, no matter how nasty and bad it seems." One of the social taboos that is broken in therapy concerns the open expression of feelings toward another person in a face-to-face situation. Patients are encouraged to tell the therapist how they feel about him: like, dislike, irritation, disappointment, and sexual attraction are all equally accepted. Patients can rarely use this new opportunity at first, for it is strange and incredible. But they try it gradually by telling about their "bad" feelings and actions towards other people.

Another norm of therapy that supports those just mentioned is "nonretaliation." The therapist will not use what he learns about the patient to strike back at him. Nor will he exploit the patient's dependence upon him in order to take advantage of his weaknesses, fears, or coercive appetites. The norm of nonretaliation is enforced partly by the ethics accepted by psychotherapists, partly by their understanding that retaliation would seriously interfere with therapy. One way that therapists avoid coercion is to avoid treating persons over whom they have power.

For example, a teacher will ordinarily not administer therapy to one of his students. He does not want to complicate the therapeutic relationship by his power to pass or fail the student. In industrial and military settings, the power of the therapist over the patient may become a serious problem. Special arrangements must be made to separate the command function from the therapeutic relationship. The therapist wants to guard against any unwitting tendencies to retaliate by using his power, and he wants to make it clear to the patient that he actually *cannot* damage him.

Therapy as a Social Unreality. Together, these norms sketch the pattern of an unusual social relationship. It is one that permits the patient to think, to feel, and to express himself with childlike spontaneity and irresponsibility. We are tempted to describe it as a parent-child relationship without the enforcement of demands and prohibitions. But calling the therapist a completely tolerant parent-figure neglects a crucial difference between therapists and parents: Therapists have no responsibility or desire to fulfill the basic biological and social needs of their patients. In this respect they are also different from husbands, wives, friends, and kinfolk. They cannot provide companionship, productive employment, social status, "nor meat, nor drink, nor slumber, nor a roof against the rain."

The fact is that the enduring satisfactions in life must be found outside the therapeutic relationship. Only by changing into some other kind of relationship could therapist and patient gratify each other's biological and social wants. And this is perhaps the deepest distinction between therapy and other significant social relationships: in therapy we actually risk little and hardly obligate ourselves socially; but in the other relationships we risk much and obligate ourselves greatly. It is in these other relationships that we really love, fight, give, take, and enjoy ourselves. And it is to them that we must ultimately return from therapy.

Compared with most social relations, then, therapy is not very real. That does not make it less valuable. But therapy is not merely a social fantasy. As a personal experience it is intensely real and involving. The hostility, tenderness, affection, and sadness felt during the sessions are actual events. Visceral changes take place during the emotions of therapy just as they do in any other emotions. The difference between the emotions of therapy and so-called "real feelings" lies only in their social consequences. In the relationship of therapy, the patient is free to announce his feelings without having to accept the usual social results of such announcements. If he criticizes the therapist, he will probably provoke irritation but not retaliation. If he says he feels sexually drawn to the therapist, he may provoke interest but not sexual relations.

The fact that the expression of wants and feelings in therapy does not entangle the patient in social complications has two important results for him. In the first place he can freely search for what he really feels and wants—explore his internal realities more thoroughly than is possible elsewhere. In the second place, he can experience the fact that feelings and wants do not have magic potency even when announced. Few patients really understand that a feeling or a desire has no consequences by itself. They assume (without being aware of it) that to feel love or hate for someone automatically establishes a relationship with that person. If they feel affection for another person, they believe that this feeling entails obligations and responsibilities for both parties. If they feel critical, they assume that the other person will want to mend his ways. The reverse is also true for these patients: other people's feelings about them impose obligations, responsibilities, and self-corrective measures. In the light of these unspoken assumptions, you can see why a patient finds it surprising and releasing when a criticized therapist accepts the patient's feeling without trying to justify, to retaliate, or to change himself.

Effects of the Novel Relationship. We can dramatize the novelty of the therapeutic relationship by saying that the patient who enters therapy is entering a new culture. It permits, even encourages, expression of emotions and of motives that are ordinarily checked. Of course, the patient does not discover the characteristics of the new culture immediately. And when he does discover them, he cannot believe that they exist. He continues to meet the novel arrangement with the assumptions and behavior he ordinarily uses. At the same time, however, he vaguely realizes that it is not really necessary. This discrepancy makes the therapeutic relationship a powerful tool for forwarding self-understanding. In fact, it is not too much to say that the chief instrument of psychotherapy is the relationship between therapist and patient. Let us see why it is so important.

In the first place, the patient can experience directly his difficulty in adapting to the new relationship. Obviously, it offers great freedom, but he discovers he cannot use this freedom. For example, it does not take long for patients to learn that they may speak freely—at least, they know this in a kind of intellectual way. But when they are offered a clear opportunity to express irritation, they refuse it. The discrepancy between what they *know* is permitted and what they allow themselves to do is directly experienced. This experience can be developed in many directions, but often the patient comes to see that he actually limits his own behavior, although he has usually believed that it is others who impose limits on him.

In the following transcript of part of a recorded interview, we can watch this self-limiting process develop. The patient is an unmarried woman in her twenties who has consistently sacrificed for others, has felt guilty about anything that seemed self-indulgent, and has repressed her hostile impulses. As this excerpt begins, the therapist reacts to an irritated tone in the patient's voice.

T: You do want to fight with me today, don't you?

P: I guess so. [*Laughs.*]

T: Tell me, what is it?

P: [*Laughs.*] Well, I ain't gonna take it out on you. [*Laughs.*] The fact that I'm lonesome. [Portion omitted.]

T: What do you want to take out on me?

P: I don't, I shouldn't want to, though.

T: Who says you shouldn't want to?

P: The rules, okay, you know who says, who I mean when I say "they" or "you shouldn't"? Not meaning any particular "you"?

T: Who do you mean?

P: I mean, the rules of life is what I mean. That's just a rule of life. You don't take out, you aren't mean to one person just because somebody else across the street was mean to you. You don't walk down and be mean to the next person.

T: Whether you should or whether you shouldn't, you do want to be mean to me today.

P: Yeah.

T: Go ahead.

P: [*Laughs.*] I don't exactly know how.

T: You don't know how to be mean to me?

P: I could just not talk, but then I'd be hurting myself too. Then I'm not getting my hour's worth, if I just be quiet.

Notice that, at the end of the excerpt, even when she considers violating the "rules of life" she can think of no way to be mean except by controlling her own behavior, by not talking. Such experiences, as they accumulate, help the patient to feel his own inflexibility and to discriminate between appropriate and inappropriate occasions for the release of feelings.

In the second place, the novel relationship with the therapist opens the way for disclosing the implicit assumptions the patient makes about people. The very great contrast of this relationship with others in the patient's life is one reason for this effect. The therapist makes fewer demands than most other people, he is more ready to listen, and yet at the same time he is less polite (in the sense of avoiding painful topics) and less willing to give advice and direction. In the course of finding out what the new relationship is, the patient sees more clearly what his other relationships have been.

But more important than this contrast is the fact that the novel relationship leads to the examination of assumptions about the therapist. Over and over again, the patient discovers that he is trying hard to please the therapist, or to irritate him, or to shut him up, or to prevent him from pursuing a painful topic. All this is usually done in some roundabout way. When it is made clear that the patient could have expressed himself directly, then the patient can find the assumptions lying behind his disguised social operations. But in finding out the beliefs he implicitly holds about the therapist, he is at the same time finding out beliefs that he holds about helpers, about authorities, about members of the same or of the opposite sex, and even about himself.

To illustrate how an assumption about the therapist becomes explicit, we shall use an excerpt given by Colby (3). A long silence had just occurred.

THER.: It seems you are having some difficulty talking today.
PT.:　　It does, doesn't it? I know I must try to be honest and tell you everything, but sometimes it's so hard. I don't know quite how to go about it. [*Silence.*]
THER.: Is it something to do with me?
PT. [*Laughs.*]: It is. I think the main thing that bothers me is how you will take it. Not that you will do anything about it. I know by now that you won't laugh at me. But you will think this is so childish.
THER.: Why would I?
PT.:　　It's something anyone would think a grown woman should have gotten over by now. Once a few years ago I told my mother about it and she scorned me, saying I sounded like a bobby-soxer.
THER.: And you're afraid I will react like your mother? (3, pp. 116 f)

In this excerpt, we see that the patient not only fears the assumed ridicule of the therapist but also relates it to her mother's attitude. It is not likely, however, that she realizes that she herself is actually evaluating what she wants to say as childish; nor does she see that she is trying to forestall the therapist's ridicule by telling him she expects it. These realizations will come later.

Another result of the novel relationship depends upon the gradually increasing sense of safety acquired by the patient. As he discovers that nothing happens to him when he expresses some thought or feeling that is ordinarily taboo, he becomes less cautious, less alert to inspect and censor his remarks. Then he says things that surprise him. Unexpected remarks seem to "slip out," and, although he may deny that he meant them, he cannot deny that he made them. The same thing can sometimes be noticed in a more dramatic way when the patient is casually modeling clay as he talks. If asked to describe what he has made, he will be surprised that it resembles a penis, a bowel movement, or a mutilated human figure. These unexpected "slips" provide new material for discussion and reveal to the patient that he is capable of a wider range of behavior than he believes.

Finally, the safety of this novel relationship is enjoyable in itself. Despite the anxiety evoked by therapeutic exploration, patients find real comfort in the continued acceptance and interest of the therapist. The relief from feelings of having to live up to the expectations of others or of having to refrain from expressing illogical thoughts is important in holding the patient in the therapeutic situation. And the continued attention of the therapist slowly builds an attitude of self-esteem and a sense of individual worth.

Problem 1. The fact that a patient pays for treatment is part of the therapeutic relationship. Many therapists believe that payment actually has therapeutic value in itself; it is also evidence of a real desire for treatment. They suggest that, even in publicly supported clinics, every patient should pay something for his treatment. For the following questions, however, assume that the patient receives private treatment costing from $15 to $25 a session.

1. What values does payment of fees have for the therapist?
2. What values does payment of fees have for the patient?
3. Does payment add to or detract from the "social unreality" of therapy?

BUILDING THE THERAPEUTIC RELATIONSHIP

We have pointed out that the patient does not immediately understand the norms of the therapeutic relationship nor the attitudes of the therapist. The early phases of therapy must be devoted primarily to the task of helping the patient develop an understanding of and a desire for such a relationship. Only when the bond between therapist and patient is strong can the two explore the patient's intense self-hatred, antisocial sexual desire, hostility toward beloved persons, and the like. Furthermore, not until the patient can become emotionally involved with the therapist will he show, in the therapy sessions, the techniques he employs in his most important interpersonal relationships. The building of a strong relationship is not accomplished by explanation or carefully worded permission. It must be brought about by time, by the arrangements for therapy, and by the behavior of the therapist. The patient's beliefs and feelings about the therapist are determined by what actually happens to him in the sessions, not by what he is told.

Arrangements for Therapy. In the very first session the patient experiences the fact that he is the complete center of the therapist's attention. The length of the session is usually about an hour, although some therapists may use up to two hours with patients they see only once a week. There are no interruptions, and the therapist is unhurried. Most patients are surprised to find how short the session seems. At the end of the hour, arrangements are made for another appointment; and the therapist usually tries to set a time that regularly will "belong" to the patient. Thus, even if the patient has not inquired about the length of therapy, he learns that the therapist plans to make himself available on a continuing basis.

In traditional psychoanalytic therapy, sessions are held five days a week. In many of the modern variants of psychoanalysis, however, patients are seen only once or twice a week. Sometimes a patient becomes emotionally upset between appointments and asks for an extra session. Whether or not this request is granted depends upon the therapist's schedule, on the intensity of the disturbance, and on the kinds of therapeutic problems that are being worked on at the time. At times, the therapist may refuse, because he would like to have the patient find out that he can stand such upsets; or he may grant the request because the preceding session brought out emotions that left the patient with considerable unresolved guilt. As in all the work of therapy, much depends upon the sensitivity of the therapist.

Another arrangement in psychoanalysis has been for the patient to lie down on a couch. While this position has many advantages, it may not be wise to introduce it in the first few interviews. Some patients find the supine position somewhat threatening; it tends to start off therapy in a way that does not suggest mutuality and friendly acceptance. Many therapists, therefore, seat patients in a comfortable chair at the beginning of therapy. Whether the couch is used later depends upon the skill and orientation of the therapist. Some therapists encourage patients to use the couch for every session; others indicate that both couch and chair are available. Guided by the patient, they decide which to use during different sessions, or even during different parts of the same session.

As therapy progresses, patients may invite the therapist to their homes or to social events. Generally, therapists do not accept such invitations. They avoid social contacts with their patients in order to preserve the clarity of the therapeutic relationship. Therapist and patient cannot very well maintain the roles of mutual friends during therapy, although they may feel friendly and enjoy each other's presence. All this does not mean, of course, that the therapist is aloof when he happens to meet a patient in some social situation. But he does keep such chance meetings on a superficial, pleasant level.

The Nature of the Interview. During the first few interviews, the patient is encouraged to tell his story: what brought him to therapy, the nature and severity of his problems, previous efforts to relieve his distress, and something about his development during childhood and adolescence. These interviews provide useful diagnostic information, but they also permit the two participants to "get the feel" of each other. Any new social contact has its "getting acquainted" phase, and therapy is no exception. During this phase, the therapist often proceeds by using the semidirected interview methods described in Chapter 6. He does little probing, preferring to let the patient take the lead in bringing up material. His comments encourage the patient to talk and to elaborate on unclear points.

After this beginning period, there are various ways of proceeding. If the patient is working with an orthodox psychoanalyst, he will probably be introduced to the method of free association (5). The analyst will instruct the patient to let his thoughts run freely and to say everything that he thinks. He is asked to refrain from holding back anything and is told that he does not need to be logical or sensible in what he says. Usually the patient lies on a couch, and the analyst sits to one side and slightly behind him. The analyst is quiet for long periods and only rarely interrupts the flow of associations. Sometimes, at the end of the hour, the analyst will briefly comment on a few significant points.

Free association is not as easy as it may sound, and it is rarely free and smooth-flowing. The patient discovers that he feels blocked for no apparent reason, or he may find that he is unaccountably anxious or angry. Again, he may attempt to be completely logical, screening out marginal associations despite the analyst's instructions. Sometimes the flow of associations is fragmented, disorganized, and nonsensical. All these events yield material that needs to be understood, and, later in therapy, the analyst will forward understanding with interpretive comments and questions.

Of course, the associations contain a vast amount of information about the patient's attitudes toward himself, about his early life, about his parents, and about the events of his daily life. He discovers that certain clusters of ideas recur frequently and becomes interested in tracing out the connections between seemingly unrelated associations that occur together. The analyst, too, is noting the information and the patterns of associations. On the basis of his theory of personality and his experience, he formulates to himself ideas about the origins and nature of the patient's anxieties, of his defenses against anxiety, of his repressions, and of his frustrated desires.

Many therapists, however, choose to proceed with a more conversational approach (1, 7). Instead of instructing the patient to freely associate, they begin sessions by asking the patient what he would like to talk about; or they may simply wait for him to begin. Some say very little and behave much like the orthodox analyst. Others may use open-ended questions from time to time and comment occasionally on what the patient says. Those who follow a "client-centered" approach will try to clarify what the patient is feeling as he talks, but they refrain from questioning. And there are some who use many questions which center around the patient's awareness of his bodily sensations, of his voice and gestures, and of his attitudes and behavior toward the therapist.[1]

These various kinds of interviews produce somewhat different therapeutic atmospheres, and probably therapists end by creating the kind of situation that enables them to work most comfortably. But the patient must also be considered, and it seems likely that different patients need different kinds of interviews. Some, for instance, may not be sufficiently imaginative and verbally facile to use the free-association method effectively. Others, who depend too heavily on authorities for guidance, may welcome continued questioning although they would profit more by methods that leave the initiative to them.

What the therapist needs, then, is flexibility and sensitivity. In the early interviews, he must do what seems needed to make the patient feel accepted and interested in continuing treatment. As treatment progresses, he must do what seems needed to provide emotional experiences that will increase the patient's insight, decrease his anxiety, and promote a sense of being able to choose and to reject courses of action. To be able to do this requires experience with actual patients as much or more than theories about the best way to do therapy in general.

Total Listening. One of the most elementary techniques used to build the relationship is total listening. The therapist constantly attends to the patient's talking. He notices not only what is said but how it is said. He notes gestures and emotional responses. And he shows that he is listening. The patient can see him nod occasionally, note a sympathetic smile, hear him say "Yes," or "Please go on."

The first few interviews will be taken up with fairly long recitals of the patient's story and his account of his distress. Even therapists who will be fairly active in later interviews usually want to establish early the primacy of the patient's right to talk and be listened to. This total listening tells the patient: "What you say is important and I am interested. You are expected to tell me whatever you want to."

"Staying with the Patient." In all phases of therapy, it is very important for the therapist to follow closely what the patient is saying and to respond, if response is needed, to the flow of feeling and of talk. This skill will be needed later, when interpretive activity starts, but it is also

[1] The value of dealing with bodily activities in therapy has been described at length by Braatøy (2). A somewhat similar approach has been proposed by Perls, Hefferline, and Goodman (6). They suggest a number of exercises to increase self-awareness and show their value as therapeutic methods.

a sign of total listening that helps establish the relationship in the early sessions. Untrained therapists do this poorly, as the following excerpt will show. It is a partial transcript of a training session for an untrained counselor. He was interacting with a man who was playing the part of an apathetic, depressed patient. This session was supposed to be the first interview. After a greeting, the interview proceeded:

T–1: Well, something on your mind? What's your first name, by the way?

P–1: Well, uh, a lot of people call me Jim.

T–2: Jim, uh-huh. Well, I'll call you Jim, if you don't mind. Something, uh, uh, perplexing you?

P–2: Well, there's something wrong with me, and I, I don't know what to do about it. And I thought maybe if I'd drop in to see you. I, uh, I'm in a lot of trouble. I don't really know what's wrong with me.

T–3: Well, tell me, Jim, how old are you?

P–3: Oh, forty.

T–4: Forty, mm-hm, uh, I take it you're married?

P–4: Yeah.

T–5: Mm-hm. Well, have a family?

P–5: Yeah, I got a coupla kids.

T–6: Well, how long have you been married?

P–6: [Pause.] Sixteen years, I guess. I don't know, things look awful hopeless to me. And I think that things are going down hill for me. I don't seem to have any interest in anything anymore. And uh, well, I didn't know whether it was a religious thing or not, but I would say this, life's got no point for me. And I, uh, I'm slipping on my job. And I'd just like to know whether something can be done about it.

T–7: Well, Jim, how long have you been feeling this way? Has it been over a period of time or did it just suddenly come on?

P–7: Well, I suppose it's been coming on me for a couple of years.

T–8. Well, uh, have you within the past five or eight years had any major sickness or operations or accidents? Something that would——

P–8: Well, I had——

T–9: Involve your physical self?

P–9. I had a bout with the flu four or five years ago, kept me out for about three weeks. But I don't know what the trouble is. There are days when I don't even get up to go to work. I just don't even feel like moving. And the boss has been pretty good about it, but I can tell that things are slipping, and, uh, I just have a feeling that I'm letting everybody down all the way around. I'm no good for my wife. I'm no good for my kids.

T–10: Are you a drinking man, Jim? I mean, do you take more than one snort a day?

In T–1 and T–2 the therapist injects a note of false personal intimacy and informality. There is no reason to suppose that the patient will feel more relaxed or accepted if called by his first name so soon; some people would feel alienated by this approach. In P–2 the patient expresses his distress in a vague way. The therapist, however, pays no attention to the obvious difficulty the patient has in stating his problem. Instead, he asks the patient's age. While this information is necessary, there will be plenty of time to get it later. It is not relevant here.

In P–6 the patient finally gets a chance to tell how he feels, but the therapist, instead of drawing him out further, continues taking a history. A number of possibilities are open to the therapist at T–7. He would have been closer to the patient's thought and mood with any of the following remarks:

"Things really seem hopeless."
"Everything seems to be slipping."
"Life's got no point?"
"How do you mean, whether something can be done?"

The therapist, from T–7 to T–9, continues to disregard the patient and follows his own rigid ideas as to the proper topic. The separation between the two becomes painful at T–10. Despite the patient's persisting effort to communicate his misery to the therapist, the latter asks about drinking!

The responses of this therapist do not tell the patient: "I am interested in your feelings and I want to understand your unhappiness. Feel free to express yourself." Instead, they tell him: "I'll ask the questions here. You keep bringing up irrelevant matters, so I'll just get on with really important things." They hinder the growth of a warm therapeutic relationship.

Permissiveness. Besides listening and staying close to the patient's thoughts and feelings, therapists do other things to build a relationship. These can be grouped under the heading of permissive behavior. While therapists agree on the importance of permissiveness, they vary in what they regard as permissive behavior.

We are fairly sure of one thing: criticizing a patient for what he expresses tends to destroy his freedom to express himself. If he says that he hates his parents or that he is having an extramarital affair, and we tell him that this is shameful or dishonest, he is less likely to report other socially disapproved feelings or deeds. People simply will not talk freely when they expect moralizing or condemnation.

Therapists usually avoid moralistic criticism quite easily. Trouble is more likely to come when the patient finds fault with the therapy. He may object to the way the therapist behaves ("You act so damned smug."), to his fees, or to the slim benefits he is getting. He may criticize the therapist for his youth, his age, his inadequate knowledge, his excessive knowledge, or for a thousand other things. The experienced therapist maintains his permissiveness in the face of these accusations and generally refuses to argue or to justify his acts.

A subtler way of blocking expression is praise or approval for doing the "right thing." Such remarks can hinder permissiveness, for the patient may, in his efforts to please the therapist, refuse to bring up "bad" feelings. When a patient tells of some improvement, therefore, therapists focus attention on the patient's own feelings of satisfaction rather than praise him.

Problem 2. Some therapists praise patients for their efforts during the therapy session. Perhaps the patient is quite upset, yet he persists in exploring thoughts and feelings and reaches new understanding. At the end of the session the therapist may express approval of the patient's willingness to work hard at therapy.

1. Will this kind of praise interfere with permissiveness? Explain your answer.

2. After struggling to hold back tears and intense feelings of sadness, a patient finally weeps, expresses deep loneliness, and talks very sincerely of a desire to feel closer to people. At the close of the session, the therapist tells the patient that he has been deeply moved and has felt very close to the patient during this experience. Is this praise? Is it likely to interfere with the permissiveness of the situation? Why?

Permissiveness goes even beyond accepting the patient without criticism or moralistic judgments. To reach permissiveness in its deepest sense requires the therapist to do more than be gentle and restrained. He must be able to show by his own behavior that emotional expression is not dangerous. An illustration of this point is given by Braatøy (2, p. 158). He suggests that a soft, low voice is needed in the early interviews with overinhibited people. He goes on, however, to point out the risk that such patients may easily come to see this as a rule of therapy to be obeyed always. They may believe that all emotional expression in the sessions must be muted and reasonable. One way of meeting this self-imposed restriction is to encourage the patient, in the later interviews, to try talking loudly or even to shout. But another way is for the therapist to express himself occasionally with more than his usual mildness. Obviously, this is risky business and demands that the therapist be sensitive to what the patient can stand at any particular time. When the therapist can appropriately express some dissatisfaction with a patient's evasiveness, for instance, he may bring a very great sense of security to the patient. But this can happen only when such an expression works to release the patient's anger toward the therapist. That outcome is ordinarily possible only after some months of therapeutic work. Therapists who express their feelings early in therapy may frighten the patient.

EMOTIONAL PARTICIPATION OF THE THERAPIST

At the close of the section on permissiveness, we touched on the problem of whether an effective therapist can express his own feelings in the session. This issue is an important one in therapy, and there have been a number of different points of view about it. We want to explore some of these differences and to indicate some of the decisions that must be faced by the therapist.

There is some research evidence pointing to the conclusion that expert therapists are able to maintain an appropriate and effective emotional interchange with patients much better than inexperienced therapists (4). Apparently, long experience counts for more in this respect than adherence to a particular system of therapy. This "appropriate emotional distance" has been described as "capacity to show interest and warmth without becoming overly involved" (4, p. 37). Inappropriate emotional distance, by contrast, may be seen in coolness, in aloofness, in talking down to the patient, in tenseness, in rigid use of particular techniques, and in failure to understand the patient's emotional communications. This evidence does not tell us, however, about the extent to which the therapist may usefully bring his own feelings into therapy.

The Traditional View. It has been widely believed that the therapist should be relatively passive and should refrain from any kind of emotional expression. Kubie says: "The psychoanalyst as an individual must be unknown to the patient. Therefore he keeps himself as much in the background as possible, out of clear focus and definition, quietly friendly, but always impersonal and reserved" (5, p. 64). Orthodox analysts keep themselves in the background by limiting what they say and by sitting so that the patient on the couch cannot easily see them.

This arrangement deprives the patient of many external cues that could help him accurately interpret the therapist's reaction. Consequently, the way is open for him to make a variety of assumptions about the therapist. It soon becomes clear, however, that the attitudes and feelings attributed to the therapist lack external validation, and the patient must recognize them as creations based on his own needs and expectations. Thus, his unwitting assumptions about others become explicit and open to examination. At the same time, the therapist's passivity provokes the patient to demand reassurance, help, or suggestions, if these are his characteristic reactions to interpersonal frustration. Or the passivity may provoke criticism, resentment, and charges of incompetence. Of course, such reactions during therapy are veiled and cautious at first, but they can become quite intense later.

Although there are advantages in keeping the therapist passive and invisible, the arrangement has some serious drawbacks. For one thing, it makes the whole therapeutic atmosphere mysterious and too remote from life (1, pp. 84–87). Possibly some patients are alienated by this atmosphere and discontinue treatment sooner than would otherwise be the case. More important, however, is the fact that this technique does not help the patient transfer his new learning to daily life situations. If the therapist is visible and active, therapy resembles the usual inter-personal relationship more closely; then it is easier for new attitudes and emotional reactions to generalize to relationships outside therapy.

We may make this last point clearer by an illustration. Suppose that a patient criticizes his father but anxiously expects the therapist to dis-approve. When the disapproval does not occur, the anxiety connected with verbal expression of criticism is weakened a little. This effect can occur even when the therapist is invisible and silent. But when the therapist is visible and interacting, the absence of disapproval weakens anxiety about *verbal criticism in a face-to-face, mutually active social contact.* Furthermore, the absence of disapproval is more obvious when the patient can see that the therapist does not frown, shake his head, or become tense. This way the patient learns that even unspoken social punishment does not follow his critical words.

Another illustration is provided by the case where a patient makes a demand or request that the therapist cannot or will not fulfill. He may want advice or approval of a certain plan. If the therapist remains invisible and silent, the patient may feel that the therapist does not like the open request, and may interpret the silence as coolness and with-drawal. When the therapist is visible and continues to interact with the patient in an interested, friendly way, such an interpretation is hard to maintain. Then the patient has an opportunity to learn that his open requests may not disturb others and that refusal to fulfill them does not imply total rejection. The therapist has demonstrated that it is possible to refuse a request without losing the warmth of the relationship. Re-peated experiences of this kind can bring both insight and increased spontaneity to persons who repress their own demands because they assume that expressing their own wants would either enslave or alienate others.

Participation in Client-centered Therapy. How can the therapist re-main visible and active and yet not give the patient a realistic basis for attributing resentment, jealousy, seductiveness, and other impulses to him? One way of answering this question has been developed by the client-centered therapists (7). In this kind of therapy, patient and ther-apist sit facing each other, and the therapist is quite active verbally. His utterances, however, are sharply limited by his training and philosophy. He responds as much as possible to the patient's immediately preceding remarks and feelings. His statements show interest and often summarize or reflect what the patient has expressed. Rarely does he try to explain something to the patient, suggest an hypothesis linking cause and effect, probe for further data, or express a feeling aroused in him by the patient's activity. His activity may be described as both acceptant and mirror-like. As Rogers puts it:

The counselor says in effect, "To be of assistance to you I will put aside myself—the self of ordinary interaction—and enter into your world of perception as completely as I am able. I will become, in a sense, another self for you— an alter ego of your own attitudes and feelings—a safe opportunity for you to discern yourself more clearly, to experience yourself more truly and deeply, to choose more significantly" (7, p. 35).

With this point of view, the therapist can interact with the patient in a way somewhat resembling ordinary social behavior; at the same time the therapist gives the patient no basis—in words at least—for viewing him as a disciplinarian, competitor, manipulator, or as a critic. Published interviews (9) leave no doubt that this kind of therapy provides an extremely permissive atmosphere, comfortable and anxiety-relieving. It also communicates a belief that the patient can make responsible, satisfying decisions about his own life.

It seems, however, that clients often wish a fuller, more emotionally colorful relationship with the therapist than client-centered therapy provides. The client-centered therapist avoids expressing even mild feelings of his own, and there is rarely any discussion of the relationship by either client or therapist. The resulting conversation conveys the impression that the patient talks *about* feelings instead of talking *with* feeling. This emotional nonparticipation of the therapist has concerned some of the client-centered therapists. Rogers quotes a lengthy statement by one of his staff members who comes to grips with this issue. Among other things, Dr. O. H. Bown says:

At this level I was literally stuck for a long time, fearing the worst if I should let any kind of personal involvement enter into my relationship with my clients. . . . I appeared to them to be a professionally adequate person who was dealing with them in an understanding and empathic way. This may have been true at the client's level of consciousness, but unconsciously, I think, he was learning directly from me, "Do not be free in this relationship. Do not let yourself go. Do not express your deepest feelings or needs, for in this relationship that is dangerous." (7, p. 162)

Bown continues by pointing out that, as he became less afraid to be emotionally involved, his patients began to discuss and to experience feelings hitherto avoided.

In addition to enriching the therapeutic experience as Bown suggests, the emotional participation of the therapist seems to have some other advantages. For one thing, it probably generates many interpersonal events that can be effectively used for interpretation. That is, instead of interpreting the events occurring between the patient and his family or friends, the therapist can call attention to the events that are actually happening in the therapy session. A second possible advantage of therapist participation is that it increases the resemblance between the therapeutic situation and "real" situations. In view of what is known about transfer of learning, this increased resemblance should make for more effective transfer of whatever is learned in therapy to life outside of therapy. A third reason for therapist participation is that patients need "feedback information" about the social effects of their behavior. If the therapist is continually neutral and unemotional, it is hard for patients to find out that they are acting in an irritating, seductive, whining, or dominating way. If the therapist is aware of how the patient is making him feel, and if he can express these feelings, then the patient has valuable data for finding out how he affects people. Giving such feedback information is clearly a delicate matter since it can provoke a great deal of anxiety. But it can be done by a skilled and sensitive therapist.

Objections to Therapist Participation. Some people feel that therapist participation means giving advice, using persuasion, or "selling" a point of view. They properly point out that advising a patient to stay married, to take dancing lessons, to confess an indiscretion, or to join social clubs is not very helpful. Most advice has been heard or thought of by the patient before he ever came for therapy. The trouble is that his attitudes and anxieties prevent him from really accepting it. He may try to go through the motions of carrying out "good" advice, but he acts so that it would fail to benefit him. His own anxiety or half-hearted interest leads to awkward, inappropriate behavior and to failure. But advice is not the kind of participation we have been discussing. There are many ways a therapist can be involved with a client besides being an adviser.

Another objection to therapist participation is that it enables the patient to find realistic grounds for the feelings and attitudes he attributes to the therapist. Once he has discovered a seemingly factual basis for his judgments, it is impossible to demonstrate that his own wishes and fears influence his perception of others. This objection is valid in so far as it concerns the intimate information that a friend could acquire about the therapist (5, pp. 65 f). But we know now that there are ways for a therapist to participate actively and still demonstrate the patient's unrealistic notions. We shall give an example of how this can be done. The example is fictitious but based on many actual interactions of this kind.[2]

[2] The problem of how the therapist can be active and still expose unrealistic social perceptions probably has several kinds of solutions. The example used here is based on the kind of solution developed by Dr. Frederick Perls at the New York Institute for Gestalt Therapy. While the method stems from important theoretical conceptions, our aim here is simply to show a possible technique.

Suppose, in the third or fourth month of therapy, that a patient spends a half hour in social chitchat. Therapists will vary in their emotional reactions to this, depending on the patient and the nature of other sessions. In this case, however, the therapist feels blocked and says so:

T: I feel blocked right now.
P: What do you mean?
T: I don't know what to do with what you have been telling me.
P: Now I think you're irritated with me.
T: How do you know?
P: Well, you said you felt blocked.
T: Does that mean I'm irritated?
P: Probably. You want me to talk about something else.
T: Must you do what I want you to?
P: Well, I suppose I should.
T: Why should you?
P: Well, uh, it would, you would feel better. You wouldn't feel blocked.
T: Are you required to make me feel better?
P: Sure.
T: Who requires you to do this?
P: Well, you do. [Pause.] I mean, nobody said I had to. Maybe I tell myself to do it.

The therapist here has been quite active and has even injected a feeling of his own. But notice that he gives no grounds for the patient to think that he requires him to change the topic. The result is to explore the patient's assumption that he must obey and please the therapist. This assumption is completely unrealistic, for the patient "knows" that the therapist is not demanding anything. Cooperating with the therapist is simply a means to the patient's own goals. Therapy is not being forced upon him, even though he may prefer to think so. In the same way, this patient has felt that other people required him to please them, although the fact is that he really wants to regard them as imposing on him. Much more work must be done before he can see why he needs to regard them in this way. It is enough for now that he should understand how he is trying to live up to requirements that he incorrectly attributed to the therapist.

A more serious objection to therapist participation is that, unless the therapist's own neurotic needs are somehow held in check, he may harm the patient. If a therapist unwittingly seeks dominance, sexual conquest, or emotional exploitation in the relationship, he may make neurotic patients worse. For example, a therapist may encourage a patient to dwell on the details of clandestine adventures in order to satisfy his own repressed interest in antisocial actions. He then follows this with subtle moralizing which quells his own sense of guilt but increases the patient's feeling of shame. Or a therapist may continually uncover more "problems" in an unwitting effort to bind the patient to the therapeutic relationship.

Rigidly limiting the interaction of the therapist with the patient is not likely to prevent trouble, however. A better solution was proposed early in the history of modern psychotherapy: the therapist himself needs therapy. A therapist who is aware of his own assumptions about people and of his own ways of manipulating relationships will be able to choose helpful ways of dealing with his patients. That is why psychological study, supervised practice, and experience as a patient are all important parts of the therapist's preparation.

We should remember, too, that the neurotic needs of the therapist are not the only forces that motivate his actions. He has other motives, such as wanting a successful outcome, wanting other patients in the future, and wanting the respect of his professional colleagues. In addition, he is aware of the unique character of the therapy session. It is not a casual social contact, but a planned and purposeful meeting. There are time limits for each session, and the eventual aim is to make the therapist unnecessary to the patient. All these factors play a part in determining what the therapist does. As he understands his position fully, he can afford to be spontaneous and expressive in the therapeutic session.

A good example of spontaneous responses can be found in the changes that a therapist will undergo in the way he expresses irritation. Suppose that in the first few sessions a patient engages in lengthy, abstruse, intellectual analysis of his problem. The therapist may sense that these are evasive tactics; the patient is not ready to feel the intense concern and anxiety attached to his human relationships. But the therapist feels no irritation at this evasiveness. Without thinking about what is involved, he simply accepts this behavior as part of the patient's style of living. As therapy continues, the patient realizes what he is doing and wishes to give up this arid analysis. He becomes capable of occasionally expressing some feelings in a simple and direct way. At this stage of therapy, the therapist may experience some irritation when the patient uses these evasive tactics. At the same time, the therapist is not greatly motivated to express his irritation. He sees that the patient is still struggling to find his own way and is not prepared to deal with a direct irritable remark from the therapist.

Still later in therapy, the patient becomes able to admit both critical and friendly feelings toward the therapist. He is aware that therapy will continue even though he openly criticizes the therapist. At this point, a reversion to sterile, intellectual analysis may elicit an irritated remark from the therapist: "This stuff is just words, words, words." Such a remark, given at this time, often brings a direct emotional response from the patient. The evasiveness stops abruptly, and the patient interacts with the therapist on the level of feelings as well as on the level of words. This outcome is, of course, exactly what patient and therapist have been interested in reaching, but the therapist's emotional participation was needed to release the emotion in the patient.

In considering the illustration we have just given, you should not suppose that the therapist carefully planned how and when he would react to the patient. His behavior at each stage of therapy was determined by a complex set of perceptions and motives. He perceives the patient as stronger, he feels his own irritation more keenly, and he wants more emotional response from the patient in the later stages of therapy. All this organizes his behavior, provided he is not restricting himself by rules that prevent spontaneity. On the other hand, his behavior in the early phases of therapy is spontaneous, too. At that period, he sees the patient miserable, emotionally handicapped, and unable to deal with irritation. He, himself, is not irritated, and is interested in helping the patient feel comfortable in the therapeutic setting. Thus, the "natural" thing to do is to wait, to notice how the patient handles the situation, and to communicate interest in him.

The extent, the quality, and the timing of the therapist's participation both in terms of comments and in terms of expressing his feelings cannot be determined by rule. Overeager beginning therapists may participate too much, and yet, if they are really being themselves, the patient may sense the interest and concern of the young therapist and respond to it. But if a therapist is anxious, worried about how the patient will accept him, and preoccupied with planning his next move, he will probably keep the patient at a distance. Such a therapist is not really sensitive to what is happening between him and the patient, and he will have little therapeutic success.

INTERPRETATION

Almost every important method of psychotherapy since Freud has stressed the importance of extending the patient's awareness or of "making the unconscious conscious." The problem is to find ways of bringing repressed processes (motives, feelings, assumptions) into awareness. We have already suggested that one way to accomplish this task is to decrease the patient's anxiety about the therapist's opinion of him. As the patient finds that the therapist is not frightened by, nor critical of, his words and actions, he can feel, think, and say things that he has previously avoided. Theoretically, if the permissive situation reduced anxiety sufficiently, repression would cease and the patient would make all his own discoveries. In that case, the therapist's whole concern would center around building a nonanxious therapeutic relationship. It is not likely, however, that even the most comfortable relationship will diminish all the anxiety that produces repression. For one thing, some anxiety is due to the patient's own self-evaluations and not to his fear of social disapproval. He may feel the therapist's complete acceptance and still be unable to accept certain wants or feelings within himself. For another thing, the comfort of the therapist's permissiveness may be so rewarding that the patient wants to keep it undisturbed. That is, the relationship may became valuable primarily as a source of relief instead of as an opportunity for discovery and exploration. Then the patient will seek to protect this valuable possession and will repress whatever could threaten to destroy it. For these reasons, the therapist must supply some of the motivation to extend the patient's awareness. One of the most important techniques for doing this is interpretation.

Interpretation consists of comments or questions that are related to repressed psychological activity. These remarks suggest that the patient is feeling or wanting something that he does not know about. And, of course, interpretations provoke anxiety or defensiveness, because they touch matters that have been repressed in order to avoid anxiety. Interpretations may often seem like accusations to the patient. You can see that merely telling a person *why* he acts servile and submissive will not really convince him if he must avoid knowing the reason in order to retain his self-respect. In addition, interpretations are threatening because they indicate that the therapist knows secrets about the patient which he himself does not know. Thus, the therapist seems to have a magic power over the patient. He may, so it seems to the patient, refuse to share these secrets or may even use them to manipulate and influence the patient. Obviously, making effective interpretations is difficult. When it is done unskillfully it may seriously damage the therapeutic relationship.

The Content of Interpretive Remarks. One of the simplest kinds of interpretations consists of an inference about the patient's emotions or motives. For example, a patient may say that he was hurt by an unfair remark that his wife made. He continues talking about his disappointment and his belief in fair play, but he does this in an excited and bitter way. The therapist may say: "Maybe her remark made you angry, too." Or, "Do you think that, besides being hurt, you felt some resentment?" An example of a more tenuous inference is the following effort to interpret a motive: A patient has been describing a committee meeting where he felt left out of the social interaction. He tells how he decided to shut up and say nothing because the group wasn't interested in him. On the basis of his story and on other information, the therapist replies: "I wonder if your silence was a way of trying to make the group show some interest in you?"

Another kind of interpretation consists of pointing out similarities in two situations. Here, the therapist may not comment on the meaning of the similarity, but his comparison brings out features that are not obvious to the patient. As an illustration, take the following comment: "It seems that both of these situations that caused you trouble were ones where you were dealing with a dominant person. And you felt helpless both times."

Other, and more complex interpretations, deal with cause-and-effect relationships in the patient's life. Commonly, these connect current happenings in the patient's life with events in his past. Thus, a therapist may point out that the patient's reactions to dominant people are similar to those elicited by the patient's father many years ago. Or that guilt over sexual desires toward his mother is related to difficulty in a current love affair. Usually, this kind of interpretation is based on some theory about the development of personality and the significant events in the life history.

A fourth kind of interpretation is the revelation of hidden meanings or the significance of symbols. You are familiar with this kind of interpretation mostly in connection with understanding dreams. Of course, the possibility of symbolic representation is not limited to dreams. Many events and objects can take on symbolic significance. Sometimes images that spontaneously arise during the interview symbolize the patient's feeling about the relationship, and gestures (clenched fist, unfastening a button, dropping a pencil) may have symbolic significance.

The Patient's Acceptance of Interpretations. Since most interpretations are inferences, there is usually some reasonable ground for patients to doubt their correctness. In addition, since they communicate information that the patient finds disturbing, they are likely to seem condemnatory. Consequently, the patient will often deny the validity of an interpretation or will distort its meaning. Sometimes the very intensity of his denial suggests that the interpretation is close to the truth. But we must remember that when the therapist confronts the patient with painful ideas, refusal to accept them may indicate the patient's efforts to retain his self-respect and self-confidence. As Kubie points out:

Confrontations which reach to deeper levels, challenging the patient to recognize some of the buried sources of his difficulties, *must* be rejected by the patient if they are not to precipitate him into unmanageable terror, guilt or depression. One learns slowly not to force a patient to look at painful facts about himself until some understanding of their origins and purposes have been achieved. Sometimes, therefore, one may have to withhold interpretations during many months of patient exploration (5, p. 31).

For these reasons, interpretations are made sparingly and are presented in a tentative way. Moreover, the therapist does not argue or try to prove his point when the patient resists the interpretation. Even though argument succeeded in convincing a patient that an interpretation was true, the interpretive effort could still be a failure. The primary aim of interpretation is to extend the awareness of the patient; *it is not to persuade him to believe something about himself, but to enable him to perceive something about himself.*

To understand this point more thoroughly, consider this example: A man is excessively independent, rejects help and sympathy, and feels constantly driven to achieve success. The therapist, building a case that is logic-tight, convinces the man that his independent behavior is a reaction against his great desire to be taken care of, to be protected, and to be tenderly nurtured. However, even though the man is convinced, he does not actually feel or experience this desire. His knowledge of himself has been increased, but his perception of himself remains unaltered. He still cannot tell those moments when the desire is actually present and paramount; consequently he cannot relate any sense of frustration to the unsatisfied desire nor take steps to satisfy it. His belief in the therapist's explanation does not enable him to feel what it is like to want loving care; he cannot identify the distinctive bodily processes and interpersonal situations that are called "wanting to be taken care of." Effective interpretation should make it possible for him to differentiate and to label these feelings.

Problem 3. An eighteen-year-old boy who has been deeply attached to his mother arrives at a point in therapy where he is ready to experience his repressed resentment toward her. The therapist makes an interpretive remark suggesting that the boy really feels strong resentment toward his mother. The patient agrees. This agreement could mean either that the boy actually experiences his resentment or merely that he believes it is a valid explanation of his behavior. What could the therapist notice that would indicate that the boy actually feels his resentment?

INTERPRETIVE OBSERVATIONS

Using Therapeutic Events to Extend Awareness. The events discussed by patients can be roughly grouped with reference to the time of their occurrence:

1. Events, feelings, and motives that took place in the past, say more than a few months ago
2. Events that are current but outside the therapy session
3. Events that occur during the therapy session itself

The time order of these events is approximately the same as the clarity, vividness, and freshness of the experiences as they are recalled. If you are to learn what it is like to feel hostile, dependent, or seductive, your task will be easier if the experience is clear and recent. It is a plausible hypothesis, then, that awareness can be extended more rapidly by helping the patient identify those motives and feelings that take place in the therapy session than by helping him identify those that occurred a long time ago. It is equally true that the events of the therapeutic session can be used to extend awareness of the patient's ways of dealing with people, his assumptions about them, and his "security operations" (i.e., his techniques for avoiding anxiety). The problem is to arrange the therapy session so that significant emotional and motivational events can take place and be utilized.

One of the discoveries of psychoanalysis concerns the therapeutic use of feelings in the therapy session. That discovery was of "transference." In transference, the patient manifests intense but inappropriate feelings toward the therapist. Usually they take the form of strong affection or marked hatred, both of which are unjustified by anything the therapist has done or said. Psychoanalysts feel that transference reactions are essentially repetitions of significant relationships that the patient experienced early in life. When, through the interpretation of tranference reactions, the patient gains insight into the relation between these early experiences and the present emotion, the transference is dissolved.

Transference reactions occur in daily life as well as in therapy. In their less intense forms, they correspond to what we have called "unwitting assumptions" about people. Many of us react to others as if they were dangerous, untrustworthy, rejecting, or domineering, and these reactions occur before we have factual evidence to support them. In daily life, such reactions go unnoticed and unanalyzed. In therapy, they become the most significant material for analysis and interpretation. For some therapists, transference provides significant material because it duplicates relationships of the remote past and thus permits the patient to understand present desires and emotions in terms of the past. For other therapists, the significance of transference is that it arouses the patient's distinctive motives and emotions during the therapy session. By focusing on these, the therapist can help the patient become aware of what he wants and feels and how he expresses these wants and feelings.

Therapist Activity in Dealing with the Events of the Therapy Session. One way the therapist can extend the patient's awareness is to make interpretations, which we described in a preceding section. If a patient suddenly becomes silent and the therapist believes that the patient is irritated, he may say: "Perhaps your silence shows irritation toward me." This kind of remark is easy to deny, and the patient may insist that he is simply thinking to himself. But there are other things that a therapist can do.

Some remarks by the therapist are not inferential interpretations and yet they are based on observations that could lead to interpretations. We may call these remarks interpretive observations, because they have the same purpose as interpretations but do not contain grounds for argument. There are several kinds of these observations.

One is a descriptive comment by the therapist. Thus, with an irritated, silent patient, the therapist may describe something the patient is doing: "I notice your jaw is tense," or "Your fists are clenched." Here, the therapist calls attention to an obvious or "surface" aspect of the pattern of irritation but leaves the labeling up to the patient. If the emotion is repressed, the patient will not experience it as irritation. He may simply reply that he feels tense. Then the therapist helps the patient elaborate the qualities of this kind of tenseness, or he may ask what is causing the tenseness. The patient may discover that it began when the therapist made a remark that sounded critical. Eventually, he may experience his tenseness as irritation.

Another way to bring about interpretive observation is to ask the patient to describe what he is doing. Or he may say: "How would you describe what is happening at this moment?" The patient may choose to describe his feelings, his thoughts, his posture, or the therapist's behavior. The therapist notes what is observed and what is omitted and encourages the patient to make a fuller description. Resistance to certain kinds of observation can be noticed and made the object of attention.

A third kind of observational comment is a statement of the therapist's own feelings. He may say to the silent, irritated patient: "I feel shut out." This remark is not an inference. It is a report of the therapist's observation of himself. If the patient insists he did not intend to produce such a feeling, the therapist makes it clear that he is not accusing the patient of anything. He is simply reporting his own feeling, but it modifies the interpersonal situation.

These remarks have several advantages over inferential interpretations. First, they extend the patient's awareness of what is actually happening. The verbal summaries and causal hypotheses can come later. Secondly, these remarks give no basis for logical refutation. The patient may claim that the therapist had hidden motives for picking out an observation, but the remarks themselves do not give a clue to the motives. Thus projections and other kinds of assumptions about the therapist can be made explicit and can be examined. Third, such remarks avoid premature interpretations. The patient has ample opportunity to draw his own conclusions. He can proceed to accumulate new perceptions and insights at his own rate, while the therapist is actively stimulating the work of therapy. Finally, since these remarks allow patients to come to their own conclusions about the meaning of their actions, new insights are usually accepted and acted upon better than those the therapist makes to the patient.

We must remember that even interpretive observations are somewhat threatening to patients and must be used with care. The mere act of calling the patient's attention to something that he is doing may be construed as criticism and thus may arouse defensiveness. The therapist's problem, then, is to keep the work of therapy going ahead without destroying the security of the relationship for the patient.

USING NONVERBAL FORMS OF EXPRESSION

One of the themes running through this chapter is that therapy consists of experiences rather than intellectual information. The patient grows, not so much by being able to give accurate verbal explanations as by having experiences that contradict and expand his previous perceptions of self and of others. Here is a simple example from an actual therapy session: A patient says that she fears the demands that other people make upon her, and that she wishes they would stop demanding so much. The therapist replies that he is willing to stop asking questions. He becomes silent. At this point, the patient becomes quite uncomfortable. After a silence, she remarks that she doesn't like this situation. And she tells the therapist: "If you don't demand anything of me, then you won't give anything either. In other words, the things I would demand wouldn't be gratified because I wouldn't have to do anything for you." The important outcome of this episode is that the patient discovers a new feeling: discomfort because of the absence of external demands. No matter what the explanation may be, she is faced with a new perception of herself which must somehow be integrated with older ones.

Perhaps we can now understand better the task of the therapist in arranging for the patient to have new experiences. We have already pointed out how the transference phenomenon leads to these experiences, but it is possible to see other methods too. Clay, finger paints, and drawing materials permit expression on nonverbal levels, and patients may derive useful experiences from working with them.

To show how patients can utilize these materials, we can report an episode that occurred during the fifth month of therapy with a twenty-four-year-old single woman. She had been struggling with the problem of her conscience. She had come to feel that she was incapable of spontaneity and joyfulness, because she continually gave herself orders to do what was proper and correct. In one of the sessions, the therapist gave her some modeling clay and asked her to play with it while she talked. After a few minutes, she rolled it into a ropelike form, partially coiled.

When the therapist asked what she had made, she hesitated and finally replied with a giggle that it was a bowel movement. Then she dropped it on the floor and laughed.

The therapist smiled but did not comment on what she had done. He felt the experience by itself was sufficient. What had the patient discovered? First, she actually experienced the fact that she had produced a model of something not discussed in polite society. Secondly, she found that there was more permissiveness in the therapeutic relationship than she had hitherto experienced. There was no need to try to find more meaning in the experience. For this inhibited woman it was enough to discover that she was capable of doing something "nasty" without being asked to explain it.

Art materials are not brought into therapy as tasks imposed on the patient but as avenues for expression or as experiments "just to see what will happen." When a patient says he has a feeling he can't describe, the therapist may suggest trying to put some colors on paper to represent it. Or the therapist may ask for elaboration of a feeling by means of a drawing. Suppose a patient describes his mother as a "monster." Then he may be asked to draw a crude picture of the kind of monster she is. Such a request may be surprising and may bring protests that he didn't really mean a monster and couldn't draw anything. Even this kind of response is useful, however, since it opens the question about the difference between calling his mother a monster and actually drawing her as one.

Sometimes the therapist will encourage the patient to tell what he is feeling as he makes a picture or a clay figure. At other times the emphasis will be on the way the patient goes about expressing himself nonverbally: carefully, impulsively, hesitantly, intensely, and so on. Then, too, it is useful to call attention to the disposition that is made of the art product. A patient may make a figure and quickly destroy it; or he may hand it to the therapist. Occasionally he may continue to hold it and stroke it. Art work widens the range of tactual, muscular, and visual experiences that therapy can provide. And, just as the verbal expression of fear or anger can bring some relief, so the making and destruction of a clay figure or drawing can bring relief.

PROBLEMS OF THE BEGINNING THERAPIST

We have tried to show you something about the way therapy is carried out, but there is obviously much more to learn. Further reading will help prepare you for therapeutic work, but it cannot make you feel entirely ready for your first attempt at treatment. Any beginner is likely to feel confused and unsure of himself as the concrete details of a patient's feelings and actions are revealed. How shall he select the important material for interpretation? When and how shall he interpret it? How can he know whether he is building a solid therapeutic relationship? These questions are important, but they cannot really be answered in advance for any case.

We can, however, point out some of the attitudes that often interfere with the effectiveness of the beginning therapist. Pointing them out will probably not change them, but at least beginners can try to be aware of their effects and perhaps can modify their overt behavior somewhat.

Preoccupation with Theories about the Patient. The beginning therapist has been exposed to a great deal of information about the causes and meanings of symptoms. He has learned about projection, rationalization, reaction-formation, undoing, and about other defensive maneuvers. He has acquired labels for various kinds of people: oral-dependent, cycloid, cerebrotonic, and the like. It is understandable, therefore, that in his therapeutic work he should try to figure out which labels apply. And he will try to solve the puzzles presented by the patient's symptoms. He wants to find the causes of the overanxious and ineffective behavior that he sees and hears about.

In itself, there is nothing wrong about this kind of theorizing. The trouble comes from doing it during the actual conduct of the therapy session. A therapist who is taken up with thinking about his patient is not really listening to nor observing his patient. It is also safe to assume that the theorizing therapist is not aware of the feelings the patient is evoking in him. It is more valuable to stay in close touch with what is happening to the two people in the session. Then there is a good chance that certain impressions will emerge strongly and spontaneously without laboriously searching for them.

For example, a patient may spend the initial portion of a session in telling funny episodes to the therapist. The therapist laughs but would like to move forward with therapy. Suddenly, he realizes that the patient is entertaining him in order to avoid the therapeutic interaction. This realization leads him to remark: "It must be important for you to entertain me today, and you're doing a good job of it." This comment unlocks the situation and focuses attention on the significance of the entertainment. Instead of wondering whether the patient has been rewarded in childhood for clowning, he keeps close to the impact of the patient's present behavior. And instead of theorizing about the behavior, he encourages the patient to notice it.

Feeling an Obligation to the Patient. Beginning therapists are prone to explain and interpret too hastily and too often. It makes no difference whether or not their explanations are correct; the point is that they are not likely to be effective. One reason why therapists overdo their intellectual summaries is that they feel they must "give the patient something to take away with each session." And the "something" is a new insight. This sense of obligation can easily result in poorly timed interpretations. It can also bring the patient to expect that the therapist will always have some important message for him.

While it is true that the therapist does have an obligation to every patient, that is not the same as saying he must give the patient new understanding in every session. The therapist's obligation is to conduct the therapeutic process so as to help the patient, but it is unrealistic to assume that every session must represent a clear step forward. Moreover, the beginning therapist should realize that a comfortable hour spent with the therapist may often be reward enough to the patient. We frequently discover that a session in which very little seemed to happen at the verbal level may have been quite satisfying to the patient.

Eagerness for Success. Therapists are delighted when patients are making progress and feeling better about themselves. But with the long dry spells of discouragingly slow improvement, the therapist may become uneasy. Then the usually relaxed and acceptant therapist feels impelled to shove the patient forward. He may try to guide the discussion to topics that seem more fruitful than those currently discussed; he may start intensive probing; or he may begin to interpret in a heavy-handed way. All this is not likely to improve the situation or the patient.

The patience to continue therapeutic work gently when little seems to be happening is a great asset to the therapist. It helps the patient, too, for the therapist's unhurried pace at such times enables him to face his own discouragement better. These periods may not be due to mistakes the therapist has made; in fact, they may be intervals when understanding and insights are being integrated preparatory to further progress. Changing one's time perspective is a help in meeting these lulls; each session must be seen as a small part of an enterprise that can last several years.

Despite insensitivity, impatience, and uncertainty, the beginning therapist can be of real assistance to the patient. With supervision, he can minimize the effects of his inexperience. In preparation for therapy he has learned to deal with people in diagnostic interviewing and testing, and he has acquired a sense of his professional responsibility. Coupled with his commitment to the task of helping people grow through self-understanding, his training will surely function effectively.

What good is psychotherapy? As good as man's faith in his humanity. Men have always believed in their ability to change for the better and to help each other so to change—through mutual assistance, love, religion, and art. Conceived in the broadest terms psychotherapy derives from the same faith and, employing of necessity some of the same means, attempts to formulate these more precisely (8, p. 303).

REFERENCES

1. Alexander, F., & French, T. M. *Psychoanalytic therapy*. New York: Ronald, 1946.
2. Braatøy, T. *Fundamentals of psychoanalytic technique*. New York: Wiley, 1954.
3. Colby, K. M. *A primer for psychotherapists*. New York: Ronald, 1951.
4. Fiedler, F. E. Factor analyses of psychoanalytic, non-directive, and Adlerian therapeutic relationships. *J. consult. Psychol.*, 1951, 15, 32–38.
5. Kubie, L. S. *Practical and theoretical aspects of psychoanalysis*. New York: International Universities Press, 1950.
6. Perls, F. S., Hefferline, R. F., & Goodman, P. *Gestalt therapy*. New York: Julian Press, 1951.
7. Rogers, C. R. *Client-centered therapy*. New York: Houghton Mifflin, 1951.
8. Rosenzweig, S. A transvaluation of psychotherapy—a reply to Hans Eysenck. *J. abnorm. soc. Psychol.*, 1954, 49, 298–304.
9. Snyder, W. U. *Casebook of non-directive counseling*. New York: Houghton Mifflin, 1947.

Index